GENDER

A CARIBBEAN MULTI-DISCIPLINARY PERSPECTIVE

GENDER

A CARIBBEAN MULTI-DISCIPLINARY PERSPECTIVE

edited by

Elsa Leo-Rhynie
Barbara Bailey
Christine Barrow

IRP
IAN RANDLE PUBLISHERS
in association with
The Centre for Gender and Development Studies,
University of the West Indies
and
The Commonwealth of Learning

First published in Jamaica 1997 by
Ian Randle Publishers
206 Old Hope Road
Kingston 6, P.O. Box 686

ISBN 976-8100-68-0

and in U.K. 1997 by

James Currey Publishers
73 Botley Road
Oxford, OX2 0BS

ISBN 0-85255-250-5

Catalogue records for this book are available from the
National Library of Jamaica and from the British Library

Cover and book design by Michael Gordon
Print and bound in the USA

Table of Contents

Part Two Engendering Justice

Part Three Gender Perspectives in Education

Part Four Gender in Language, Poetry and Prose

Preface

This volume is the first publication of the Centre for Gender and Development Studies (CGDS) of the University of the West Indies (UWI). The Centre was established in September 1993, and is the outgrowth of the Women and Development Studies (WDS) groups which spearheaded its formation. The volume consists of articles based on a selection of the papers presented at a series of interdisciplinary and disciplinary seminars organised by the WDS groups and held on the three campuses of the UWI over the period 1986 to 1993; and at one seminar organised by the newly established Centre in 1994. The disciplinary seminars were faculty based, and the involvement of faculty members in both interdisciplinary and disciplinary seminars was part of the strategy used to stimulate the curriculum development necessary for the inclusion of women and gender issues in UWI courses and programmes. The entire seminar series was an important component of the Project of Cooperation in Teaching and Research in Women and Development Studies between the Government of the Netherlands and the UWI. The seminar series spanned an eight-year period, and some of the articles presented in the early seminars date back to the mid 1980s. Their inclusion in this volume is important, however, as the concepts and ideas are still relevant, and they provide a record of the academic thought and input which have helped to shape the mission and objectives of the CGDS.

The preparation of this publication has been sponsored by the Commonwealth of Learning (COL), and we wish to thank Dr. Dennis Irvine for approving the initial proposal, and Mr. John Steward who has greatly facilitated CGDS over the publication period. The volume is the result of the work of several persons, to whom we would like to offer our sincere thanks. These include the members of the WDS groups whose time and talents in the organization of the several seminars and whose contribution towards the establishment of the CGDS constituted 'voluntary overwork', all the women and men who presented papers at the various seminars, the women's organizations who supported the seminars, funding agencies and private sector interests who assisted with seminar sponsorship, and students who helped in a variety of ways.

Special thanks must also be expressed to Professor Joycelin Massiah who was one of the initiators of the WDS groups and who has been intimately involved in their activities over the years, for writing the comprehensive introduction to this volume, Mrs. Louraine Emmanuel of CDGS who effectively handled the administrative details, Ms. Elizabeth Johnson and Ms. Carol Thompson who provided word processing services, those persons who assisted in proof -reading, and the staff of Ian Randle Publishers Limited for their interest, cooperation and assistance.

Elsa Leo-Rhynie
Barbara Bailey
Christine Barrow

Introduction

Joycelin Massiah

The publication of this series of seminar papers by the Centre of Gender and Development Studies (CGDS) of the University of the West Indies (UWI), marks a significant milestone in the process of institutionalisation of the study of women and gender in the UWI. It represents the culmination of the important faculty development aspect of the Project of Co-operation in Teaching and Research in Women and Development Studies between the University of the West Indies and the Institute of Social Studies at The Hague (ISS).

The seminars were conceived as a vehicle for raising awareness within the University of women and gender issues as valid concerns for research and teaching; for providing a forum for those who were working on these issues to present their experiences to their colleagues; and for beginning the process of examining critically the content of their course offerings to determine what, if any, adjustments were necessary in order to reflect a balanced gender perspective. The process covered a period of eight years (1986-94) and involved a series of ten seminars, three interdisciplinary and seven faculty-based. All faculties in the University participated in the process, with the notable exception of the Faculty of Engineering.

In keeping with its participatory philosophy, the CGDS ensured that the seminars were rotated among the three campuses of the UWI. Three of the seminars were held at the Mona campus, one interdisciplinary and two faculty; three at St Augustine, one interdisciplinary and two faculty; and four at Cave

Hill, one interdisciplinary and three faculty, the extra faculty one having to be transferred from Mona on account of Hurricane Gilbert which devastated the Mona campus and indeed the whole of Jamaica. Overall design and structure of the interdisciplinary seminars were determined by the three CGDS campus groups which also appointed a seminar coordinator from the CGDS group who was responsible for actually organising the seminar. In the case of the faculty seminars, the design and structure were determined by the faculty and the three CGDS campus groups; the faculty named a seminar coordinator and selected a keynote speaker, usually from outside the region, and the faculty and the relevant CGDS group jointly organised the seminar. In both cases, a campus-based planning committee, selected by the campus faculty board and the campus CGDS, supervised the preparations. All faculty-based seminars were advertised under the joint sponsorship of the Women and Development Studies Programme and the faculty concerned.

The launching of an official programme of Women and Development Studies in the UWI was marked by an inaugural seminar held at St Augustine in September 1986. The papers presented at that seminar were published as a book entitled ***Gender in Caribbean Development***, under the joint editorship of two members of the St Augustine Group, Patricia Mohammed and Catherine Shepherd. That publication, in the words of Lucille Mathurin Mair who wrote the foreword, represented 'a prelude to a programme projected over a period of some years, to build the foundations for the integration of multi-disciplinary gender and development studies into the curriculum of the regional university.'

Until the publication of the present volume, that book was the sole formal publication of the CGDS.

The present volume represents not only the second venture of the CGDS into publishing, but also an attempt to build on that foundation in the process signalling that women and development studies has secured a firm place on the UWI curriculum. The volume presents a selection of papers from eight of the ten seminars sponsored by the UWI/ISS Project of Cooperation. The seminars excluded are the second and third interdisciplinary ones held at St Augustine and Cave Hill respectively. The St Augustine seminar entitled 'Women, Gender and Development Studies: The Theoretical and Methodological Challenge', had taken the form of a closed programme of eight days designed to train a small core of personnel for teaching and research in women's studies, and a public programme for two days aimed at exposing a general audience to some of the issues addressed by women's studies. The Cave Hill seminar, called 'Women's Studies: Interdisciplinary Readings', took the form of readings and discussions on feminist theory. Readings were selected to introduce participants to the basic concepts of feminist thought and to illustrate the recurrent themes across the different disciplines. One session was devoted to discussions with representatives from a wide range of non-governmental organizations(NGOs), the media and the Bureau of Women's Affairs; and another with representatives from the teaching and senior administrative staff of the university campus.

On average, about 65 men and women attended each of the seminars, a number that testifies to the general acceptance of their relevance and importance to the conventional course offerings. Special steps were taken to ensure the attendance of individuals and representatives of relevant groups from outside the University community. This facilitated the maintenance of links which the CGDS has always felt to be crucial to ensuring the vitality of its programmes.

The Papers

The editors of the volume faced the daunting challenge of selecting from among the vast number of papers (over 100) presented throughout the entire series. Selections were made with a view to highlighting the key issues, the wide range of Caribbean country experiences and comparative experiences from outside the region which were the subject of discussion. The selected papers take the form of presentations of research findings, theoretical and practical think-pieces and policy prescriptions. But always there is the search for ways of linking research, teaching and practice, of linking the academics with their counterparts from government and non-governmental sectors, and of linking the disciplinary findings and perspectives to the crafting of an interdisciplinary approach to the multi-disciplinary issues raised. As a result, the question of appropriate methodologies looms large throughout the volume.

The papers are presented in six parts, roughly coinciding with the seven faculty seminars and one of the interdisciplinary seminars. Part 1 carries two pieces from the Faculty of Social Sciences seminar, "Gender, Development Policy and the Management of Change", and two from the first interdisciplinary seminar, "Gender, Culture and Caribbean Development". The pieces selected reflect the programme's concern to ground the empirical and practical manifestations of gender bias into the cohesive theoretical and methodological framework. This is admirably encapsulated in Geertje Lycklama's paper. In particular, her definition of Women and Development Studies serves to anchor much of what that particular seminar, and indeed this publication, was trying to achieve: 'Women and Development Studies . . . studies the dialectical relationship in the socio-economic, political and cultural dimensions of change and represents a dynamic, comprehensive discourse which needs to be dealt with in a multi-disciplinary fashion.'

Within this framework, she offers some insights into what is involved in the institutionalisation of women's studies programmes.

Part 4 relates to the Faculty of Arts and General Studies seminar "Gender Issues in the Humanities", which sought to explore the relationship between gender and the theory and practice of the arts and the humanities. The selections are taken from literature and French linguistics. These papers do not necessarily raise the question of how to; they simply do it by employing the traditional methods of the individual disciplines to demonstrate how an understanding of gender can sharpen our interpretation of text and language.

Part 3 focuses on the Faculty of Education seminar, "Gender and Education". Here, for the first time in the volume, we begin to get a sense of the historical context in which the contemporary Caribbean Woman has emerged. We also begin to get a feel for how biases of sex, race and class infiltrate educational texts and perpetuate the traditional stereotypes. The question of how to is not asked specifically by any of these selections. However, by laying bare the obstacles, perhaps the question is being asked implicitly.

Part 5 examines gender issues in health as reflected in the Faculty of Medical Sciences seminar, "Women and Health" and includes one contribution from the Faculty of Natural Sciences seminar "Gender, Science and Technology." The selections isolate the historical and cultural factors influencing women's health and health needs; and identify the research imperatives and kind of reform required in the health-care system if women's health needs are to be adequately met. Together these papers provide a wide-ranging overview of the contemporary situation.

Part 2 addresses gender issues in law as presented in the Faculty of Law seminar, "Engendering Justice: Gender and the Rule of Law in the Commonwealth Caribbean". The selections cover the legal position of women in a number of fundamental areas: family, the home, the workplace and reproductive life. Each of the selections records how much has changed and yet how much more needs to be changed. The fundamental question raised by these papers is whether legal reform by itself can really effect significant improvements in the situation of women or whether it is not in fact necessary to take into account other factors such as cultural attitudes, the administration of justice, advances in science and technology and ethics, to mention a few. Heavy reliance is placed on public education, especially through the use of the media, to sensitise the public to the kinds of legislative reform needed to create the type of environment which will render the proposed reform effective.

Part 6 looks at gender in Caribbean agriculture. The selections are taken from the Faculty of Agriculture seminar, "Alternative Strategies for Agricultural Development: An analysis of Women and Gender Issues". These papers provide a historical overview of women's role in Caribbean agriculture and prescriptions for change in policy directions, research agenda, and strategic alliances. The question of how to is comprehensively answered by Achola Pala Okeyo in the conclusion of her keynote address. She presented a nine-point plan which incorporated an understanding of the local and international development context, use of indigenous technology and structures, organisational solidarity, research, increased donor support and South-South collaboration as the main planks.

Methodology

A reading of these papers suggests that for the CGDS the question of methodology should be relevant to its future activity in four main areas:

Research

The question here is one not only of identifying research issues, but also of designing methodologies which could adequately reflect the magnitude and complexity of the issue, the extent to which it is influenced by gender and how women are affected by the operation of the gender factor. The issue of class, for example, has been raised, explicitly or implicitly, in several of the papers in this volume (for instance, Drayton and Gordon), as critical to an understanding of the situation of women in this region. Yet a class analysis has not been applied to women. We do not know the class groupings to which women belong, how they got here or in what numbers. We do not know how their numbers relate to those of men in similar groups or if and how they move from one group to another. Nor do we know what fuels the relationship of men and women of the same class or of different classes. All we have are blanket generalisations about women of a perceived class position.

Part of the problem is that the two streams of class analysis which have prevailed in Caribbean sociology, the theoretical and the empirical, have not really merged and have certainly not addressed the question of gender and class, except in a limited way in the paper by Gordon in this volume. And the absence of that merger prevents us from knowing how social mobility transforms people's social attitudes and behaviour, or how that mobility affects the ideology governing relationships between the sexes. What available gender research does tell us is that the highly structured economic and social forces to which women are subject not only do not apply to men, but also cut across what are described as class divisions. Such things as exploitation and discrimination in the labour market, institutionalised sexual oppression such as rape, sexual harassment in the workplace, legislation confirming men as central, and the marginalisation and trivialisation of women's contributions; these are not manifestations of a class system or experiences of a single class of women. Rather they are manifestations of a gender division of labour which underpins male monopoly of power and authority and which defines and circumscribes all women.

If our concern is to relate gender and class, then we need first to find an acceptable way of defining and measuring class and secondly, to devise imaginative and sensitive methodologies to collect qualitative information about the experiences of women of different classes, however defined. Such a procedure may permit a glimpse of the operation of what the gender ideology is and how it structures gender relations across and within class boundaries. Investigations along these lines had been proposed for one of the sector studies of the ISER-sponsored Future of the Caribbean Project in 1988. The CGDS might consider exploring the status of that project and seeking ways to collaborate with ISER in any follow-up activities.

Policy

The primary undergirding of the CGDS has been correctly identified as research, primarily research which illuminates the reality of Caribbean women and secondarily research which involves theory-building. The constant concern of the CGDS should be to ensure that its research also relates to the priority development issues articulated by governments and regional development institutions. At the 23rd meeting of the Board of Governors of the Caribbean Development Bank, for example, the President identified five "windows of development" which will require constant attention if further development of the Caricom region is to attain any measure of sustainability. The five windows are macro-economic policy, physical environment, technology, human resource development and the external environment. Within each of these windows there are a number of critical issues which need to be addressed, but underpinning all of them are the prevailing social and cultural values which determine the type of social organisation we value, the goals we set and the extent to which we will attain them.

In all of this prescription, there is no mention of the differential impact on men and women of either the problems identified or the solutions prescribed. Immediately a role for the CGDS suggests itself: the provision of gender-sensitive research and information to illuminate the interior of those five windows and to identify which windows of opportunity need to be opened in order to achieve the improved physical quality of life so as to attain the heightened sense of identity, self-respect and self-reliance which are the ultimate goals.

The CGDS therefore needs to position itself, through its research and outreach activities, to provide the kinds of analytical frameworks, information and recommendations for practical action which can inform the process of development decision-making in the region. It must learn the development language. It must learn how to transform its research findings into the language and idiom which policy-makers and administrators understand. It must learn to experiment with ways of generating policy decisions and programme action from its research. It must assist its students to develop an interest in and sensitivity to the key priority areas which our development institutions are identifying. And it must equip itself to collaborate with those responsible for making the major economic decisions affecting our daily lives.

Outreach

Several papers, notably those concerned with planning (Antrobus), health (Allen, Massiah) and agriculture (French) mention the advantages of strategic alliances with NGOs and community groups as a means of furthering the goals of particular activities and ultimately of ensuring the empowerment of women.

The CGDS itself has adopted this as a regular tenet of its own programming, as the organisation of these seminars has shown. However, there is need for much more intensive analysis of which alliances are of greater strategic advantage and for which purpose. There is need to expand the circle of alliances beyond the confines of NGOs and to look to the public and private sectors, the international development community and even to private individuals. There is need to craft with each partner a particular set of activities which extends the work of both parties, while at the same time ensuring that the particular goals of each are achieved. In other words, the question of outreach is not merely a matter of inviting significant others to participate in the activities of the CGDS. It is about collaborative research, design, implementation and evaluation of action programmes. It is about developing a sustainable relationship which nurtures both parties and empowers the women whom they both seek to serve.

Management

The particular organisational format chosen by the CGDS, the participatory approach, is perhaps the most difficult one to operate successfully within an academic setting. Ideally, everything should be developed and executed collectively [operational strategies, curricula development, research proposals] and that alone creates formidable problems. When the collective is scattered across departments and faculties, across campuses which are geographically separated by thousands of miles, the difficulties multiply. And when the coordinating unit of the collective is not anchored within a specific faculty but in the administrative centre of the University, the difficulties multiply even more.

But there are two major advantages which the CGDS enjoys. The regional nature of the UWI implies a potential for the CGDS to draw on a range of resources. Thus, for example, each of the seminars which are the subject of this volume involved staff and participants from all of the campuses. When one campus CGDS was unable to organise a seminar, another was able to substitute. When this volume was being prepared on one campus, staff on the other two were called on for assistance.

By the same token, it is possible to utilise the University resources to facilitate collaborative programmes across the region. For example, it is possible for a campus CGDS to develop a training programme with an NGO or a women's bureau and to beam it across the region through the University's Distance Teaching (UWIDITE) system. This is an effective way of enabling women's groups across the region to share information with each other and at the same time to draw on the expertise of the CGDS. The CGDS, in turn, becomes familiar with the work of these organisations and is enabled to draw on that work to inform its research and teaching agenda.

The second major advantage lies in the management style of the CGDS which has emphasised collaboration, caring and sharing. It has also showed flexibility, improvisation, risk-taking and a kind of "creative makeshift" which produces enviable results again and again. It is a management style which differs radically from the rest of the academy and which needs to be analysed, documented and used as case study teaching material in both the CGDS and the Department of Management Studies. The model can become a contribution to organisational theory and an exemplar of the interdisciplinary approach to which the multidisciplinary approaches reflected in these essays aspire.

Conclusion

These papers represent a remarkable collection of thought on the issues facing Caribbean women. In many cases they provide no definitive answers to the complex questions raised. However, they are unanimous in their conviction that the answers are not unilinear. Rather, the multi–dimensional nature of the issue of gender itself demands a multifaceted response whether in terms of policy, planning, legislation or systems development.

The issue which arises now is, how much can the CGDS achieve in terms of addressing the variety of sectoral diagnoses reflected in these papers? Even on the assumption that the CGDS itself is properly equipped in terms of staff and resources, it is hardly likely that it can fully address the agenda of research and action which the papers and even this introduction imply. It might be more practical to select and concentrate on a limited number of areas where effective programmes can be established. To a large extent these should be guided by the strength of the alliances with partners outside of the University community and the possibility of successfully mounting joint efforts in mutually agreed areas. While some of this must necessarily be operative at the national level, the very structure of the CGDS demands that a significant portion of its programming be pitched at the regional level. Much scope exists at that level as has been demonstrated by the preparations for participation in the Fourth World Conference on Women (WCW) which proceeded within a regional framework.

The message of the essays in this volume has been one of the need for strategies for development in each of the sectors addressed. The message from the government and from NGOs who prepared national reports for the WCW has been one of the need for a development model which protects the areas in which women have achieved some progress and institutes measures to correct the imbalances which have been reported in many territories. The most significant imbalances have been identified by Mondesire and Dunn (1994) as:

- women's low access to the established loci of power and their inability to utilise power in areas where they have an advantage
- the use of physical and psychological force against women
- the growing impoverishment of women

Underpinning these imbalances are the growing crisis in the family, the economic development strategies adopted over the past two decades and the invisible unwaged work of women which bolsters society. The message is the need for a new paradigm of development based on a more balanced concept of social justice.

If the CGDS could review these national reports, select two or three of the most acute problem areas, link them to the relevant papers from the seminar and develop a programme of research, teaching and advocacy around them, then the organisation of these seminars would have yielded much.

References

Caribbean Development Bank. "Statement of the President". 23rd Annual Meeting of the Board of Governors. 12-13 May, 1993.

Drayton, Kathleen. "Women and Development Studies: The Cave Hill Experience". Paper presented at the 10th Anniversary Symposium, WDS, UWI, Cave Hill. 1-2 December, 1993.

Leo-Rhynie, Elsa. "Women and Development Studies: Moving from the Periphery?". Inaugural Professorial Lecture presented at the 10th Anniversary Symposium, WDS, UWI, Mona. 8-10 December, 1992.

Mohammed, Patricia and Shepherd, Catherine (eds). "Gender in Caribbean Development." University of the West Indies, Women and Development Studies Project, Mona, Jamaica; St Augustine, Trinidad and Tobago; Cave Hill, Barbados. 1988.

Mondesire, Alicia and Dunn, Leith. "Towards Equity and Development: A Report on the Status of Women in Sixteen Commonwealth Caribbean Countries." Prepared for the 4th World Conference on Women, 1995. Caribbean Community Secretariat, Georgetown, Guyana, 1994.

Thorpe, Marjorie. "Women's Rights as Human Rights". Keynote address presented at the 10th Anniversary Celebrations, WDS, UWI, St Augustine. March 1993.

University of the West Indies, Women and Development Studies Project. "Composite Report of the Three Interdisciplinary Seminars in Women and Development Studies at the University of the West Indies". Institute of Social and Economic Research, UWI, St Augustine, Trinidad. November 1987.

Part ONE

Gender and Development Research and Policy

Gender and Development

Research and Policy

Introduction

Elsa Leo-Rhynie

The papers which comprise Part 1 were presented at interdisciplinary seminars on gender and development held between 1986 and 1990. The keynote address of Johnnetta Cole was delivered at the 1986 conference in Jamaica, and it identifies a thread which runs through all the papers: the misconceptions and assumptions about women and their roles in society on which development policy, planning and practice have been structured. Geertje Lycklama à Nieholt examines theoretical and practical issues relating to activities involved in the institutionalisation of women and development studies in universities. Derek Gordon looks at the importance of including women in sociological research being used for planning. Peggy Antrobus looks critically at traditional methods of development planning and proposes an alternative analysis which is based on feminist theory. Gwendoline Williams explores the process of mainstreaming gender analysis in development planning.

Johnnetta Cole outlines some popularly accepted beliefs about developing societies such as those of the Caribbean; beliefs which centre on cultural elements, including the complex issues of gender, race and class systems, which are seen as hindrances to development. One example is female-headed households which, Cole argues, are viewed as a problem, when in fact the real problem is poverty, brought about, particularly over the past 20 years, by the policies of the International Monetary Fund (IMF). She points out that development projects do not necessarily develop women and encourages the examination of the survival value of culture and its potential for effecting positive change in the lives of women.

This theme is echoed in the presentation of Lycklama à Nieholt, who notes that in efforts to institutionalise women and development studies, a strategy utilised in any one situation cannot be slavishly followed in another, as the cultural context must be an important consideration. The process itself raises some theoretical as well as practical issues. What definition of development will be used in the women and development studies discourse? What type of institutionalisation? How and under what conditions? She urges considering development as a process of transformation and institutionalisation which seeks to bring about change at all levels, challenging particularly the methodology of knowledge generation. The process of institutionalisation in a number of countries in Asia and Africa, as well as a case study of the Institute for Social Studies in The Hague, reveal the variety of ways in which this process has responded to demand in different historical and cultural backgrounds. One factor which the author feels is very important, regardless of the way in which institutionalisation takes place, is the continued linkage and networking between academic programmes in women and development studies and activist feminist groups in society.

Omission of women from studies of social mobility has traditionally been justified on the basis of assumptions about gender and class in society, the major one being that women derive their social class positions from those of their husbands. Derek Gordon examines the inappropriateness of such a model in situations such as exist in Jamaica and the Caribbean, where a large percentage of household heads are women, and where there is widespread involvement of women in the labour force. Gordon cites his work in the Jamaica Mobility Survey which, by taking women into account, has provided a much richer database than would otherwise have been available; data which allow, for example, an assessment of intersections of race, class and gender in the formation of family units. He notes that there are special challenges to be faced when working with data where the mobility of men and women is not entirely independent of each other, and that different strategies are needed to overcome these challenges. Certain issues arise in the use of these strategies, however, such as the assumptions on which the actual measurement of occupational status ought to be based and the unit of analysis—individual or household—in the analysis of social class. Gordon discusses the use of separate measurement scales for men and women followed by cross-gender and within-gender comparisons, and advocates studying the interaction of individuals and households and the way in which this affects class formation and behaviour.

Peggy Antrobus' work is critical of women in development (WID) strategies promoted and implemented by international agencies and governments, which have been based on the assumption that women operate outside the development process and need to be integrated into the mainstream. She points to the central contributions of women to development, which were: 'the very base on which development was constructed; but in a way that was deeply exploitative of their time, labour, both paid (in the workplace) and unpaid (in the household), and their sexuality.'

Antrobus details conventional approaches to development planning and the gender ideology undergirding it. She cites, for example, structural adjustment policies, which result in reduced spending in the social sector where women predominate as key players. She proposes an alternative analysis based on feminist theory. Five criteria on which such an analysis should be based are presented and discussed, and the implications for the use of this approach are examined. She identifies three levels of gender analysis: policy, planning and action and implementation levels, and looks critically at tools such as checklists, impact statements and training approaches currently being used in this analysis. The experiences of the Women and Development Unit (WAND) of the University of the West Indies, which has shifted its focus over the years from integration of women into development to the empowerment of women, are used to demonstrate the use of this alternative analysis.

The inclusion of gender analysis in the development planning process is also addressed by Gwendoline Williams, who relates its slow progress in spite of the commitment of governments and other agencies to its implementation. Her contention is that the approach traditionally used in development planning focuses on economics, financial management and technology, to the detriment of socio-cultural and behavioural aspects. Williams identifies issues which need to be addressed in policy determination. These include the following.

1. The recognition of women as active contributors as well as beneficiaries of the development process.
2. The use of a development planning methodology which removes the invisibility of women from the development process.
3. The use of gender as a variable in data collection and analysis for planning purposes, so as to fully document women's triple role.

Three case studies—CARICOM, the World Bank and the Ministry of Settlements and Public Utilities in Trinidad and Tobago—are used to highlight the possibilities and constraints in trying to develop and use a gender 'lens' in development planning. These studies point to the vital importance of a social analysis, incorporating gender, at the stage of framing policy and designing projects, and the inclusion of gender in the social impact analysis which ought to be a component of the review and evaluation stages of both policies and projects. The potential and prospects for the inclusion of gender in community-based development planning, decision-making and implementation are also demonstrated. Williams acknowledges the challenges presented by the need to integrate gender into planning, but stresses the importance of documentation and the integration of comprehensive sets of social data with technical information to allow for the effective use of the gender variable in development planning and implementation.

Gender, Culture and Caribbean Development

Johnetta Cole

I am deeply honoured to be a part of what promises to be an intellectually exciting and profoundly significant seminar. I thank you for giving me the opportunity to participate.

I have convinced myself that there is an important reason why you asked me to give this keynote address. It is captured in a saying of an anthropologist Clyde Kluckhohn, that I am very fond of: 'It is scarcely the fish who discovers water.' Fish are so involved with just doing what fish do in water, that one does not jump out of the water and from some distance say: 'Well now, let me contemplate the nature of water.' Let me philosophically examine the very nature of H_2O. Anthropologists have built a discipline on the very notion that distance gives insights.

Perhaps my distance as an Afro-American woman of the USA can bring a particular set of lenses for looking at what is so very close to persons in the Caribbean, perhaps a little too close. We know that one sees differently from a distance as opposed to close up. And so, minimally, I can bring you a different view.

A second and related reason why you might be justified in asking me to give this keynote address is, again, something which we have learned from the discipline of anthropology: the value of the comparative method. In this paper some ideas about gender, culture and Caribbean development are proposed, partly by making comparisons with the situation of women and men in Afro-American communities in the USA.

If there are advantages in this distance, and in the use of the comparative method, there are also dangers. For example, from my vantage point, that of an Afro-American woman living in the USA, I may see something in the Caribbean that looks like a phenomenon I know in the USA, and I may proceed to compare and contrast it with a US pattern. But despite how profoundly similar the experiences of Black folks throughout the Americas, we need to fully respect the historical and cultural specificities of our realities.

The experiences of black women in the USA are strikingly similar to those of Afro-Caribbean women, but they are not identical. It seems to me that the most fundamental mistake in women's studies programmes in the USA is the assumption that if you have seen one woman, you have seen us all. In North America white middle-class women, Afro-American women, Hispanic women, Asian women and Indian and Native American women are bound by shared experiences of living in a country where sexism is a fundamental part of the ideology in the society. But the daily lives of these various groups of women can be as different as night and day.

It is particularly important then for us not to slip into the habit of homogenising women's experiences when we come to look at black women in the USA and the Caribbean. We share 'race' (whatever that is), we have a culture which is derived from an African base, and we have the common experiences of slavery, but we are not the same. There are important particularities in the experiences of women in Barbados compared with Jamaica; Antigua compared with Tortola; Haiti compared with Trinidad and Cuba compared with Puerto Rico. Having carried out fieldwork in Cuba, I am particularly aware of how similarly and differently the woman question proceeds there. And of course there are significant differences among various groups of women in a single Caribbean island, differences which are a reflection of age, colour, class, sexual preference, political views, religion, physical ability or disability, the part of the island where one lives, and other factors.

And yet, are there not those experiences, aspirations, pains, victories, which connect in serious and moving ways, black women of my country and you sisters? Yes, there are lines that divide us, Afro-Caribbean and US Afro-American women, but there are also ties that bind. When we are in relationships of marriage or other arrangements with a man, and we, like the man, are working outside the household, when we each come home exhausted from a day of work, who is it that tends the kids, cleans the house, cooks the food, washes the dishes? Guess who? I tell you, in the Caribbean or the US, the answer is the same. And whether it is black women in North America or in the Caribbean, notice these similar patterns. It is we women who are the major participants in the churches, the backbones they call us, frying the chicken, making the roti, but it is the brothers who are almost always the heads, the leaders. It is we women who take the notes at the meetings, organise the buses for the rallies, go door-to-door to get the votes, but it is almost always the brothers who are the Prime Ministers.

Is it not of interest that whether the setting is the Caribbean or the USA, when the question of black women's studies is raised, many of our distinguished brother colleagues snicker?

Yes, there are lines that divide us, but there are also ties that do indeed bind us, sisters of the Caribbean and the USA.

I think that one of the most striking points about the theme of gender, culture and development, is the currency of a myth concerning the relationship between the three components. Here of course we are focusing on the Caribbean, but it is my contention that wherever the site (and if the issue is development, then it is assumed that we are talking about a nation of people of colour), there is a myth that third-world culture (for which read backward, primitive ways) and society's gender system (for which read women) are the major obstacles to development. Development itself is romanticised as some ideal state in which industrialised, capitalist countries exist, and to which third–world countries aspire. But because of the drain of backward cultural ways, and the drag of women in the society, the road to development is going to be pretty rough going. Put in slightly different language for a different part of the world, Africa is underdeveloped because of the Africans, not, as Walter Rodney so brilliantly demonstrated, that it was and is Europe (and America) that underdevelops Africa.

Let me offer an example of how the myth concerning gender, culture and development operates with respect to the Caribbean. The Caribbean would develop faster if the people would give up a host of backward cultural notions: about birth control, about duppies, about smoking ganja, about when, under what conditions and for how much one works. The Caribbean would develop faster if women would just stop having so many babies and if they would give up their cultural propensity for matriarchal families. As a final example, the Caribbean would develop faster if the masses of black people would just work harder and behave like the culturally sophisticated brown folks, like the elite. Embedded in this mythology about development are certain notions about race and class as well as gender and culture.

This is reminiscent of the way that the state of black America is explained vis-a-vis highly developed, middle- and upper-class white America. You see, black Americans are underdeveloped because of their matriarchal families, their backward black cultural ways and their poverty.

While I am rejecting the myth that Caribbean culture and gender are the principal impediments to development, I am not suggesting that there is no relationship among the three. My argument is that there are complex and dynamic relationships among development, gender, culture, race and class. But before we can attempt to hint at characterising all of that, we need to take a tour into the land of definitions.

Race

In the Caribbean countries (as well as in the USA), the experience and legacy of slavery and the post-emancipation period gave rise to racially stratified societies in which colour and class were tied. White masters often raped or, more simply, took black women as mistresses, and the offspring of these illicit unions formed a new coloured class. In the Caribbean (as in the USA), lighter skin afforded more opportunities and these offspring of Africans and Europeans sometimes inherited land and money from the masters. This resulted in a creole society made up of the ruling planter class and the newly-created coloured middle class, while black people remained at the bottom of the strata.

In these islands ex-slaves quickly left their plantations to establish villages and economic independence from their former masters, resulting in the necessity of importing Chinese, Portuguese and East Indian labour. Later, the interaction of all these groups led to even further social stratification and friction amongst them. These historical features set the stage for a correspondence of race and ethnicity with class and status, despite calls for unity such as: "Out of many, one people".

The importance of these realities when considering development will be introduced shortly.

Class

Class and colour are closely tied in the Caribbean. But when one speaks of class in a developing country, what are we really talking about? If one is bound to a given set of terms and seeks a ruling class in the Caribbean one may not find it there, for it is largely made up of absentees. The owners of industry are in North America and in Europe. Underneath are the indigenous upper-middle class and a few rich owners of large businesses. But Caribbean economies for the most part depend upon intensive foreign investment in order to exploit their most precious resources, such as bauxite in Jamaica and oil in Trinidad. Thus there is a ruling class, so to speak, that is largely removed from the internal class structure of the islands. This does not mean that an internal class structure with an elite does not exist. It does, but occupational status and money are gained far more often from civil service careers and the professions than from "ownership of the means of production".

Culture

Few, if any, social science concepts rival 'culture' in terms of the profusion of definitions and the resultant confusion. It is not my intention to launch into a full-scale review of the hundreds of definitions found in anthropology nor the varied ways in which the term is used in the development literature in women's studies and everyday parlance.

The definition of culture is quite simply that it is a people's patterns of and for behaviour. But let us be clear: these patterns do not just mysteriously appear from somewhere, nor are they a weird collection of beliefs and practices, one set associated with this group and another set with a neighbouring group. In my view culture, as patterns of and for behavior, is best viewed as the totality of values, ideas and means by which a given people deals with its environment, geographical, social, political and economic.

When culture is looked at in this way, we realise that Afro-Caribbeans and Afro-Americans in the USA share a generalised culture that is based on a common historical past: the wretchedness of slavery, the trials of post-emancipation and the ongoing struggle against racist ideologies and forms of economic colonialism.

It is precisely because our histories and current conditions are similar in certain ways that we find similarities in the cultural expressions of black folks in the Caribbean and in the USA: matrifocal families; widespread involvement with religious organisations; a coming together of religious and political leadership; patterns of women working (dating back to the days of slavery which was the last time there was full employment for all black women and men); extended families; the importance of clubs, associations and societies in social, political and economic life; the centrality of music in our lives, and so on.

Gender

Among the few things that we anthropologists are quite sure about is that cross-culturally, gender is a meaningful concept, but because it is not biologically, but culturally and historically determined, it is not an easy thing to grab hold of. We may think that being a woman is the same all over the world in terms of expectations, mores, values and realities. But that is far from the case. Indeed, within a given society like the USA, concepts of 'womanness' and 'manness' vary considerably by race and ethnic group, by class, by region of the country, and by sexual preference. And of course in the Caribbean there are also differences, despite the overall ideology concerning what is of and for women as opposed to that which is of and for men. It is that overall ideology that is of most concern, it seems to me, in considerations of development.

Who sets out the idea that there is a traditional sexual division of labour that must be maintained? Where did the idea come from that women are the natural and in fact the only creatures designed to care for others—babies, the sick, men, older relatives? Why is it considered so strange to image a woman president of almost anything? Equally, why is it considered strange to think of men as day-care workers?

The problem with this set of ideas about who does what is that inevitably, what women are said to be good at, restricted to, designed for, is valued less than whatever is said to be man's natural sphere.

But women do hold up half of the sky, and no society can truly develop if it does not recognise and reward the fact.

Development

Finally, we turn to the question of development. What is it, for whom is it designed, how does a country get some of it? There are different ways of defining development.

I recall very vividly the way in which I came to see what development is and is not. I was working in Liberia, West Africa, from 1960 to 1962, engaged in fieldwork for my PhD in anthropology, but simultaneously involved in a research project in which Northwestern University was carrying out the first economic survey of Liberia. It was a time of considerable growth in the Liberian economy, including structural changes and transformation of the economy. But, at the same time, the men who tapped the rubber trees on the Firestone plantation were still making 25 cents a day. Women, sitting in front of the totality of their stock, were hawking five single cigarettes, eight boxes of chewing-gum, some groundnuts, a little pepper and a few kola nuts. Attempting to capture this situation, the Northwestern research team entitled its book on the economy and society of Liberia, *Growth without Development*.

The term development, as I use it, involves more than the quantitative growth of material output, especially when such growth occurs simultaneously with gross inequities in income and access to social services. I see development in terms of a process which focuses on the people for whom development is planned and on the society in which they live. Let me quote the paper; 'Referred to as a "people oriented" approach this model of development incorporates the elements of economic growth with popular participation in the process by which development is achieved. Its aim is an equitable distribution of income and social amenities in society.' Using development in these terms, one can describe black America as an underdeveloped sector within the USA; and with few exceptions, the Caribbean is an underdeveloped region.

The Roles of Race, Class, Gender and Culture in Caribbean Development: Some preliminary considerations

In this section of the paper I wish to explore-tentatively—a few examples of how development in the Caribbean is affected by race, class, gender and culture. In the process, I hope to maintain a sensitivity to differences (as raised in my introductory comments) and also to heighten our understanding through a few comparisons with the situation of black women in the USA.

Race, Class and Gender in the Caribbean

Although race and femaleness combined place women of colour in double jeopardy in the Caribbean, this combination is not expressed in exactly the same way for all women. In the Caribbean, as indeed in the USA, and throughout the world, some women are more oppressed than other women and some women can act as the oppressors of other women.

I want to make an inference from Elsa Leo-Rhynie and Marlene Hamilton's article on Jamaican professional women (1982): 'The middle-class group was able to instil this value . . . for their daughters (to obtain an education and achieve professional status) and provide the support needed for its daughters . . . (That this is the case) is evidenced by the fact that many professional women today belong to the category of second-generation middle class.' My inference is that since the lighter-skinned Caribbean middle-class woman is more likely to become educated instead of pregnant at an early age, she has a better chance of becoming a professional. And since her darker, poor sisters are more likely to be one of the relatively low-cost domestics that the professional is able to afford, there is a situation where one black woman is the employer and potentially the exploiter of another black woman. In writing on domestic workers in the Caribbean, Patricia Mohammed demonstrates what we all know, that these women are among the most exploited on the labour market today.

One of the many ironical twists in the US labour market is that today, black women born in the USA are moving out of domestic work and are being replaced by women from Latin America, the Caribbean and and less often, Asia. This means that middle-class Afro-American women are sometimes the employers and exploiters of Afro-Caribbean and Afro-Latin women. However, it is still the case that the overwhelming majority of employers of domestics are white American women.

Women in the Caribbean who work other than domestic work are mostly self-employed as purveyors of cooked foods, seamstresses and petty traders. This type of self-employment is often ignored in considerations of their country's economy.

Another contribution of Caribbean women to the economies of the region which is not recorded or fully appreciated consists of remittances sent back home from wages earned in the USA and Canada. The source of these wages is often domestic work, and they are wages received under the most harsh of conditions. Caribbean sisters are forced to put up with the exploitative working conditions and lack of respect shown them because they often do not have permanent resident status in the USA.

It should be emphasised that although there are some black women in the Caribbean (as in the USA) who become professionals, the majority of black women remain at the bottom of the labour market: ununionized and underpaid and as a group paid less than men for the same job done. Even when Caribbean women become part of an elite corps of professionals, they share the experience of discrimination on the job. For instance, one attorney-at-law/judge interviewed by Leo-Rhynie and Hamilton reported: 'The test for a female to obtain a senior post is much more stringent than for males. I had to "superperform" to warrant a break with tradition.'

Culture and Gender in Caribbean Development

A full discussion is not offered here of the complex relationships between the ideology and realities of gender and culture within the process of Caribbean development. Instead the focus is on what is perhaps the most discussed aspect of Caribbean and North American black culture: the so-called matriarchal or matrifocal, or female-headed, household. From the days of the infamous Moynihan report, to the title of the book *My Mother Who Fathered Me,* to today's commissions, studies, panels and conferences on female-headed households in the black world, there is an incredibly simple point that is missed: the problem with female-headed households is not that they are headed by females, but that they are poor. The profusion of such households in the Caribbean and among black Americans has been viewed as an expression of an African cultural retention, a carryover from patterns in West Africa of polygamous marriages which consist of several matrifocal units. This view, associated with the early work of Melville J. Herskovits, was in opposition to the ideas of scholars like E. Franklin Frazier who saw Afro-American culture as devoid of Africanisms and argued therefore that patterns such as matrifocal households were in response to economic and other conditions in the USA. It is not clear to me why female households cannot be both, that is, a choice by Afro-American peoples to maintain an African pattern, which not only permitted their survival under the most oppressive conditions of slavery, but today represents a cultural response to the oppressive conditions of racism, sexism and classism.

The problem of female-headed households exists when men, be they conjugal lovers , visiting mates or legal husbands, cannot help out with the economic needs of a family or when a woman is not able herself to carry the financial responsibilities of a family. Astronomical rates of unemployment mean that staggering numbers of Caribbean (like Afro-American) men cannot contribute to their families' material needs. In the Caribbean 75 per cent of women are mothers. Yet this tradition of self-support is being threatened by worsening economic conditions.

A. Lynn Bolles cited the disastrous effects upon working-class Jamaican women during the International Monetary Fund (IMF) destabilisation of the late 1970s. 'Due to the high rates of unemployment . . . many men who would have assumed responsibility for child support were unable to do so. In addition, single women were hurt by factory shut-downs due to the lack of raw materials.' But at the same time that these forces (that is, political and economic forces such as unemployment), external to our communities, adversely affect our families and households, there are cultural ideas within our communities which, while they may have developed in response to those external forces, we must take control of and change.

One of these is the growing incidence in the Caribbean and the USA of babies making babies. The rate of teenage pregnancy is on the rise. This trend is clearly a reflection of worsening economic and social conditions in our communities. But this is a moral issue that we must address. I do not mean a moral issue in the way that the fundamentalist, right-wing religious forces use that term, reflecting their obsessive concern about who is sleeping with whom. I mean moral in the most profound sense of that term. For is it not immoral to rob a teenager of the possibility of an education, of developing at the slow but steady pace that leads to a full, productive and happy life? And is it not immoral to deny the baby of the baby even a few of life's opportunities?

In summary, what can we say about culture, gender and development in the Caribbean? Perhaps the most important thing to say is how complex these things are.

We have suggested that any considerations of development in the Caribbean must include race and class no less than gender and culture as key elements.

Although gender roles are not the same in each colour group and class in the Caribbean, in general we can say that it is not women who are blocking development, but attitudes about what women can and cannot do. As long as society operates on the assumption that half of its population is more rational, smarter,and less capable of nurturing and caring than the other half, then how can it fully develop the potential of all, providing what are in fact the basic rights of education, health and employment opportunities? But we must admit that gender-biased attitudes are not the sole possession of men. We must recall, for example, that it is women who are the major socialisers of our children, and that includes being the major socialisers of our children in terms of what is 'proper' behaviour for men and women.

Another important point which crops up in current development literature, is that what are conceived of as development projects and schemes do not necessarily benefit women. It is rare for the particular experiences and needs of women to be taken into consideration when the schemes are concocted, so why should their results be particularly sensitive to the needs of women?

There is a duality in the development process. Of course, aspects of Caribbean culture can serve as a drain on development, but one needs to go to the roots of those cultural patterns, where one finds very often that they are responses to exploitative situations whose sources are patterns or forces outside the Afro-Caribbean or Indian Caribbean community. So culture can be, in all of its complexities, an instrument of survival, of resistance and ultimately, of course, of positive change.

So who will change biased attitudes and sexist behaviour towards women in the Caribbean? Who will consciously use Caribbean culture in the interest of positive change and development? In response to these questions, I want to draw on a story told by the great civil rights organiser Fannie Lou Hamer of Mississippi.

At a meeting of the National Association for the Advancement of Coloured People (NAACP), Mrs Hamer told this story in a speech on the role of black women in the USA.

Some kids wanted to trick a wise old man. So they plotted to ask him a question. They planned that they would each get a bird and hold the bird behind their backs. They would ask the old man 'What do we hold in our hands? Is the bird dead or alive?' If he says alive, we'll crush it. If he says dead, we'll let it fly away.

And so they approached the old man with the question: 'What do we hold in our hands, is it dead or alive?' And the old man in his infinite wisdom looked up and said, 'It's in your hands!'

References

Bolles, A. Lynne. *The Impact of Working-Class Women's Employment on Household Organizations in Kingston, Jamaica.* PhD thesis. State University of New Jersey, New Brunswick, New Jersey. 1981.

Clarke, Edith. *My Mother Who Fathered Me.* 2nd edn. London: George Allen and Unwin 1966 (first published 1957).

Frazier, E. Franklin. *The Negro Family in the United States.* Chicago: University of Chicago Press. 1939.

Herskovits, Melville J. *The Myth of the Negro Past.* Boston: Beacon Press. 1958 (first published 1941).

Mohammed, Patricia. "Domestic Workers", in Ellis Pat (ed.), *Women in the Caribbean.* Kingston: Kingston Publishers. 1986.

Moynihan, Daniel. *The Negro Family: the Case for National Action.* Washington DC: Office of Policy Planning and Research, US Department of Labor. 1965.

Leo-Rhynie, Elsa and Hamilton, Marlene. "Professional Jamaican Women: Equal or Not?" *Caribbean Quarterly,* Vol. 29, Nos. 3 and 4, 1983, pp. 70-85.

Rodney, Walter. *How Europe Underdeveloped Africa.* Dar es Salaam: Tanzania Publishing House; London: Bogle L'Overture Publications. 1972.

Women and Development

Some Theoretical and Practical Considerations

Geertje Lycklama à Nieholt

Introduction*

Over the past 15 to 20 years, we have seen a process of increasing institutionalisation of women's concerns in all kinds of institutions and structures, and in particular, those related to development. This process was and is greatly encouraged and to some extent supported by the United Nations (UN), its regional commissions and its specialised agencies. In particular, during the UN Decade for Women (1976-85), resources were made available for this in women's bureaux, women's divisions and women's centres, for example. In the same period there has also been a tremendous growth in research, carried out especially by women of the South in the South. With a few exceptions, the same can as yet not be said of teaching. So far most teaching programmes concerned with women's issues in development are found in the North; the Institute of Social Studies (ISS) in The Hague, of which I am a part, sustains one of these programmes. In teaching, a lot of shifting of resources, of sharing and of exchange still needs to take place.

*I would like to thank my friend and colleague Dr Renee Pittin for her insightful comments on an earlier draft of this paper.

The objective of this paper is to bring forward, on the basis of a comparative analysis of western and third–world experience, the relevant theoretical and practical considerations of institutionalising women and development studies in university systems. To do a world survey in a brief paper is not quite possible; therefore I shall highlight a number of experiences which seem to be relevant. Based on these, I shall raise important questions for considering how women's studies may be institutionalised which may clarify the differences and may also point to some similarities-and even lessons that can be learned in such a way as to lead to mutual strengthening.

Before any practical experiences are considered, it will be helpful to first elaborate on some of the concepts and make clear how we understand them.

Clarification of Concepts

In discussing the institutionalisation of Women and Development Studies as they are understood at the Institute of Social Studies, first it is necessary tomake clear what we understand by development. Do we see development as a process of economic growth, with or without equality? Or do we refer to far more encompassing processes of transformation at the global, the national and the household levels, which lead to the emancipation of all people? Are these processes of transformation which affect the socio-economic, the political, the legal and the cultural dimensions of life and are characterised by accountability, cooperation and sharing, instead of power play, competition and individual accumulation? The latter combination usually characterises development as it takes place in present mainstream capitalist development. A study by Gita Sen and Caren Grown has forcefully documented the detrimental effects for women of this latter type of development, which is andro-centric and strongly biased against women. The women's movement, and in particular third-world feminism, wants to transform this kind of andro-centric capitalist development and recognises that development is a highly political process involving political choices. Thus, when dealing with the institutionalisation of women and development studies, one cannot escape the political question of what kind of development is being pursued. This question should at least become part of the women's studies discourse. The answer depends to a large extent on the given socio-political and economic context in which one is working or rather 'institutionalising'.

The term institutionalisation also needs elaboration. Most of the institutionalisation of women's concerns has taken place under the auspices of the UN, and this has been promoted with the strategy of integrating women into development. The question of what kind of development must be left to the member states, although in practice this mostly leads to integration into mainstream capitalist development. Not only are women thus institutionalised within a type of development which is capitalist in nature, but also this type of development is patriarchal in nature and biased against women. Feminists have criticised this strategy and pointed out that women are already fully integrated into development, since in fact, without all the work that women are doing, there would be no development. The problem is that women's work (domestic work, subsistence prdoduction, bringing up the next generation and caring for the sick and the elderly), is not recognised as valuable work in comparison with wage work. Women are usually subsumed under the family and therefore it is thought that they, like their children, are being provided for by the husband or father. This assumption is not true for milllions of women. Such a strategy denies the conflicts of interest which often exist between women and men and the unequal distribution of power among them. The integration and institutionalisation of women into mainstream development without transformation of that type of development will in many cases only lead to a further undermining of women's socio-economic position; we have witnessed this process often during the past few decades (Sen and Grown 1987; Rogers 1980; Boserup 1970). Instituionalisation is not a neutral process. It is very important to critically assess into what one is being institutionalised, how and under what conditions. Women and development is a highly political phenomenon which needs to be recognised as such. Only by recognising its not so innocent character can we fruitfully consider and discuss the question of what has been called the institutionalising of women and development studies in university systems.

Clarification is also needed on what we mean by women's studies. Women's studies should not just mean any academic study on women. It represents an area of study which aims at realising societal change, moving beyond the boundaries of academia into direct interaction with the wider community. In this way it has the potential for changing the present power relationships in society at large (Bowles and Duelli Klein 1983: 13). Women's studies, or feminist studies as it is also called, is generally seen as the academic arm of the women's movement; in that sense it serves the movement in realising its goals. These goals are fundamental changes (see for example Mies 1983). Minnich (1982:9) puts it as follows: 'What we (feminists) are doing, is comparable to Copernicus shattering our geo-centricity, Darwin shattering our species-centricity. We are shattering andro-centricity, and the change is as fundamental, as dangerous, as exciting'. Women's studies does so by critically reviewing the explicit and implicit assumptions underlying the theory and the methodology of the various sciences. This implies radical transformations in the systems and processes of knowledge creation. By sustaining strong links with the women's movement, the reality of women's lives is brought into the scientific discourse and thus academic work, which from a woman's perspective has become quite sterile, is transformed into creative new scholarship which brings forward new, challenging theories and methodologies. This scholarly work in the true sense of science leads to a better understanding of women's reality and their everyday life and work, as manifested in the political, economic, social, legal and cultural dimensions of life. It contributes to a realisation of the goals of the women's movement: human emancipation and women's liberation. For this creative new scholarship, it is necessary to move beyond the often fragmented disciplinary approach to a much more holistic multidisciplinary approach, in order to move away from the compartmentalisation of, for instance, the knowledge concerning processes of change and development. Women's studies also challenges the usually low representation of women among scientific scholars.

Women and development studies is women's studies. Like women's studies, it transcends the boundaries of disciplines and reaches out to women's lives at grassroots level. In addition, however, its special focus is on the dynamics of the processes of global change and development. It transcends national boundaries and focuses on global processes of change as they affect women; for example, economic and social restructuring, shifts in political power and re-emerging cultural forces such as religious fundamentalism. It brings into the academic discourse the plight of women who are most affected by the economic exploitation inherent in the present dominant economic system, whereby race, class and position in the global economy are determining factors.

Its emphasis is also on the similarities of global phenomena, for example, how women's labour is exploited in putting out systems and home-working, phenomena which are found both in the North and the South, and the patterns of violence against women. It studies modernisation and the changes which lead to the marginalisation and devaluation of women's rights, values and culture (as for example in the media).

Women and development studies in this way studies the dialectical relationship in the socio-economic, political and cultural dimensions of change and represents a dynamic comprehensive discourse which needs to be dealt with in a multidisciplinary fashion. Considering the challenges that women's studies presents, it is no surprise that those in power, especially those who have vested interests in academia, mostly have not extended a warm welcome to them. The next question then is, what the experience with the institutionalisation of women and development studies has been so far, and how it has taken place.

Establishing Women's Studies: The experience

I shall share with you our institutionalisation experience at the ISS, but first I would like to refer to some general points which emerge out of experience in the North. Here, a debate has been raging about the institutionalisation of women's studies, and it still continues, which presents a sharp dichotomy between the integration of women's studies in the various disciplines and existing general courses, so-called mainstreaming, and the establishment of more autonomous departments or programmes. A good overview of the arguments can be found in *Theories of Women's Studies*, edited by Gloria Bowles and Renate Duelli Klein (1983), in a special issue of *Women's Studies International Forum* (Vol. 7, No. 3, 1984) entitled 'Strategies for Women's Studies in the '80s' and in an article by Margaret Andersen in the winter 1987 issue of *Signs*. It turns out that in actual practice, women's studies is being institutionalised in a great variety of ways, depending very much on the specific circumstances, the kind of people involved and their strategic insights. The extremes of autonomy, integration and mainstreaming are usually considerably modified (see McIntosh and Miniich, 1984). In all cases, however, it is important to be clear about goals, what changes are desired and in what time frame. Personally, I have the view that women need considerable autonomous space to realise transformations, not only in academia, but also in the wider society.

Johnella Butler, makes an important contribution to this debate:

> The term mainstream has always been used to define the American norm which we in Black Studies and Women's Studies know to be not the norm but an ethnocentric, racist, sexist, classist bias that results in a research methodology and subject content that engenders bigotry and prejudice in students in our future. Mainstreaming, though used with the best of intentions, implies that nothing is wrong with what exists that addition or inclusion and minor revision will not correct . . . What we must be involved in is social, economic, political and cultural change" (Johnella E. Butler, 'Minority Studies and Women's Studies: Do we want to kill a dream?', *Women's Studies International Forum* 7 (1984) 3: 136)

In our discussions on how women and development studies should be organised in university systems the experience of institutionalisation of black women's studies in North America seems to me very relevant.

Experiences with Women and Development Studies in the South

According to UNESCO, 'It is a common complaint that research done on women has remained largely unutilised both by policymakers and by the educational system' (UNESCO, Office of the Regional Adviser for Social Sciences in Asia and the Pacific, 'Women's Studies and Social Sciences in Asia', Meeting of Experts, New Delhi, 4-8 October, 1982, p. 25). In Asia, however, the situation is changing rapidly for women and development teaching. Most countries in this region have a rich tradition of girls' education, both at the primary and secondary level, and at the college level. However, as Sister Mary Braganza complains about India: 'With passing of time . . . women's colleges more or less become grooming schools for the marriage market.' (*Samya Shakti* 1(1983) 1: 46). Reflecting on the performance of these colleges has led to an awareness that these colleges are not responsive enough to the needs of women in rapidly changing societies (*ibid.*). Since the early 1980s changes have been taking place and rapid institutionalisation of women's studies can be observed.

In Korea, for example, the first women's studies programme was established at Ewha Women's University in 1976 (Soon Young Yoon, 1983). Since then, at least a dozen colleges and universities have established Women's Studies courses with varying emphases and approaches. The Ewha Women's University started a graduate programme in women's studies in 1982 (UNESCO, 1983: 12-13).

In Japan, through the activities of the the UN, a great interest in women's studies has emerged. In 1982 already 25 institutes of higher education were sponsoring women's studies courses (Junko Wada Kuninobu *Women's Studies International Forum* 7 (1984) 4: 301-5).

In India the situation is changing very rapidly; the Fourth National Conference on Women's Studies was held October of 1986. A review of curricula undertaken by the organisers of the First National Conference in 1981 showed that women's studies were virtually absent from social science curricula in the country (UNESCO, 1983: 51) and 137-9). Since then steps have been taken to introduce a feminist perspective in academia (see Nandita Gandhi, *Economic and Political Weekly*, 7 April 1984, 586-7). The SNDT Women's University in Bombay was the first to introduce a women's studies course as part of its graduate work in sociology and it has introduced a women and development course at the MPhil level. The constraints of setting up new disciplines in the Indian system of higher education have led to the strategy of incorporating and integrating women's studies within the existing courses (UNESCO 1983: 52). Women's Studies should, however, not be just another theoretical academic exercise. According to Braganza, a new term needs to be found, expressing:

> Women's concerns, issues, studies-reflected on in their historical context; in this context a growing awareness of women's responsibility towards herself and others; leading to an understanding of solidarity with the millions of faceless, invisible, voiceless women of India, a solidairty that would lead to sharing and communion; leading to a realisation that the women's movement is not restricted to India alone, but is part of a larger Asian, African, worldwide movement. (Braganza, 1983: 47)

Women's studies is advancing rapidly in India, due to the national conferences on women's studies, the Regional UNESCO Conference, the establishment of the Women's Studies Association and not least the appointment of Dr Madhuri Shah as the chairperson of the University Grants Commission (UGC). Dr Madhuri Shah is a staunch supporter of strengthening women's studies and it is through the UGC that from 1984-85 an additional 24 colleges received support for establishing women and development centres. This development underscores the strategic role that women's studies can play in supporting women who are committed to women and development in filling powerful posts in the university system.

The situation in Africa is very different. The Association of African Women for Research and Development (AAWORD) has for many years been active in stimulating work by African female researchers. Teaching so far has received less attention. At the ISS-UNESCO International Seminar on Women's Studies Curricula and Programme in Higher Education, held in The Hague in April 1985, Ayesha Imam reported that an undergraduate course, 'Women in Society', and a postgraduate option given at the Ahmadu Bello University, Nigeria, in the Department of Sociology, are the only women's studies courses offered in West Africa. In southern Africa Patricia McFadden at the same seminar deplored the sexist, elitist and chauvinist nature of formal education, and the persistent belief that education for women is a privilege granted by men rather than the result of a struggle fought by women (1985: 1). Most women in southern Africa are workers and peasants, deprived of educational or other means to break out of their poverty. In a country like Swaziland with a strong state-sanctioned patriarchal ideology, it is difficult to raise the issue of women's studies at faculty level. Women's studies is perceived as both a feminist and a political issue, and, according to McFadden (*ibid.*, 3), there are few women who are ready to challenge male dominance. It is easier and better for a female academic's career to accept the *status quo*. She considers it, however, to be of crucial importance to create the structures through which women can start to tackle the problems they face and so women's studies courses and departments are very much needed.

An example of how a women's studies perspective is introduced into a sociology course can be found at the University of Zimbabwe in Harare. Here Rudo Gaidzanwa teaches a course in industrial sociology, unravelling with her students the false assumptions of the general literature in this field which holds that women are housewives and husbands are wageworkers, an assumption which does not fit at all the reality of the Zimbabwean situation.

A new and exciting development in the southern African region is the possibility of a Women and Development Studies course at the UN Institute for Namibia (UNIN). This highlights the direct relationship of Women and Development Studies to the people's struggle for liberation. In 1985, the ISS designed and supported a training course in cooperation with the SWAPO Women's Council, the women's arm of the Namibian liberation movement. The aim of the course (funded by the Commission of the European Communities, the Netherlands Ministry of Foreign Affairs/Development Cooperation and UNESCO) is to provide students with practical and theoretical training through coursework and research in women and development issues, including policy analysis and the assessment of projects aimed at improving women's conditions, as women are playing a vital role in the struggle for Namibian national liberation and the construction of a new society. Again, this is an example where women and development studies is transcending academic and disciplinary boundaries by directly relating teaching to the struggle for liberation of the Namibian people. In the proposal for restructuring UNIN from a three-year to a five-year education and training programme, plans have been submitted to the UNIN governing board to develop within this expansion of UNIN a two-year specialisation on women and development, plans for which already have the support of the SWAPO leadership. The ISS/SWAPO Women's Council training course has provided a starting point, and research and documentation are planned as an integral part of the teaching programme. The everyday lives of women as workers and peasants will be at the centre of such a programme.

I shall not refer here to the institutionalisation experience in Latin America and the Caribbean, assuming that you are familiar with these developments. The establishment of CAFRA, the rich research material produced through the Women in the Caribbean Project, the excellent outreach of WAND, the UWI/ISS project and the various meetings held in cooperation with UNESCO, are witness that women's studies is very much on people's minds in these parts of the world, and serve to confirm the leading role that so many Caribbean women play when it comes to women in a changing world.

Development Training

A trend which may have quite a shaping influence on women and development studies is development training through which development agencies, the UN, bilateral donors and private development agencies seek to incorporate gender roles in training courses for development planning and management. These courses are meant to transfer skills to women in managing income-generating projects, small-scale businesses and appropriate technology projects. In 1986, the Population Council published a document which gives an overview of such training courses (Arunashree P. Rao Council, 1986).

Such courses are often short and thus give little scope to go into depth. However, the courses are part and parcel of the dominant development ideology and structure. This raises the question whether this mainstream development is the kind of development women want. Feminist voices from the South had already given a negative answer and had been pleading for another sort of development for women (see Dakar Declaration of 1982 and the work of the DAWN group since 1984). Andro-centric development, the unjust socio-economic and political world order and cultural hegemony are usually not questioned in such training courses, so that they may well work out to the disadvantage of the women they are supposedly serving. These courses throw up large problems and through the national and international networking of women involved in women's studies and women involved in development organisations (both at governmental and non-governmental level) ways should be found to restructure these training courses so that they serve women's real needs and interests, especially those women from the poorer and most disadvantaged sectors of our societies.

Issues arising

Reviewing the literature on the institutionalisation of women and development studies, three preliminary observations can be made. First, after the substantial increase in research carried out by women of the South during and after the UN Decade, there is an increasing demand for women and development teaching, both inside and outside academia. Second, from the experience so far, it seems that there is no blueprint for how such teaching should be institutionalised in university systems or elsewhere. Its form and content depend very much on the specific historic situation and on the people involved. Third,there is a strong awareness that women's studies and women and development studies have to be organically linked to the women's movement, so that women's needs and interests are centrestage in the academic discourse.

With respect to content, the following issues are important The first is the issue of development's andro-centricity and the asymmetric power relations between women and men. This issue should be central to research, teaching, documentation and the outreach of women and development studies. Related to this is the issue of societal change, the need for transformations at the various levels of society which should lead to the emancipation of all people, to include women's liberation. Processes of transformation which involve the socio-economic, political, legal and cultural dimensions of life must be priorities and should be motivated by a vision of accountability, cooperation and sharing, instead of powerplay, competition and individual accumulation.

Such issues demand that women's studies move beyond the often fragmented disciplinary approach to a more holistic interdisciplinary approach, thus moving away from segregated knowledge in segregated disciplines.

Thus a major issue of organisational form is whether to establish separate autonomous programmes or integrate women's studies into existing disciplines and courses. With regard to these issues, I should like to share with you some of the experiences of the women and development programme at the ISS.

Conclusion: The ISS experience

The ISS is an institute of postgraduate development studies with a problem-oriented approach in which disciplines play a secondary role. Instead of disciplines, areas of study is the term used, as for example, agriculture and rural development, economic policy and planning, labour and development. In addition the ISSS focuses on the socio-economic, political, legal and cultural dimensions of development.

In such a setting, it was possible, though not easy, to institutionalise women and development as a study area. The programme emerged within the framework of the international women's movement as it developed in the late 1960s and 1970s. As a follow-up to contacts made by an ISS staff member, Mia Berden, with participants at the 1975 UN Conference in Mexico, a three-month workshop on women and development was held in 1977 at the ISS. The great majority of the participants came from Africa, Asia and Latin America and the Caribbean. One of the results of this workshop was the participants' request that the ISS institute a fully fledged postgraduate degree in women and development. This was initiated in the academic year 1978/79 with the introduction of two courses on the ISS MA programme in development studies. In 1979/80 the first ten unit sub-specialisation was offered under the guidance of a newly appointed staff member, Dr Maria Mies, who was lated joined by Dr Kumari Jayawardena. Subsequently, a full specialisation was developed, one of the seven specialisations in the MA programme. By 1986, the programme had five full-time staff members, and some six or seven other contributing staff members. Besides instruction, the programme involves research, and outreach activities are linked to both teaching and research.

The content of the teaching programme, is perhaps best outlined by the four basic principles underlying the teaching as formulated by Rhoda Reddock in 1985.

1. That Women's Studies emerged from the women's movement and thereafter that link should always be actively maintained if Women's Studies is to maintain its relevance and dynamism within the society.
2. That the aim of Women's Studies is to understand the mechanisms through which asymmetrical and hierarchical power relations of sex, race and class developed

within human society and how they have been reproduced, and to work out strategies for their transformation.

3. That the women's problem is an international problem, common to all countries but it has to be understood within the historical and socio-economic context of each society or group of societies within the international setting.
4. That Women's Studies by definition is interdisciplinary although specific aspects can be more closely related to specific disciplines. It can therefore be seen to be both interdisciplinary and multidisciplinary. (Reddock 1985: 3-4)

Content and form are closely linked and it was strongly felt that only through the establishment of an autonomous women and development specialisation could these principles be realised. Autonomous space is needed to work towards creating a vision of what kind of society we want, and what we want for women. Strategies need to be developed which will bring us there as well as methods for actualising our visions and strategies, which will empower women (Sen and Grown, 1987: 78-9).

In the particular ISS context, this led to the struggle for special courses for women, for the appointment of feminist staff, for fellowships for women, etc. Various strategies were developed. In retrospect, two major ones can be distinguished. One was using the ISS instruments for innovation, in particular, the so-called policy workshop, where for a period from six weeks to a few months, knowledgeable people from all over the world are brought together to explore new areas of common interest. The other strategy is the building of networks and support groups within the ISS, but also in the Netherlands and internationally. Instruments used to sensitise a wider audience to the work we are doing are:

1. Seminars which are open to all staff and students;
2. debates and open fora among students of the wider ISS;
3. public lectures which are aimed at attracting a wider audience from outside the ISS; and
4. the organisation of an Open Day which usually involves the presentation of audiovisuals, photo exhibitions, songs, poetry, discussion groups, theatre, book displays, etc.

It is in these various forms that our visions have crystallised into strategies, methods and instruments. So far, these efforts have been quite effective, and in spite of a few years of serious budget problems, staff and other resources of the programme have been increasing. Crucial in this respect has been the growing interest of students in the programme and the generous fellowship policy of the Netherlands government. Around 25 postgraduate students yearly enter the programme for the 16-month MA degree in women and development studies. It is from this base of a comparatively autonomous programme that staff and students increasingly challenge and contribute to the other MA teaching specialisations.

Throughout our history, we have seen and still see feminism as a political force that transforms patriarchal society. The historic specificity of patriarchy demands that women in their own situation acquire autonomous space to do such work. This is what the institutionalisation of women and devleopment studies is all about. Its purpose is: to analyse how andro-centric development, the unjust socio-economic and political world order and cultural hegemony relate directly to women's daily reality, in particular to that of the most disadvantaged among them; and to create networks of mutual support and learning, thus transcending differences of race and class, and moving beyond the boundaries of disciplines and academia themselves.

References

Andersen, Margaret L. "Changing the Curriculum in Higher Education". *Signs* 12 (Winter 1987), 2: 222-54.

Boserup, Ester. *Women's Role in Economic Development*. New York: St Martin's Press. 1970.

Bowles, Gloria and Klein Renate Duelli (eds). *Theories of Women's Studies*. London: Routledge and Kegan Paul. 1983.

Braganza, Sister Mary. "Women's Colleges and Women". *Samya Shakti* 1 (July 1983), 1: 46-50.

Butler, Johnella E. "Minority Studies and Women's Studies: Do We Want to Kill a Dream?". *Women's Studies International Forum* 7 (1984), 3: 135-8.

Development Dialogue. "Another Development with Women". 1982: 1/2.

Gaidzanwa, R.B. "Introducing Women's Studies Perspectives in Basic Courses in Social and Human Sciences in Higher Education: Reconstructing Knowledge". Paper presented at ISS-UNESCO International Seminar "Women's Studies Curricula and Programmes in Higher Education". Institute of Social Studies, The Hague, 1-4 April, 1985.

Gandhi, Nandita. "Introducing Feminist Perspectives in Academia". *Economic and Political Weekly* 19 (7 April 1984), 14: 586-87.

Imam, Ayesga. "Women's Studies in Nigeria, West Africa". Paper presented at ISS-UNESCO International Seminar "Women's Studies Curricula and Programmes in Higher Education". Institute of Social Studies, The Hague, 1-4 April 1985.

INSTRAW News Women and Development, special issue, "Training Women in a Changing World" No. 7, Fall/Winter 1986.

ISS-UNESCO. "International Seminar on 'Women's Studies Curricula and Programmes in Higher Education". Institute of Social Studies, The Hague, 1-4 April 1985. SHS/POP/ST/85.

Junko, Wada Kuninobu. "Women's Studies in Japan". *Women's Studies International Forum* 7 (1984) 4: 301-5.

McFadden, Patricia. "Women's Studies: Regional and National Perspectives—Focus on Swaziland and Southern Africa". Paper presented at ISS-UNESCO International Seminar "Women's Studies Curricula and Programmes in Higher Education". Institute of Social Studies, The Hague, 1-4 April, 1985.

McIntosh, Peggy and Minnich Elizabeth Kamarck. "Varieties of Women's Studies". *Women's Studies International Forum* 7 (1984), 3:139-48.

Mies, Maria. "Towards a Methodology for Feminist Research". Bowles, Gloria and Klein Renate Duellli, *op. cit.*, pp. 117-39.
Minnich, Elizabeth. "A Devastating Conceptual Error: How Can We *Not* Be Feminist Scholars?" . *Change* 14 (1982), 3: 7-9.
Rao, Aunashree P. (ed.). *Incorporating Gender Issues in Development Training*. Population Council, Regional Office for South and East Asia, Bangkok, Thailand, December 1986.
Reddock, Rhoda. "The Institute of Social Studies Women and Development Teaching Programme and its Relevance to the Caribbean: A Discussion Paper". UWI, St Augustine, February 1985.
Rendel, Margherita. "A Worldwide Panorama of Research and Teaching Related to Women". *Futures, Dialogue between the People of the World* 8 (1982), 3: 102-20.
Rogers, B. *The Domestication of Women. Discrimination in Developing Societies*. London: Kogan Page 1980.
Sen, Gita and Grown Caren. *Development, Crises, and Alternative Visions. Third World Women's Perspectives.* New York: Monthly Review Press 1987.
Soon Young Yoon. "Women's Studies: Is it Relevant?" *Samya Shakti* 1 (July 1983), 1: 1-10.
UNESCO, Office of the Regional Adviser for Social Sciences in Asia and the Pacific: "Women's Studies and Social Sciences in Asia". Report of a Meeting of Experts, Bangkok 1983.
Women's Studies International Forum. 6 (1983) 2; 6 (1983) 3; 6 (1983) 4; 7 (1984) 3; 9 (1986) 2.

Integrating Gender into Sociological Research

Derek Gordon

This paper presents an overview and a critique of recent attempts to incorporate gender into sociological research on class, status and social mobility, as a contribution towards bridging the continuing gap between abstract theory and empirical research in this area. Where possible, the issues are illustrated with examples from my own ongoing empirical work on social mobility in Jamaica.

First, the crisis in social mobility studies deriving from the exclusion of the social mobility of women is discussed. We shall see how this exclusion has been justified and consider some of the new research directions inspired by criticism of the conventional approach. Whatever the deficiencies of the new approaches, we hope to show that they do provide new information and new ways of understanding the relationship between gender and class.

The second major area in which a ferment is taking place is the traditional study of occupational status, where consideration of the effects of gender on the division of labour and the occupational status hierarchy is leading to a reconsideration of earlier empirical work. A crucial issue here is the extent to which the generation of occupational or class places and the allocation of persons to these places can be treated as conceptually separate issues. Gender has been seen traditionally as having to do with the second and not the first.

One of the main controversies in recent research concerns the relevant unit of analysis for the study of class and status: individual, household, or larger collectivity. The close relationship of this issue to differing theoretical conceptions of the nature of social classes is also examined.

The Crisis in Social Mobility Studies

The modern study of social mobility, involving national samples, is basically a post Second World War phenomenon. Data have been gathered on the occupational and educational attainments of men and these have been compared with the occupational attainments of their fathers at an age just prior to the entry of the sons into the labour force. Even when data on women were gathered, as in the classic 1949 study of mobility in Britain by Glass and his associates, which interviewed 10,000 adults aged 18 and over, they were not analysed. The 1962 US study by Blau and Duncan in which 21,000 men aged 20-64 years were interviewed and the 1973 study by Hauser and Featherman in which 34,000 men were interviewed did not collect data on women unless they were the spouses of men. In the 1972 study of mobility in England and Wales conducted by John H. Goldthorpe and his associates 10,000 males aged 20 to 64 were interviewed.

Justifying the study of Male Mobility

The justification for the omission of women usually given is that their presence would add nothing to the understanding of class inequalities or class formation. This position, most persistently defended by the UK sociologist John H. Goldthorpe, is that the family or household is the basic unit of the class structure. The articulation with the class structure is predominantly through the male head of household, who is traditionally the main participant in the labour force and the main income earner. The class position of women is largely derived from that of their husbands. Despite changes in the labour force participation of married women, Goldthorpe argues that this participation still retains a secondary and derived character, and does not affect the class position of the household. In a series of papers Goldthorpe has tried to show that even when we have data on women, their work history does not make a difference to the basic class position of the family (Goldthorpe 1983, 1984, 1986).

A basically similar version of this argument is put forward by the UK Marxists John Westergaard and Henrietta Resler in their classic account of British class structure, *Class in a_Capitalist Society*. They argue that the socio-economic position of men is still far more important than that of women for the character of the class structure. They maintain that not only is the basic pattern of class inequalities the same, but gender inequalities in occupational position and earnings reinforce class inequality because gender inequality is more extreme in the working classes. In their desire to show that gender inequalities do not negate or reduce class inequalities and antagonisms, Westergaard and Resler come uncomfortably close to reducing gender to class.

Critique of the Conventional Position

The criticism of Goldthorpe's position and related positions taken by US stratification theorists and researchers is made from a number of angles.

First of all, even within its own terms, the defence of male mobility studies is defective. Even if all heads of families were male, there would still be households in which women active in the labour force were the only members. Quite apart from these cases there would be some cases, where the husband's inactivity through illness, handicap, etc, would lead women to become the *de facto* heads of the household. In critique, it has been pointed out that perhaps as many as two-fifths of US households were headed by women either living alone or in households where the man was not economically active. This is probably even more the case for the English-speaking Caribbean. Our own analysis of the Jamaican data showed that only 31 per cent of all women in the labour force were partners of male heads of household. Thirty–five per cent of all household heads (at a minimum) were women, while 33 per cent of all women (similarly at a minimum) were household heads (Gordon 1987). Where the labour force participation, occupational status and earnings of the wife consistently exceed those of her partner, her status should be used to designate the class position of the household.

Secondly, even if the assumptions of the conventional approach were to be upheld and the basic findings vindicated, the basic information on women's labour force involvement and class background is still necessary. Fundamental assumptions about the link between class structure and households should not go untested.

There has been a considerable increase in the labour force participation of women, particularly married women, in advanced capitalist countries. In the US for example, the proportion of women in the workforce had moved from 20 percent in 1900 to 43 percent in 1970, and it is continuing to rise. The same trend is evident in Europe. Such levels are not at all unusual in the Caribbean. In Jamaica approximately two-thirds of all women were working, looking for work, or wanting and able to work at the time of our mobility survey, in 1984. This raises the strong possibility that assumptions about female marginality in the class system may not hold today, even if they might have been more or less valid in some advanced industrial countries in the past. Goldthorpe has denied that these facts change anything, and has argued, on the basis of new data on the mobility of women, that his basic findings on class mobility and class formation remain valid. But his conclusions have been fiercely disputed, on the basis of the same new data (Stanworth, 1984). Using arguments based on male mobility patterns would not have forced the debate to confront new data.

Thirdly, a number of new and interesting findings have merged as a result of incorporating women into the analysis. Whether these findings are significant for our understanding of the formation of social classes, or whether they are mainly of interest for the understanding of other aspects of stratification and occupational mobility is hotly disputed.

New Directions: Men and Women as Independent Subjects

The first major departure from the conventional approach was the analysis of data from secondary sources such as the General Household Survey in Britain and the NORC annual surveys in the USA which contained information on the social mobility of women. In Europe and Canada, material on women was available as part of the design of detailed mobility studies.

The data from these analyses compared the intra- and inter-generational mobility of working men and women. The most important findings from these studies (such as Heath 1981; Portocarero 1983) were that the major differences between men's and women's mobility lay first in the patterns of occupational segregation which channelled women into certain occupations regardless in some ways of social origins. Gross patterns of mobility therefore differed considerably. Secondly, men were much more likely to inherit the occupations of their fathers than were women. This allowed men to maintain their advantages in professional, managerial, petty bourgeois and skilled worker occupations. Thirdly, when occupational segregation is taken into account, the class distances between occupations are substantially similar for men and for women, thus upholding in a modified form the arguments of Westergaard and Resler.

The Jamaican Mobility Survey included information on the mobility experiences of women. To our knowledge this was the first mobility survey in a developing country to do so. We found that women have been more mobile than men in Jamaica, because men have been able to inherit their class positions to a greater degree than women, and some sex-segregated occupations like clerical labour have expanded considerably in the postwar period. For example, we found that men from higher-level managerial and professional backgrounds were nearly 28 times as likely to be found in these occupations than other men, while women from the same background were only 12 times as likely to end up there as other women. Men were therefore more than twice as likely to inherit higher managerial and professions than women. Despite these differences, the intrinsic gap between the most impoverished groups like small farmers and unskilled labourers, on the one hand, and higher managerial and professional groups, on the other, was much the same for men and women. (Gordon 1987a; 1987b).

A major problem with this approach is that the class behaviour and opportunities of men and women are not totally independent. Although the actions and possibilities of both men and women in families are conditioned by each other, there is still an asymmetry in these effects. Women are more dependent than men on the fortunes of their spouses. The same issue logically arises in the study of social origins, where either the father's occupation or the head of household's occupation traditionally indexes class position. Sometimes women do not engage in paid work or own-account activities at all, and in that case are either excluded from the analysis, assigned the highly ambiguous category of housewife, or given the position of the male partner, if that information is available. This procedure has been implemented in the study of what is called marital mobility, or the social mobility made possible by marriage, where wives are classified by the position of their husband and their mobility is measured as movement from their own social origins to their husband's social position. Not surprisingly, it is found that the marital mobility patterns of women are similar to male social mobility patterns, assuming, therefore, what it sets out to prove. In its simple form, it treats as hidden the occupational position and earnings of the wife, although studies have demonstrated that this has an effect on the class position, class behaviour and class chances of the household.

One solution to this problem has been proposed by Erickson (1986). Men and women who are single are assigned class positions on the basis of their own employment. Men and women in families are assigned a family or household class position based on the household member (who need not be male) who has the dominant economic position defined along two axes: degree of commitment to the labour force and occupational status. This method is actually the one implied but not implemented by Goldthorpe. It also prevents us from fully exploiting the information that we have about a household's class position.

A full understanding of the patterns of dependence and interdependence requires us to study the role of partners in affecting the class chances of their spouses.

New Directions: The Interdependence of Partners

With the increasing availability of data on women, it is possible to carry out quite complex analyses which consider both partners in a household simultaneously: present occupational positions; the social origins of both partners; the relation between the present class occupational positions of both partners and their social origins; and the relationship of all status indicators. Much work has already been done on the homogeneity of partners' occupational positions in the USA and Europe (Portocarero 1985). This work demonstrates quite clearly that, while there is a very strong association between occupations and therefore a considerable degree of class homogeneity or class endogamy, there is also much dissimilarity, arising largely from the sex segregation of occupations. This creates cross-class marriages in which working class spouses have middle-class or self-employed mates or middle–class spouses have working-class partners.

The treatment of these cross-class marriages has led to much debate. Goldthorpe argues that the class positions are not really different when we consider market and work situations, as in the case of a working-class man married to a female clerical or sales worker, and that the class positions of women are secondary and temporary, and should not be given major weight when we find discrepancies between the class positions of men and women. Heath and Britten (1983, 1984) on the other hand, present data to show that the voting and fertility behaviour of women is affected by their jobs to a degree over and above the effects attributed to their husbands' class positions.

The data for studies such as these are still largely confined to the industrialised countries. Although our enquiry does not ask men and women to supply information on their partners, it has been possible to reconstruct this information by manipulating the database, which included records on all adults in a household, to match the records of heads and their spouses. The resulting data set has created a record which provides data on heads' and spouses' occupations, occupational origins, education, race, etc. Preliminary analysis has been conducted. Although it is not presented here, it might be appropriate to indicate the directions in which it is taking us. The analysis underlines the very strong association between the occupational statuses of married and common-law couples. It is highly unlikely that men and women from the extremes of the class structure will be living together. Even if we consider occupational rather than broad class endogamy, we find a great probability of in-marriage. This is more accentuated for higher status occupations (the odds of persons with higher managerial or professional occupations living with partners having the same occupational level is about 57 times as likely as either of them living with persons from a lower occupational level), and it is considerably greater than we might expect for all other occupations.

Our data show that this high class association between the class and occupational positions of couples is compatible with a considerable number of cross occupational and even cross-class unions. An important reason for the large number of cross-class unions lies in the imbalance or segregation of occupations, which increases the overall likelihood of such unions. These imbalances have already been documented. There are considerably more male small farmers than female, and considerably more female clerks than male. Women are more likely to be concentrated in unskilled labouring occupations while men are more likely to be artisans and industrial operatives. Men are more likely to be in the managerial and professional occupations than are women, despite the fairly large numbers of women occupying lower-level professional and supervisory occupations.

Once we take into account the imbalances deriving from the sexual division of labour, the chances of women of any occupational or class group marrying into a particular occupational or class group are no different from the chances of men of that group marrying into the same occupational or class group (that is, the log-linear model of quasi-symmetry holds in this case). There is no intrinsic propensity for cross-class marriages to be of one particular combination of occupations or classes for men and another for women. This is an interesting finding, which interprets the observed proportions of men and women out-marrying as a function of both the class composition of men and women and the intrinsic social distances between the occupations and classes.

These observed proportions are of interest in their own right. Working-class women were somewhat more likely to have middle-class spouses than working-class men. For example, 12 per cent of female industrial workers were found to be likely to have a spouse with professional, managerial or supervisory responsibilities compared with 7 per cent of male industrial workers. Middle-class women were more likely to have middle-class spouses than were middle-class men. Women with higher managerial and professional occupations were more likely to have spouses from the same group than men (53 per cent to 23 per cent), and to have more spouses from the broad professional managerial and supervisory group (82 per cent compared with 56 per cent). A large proportion of the partners of female traders, artisans, unskilled labourers and farmers were farmers (39, 26, 36 and 88 per cent respectively), indicating the domestic economic structure of the small farming household, while the partners for male traders, artisans, unskilled labourers and farmers were more widely recruited from the female working class.

Analyses like these will allow us to assess the interaction between race, class and gender in the formation and consolidation of family units. A study is being carried out on whether there are any fundamental asymmetries in the racial make-up of couples, considered in comparison with the respective social origins of couples or their present occupational positions. This should help us to illuminate how much has changed and how much remains the same in the historical formation of these domestic groups.

Ferment in the Measurement of Occupational Status

Most classifications or scales developed to study class structure or social status have relied on occupational data, either alone or in conjunction with employment status, size of establishment, authority, skill, educational qualifications, income and subjective evaluations. There are two main traditions. One is based on the attempt to create a ranking or continuous scale of occupational position, and the other is based on the discrete classification of occupational data into a limited number of groups.

The attempt to develop a continuous scale has been most intensive in the USA and Canada. There two closely related routes have emerged. The first is based on the relationship between people's evaluation of the goodness of a limited number of occupations, and the attempt to extend the results of this rating to the full list of census occupational categories by an estimation procedure relating the educational and income requirements of the occupation to its prestige score (The Duncan Socio-Economic Index). A variant of this method attempts to develop prestige ratings directly for all major occupational groupings (Goldthorpe and Hope 1974). The second method attempts to develop scores directly from information on the income and educational characteristics of occupations (Nam and Powers 1965; Blishen 1958).

It might be worthwhile to speculate on the reasons for the intensive development of these scales in North America and their use in status attainment studies since Blau and Duncan's landmark (1967) study, *The American Occupational Structure.* Goldman and Tickamyer (1984) argue convincingly that this tradition:

> reflects a system of stratification structured according to the logic of the commodity form and instrumental rationality . . . .The origins of status attainment forms of stratification are rooted in the advent of market relations . . . Socially organized around market practices, the allocation of status becomes individuated . . . . Status is defined as possession of quantified units of positional measures. One moves up and down the stratification hierarchy by gaining or losing increments of education, income and occupational prestige.

Examples of this approach to social stratification in the Caribbean can be found in the work of Graham and Gordon (1977).

The second major approach has been to develop classifications based on occupational data, usually in connection with other criteria such as employment status, authority and skill. This has been done for example by Blau and Duncan in the USA and Goldthorpe (1980) in the UK. The Jamaican Mobility Study developed a 16-category classification which utilised information on employment status (employer, self-employed, employee) and occupational characteristics. Such classifications have a hierarchical aspect, but they also attempt to capture aspects of the class structure which are not simply to be put into a uni-dimensional scale.

In both cases the omission of women has produced some problematic results. In the case of socio-economic scales, these have been constructed either implicitly or explicitly on the basis of information on male occupations (for instance, the Duncan SEI and the Goldthorpe-Hope Scale). They therefore reflect the evaluation of male occupations and produce a male hierarchy. Occupations which have a high proportion of females, such as secretarial work, receive scores based on the educational and income characteristics of male incumbents. The sample of occupations which has been evaluated has tended to under-represent occupations with a high female concentration, although there were conscious efforts to alleviate this problem, starting in the 1960s. Finally, it seems possible that the perception of the sex composition of occupations or the appropriate sex incumbents of an occupation could have an effect on the occupation's rating. Comparisons of the status attainments of men and women using the male based SEI have found roughly average levels of attainment and similar processes of status attainment (Featherman and Hauser 1976) although to many critics this is incompatible with what we know of sexual inequalities in work.

In the case of discrete classifications, these have produced analyses of the changing occupational structure which are based solely on males (Blau and Duncan 1967; Hauser and Featherman 1978; Goldthorpe *et al*, 1980). Data on women began to be analysed as they became available, using the classifications based on men, without taking into account the specifics of the female work world. In many cases this understated male-female disparities. Occupations which were highly segregated were included in broader classifications which had a bias towards men. This problem, frequently demonstrated in occupational sex segregation studies, means that the less finely detailed the classification, the lower the level of reported sex segregation. Critics argued that the difference in the distribution of detailed occupations and jobs within major classification groups invalidates comparisons of male and female mobility based on these classifications as such comparisons 'all assume that major categories include the same variety of occupations for the two populations.'

Critique and Empirical re-direction

Defenders of the conventional approach tend to argue that there is really one occupational hierarchy or one gender neutral class system. The assumption is that the places in the division of labour and the class system are generated by principles which are technological or economic, but not sex-specific. It is in the filling or allocation of these occupations that gender-specific segregation and inequalities are concentrated.

This position is under varying degrees of challenge. Murgatroyd (1982) and Scott (1986) have argued that gender roles are embedded in the division of labour and affect the construction of occupational categories. Murgatroyd argues, for example:

> whether a job is mainly a 'man's job' or a 'woman's job' is an inherent characteristic of the occupation. As we have seen, both the degree of segregation within an occupation and the sex-group which dominates it are important indicators of the market position of, and social relations engaged in by, men and women in that occupation.

The distinction between the processes shaping occupational and class places and the allocation of people to these places on the basis of sex, education, race and other qualities is in fact submerged in the actual construction of socio-economic indices, based as these are on the characteristics of the people who occupy these positions. Recognition of this fact has in fact spurred attempts to modify the traditional indices. This modification takes a number of forms.

Among those who continue to believe in the value of a common index of occupational roles which would apply equally to all incumbents, there is a greater attention to the need to incorporate sex-specific patterns in the scales or to develop scales which are genuinely sex-neutral. In the first case, scales have been developed based on the characteristics of the total labour force. These scales typically give a more faithful representation of gender inequalities. A related strategy is to develop a single scale which allows for sex-specific differences in the effects of education and income in the estimation procedure. In the second case, the aim is to continue the search for more detailed, task-based job and occupational classifications which do not obscure gender differences. This attempts to preserve the technological or economic conception of the division of labour.

Construction of separate male-female scales does not by itself indicate a departure from the unitary conception if the same scale is used to compare men and women. A number of researchers have done this (in fact this was the original approach to comparing men and women using the male SEI scale) and the results are fairly similar in their tendency to mask male-female differences.

A more radical solution is to develop separate scales for men and women and to compare men using the male-derived scale for men and women using the female-derived scale for women. This approach assumes that the occupational structure is dual, or parallel, not unitary; that is, it is not independent of the characteristics of incumbents.

As Boyd *et al.* (1985) report, when this assumption is adopted, the sex differences in the attainment process sharpen relative to what is observed when only a single socio-economic hierarchy is assumed.

In a related development in the area of discrete occupational classifications, Dale, Gilbert and Arber (1985) have developed a classification of the female occupational structure which takes into account the differing market capacities of women even in the same occupations as men. Some of the traditional male-oriented distinctions between levels of skill and manual and non-manual work do not appear, while in other areas dominated by men such as office, clerical and service work, sufficient distinctions based on skill are not made. Dale *et al.* nevertheless propose a 'reformist' solution: to use the more detailed information provided by their classification to construct a unitary classification which would be appropriate for women as well as men.

Individual and Household in the Analysis of Class

A central issue in all of the controversies we have reviewed is whether the individual or the household is the proper unit of class analysis. Goldthorpe, for example maintains that it must be the household. Yet all theorists say that the link with the economy in modern society is made by individuals through the labour market. Theorists like Goldthorpe solve this question by maintaining that the link is through the person in the household with the dominant economic tie to the labour market; usually the head of the household, and usually the man.

However it is not only the head of household who becomes a wage labourer. Other members have always participated in the labour market, and this trend has accelerated in the second half of this century. The many critics of Goldthorpe's approach share his theoretical terrain, which is predominantly Weberian. For Weber modern social inequalities derive from the market, not directly from production. Those who do well in the market improve their life chances and the position of their household. Ultimately, classes do not spring from exploitative production relations but from the resources people bring to the market and the outcome of market forces in terms of income, possessions, etc. Classes are ultimately rooted in distribution and consumption, not production.

The adherence to Weber's theories of social class leads to the employment relation being played down as the source of classes and the elevation of consumption as the criterion of class. The formulation that is becoming widespread is that the work situation is an aspect of class that pertains to the individual while the market situation pertains to the family or household. The individual here is performing as an individual owner of the commodity labour-power and not as a member of a class exploited in the production process after selling his or her labour power. The family emerges as the dominant partner in this bifurcation. As Dale *et al.* put it:

> In capitalist society, because the labour contract is made between individuals and their employers, the relevant unit of analysis for the labour market dimen-

> sion of stratification must be the individual. But ownership or private education can be measured only at the level of the family as a whole, and so the appropriate unit for analysing relations to the consumption market is not the individual but the family.

Erickson (1984) forthrightly draws a conclusion from this:

> It therefore seems that we need two class concepts, one work-related with individuals as the unit of classification, and one market-related with families as the unit of classification. From my perspective, the nuclear family is the basic element of the class structure of modern industrial societies because of the dependence of family members upon each other and the largely shared conditions within the family. Class society also embraces everybody: all of us have a class position, regardless of whether we participate in the labour force or not. I therefore suggest that we use the term work position for the work related concept and the term class position for the market related concept.

Goldthorpe has no trouble with this. He allows that the study of the occupational mobility of women might be interesting from the view point of labour force dynamics; and that the demonstration that the occupation of women makes a difference to voting behaviour might be interesting to political sociologists, but it does not affect the fundamental class position of the household or the formation of classes as stable collectivities.

In giving theoretical priority to the household and consumption it seems to me that the critics of conventional approaches are conceding too much. What is needed is a study of the dynamic interaction of households and individuals in their effect on class formation and class behaviour.

The separation of the individual from the household is part of the whole process of separation set in motion by the capitalist mode of production. The household is transformed from a unit of production and consumption into a centre of consumption with the development of wage labour. Productive consumption is sharply separated from individual consumption. It is the individual labourer, not the household, who contracts with the capitalist to work for a wage in the production of commodities.

Nevertheless, the individual's link with the household and the family is not severed. If we consider production in its totality as a process of reproduction, then a vital moment in that process is the reproduction of the labourer (and the labourer's replacements). This involves individual consumption and the relations involved in biological reproduction and childrearing. This, alongside the involvement of the individual in the production process outside the household, obviously involves the reproduction of the social relations in which the labourers find themselves, and thus of social classes. Both household and individual are involved in the formation of social classes.

A purely individualistic approach would not be adequate to this complexity. Neither would an approach that singles out the head of household and neglects to study intra-household dynamics. In some respects, economists, particularly those studying female labour supply and household welfare, are ahead of us.

The lesson is clear. To understand the actions of individual women (and men) we must take the household into account, and *vice versa*. The only surprise is that we have done this so infrequently.

References

The references for this paper are incomplete. Dr Gordon died in 1992 and although efforts were made to compile a complete list of references, it was not possible. The quality of the paper, however, was such that it was decided to include it and seek readers' understanding of the omissions.

Blau, Peter and Duncan, Otis Dudley. *The American Occupational Structure*. New York: John Wiley & Sons.1967.

Blishen, Bernard R. *Et al. Canadian Society: Sociological Perspectives*, Toronto: Macmillian of Canada. 1961.

Boyd, Monica *et al. Ascription and Achievement: Studies in Mobility and Status attainment in Canada*. Ottawa: Carleton University Press. 1985.

Featherman, David L. Jones, F.L. and Hauser, R.M. *Assumptions of Social Mobility Research in the US: The Case of Occupational Status*. Wisconsin: University of Wisconsin. 1974.

Glass, Davis Victor '*Social Mobility in Britain*' 1954.

Goldthorpe, John H. The Affluent Worker: *Political Attitudes and Behavior*. London: Cambridge University Press. 1968.

____*Social Mobility and Class Structure in Modern Britain*. Oxford: Clarendon Press. 1980.

____and Hope, Keith. *The Social Grading of Occupations: A new approach and Scale*. Oxford: Clarendon Press. 1974.

Gordon, Derek. Class, Status and Social Mobility in Jamaica. Institute of Social and Economic Research 1987a.

'The Sexual Division of Labour and Intergenerational Mobility in Jamaica' In Robert V. Robinson (ed.), *Research in Social Stratification and Mobility*. Greenwich: Jai Press, 1987b. pp. 215-38.

Graham, Sara and Gordon, Derek. *The Stratification System and Occupational Mobility in Guyana*. Mona, Jamaica: Institute of Social and Economic Research, UWI.

Hauser, Robert M. And Featherman, David L. *Opportunity and Change*. New York: Academic Press 1978.

Health, Anthony Francis. *Social Mobility* . London: Fontana Paperbacks. 1981.

Nam, Charles B and Powers, Mary G.. The Socio-Economic Approach to Status Measurement. Houston, Texas: Cap and Gown Press. 1983

Portocarero, Lucienne. *Social Mobility in Industrial Societies: Women in France and Sweden. Department of Sociology, University of Stockholm*: Almquist and Wiksell International. 1987.

Scott, A. M. "Women and Industrialization: Examining the 'Female Marginalization' Thesis" . Journal of Development Studies Vol. 2, No 4, 1986. Pp.650-80.

Stanworth, Michelle and Janet Siltanen (eds). *Women of the Public Sphere: A Critique of Sociology and Politics*. New York: St. Martin's Press. 1984.

Weber, Max. 'Status Groups and Classes' in Guenther Roth and Lass Wittich (eds.), *Economy and Society*, Berleley University of California Press, 1978.

Westergaard, John and Resler, Henrietta. *Class in a Capitalist Society: A Study of Contemporary Britain*. London: Heinemann Educational. 1975.

Women and Planning

The need for an alternative analysis

Peggy Antrobus

Introduction

Within the framework of the United Nations (UN) Decade for Women (1976-85) the goal of integrating women in development became the focus of work carried out by both governments and non-governmental organisations. The assumption underlying this approach was that women were outside the process of development and needed to be integrated into the mainstream (Tinker and Bramsen 1976). A number of strategies aimed at documenting and quantifying women's work, making it visible to planners, were proposed (Beneria 1982; Tinker 1982). Underlying these was the assumption that if policy-makers and planners could be made aware of the importance of women's contribution to development, women would receive more of the benefits of development; for example, access to the resources and services required to build their capacity to contribute more fully and effectively to development efforts.

Within the framework of this women in development, (WID) approach, special machineries- units, divisions and programmes-were established within government bureaucracies and international agencies. Laws and policies were changed, income-generating projects were implemented, and new programmes for increasing women's access to health and education services were launched

(Fraser 1987). Many of us used this approach, which I have characterised as the expediency approach (Antrobus 1983).

However, a great deal of the research generated by the UN Decade for Women showed that women were not outside development (Deere and Leon 1987). Indeed, it was becoming clear to many activists and practitioners that women's contribution was central to development, was the very base on which development was constructed; but in a way that was deeply exploitative of their time, labour, both paid (in the workplace) and unpaid (in the household), and their sexuality. This has been clearly illuminated by the policies of structural adjustment which most third–world governments have been forced to adopt to deal with the financial problems of unpayable debts, chronic balance-of-payment shortages and fiscal deficits in the 1980s (UNICEF, n.d.).

Critique of Structural Adjustment Policies

When I first started working on a gender analysis of the impact of structural adjustment policies on Jamaican women, I argued that these policies were an example of policies which failed to take women into account (Antrobus 1987). Today, after further analysis and a better understanding of their theoretical and ideological underpinnings, I would argue that, far from not taking women into account, these policies are actually grounded in a set of assumptions, a gender ideology, which assigns certain roles and characteristics to women. Indeed, it is clear to me that both components of existing structural adjustment policies-those aimed at reducing consumption (the austerity measures reflected in the cuts in government expenditures on social services) as well as those aimed at increasing export-oriented production (the emphasis on the promotion of export processing zones)-depend on assumptions about the roles into which most women have been socialised. These gender roles are mediated by class, race, ethnicity and the level of development of society. For this reason I prefer to speak of gender roles rather than women's roles, so as to give specificity to the analysis and to reveal the differences between women of different social groups (Oakley 1972).

It is because of the central importance of these roles in social reproduction, especially for the poorest sectors of the society, that policies which place them in jeopardy have negative consequences for the whole society, and ultimately for production itself, for production is not only dependent on the availability of capital, technology and markets, but also on the physical, psychological and intellectual capacities of the labour force. Such capacities are determined in the social sector, the sector in which women are the key actors (and not the passive recipients of welfare services, as they are often perceived). Unfortunately, this critical link between women's productive and reproductive roles is one which is typically overlooked in conventional, growth-oriented models of development (Beneria and Sen 1981).

In fact, structural adjustment policies call into question the fundamental assumptions of the WID approach. Firstly, the recognition of women's work has been used to justify cutting resources to them (UNICEF 1987); second, even the practical gains made in social development during the 1970s have been reversed in the wake of depleted resources, despite the fact that many governments have continued to find resources to increase their budget allocations to defence and of course to debt-servicing. This recognition of the limitations of the WID approach should alert us to the need for an alternative analysis of issues relating to women and development planning (Maguire 1984).

Conventional Approaches to Women and Planning

Since 1975 many people and agencies have attempted to address the problem of how to incorporate women's concerns into development planning. Special mechanisms have been established within both governmental and non-governmental agencies at national, regional and international levels, and checklists, guidelines, policy statements and analytical frameworks have been developed for dealing with how to incorporate gender into planning processes, and in programme and project design (Antrobus 1988b).

Despite these laudable efforts, and many approaches such as personal and national commitment, relevant policies and the allocation of small but qualitatively significant resources, as well as ongoing monitoring and evaluation, the results have been disappointing (INSTRAW 1987). The goal eludes us as we witness continued deterioration in the situation of women worldwide.

After reviewing some of the past experience in the approaches adopted to integrating women in development planning, including my own experience in the Women and Development Unit (WAND) of the University of the West Indies (UWI) School of Continuing Studies, my conclusion is that the problem is not how to do it, but who does it, in what socio-economic and political context, and within what framework of assumptions and values: within what paradigm.

Chhachhi (1989) provided an excellent overview of the feminist critique of prevailing social science concepts and methodologies. It is against this background that this paper seeks to examine the issues of gender analysis and planning and the arguments for an alternative analysis. It also attempts to suggest the elements of such an alternative analysis, one that is grounded in feminist theory and so addresses the issue of women's subordination or oppression within society. However, since we currently operate within the framework of the dominant paradigm, I hope to suggest approaches which can be used within these constraints to open up some spaces—intellectually, politically and practically—for alternative approaches to the issues of women and to development.

Elements of an Alternative Analysis

The following elements should form the basis of an alternative analysis for the purpose of planning for women in development activities.

1. The analysis should be grounded in theories of development and social change which recognise the differences between those that aim to maintain the *status quo* (those located in the dominant or integrative paradigm), and those that seek to

promote social change (those which fall within the alternative or 'liberative' paradigm) (Paulson 1976). Secondly, the analysis should recognise both the relevance and limitations of the alternative or liberative paradigm and the need to integrate feminist theory into this paradigm to form a feminist alternative paradigm (Jain 1983). I would argue that lack of explicitness about theoretical frameworks has been a major contributor to the blurring of our analysis of the problems of integrating women's and gender concerns into development planning (Maguire *ibid.*).

Indeed, I have argued that the problem with the array of guidelines, checklists, and methodological tools that have been formulated has less to do with their technical qualities and shortcomings than with the conceptual frameworks and paradigms within which they are situated and by which they are constrained (Antrobus 1988b).

2. The analysis should attempt to relate experience at the micro level of the sector, community, project or household, to that of macro-economic analysis: it should attempt to address issues of both human agency and structure. A gender analysis of structural adjustment policies illustrates the ways in which macroeconomic policies affect women's experiences at the level of the poorest household. Unless experience at the household level is used to inform macro-economic policies, and *vice versa*, unless people at the micro level can analyse and understand their situation within a structural analysis, no meaningful change can be effected.

3. The analysis needed is one which is holistic, seeking to integrate social, cultural and political dimensions into economic analysis. This idea has been borne out by analysing the social, economic and political consequences of current economic policies which reveal the linkages and the futility of focusing on economic production at the expense of the social sector (reproduction) (UNICEF 1987; Antrobus 1988a).

4. The analysis should recognise the political nature of the processes of development; that the concepts and causes of development and underdevelopment reflect imbalances of power within and between countries rather than the presence or absence of resources (Frank 1967; 1973; Rodney 1972; Gutierrez 1983). The failure of more than 30 years of development experience should have convinced us of the limitations of strategies based on technical, rational approaches which focus on growth and modernisation in areas such as production, education or health.

5. Finally, the analysis must be feminist, rejecting the dichotomy in the private and public domains: the household from the economy, personal from political realities, the realms of feeling and intuition from those of rationality. Above all, we need an analysis which seeks to validate all women's work, and not only that which lies within the monetised sector of the economy (Anand 1983). The contradictions outlined above, and the exclusion of much of women's work in national income accounting systems, lead to analyses which are fundamentally flawed and inadequate for the task of efficient and effective policy-making.

Towards an Alternative Analysis

In order to implement an alternative analysis, the tools for incorporating gender into planning, and the necessary approaches must be considered.

A distinction must be made between gender analysis and gender planning. Gender analysis, like any other form of social analysis, 'examines causes, probes consequences, delineates linkages, and identifies actors. It helps make sense of experiences by putting them into a broader picture and drawing the connections between them' (Holland and Henriot 1985: 8). Adapting this formulation, we can say that gender analysis is the effort to obtain a more complete picture of a social situation by exploring its historical and structural relationships. Gender analysis considers issues, policies and structures and ultimately the cultural, social, economic and political systems which shape the relationships between men and women in their gendered roles. It includes gender planning, but it can also be done by women at every level of society; and it needs to be done, if a constituency for alternative development or social change is to be created.

Gender planning is 'a planning approach, which in taking into account the fact that women and men play different roles in Third World society and therefore often have different needs, provides both the conceptual framework and the methodological tools for incorporating gender into planning'. (Moser 1988: 1)

Three levels of gender analysis might be distinguished along with the key questions that need to be addressed:

1.	Policy	Why is there need for special attention to women and/or gender roles in development?
2.	Planning	How can gender be incorporated into the design of programmes and projects?
3.	Action and implementation	How to engage women within the target area in: » the analysis of their own situation » the definition of the long-term requirements for social change and transformation and meaningful development » the social action required for the realisation of their vision

At the policy level, the rationale may be put in terms of an approach which focuses on a number of concepts, depending on the context. Since the 1950s, when the international community first started to focus on development, many different approaches have been used. Caroline Moser (1989) has outlined five historical approaches, starting with the welfare approach, and continuing with the equity, anti-poverty, efficiency, and empowerment approaches.

Within the framework of the Decade for Women, I also have identified approaches linked to the goals of equality, development and peace (Antrobus 1983). These are as follows:

1. The justice approach (corresponding to the goal of equality): if women constitute 50 per cent of the world's population, then it is only fair that their gender needs be met.
2. The expediency approach (corresponding to the goal of development): if we are to achieve our development goals, then women's contribution is important, and their

(practical) needs and concerns must be addressed; moreover, if societies are to show gains in health, nutrition, food production, literacy and other areas, then women must benefit.

3. The wisdom approach (corresponding to the goal of peace), an approach which comes closest to the feminist approach: if we want a more humane and safer world, then women's visions, values and perspectives must take their rightful place at the centre of decision-making, at all levels from household to policy.

The planning level is the one with which we are most concerned in this paper. It is possible to identify two categories of approaches to this:

1. An institutional approach focusing on the preparation of policy statements, guidelines and checklists.
2. An approach which emphasises both formal and non-formal training and focuses on the use of case studies, evaluation exercises, conceptual and analytical frameworks and methodological tools.

The action/implementation level helps to ensure that the programme or project actually meets the practical and strategic needs of women. Here we see a limited but significant role for planners, a role that has not always been clearly understood or articulated. In this paper both the planning level and the implementation level are briefly examined.

Planning Level: Guidelines and Checklists

In order to fulfil the numerous resolutions, mandates, policies and recommendations generated within the framework of the Decade for Women, as well as in response to the imperatives of the feminist and personal commitment of the countless women inspired by the vision and energy of this period, many of the agencies working on issues of international development formulated and adopted WID guidelines and checklists. These included governmental bilateral and multilateral programmes and private agencies including donors as disparate as the International Planned Parenthood Foundation (IPPF), the World Council of Churches and the World Young Women's Christian Association (YWCA).

The following definitions are contained in the report of a meeting co-sponsored by the Food and Agricultural Organisation (FAO) and INSTRAW in 1985 to evaluate bilateral and multilateral experiences in the development and use of WID guidelines and checklists and their implications for national use in formulating agricultural projects for women (INSTRAW 1985).

Guidelines are intended to provide a general framework for bringing significant aspects of women's concerns to the attention of development agencies. In a broad sense, guidelines are indicators for translating policy mandates on women and development into action at the programme and project level. They can be used by planners, policy-makers and project designers in governments and agencies. They recommend or direct action at the programme or project level and may be used both at headquarters and in the field.

Checklists are more specific and aim to provide a more detailed memory aid, giving conceptual clarification and practical suggestions. They are usually in the form of questions prompting the reader to include women in very specific activities.

The functions of Guidelines/Checklists are manifold but in general, they focus on the following broad issues:

1. Measuring, assessing, and monitoring the extent of women's integration in development programmes. This requires:
   (i) collection, during the project, of socio-economic data regarding political and economic structures, division of labour, the structure of the household and the decision-making process therein, women's access to resources, etc.
   (ii) assessment of the effects of the project on the situation of women, in particular time allocation, work load, income-generating activities, health, control over food supplies, self-sufficiency and access to resources; determination of possible adverse side effects of the project on women who are not in the target group.
   (iii) monitoring of women's participation in planning, implementation and evaluation of the project.
2. Ensuring that women's interests are represented and their needs met by projects.
3. Making the tasks of women more efficient; easing their work load etc.
4. Supplying information needed by agencies to orient their programmes correctly. (INSTRAW, ibid.: pp. 16-17)

The Impact Statement

Within the category of planning strategies, the impact statement is an interesting approach, as imprecise as it is, since it sets people thinking about the consequences of their interventions. Unlike USAID, where a boiler-plate impact statement was sufficient to satisfy the requirements of the Percy Amendment, the UK's early version of this was more detailed and contained the following prompts for officials of the Ministry of Overseas Development (Spens 1986).

- How will the project affect women's access to economic assets and cash incomes? Will they lose any of the following:
  - access to land?
  - opportunity for paid employment or other income-earning activity?
  - assistance with economic activities from other members of household?
  - control over sale of products, etc.
- Are any gains expected other than those stated in Objectives?
- How will the project affect women's allocation of time?

- Will their workload increase or decrease as a result of innovation or change? For example:
  - mechanisation;
  - new agricultural inputs and cropping patterns;
  - withdrawals of labour by other household members;
  - agricultural advice, nutritional or health teaching, if implemented;
  - changes in distance to farms, workplaces, water supply, firewood supply, etc ;

- If workload is decreased, does this involve loss of income for women?

- How will the project affect subsistence within the target group and women's control over food supplies for household? Will promotion of commercial agriculture affect:
  - availability of land for food grown mainly for use?
  - women's access to land?
  - labour inputs (male and female) on food crops, etc?
  - the removal or decrease of the source of food?

- Is the project likely to have any adverse consequences for women within groups and categories not immediately affected?

I have quoted these at length, not only because they reflect an understanding of the issues which need to be considered, but also because they illustrate the fundamental difficulty with these devices, both the financial and methodological problems posed if accurate answers are to be sought, as well as their failure to recognise their political limitations. None of these considerations are likely to prevail against the determination of the powerful interests in favour of appropriating either women's time or resources for their own purposes. For example, knowledge that the structural adjustment policies would reduce the access of poor women to food and essential services was no impediment to their introduction.

Training Approaches: Case studies

Another method used for sensitising planners about gender issues is the preparation of case studies for training purposes. The Population Council was one of the earliest agencies to use a case study (the Nemow case) to illustrate the costs and benefits to development projects of incorporating women's and gender concerns. In 1982 the council also worked with WAND and other agencies to develop a planning-centred approach to the development of case studies which could be used to sensitise planners to the work that women do and its relevance for development. Recognising the limitations of research-centred policies and planning-related research methodologies 'in which academics initiate the research, formulate the research design, and draw planners into the process too late' (Staudt 1983:4), this project developed a set of guidelines from a planning-centred, participatory approach to research, 'assessing the impact of rural development schemes on low income households and the role of women'. (WAND/Population Council 1983 pp. 100-103)

Another currently popular use of case studies has been the Harvard case studies on gender roles in development projects (Overholt *et al.* 1985). The project was first developed by the Harvard Institute for International Development (HIID) in collaboration with the WID Office of USAID. It drew on studies of USAID-funded projects as a data base for the introduction of new analytical and conceptual skills to senior-level USAID staff. It was later used with the staff of the World Bank, and the Canadian Agency for International Development (CIDA). Later this framework was introduced to the staff of UN Development Programme's offices in the Caribbean, and later extended to those of other development agencies based in Barbados, along with representatives of women's units and planning units from the Organisation of Eastern Caribbean States (OECS) countries. WAND plans to use this framework in its fieldwork in the future.

The case book represents an analytical framework for facilitating the process of integrating women into project analysis. There are four interrelated components: an activity profile; access and control profile; analysis of factors influencing activities, access, and control; and project cycle analysis. It describes these components as follows:

The activity profile 'is based on the concept of a gender-based division of labor . . . it . . . delineate(s) the economic activities of the population in the project area first by age and gender and then by ethnicity, social class, or other important distinguishing characteristics. In addition, it . . . indicates the amount of time spent by individuals to accomplish these activities.'

The access and control profile identifies 'what resources individuals can command to carry out their activities and the benefits which they derive from them.'

The analysis of factors influencing activities, access, and control 'focuses on the underlying factors which determine the gender division of labor and gender-related control over resources and benefits. These analyses identify the factors which create differentials, opportunities or constraints for men's and women's participation in and benefits from projects.'

The project cycle analysis examines a project in light of the basic data generated by the other components. (Overholt *et al.* 1984: 4-5)

Special reference should also be made to CIDA's workbook, *Women in Development and the Project Cycle* (1986), which builds on the agency's earlier policy guidelines (1977). It is intended to promote a 'corporate strategy' in support of the operational objective 'to develop explicit plans to include and to benefit LDC women and girls in operational plans ... Country Program Reviews, program and projects design and in sectoral policies and guidelines.' (ibid. p.2)

Training Programmes

An interesting training programme is *Planning with Women for Development* conducted by Caroline Moser of University College, London (1983-86). In an extremely valuable insight on her experience in incorporating gender in courses on planning, Moser writes: 'Efforts to make . . . planners (engaged in sectors such as transport, housing, employment, land-use and infrastructure) aware by 'grafting' on gender to their particular planning disciplines met with little success, and led to recognition of the necessity of distinguishing between a gender-aware planner (in say transport planning) and gender planning, a specific planning approach in its own right.' (Moser 1988: 47)

The approach provides both the conceptual framework and the methodological tools for incorporating gender into planning. In this framework Moser draws attention to the need to challenge 'planning stereotypes' relating to the structure and the division of labour within low-income households, and to distinguish between practical and strategic gender needs. She points out:

> When planners are blind to the triple roles of women, and to the fact that women's needs are not always the same as men's, they fail to recognize the necessity of relating planning policy to women's specific requirements. In particular, development planning based on a sectoral approach does not provide the integrative strategies women require (e.g. health facilities are frequently undersubscribed because their opening hours are inappropriate for working mothers. (1988: 8)

She views the distinction between strategic and practical gender interests and needs (Molyneux 1985) as being 'of critical importance . . . if realistic parameters are to be identified as to what can be accomplished in the planning process, as well as the limitations of different policy interventions'. (Moser, *ibid.*, 10). She makes the important point that practical gender needs such as food, shelter and water are required by all the family, and are identified as priorities both by the women themselves, and by 'policy makers concerned to achieve developmental objectives'. However, while these 'practical' objectives help to ease the immediate burden of women's work, they also serve to preserve and reinforce the sexual division of labour, and in that sense work against the achievement of strategic gender needs.

Moser suggests that the identification of the triple role of women, and the distinction between practical and strategic gender needs, also might make support for women's work more palatable to policy-makers since they can be dissociated from the feminism of the pursuit of strategic gender needs, and the distinction "may assist in diffusing the criticism of those who find 'feminism' unacceptable."

At the same time she recognises the need for the 'selection and adoption of more challenging solutions'—and gives a number of examples of intervention, in such sectors as employment, housing and basic urban services, to illustrate the potential and limitations of different planning practices for addressing practical or strategic gender needs.

The possibility of building on practical needs to achieve strategic gender needs is the key issue for those who recognise the need for the transformation of existing oppressive structures and relationships. The adjustment policies, with the crushing and inequitable burden which they place on poor women, illustrate the danger of leaving gender ideology unchallenged and demonstrate that even practical gains are easily reversed if women (with a feminist orientation) lack the power to influence policy options. The existence of strong feminist groups among poor women in third–world countries and the clear articulation of feminist perspectives by the Development Alternatives with Women for a New Era (DAWN) group are indications that feminist consciousness has developed too far to be discouraged by the resistance of male (and female) planners. Rather than deny the relevance of feminism to the achievement of meaningful development goals, feminist planners ought to seek opportunities to help progressive, non-feminist colleagues to understand feminism as a transformational politics (Bunch 1985).

An analysis by the network of third-world feminists promoting DAWN shows clearly the links between the subordination of women and the interlocking global crises of economic disarray, deteriorating social services, food insecurity, environmental degradation, cultural fundamentalism, violence against women and militarism (Sen and Grown, 1987), and relates all of this to the type of economic model currently being promoted (entrenched) through policies of structural adjustment (reinforcement). We need to recognise that while the concentration on practical gender needs might help to alleviate the gross deprivation of the poor, we need policies that will move poor women beyond mere survival towards determining the long-term requirements for the creation of a more equitable society. Policies must create the space for women to pursue strategic gender interests.

In 1981 the Economic Commission for Latin America and the Caribbean (ECLAC), in collaboration with WAND, addressed this concern by developing a training programme for women working in agencies, community development departments, institutions (macro-level), and other community organisations such as non-governmental organisations (micro-level). The unique feature of the programme manual—*Women and Development Guidelines for Program/Project Planning*, was its experiential approach, stated as follows. 'The Guidelines are intended to recall to mind past learning experiences, to assess the gaps between what the situation is and *what we have a right to expect it to be*, and to stimulate new ideas of *what we can do about it* (my emphasis). They are not intended to be a step-by-step, how-do-do-it manual, but rather to point out steps in the planning process-with blank spaces to be filled in by the users, based on their reality and choices.' (Pezzullo 1981: 8)
The conceptual framework for this approach is also unusual, as illustrated by other statements in the introductory section.

- 'Development planning has traditionally been confined to meeting economic goals. We seek "Women and Development" *perspectives that go beyond this tradition* by involving women at all stages and at all levels of program/project planning and in the formulation of strategies for change *to ensure that our objectives of freedom, dignity, equity, and autonomy are met* '(my emphasis).

This section quotes the Jamaican economist George Beckford's definition of development:

> Meaningful development for Third World countries must not only lead to increased real per capita income, but also requires more equitable patterns of income distribution, and (that) countries at least have control over their resources and the environment in which they live. This is a basic precondition for the achievement of full human dignity, which is of crucial and ultimate importance to all people. (Beckford: 1972)

- Women along with the poor have been seen as targets requiring integration into the existing process in passive rather than active roles.

- *Women must unlearn their habits of dependence and strive toward self-reliance.* (my emphasis).

- Positive action by government and the private sector is *necessary to assist this 'unlearning' process.* (my emphasis).

- Economic growth has traditionally been accompanied by industrialisation and urbanisation, which have brought more harm than benefits to women. Women's roles have been changed *without their having had anything to say about it* (my emphasis).

- *Tactical approaches* for working with existing institutions which embody this industrialisation and urbanisation (approach) must be developed even as work goes on *to change these institutions* (my emphasis).

- To participate fully in the development process, it is imperative to know how and why specific choices are made in development planning and programming.

- Women must be afforded the possibility of *knowing the options open to them, of exercising freedom of choice in selection of options,* and of having access to the resources needed to carry them out (my emphasis) .

- We reject the 'information trickle-down,' i.e. the idea of *special groups parceling out knowledge* (my emphasis) (Puezzullo 1981: 8).

These sections are quoted at length to demonstrate that it is possible to incorporate radical or alternative feminist approaches into a process normally viewed as purely technical.

A final approach, which is not normally used with government agencies, is mentioned below to illustrate the action and implementation level of intervention at which the question to be asked is how to engage women within the target area in the processes of (gender) analysis, that is, analysing, defining, and acting (in other words, praxis, participatory research, etc, empowering women).

This approach was through the *Pilot Project on the Integration of Women in Rural Development* implemented by the Women and Development Unit (WAND) between 1981 and 1983 (Ellis 1983: 84-99). A community-based, three-week training programme, *Participatory Activities for Field Workers, Getting the Community into the Act* (WAND 1983), brought together women and men from the community along with fieldworkers from the key ministries of agriculture, health, education and community development, and field representatives of NGOs working in the community, for training in participatory methods in needs assessment, programme planning, and evaluation.

Among the spin-offs from this training programme were the following:

1. A challenge (through an editorial and letter-writing campaign in the local media) to the government and the minister responsible for women's affairs to clarify their policy, after the minister had used insensitive, derogatory language at the opening session.
2. A new level of respect from the ministries for the independence and autonomy of the women of the community.
3. A new level of self-confidence and self-esteem among the women of the community, as they took control of what happened in their community, and recognised their ability to achieve goals set through a process of community participation, by their own efforts.
4. A new spirit of cooperation between men and women in the community.
5. A new focus on the welfare of children, youth and the elderly in the community.
6. A new spirit of self-reliance throughout the entire community.

The assumptions underlying this approach were that

1. The empowerment of women with the confidence, skills and access to resources within their community as well as nationally, regionally and internationally would enable them to define and implement their own programmes; and that
2. The empowerment of women at community level—to make government and public servants accountable to their constituencies—is also the most effective way to influence policy-makers, planners, project managers and key change agents.

While the first has been validated, the second has not. The empowerment of women at community level, through a training process focused on the provision of technical skills, was not sufficient to protect the community from the adverse effects of macroeconomic policies adopted by their government even without the pressure of having to meet IMF conditionalities. This brings us back to these issues:

1. How to link the micro-level of experience with macroeconomic analysis;

2. How to ensure in this analysis that explicit attention is given to the different world views of the different theoretical frameworks within which we operate; and

3. How to recognise and take into account in our planning strategies the limitations of purely technical approaches; how to create the space for the political and counter-cultural elements necessary to enable the poorest most powerless women to determine and realise strategic as well as practical gender interests (Crowfoot and Chesler 1974).

Approaches to an Alternative Analysis

Over the ten years of its operations WAND's approaches have changed as it has responded to the insights gained both from its own work, and the changing socio-economic and political context in which it has functioned. As I have pointed out above, this changing context, symbolised by current policies of structural adjustment, highlights the limitations of approaches which seek to integrate women in development. WAND is responding to this by seeking to change its goal from one of integrating women in development into one which increasingly seeks to empower women to promote social change.

In a sense, these changes in WAND's analysis of the problems of women and development represent a shift from the assumptions and approaches of the dominant paradigm of development and social change toward an increasing search for feminist perspectives within the alternative paradigm. However, there are numerous constraints on the shift in focus from the integrative to the liberative paradigm: political, psychological (professional and personal) and institutional.

Politically, we operate within the space allowed within a paradigm which seeks to maintain control by simultaneously labelling (as Communist, for example) and discrediting any attempt to challenge the capitalist system. Attempts to break out of this system are inevitably met with repressive measures (Labelle 1976).

Psychologically, at a personal level, one has to confront women's collusion in their own oppression and subordination due to their lack of consciousness of their oppression and their fear of change.

Professionally, we are constrained by a foundational epistemology which defines both the method and content of knowledge, maintaining the separation of subjects and objects of research, and at the same time ascribing to academic knowledge the status of truth (Rorty 1976).

The implications of these constraints for an organisation dedicated to releasing the energies and creativity of ordinary (unschooled) people, but located within academia itself, are enormous. Institutionally, mainstream organizations and staff processes tend to reflect integrative analysis and commitment and to act consistently within this framework. This makes it especially difficult to create the space within which real options can be addressed. And yet a central part of any project for social change towards alternative development strategies must be the transformation at individual (personal and professional) as well as institutional levels. This entails helping the staff to develop (individually and collectively, that is to say, institutionally) a critical consciousness of the need for a paradigm shift. This is the task which we are in the process of undertaking. As we engage in it, we will not only be using it as a strategy for the transformation of our own programme, but we will also be learning about the factors which facilitate or impede such a process, and about the consequences of attempting this shift. If we survive we will have something to share with the agencies and groups with whom we work.

Conclusion

> There is no easy approach to WID issues. The interrelationships of the productive and reproductive activities of women, the inter-linkages between the macro- and the micro-levels of the economy, the web of international and regional factors affecting the lives of women, collectively or as individuals, all of these combine to weave the complex relationship of women and development that sometimes baffles planners. (INSTRAW 1987: 2)

> Checklists and guidelines can be effective only as part of a larger information system - one complemented by strategy or goal statements, directives, responsible personnel, resources and training, and involving monitoring and evaluation procedures. (Finney 1985: 8)

> Checklists are mechanistic nonsense. (AWID, unnamed participant at 1988 meeting on gender issues in development cooperation)

These quotations are a measure of the complexity of integrating gender concerns into development planning. Given this state of affairs and the requirements listed by Ruth Finney in her statement at the 1985 meeting (quoted above), some third-world feminists might well question the value of expending limited resources on activities whose impact are so problematic. My own position is that their value might be enhanced if they could be used to raise fundamental questions about the development process itself, as for example, the work of DAWN has done. For the most part, the checklists and guidelines, analytical frameworks and methodological tools are limited by the fact that they are situated within the dominant liberal paradigm and therefore never challenge the assumptions on which this particular model of development is based.

As I have argued, this model of growth-oriented development is grounded in a gender ideology which assumes, indeed depends upon, an inequitable distribution of resources, power and work between men and women. It never questions the sexual division of labour, which provides the rationale for a special attention to gender in development planning. It continues to assume that sensitivity to gender differences, and well thought-out methodologies, will take care of the problems posed by the failure to take women's specific practical gender needs into account. Above all, it persists in suggesting technical solutions to what is essentially a political problem.

My own experience in the Caribbean demonstrates that even when there is awareness and methodologies for taking women's needs into account, the results are not always what one would anticipate. The establishment of special mechanisms and procedures, the use of checklists and guidelines, the application of carefully constructed conceptual frameworks and methodological tools, have too often been to no avail. On the contrary, awareness of the important role played by women, for example in meeting basic needs, is (within adjustment or austerity programmes) used to justify cuts in government expenditures on basic social services (UNICEF 1987). The services which are cut include not only health, education and social security, but also expenditures on feeder roads, water supplies and low-cost housing, all of which are essential support services for women as they struggle to perform their multiple roles.

An assessment of the programmes in which WAND has been involved since 1976 demonstrates that the greatest impact both in terms of their capacity to lead to improvements in the quality of life in Caribbean communities, as well as to generate greater responsiveness on the part of the government agencies to women's needs and concerns, has come from those projects in which we worked directly with the women at community level. The inclusion of the extension staff (mostly men) who worked in the community in the initial training programme in the use of participatory methods for *Getting the Community into the Act*, also helped to sensitise them to women's capacity for leadership and facilitated follow-up contact between the women and their agencies.

Experience suggests that the methodologies required are those of participatory research, social analysis and popular education. Such methodologies help poor people — especially women — to analyse their circumstances in order to understand the steps that need to be taken to protect and enhance the quality of their lives. What this suggests is that it is only when women are empowered by the building of self-confidence, skills and access to resources that they are able to negotiate both the time and resources required for improving their own lives and the quality of life in their communities.

Nevertheless, not even these advantages were sufficient to protect the community from the devastating effects of some of the cuts in government services introduced as part of the country's adjustment policies. This points to the need to address macroeconomic policies as well as approaches at the micro-level, and to incorporate social analysis (including gender analysis) as well as skills in organising into our training programmes with women at community level.

The overwhelming conclusion from all of this is, therefore, that the most important requirement is the need for planners to recognise that development is not a technical matter, but a deeply political process requiring political and cultural sensitivities, as well as the technical skills at their command. The best approach for feminists concerned with gender issues in the planning process is to help to create the space which might link the experiences of women at the level of their communities to the processes of sectoral and national planning.

We must also try to ensure that the necessary resources are provided to enable the women to act in their own best interests; and then, if possible, work to offer the protection that may be needed for people who risk their lives in the struggle for survival, and justice.

References

Anand, Anita. "Rethinking Women in Development". In *Women in Development: a Resource Guide*. Geneva: ISIS Collective. 1983

Antrobus, Peggy. "Equality, Development and Peace: A Second Look at the Goals of the UN Decade for Women". Paper presented at the Conference of the Associated Country Women of the World (ACWW) Vancouver, BC, June 1983.

______. "The Impact of the Debt Crisis on Jamaican Women". Paper presented at the First Meeting of Caribbean Economists. Jamaica. June 1987.

______. "Gender Implications of the Global Economic Crisis". Presentation sponsored by the Women's Studies and Latin American Studies Program at the Woodrow Wilson School of Public Administration Princeton University. April 1988a.

______. "Gender Analysis". Comprehensive Paper for the Doctoral Program at the Center for International Education, University of Massachusetts, Amherst. 1988b.

Beckford, George .*Persistent Poverty: Underdevelopment in Plantation Economies of the Third World.* Oxford: Oxford University Press. 1972.

Beneria, Lourdes. "Accounting for Women's Work". In *Women and Development: the Sexual Division of Labour in Rural Societies.* New York: Praeger. 1982.

______ and Sen, Gita. "Accumulation, Reproduction, and Women's Work in Economic Development: Theoretical and Practical Implications", *Feminist Studies,* V.8, No. 1, Spring, 1981, pp. 157-176.

Bunch, Charlotte. *Passionate Politics: Feminist Theory in Action.* New York: St Martin's Press. 1987.

Chhachhi, Amrita. "Women, Development Policy and the Management of Change: a Critique of the Social Sciences". Keynote Address at the second disciplinary seminar in Women and Development Studies (Social Sciences). The University of the West Indies, Cave Hill, Barbados, 3-7 April 1989.

Canadian International Development Agency(CIDA). *Women in Development and the Project Cycle: A Workbook.* Ottawa: 1986.

Crowfoot, James E. and Chesler, Mark A. "Contemporary Perspectives on Planned Social Change: A Comparison". In *Journal of Applied Behavioural Science*. Vol. 10, No. 3, 1974.

Deere, Carmen Diana. "Rural Women's Subsistence Production in the Capitalist Periphery" *Review of Radical Political Economics,* Vol. 8, No. 1, 1976, pp. 9-17.

______ and Leon, Magdalena. *Rural Women and State Policy: Feminist Perspectives on Latin American Agriculture.* Boulder: Westview. 1987.

Ellis, Patricia. "The Rose Hall Experience—Bottom-up planning". In *Planning for Women in Rural Development: A Source Book for the Caribbean.* Barbados: WAND/UWI. 1983. pp. 84-99.

Finney, Ruth. Quoted in INSTRAW (see below). 1985.

Frank, A. G. *Capitalism and Underdevelopment in Latin America.* New York: Monthly Review Press. 1967.

______, "The Development of Underdevelopment". In Weiler, C.K. (ed.) *The Political Economy of Development and Underdevelopment.* New York: Random House. 1973.

Fraser, Arvonne. *The UN Decade for Women: Documents and Dialogue.* Boulder: Westview. 1987.

Gutierrez, Gustavo A. *Theology of Liberation.* New York: Orbis Books. 1973.

Holland, Joe and Henriot, Peter. *Social Analysis.* New York: Orbis Books. 1985.

INSTRAW. 'Evaluating Bilateral and Multi-lateral Experiences in the Development and use of Women in Development Guidelines/Checklists: Implications for National Use in Formulating Agricultural Projects for Women'. Santo Domingo, Dominican Republic. 1985.

______, *Selected Guidelines and Checklists for Women in Development.* Santo Domingo, Dominican Republic. 1987.

Jain, Devaki. *"Development as if Women Mattered: Can Women Provide a New Paradigm?" Address to OECD, Paris. 1983.*

Labelle, Thomas. Non-formal Education and Social Change in Latin *America.* California: UCLA Latin American Center Publications. 1976.

Maguire, Patricia. *Women in Development: an Alternative Analysis.* Amherst: Center for International Education. 1984.

Molyneux, M. "Mobilization without Emancipation? Women's Interests, State and Revolution in Nicaragua". *Feminist Studies,* Vol. 11, No. 2, 1985.

Moser, C. O. N. "Gender Planning for Women in Development". *World Development.* Washington. 1988.

Oakley, Ann. *Sex, Gender and Society.* London: Temple Smith. 1972.

Overholt, Catherine *et al. Gender Roles in Development.* West Hartford, Connecticut: Kumarian Press. 1984.

Palmer, Ingrid. "The Nemow Case." In Population Council Series, *Women's Roles and Gender Differences in Development — Cases for Planners.* West Hartford, Connecticut: Kumarian Press. 1986.

Paulson, R. *Conflicting Theories of Social and Educational Change: a Typological Review.* Pittsburg: University Center for International Studies. 1976.

Pezzullo, Caroline. *Women and Development: Guidelines for Program/ Project Planning.* Santiago: ECLA. 1981.

Rodney, Walter. *How Europe Underdeveloped Africa.* Dar-es-Salaam: Tanzania Publishing House. 1972.

Rorty, Richard. *Philosophy and the Mirror of Nature.* Princeton: Princeton University Press. 1979.

Sen, Gita, and Grown, Caren. *Development, Crises, and Alternative Visions: Third World Women's Perspectives.* New York: Monthly Review Press. 1987.

Spens, Teresa. *Studies on Agricultural Extension Involving Women.* UNIFEM. 1986.

Staudt, Kathleen. "Methodological Overview". In Planning for Women *in Rural Development: a Source Book for the Caribbean.* Barbados: WAND/UWI. 1983. pp.4-14.

Tinker, I. and Bramsen, M. (eds). *Women and World Development.* Washington, DC: Overseas Development Council. 1976.

______, "The Adverse Effect of Development on Women". In *Women and World Development.* Washington, DC: Overseas Development Council. 1976.

Mainstreaming Gender Analysis in the Development Planning Process

Gwendoline Williams

Much has been said about the need for the integration of women into the development process. To this end, by 1985 some 90 % of national governments around the world had established what the UN terms national machineries intended to put the issue of gender squarely on the public planning agenda. The espoused goals have been to correct the socio-economic and political inequalities faced by women. The position was summed up in the statement from the 1980 Copenhagen Programme of Action: half the world's population performs two-thirds of the world's work; receives one-tenth of the world income; and owns less than 1 % of the world's property.

Notwithstanding the positive political and organisational response to the Women in Development (WID) initiative through the setting-up of bureaux, ministries, women's desks and advocacy groups, gender inequity is not far along the road to being de-institutionalised. As the twentieth century draws to a close, this has created an increasing sense of bewilderment, frustration as well as anger among WID advocates, both male and female.

Staudt (1987, pp. 3-6) listed some of the likely reasons for the failure to 'dismantle male privilege'. These include: gender-biased ideologies of production, reproduction and household management which characterise public policy planning and implementation at the national, regional and international levels; the scarce financial, material and human resources allocated to governmental and non-governmental agencies set up to address the concerns of women; and the deficiencies in organisational and political skills of women who have to function in male-dominated, bureaucratised public institutions and women's organisations. There are also obstacles placed in the path of women who legitimately seek to gain entry into the executive management arenas of public- and private-sector bureaucracies where they may be able to affect the policy planning process.

In this paper yet another delimiting factor will be identified: the approach to development planning within national, regional and international agencies, particularly in developing countries.

It will be argued that development planners, who are invariably male, exercise ideological, technical and cognitive or intellectual hegemony over the planning process. These planners, trained and often over-indoctrinated into their particular lead discipline, are usually convinced of the centrality of the disciplines of economics, financial management and technology studies. As a result, the planning methodology devised—models, methods, techniques and organisational structures in use—emphasises what Kardam (1986, p. 1) calls 'technical control'. There is, therefore, a corresponding lack of emphasis on the socio-cultural and behavioural aspects of the planning process, which may be explained by the underplaying of the inputs of sociology, anthropology, psychology and other people-focused disciplines into the various stages of development planning.

The overall position taken in this paper is that political and organisational initiatives to 'integrate' women into the development process are necessary, but these are not sufficient to bring about gender equity. A viable methodology which reconciles technological, economic and financial concerns with those of gender awareness, social analysis and social impact analysis is needed in order to achieve gender-sensitive public policy planning. Success in this regard would move the WID initiatives beyond rhetoric and advocacy to the mainstreaming of gender analysis in the policy planning process.

Gender in the Planning Process

Hogwood and Gunn (1984) see public policy as a process that has several facets which include the various stages of planning and action. For example, policy determination in its earliest phase is conceived of as expressions of general purpose or desired states of affairs. They note that:

> 'It expresses the broad purpose or "ends" of government activity . . . and also describes the state of affairs which would prevail on the achievement of those purposes' (p. 14).

Contingent on these broad statements of intent are specific proposals which constitute the specific policy measures relating to a particular sector or sectors that are institutionally linked. The measures are the formal authorisations which, when legitimised by social and legal processes in the realm of public decision-making, are converted into specific economic and social programmes and projects. The outcomes of these are assessed in order to evaluate the effectiveness of the public policy in the given setting.

The effectiveness of public policy directions and measures, programmes and projects is coming to be determined among other factors by the extent to which there is explicit consideration of gender in the development planning process, from the expression of intent to outcomes.

The extensive role played by women in economic, political and social life, as well as in domestic household management, requires that policy statements of intent, programmes, projects and outcomes reflect the contribution as well as the interests of women as a separate constituency of interest involved in and affected by the decision-making that takes place in the policy environment. What is required is a world view that directly recognises the existence of this group as both contributors and beneficiaries of development.

In a colloquium report, *Gender Issues in Development Cooperation*, reference was made to the utility of a 'gender lens' that could be used to modify the existing methods of policy planning, so that the variable of gender could receive specific treatment at each stage of policy determination and implementation. The report noted that the idea of the gender lens represents a very different approach from that of treating women as a special interest group. It opens up the real possibility that with the use of the lens, which reveals the triple contributing role of women in development, in the areas of economic management, population management and household and community management, will result in the emergence of a governmental and professional responsibility to take the economic and social relations of gender into account in the shaping of public policy. The report continues: 'Instead of looking at "impacts on women", we must look at gender differentials in *benchmark planning data* and in evaluation impacts . . . Gender differentials can be a technical tool . . . sex disaggregated data an *institutional strategy*. (p. 19)'

Data analysis that is gender-sensitive in the way described above helps in the policy planning process in these ways:

1. the identification of critical policy issues as these reflect development planning with a human face;
2. forecasting, needs assessment and problems;
3. the determination of objectives and priorities;
4. options analysis in the light of priorities set and available resources; and
5. policy implementation, control, evaluation and review.

A more gender-sensitive approach takes shape, therefore, after there is a clear world view of women's role in the development process as active contributors and beneficiaries. This is followed by a development planning methodology which systematically removes the invisibility of women in the various stages of policy studies and analysis. To do this, gender is used as a technical variable that guides data generation, analysis and use so that the triple role of women will have its effect on policy decision-making programmes and outcomes.

Gender as a technical variable is best used in public policy planning when the methods of forecasting and analysis employed include a direct focus on social analysis, social feasibility analysis and social impact analysis. This approach is needed to assist formulation, implementation and evaluation. It must also influence the policy planning process conducted by the political and technical directorates in bodies such as national planning commissions and quasi-autonomous public-sector agencies. The evidence reveals, however, that in both these realms the planning process is not explicitly cognisant of the issue of gender.

The conceptual, procedural and organisational constraints on devising a gender-sensitive approach to the policy planning process will be highlighted through a brief reporting on three case studies from international, regional and national organisations. These are the World Bank, CARICOM and the Ministry of Settlements and Public Utilities in Trinidad and Tobago.

The World Bank experience

Michael Cernea, editor of the 1985 World Bank publication, *Putting People First*, noted in the preface that 'people are — and should be — the starting point, the centre, and the end goal of each development intervention'. This requires making social organisations the explicit concern of development policies and programmes. It includes constructing development projects around the potentials of the populations in the project area. Cernea summed up the position in the following way:

> '"Putting people first" in development projects may be regarded as an appeal to planners' humanitarian feeling. If only this meaning is ascribed to it, however, the slogan will walk on short legs and stumble fast . . . [It is] in development — people . . . Non-economic social sciences which study people, cultures and societies and are vitally necessary.' (p. 3)

The Bank has often acknowledged in its reports that one of the reasons for the ineffective implementation of development projects has been the fact that many were 'socially ill-informed and ill-conceived' (p. 3). They failed to take explicit account of the way in which cultural variables such as class and status, race and ethnicity, geographical region, age and gender serve to shape as well as influence development efforts.

Putting People First is essentially an amalgam of evaluation reports which acknowledge the project planning deficit, albeit for rural development projects. An in-depth analysis of this deficit as it affects the WID initiative has been provided by Nuket Kardam of the World Bank staff.

The Bank displayed its commitment to integrating women in the development process by articulating a WID policy with supporting programmes and projects. A WID office was established to provide institutional and administrative support for the Bank's initiative. Kardam reports on interviews with Bank staff, including those who were interested in WID and wanted to integrate it into their planning and programme developments. There was widespread feeling that the consciousness–raising strategies for promoting WID were not being followed up by research and development as well as planning to make WID 'more operational' (p. 5).

Respondents felt that the operationalising of the gender variable in the policy and project planning process was not possible owing to a lack of emphasis on social planning which would have shown the need for the use of the gender lens in social analysis, for example, an analysis of women's access to and control of resources and benefits from the productive sector.

The Policy Focus

The central policy issue has focused on education and population, health and nutrition. This emphasis can be attributed to the pervasive ideology of reproduction, child-rearing, household management and community action which set the parameters on the policy issues which concern women.

Kardam (p. 13) noted that the Bank's initial involvement in the UN WID activities was in the area of women and population planning. The 1970 resolution of the General Assembly on international action for the advancement of women led to the Inter-regional Meeting of Experts on the Role of Women in Economic and Social Development, and was sponsored by the UN Division of Human Rights in 1972. As part of the activities of World Population Year in 1974, another inter-regional seminar was held on the role of women in population development. In this forum the World Bank participated in its president's speeches on fertility decline and development.

The policy of the Bank took as a result a direction on WID that emphasised women's reproductive role, and its productive activities, existing largely in the informal sector, centred on supplementing incomes for the purposes of improving household management.

The Bank's policy direction has meant that the integration effort has segmented development planning into women's issues and *bona fide* economic planning that is male-centred. WID therefore became a sideline policy issue.

Alternatively, the mainstreaming of the gender variable in development planning requires a different kind of policy focus and methodological approach in the research and development dimension of the planning process. The central question to be posed then is, what level of access and control over financial, material and organisational resources do women (who constitute more than 50% of the world's population) have? Also, what is the distribution of economic and social returns on investment proportionate to levels of productivity by the respective genders?

The recasting of the development perspective and policy directions must be followed up by a suitable mix of technical and social assessment methods and techniques of research, policy and project formulation. These methods and techniques are to be employed at all stages of the planning process and project preparation, from conceptualisation to implementation and review and evaluation.

In *Putting People First* Cernea revealed that the technical and sociological mix of methods has been difficult to effect and to time. For example, the social assessment inputs have been very difficult to incorporate at the preparation or design stage in the project cycle, of project identification, preparation, appraisal, implementation and evaluation. Each stage requires a substantially different 'contribution (informational, analytical, or predictive) from sociologists and anthropologists. The sociological input is thus determined by the timing of their contribution—that is, the stage at which it is made and the implicit requirements at that stage.' (p. 7).

Yet the evaluation reports consistently show that usually the first entrance point for social analysis and social impact inputs has been at the evaluation of project outcomes. This is usually at a stage when it is difficult, if not impossible, to deal with the emergent problems of culture, politics and social differentials such as class and status, race and ethnicity, age and gender.

Technical Control and Professional Hegemony

Respondents in Kardam's study substantiate Cernea's explanation for this state of affairs. They point to the control that technically-oriented researchers, planners, politicians and administrators have over the planning process. The World Bank staffers corroborated the view that gender-sensitive development planning and project formulation are not pursued owing to the supreme concern with meeting efficiency criteria. This is facilitated by technical, objective, value-free knowledge and planning techniques. Kardam concludes that technical control and the resultant tidy approach to development planning takes precedence over all else. 'The goal of technical control requires technically rigorous analysis that is expressed by quantitative measures of returns on investment . . . . Emphasis is put on technical, economic and financial analyses because they are "rational", and scientifically grounded.' (p. 4)

Therefore social analysis and other social assessment methods are less determinate, less conclusive and are not compatible with the goals of technical control.

Apart from model-building and methods, there is the issue of maintaining the pre-eminence of the technical- over the human-oriented social sciences. Such pre-eminence ensures the continuing intellectual hegemony and professional status enhancement of the development planners who control the policy environment at the World Bank.

Time Pressures

At the same time, the effects of time pressures on project development should not be played down. Meeting Bank deadlines and recipient country schedules usually create a degree of impatience with field-based, costly social planning which would force researchers and planners to treat the gender variable.

The overall picture of development planning at the World Bank up to 1986 reveals the non-institutionalisation of sociologically influenced planning. The quest for maintaining intellectual and organisational hegemony by the technically-oriented planners is matched by the ideological emphasis on WID as a forum for reproductive or productive policy determination. The call for a methodology that would put the key relevant questions on gender equity in the economic, financial and political arenas, instead of merely in health, education and population management has so far gone unheard. The legitimation and incorporation of social planning and social assessment methods that would treat explicitly the gender variable are yet to be realised. The politics of professional pre-eminence among technically-oriented planners adds to the factors which hinder gender-sensitive planning at the Bank.

Caricom: A Gender-sensitive Training Programme for Women Administrators

In February 1988 the Administrative Staff College of Jamaica conducted, on behalf of the CARICOM Secretariat a seminar for senior women administrators called *Gender Issues and Regional Politics*. In April 1988 a Train the Teachers Workshop was mounted by the CARICOM Secretariat for senior trainers in both the public and private sectors in the Caribbean. This workshop was entitled *The Management of Change: A Gender Perspective* and was organised directly by the Women's Affairs Division of the CARICOM Secretariat.

Both exercises were mounted with the intention of raising the consciousness of women administrators as well as male and female Caribbean trainers on the necessity for institutionalising gender awareness in policy planning and management training programmes. The CARICOM Secretariat organised the seminar and workshop with funding from the *Management for Change Programme* of the Canadian International Development Agency (CIDA) and the Commonwealth Secretariat.

Gender issues and regional policies: report on two seminars

The aim of the first seminar was to give senior women administrators the opportunity to:

1. seek ways of integrating family and work aspects of women's lives;
2. direct energies towards overcoming obstacles to career growth; and
3. consider techniques for encouraging policy-makers to incorporate women's issues into national policies (p. 1).

Among issues which formed part of the course content were :

(i) women in national and regional development;

(ii) organisation and management; and

(iii) the interface between self, family and workplace.

Some of the major constraints on the mainstreaming of gender analysis in the policy planning process in the region included: the bureaucratised and formal structures of national and regional institutions and agencies; and the linkages between the region and external funding agencies, in the latter of which the technical control function of project planning, implementation and evaluation dominates; and budgetary constraints.

The strategies suggested for removing the obstacles to gender-sensitive development planning included improved data collection, analysis and dissemination. This database would then be used to bring visibility to gender, and by extension women's issues in economic and social planning. In order to facilitate this process of devising a gender lens for use in policy planning, emphasis was to be placed on training and community education. This particular recommendation called for the sensitising of trainers and public- and private-sector top-level personnel to gender issues.

In the training process, use was made of approaches that would create an acceptable level of gender awareness among the participants as individual professionals and as policy-makers. The Seminar Report listed and explained the approaches (pp 4-5). These were: the experiential, where participants shared their worklife experiences with each other; the interactive/analytical, in which participants engaged in open discussion after completing a managerial role matrix designed and developed by Dr Indira Parikh. The analyses revealed individual strengths and weaknesses within the given organisational setting. In the cognitive realm, there were discussions on development planning perspectives; research and development; and approaches to policy planning.

The second seminar, which dealt with a gender perspective on the management of change, aimed to:

1. develop case studies on information and recommendations arising from the first seminar which dealt with gender issues and regional policies;
2. re-design and modify training programmes to include modules related to WID; and
3. develop training methodologies for transfer of knowledge on gender issues to participants in future training programmes.

The workshop plan focused on an international viewpoint on women in development. This viewpoint revealed the top-down policy-making methodology of international funding agencies in providing support for the process of social change in the region. Additionally, the institutional structures in both the public and private sectors made top-down as opposed to participatory changes more probable.

Another important workshop session dealt with the extent of gender awareness in the public sector administration reform process in Jamaica. What was evident from the account was that basically a gender-neutral approach was adopted.

The last session centred on new techniques in the CARICOM context of training managers for participating in gender-sensitive development planning.

This second seminar was participated in by the writer as a resource person. There was no doubt about the programme intent, which was that participants were to become more gender-sensitive in carrying out the management function in their respective organisations.

The training process focused on the problem of gender-aware management and development in the Caribbean. This had several dimensions: the diagnostic/analytic; the treatment of the problem by intervention strategies that would impact on participants in the cognitive, affective and behavioural realms; the development of action plans for ensuring institutional and societal change; and the evaluative.

Much of the training experience remained centred on the diagnostic/analytical aspect of the problem. There was, for example, much discussion on the top-down approach to development and the reasons for this. The treatment dealt with modes of consciousness-raising and advocacy as strategies for affecting public decision-making. Not much progress was made in the realm of research and development and policy planning in terms of the development, acceptance and use of the gender lens as a technical tool of gender-based policy planning, analysis and evaluation.

In the practical area, the workshop participants were asked to do the following:

1. develop case studies that were gender-sensitive and based on recommendations arising from the first regional workshop;
2. re-design and modify training programmes to include modules relating to WID issues;
3. develop training methodologies for transfer of knowledge on gender issues to participants in future training programmes.

A discernible feature of this part of the workshop was the evident search for a specific approach to the development of gender-based or gender-sensitive cases. In part, this seemed to have stemmed from the differing levels of expertise in case-writing. Critically, however, the mechanics of the cognitive or intellectual aspects of the gender lens, for example, the gender-based division of labour; the variable of access to and control of productive resources and property assets; and the stereotyping of personality systems along lines of gender were not easily assimilated and utilised in the case-writing session.

While the discussion sessions on the development of a gender-aware approach to the management of change in the Caribbean were informative and lively, the translation, application and actual use of the variables that provide the channels for the gender lens still had to be crystallised. It was one thing to have a cognitive and effective hold on the process. The real challenge continued to be the analytical and, more importantly, the experiential.

The quest for actual training strategies and techniques in gender-sensitive institutional development and institutional strengthening must be advanced rapidly. This would remove the focus from the present emphasis on advocacy and problem diagnosis. The rhetoric on the need for WID would be substantially replaced by a genuine pursuit of strategies that would be readily used in training sessions and organisational development programming. In short, the training and development agenda in the WID requires a praxis, that is, an analytical and experiential mode which reflects the process of theory into practice. Such an approach would provide specific action plans for incorporating social analysis and social impact into the development planning process along the lines of gender.

The Sou Sou Land Concept

In June 1988 the Women Studies Group on the UWI St Augustine Campus accepted an invitation to participate in the Regional Seminar on Women in Human Settlements Development and Management hosted by the UN Centre for Human Settlements (HABITAT) and the government of St Vincent and the Grenadines.

In a paper on public policy and settlements, the St Augustine representative examined the settlements policy of the government of Trinidad and Tobago from 1986 to the present. It was found that the defining characteristic of the policy is the Sou Sou land concept. This concept has been spelt out in the official policy documents, for example: the National Housing Authority: Towards a National Settlements Policy 1987; Settlements: Perspectives, Achievements, Projections (1988 Budget Debate Summary Statement); and the revised draft of a Macro-Planning Framework: Outline of a Medium-Term Seven-Year Plan for Trinidad and Tobago, 1988-1994.

The concept was also described in the election manifesto of the political party, the National Alliance for Reconstruction (NAR), which was the government of Trinidad and Tobago at the time. Documentation is also contained in a booklet prepared by Ivan Laughlin, the Sou Sou land senior planner, called "The Sou Sou Land Story—A Non-Governmental, Non-Profit Land Initiative in Trinidad and Tobago".

The NAR manifesto incorporated the Sou Sou land concept as part of official public policy on human settlement. It stated that the Sou Sou land concept would be used as 'part of a state initiative in its Immediate Action Plan, its Recovery and Reconstruction Plan, and its Human Dignity and Social Progress Programme'. In the immediate Action Plan the Sou Sou land concept would be used as a base 'to commerce a nation-wide programme to provide agricultural and building lands, housing and job opportunities'. The Recovery and Reconstruction Plan, based on the concept of Sou Sou land which integrates finance, idle capacity and social needs, new land and housing development would be pursued. A national plan for land development and distribution would be drawn up to structure economic activity and generate employment and social benefits. In the Human Dignity and Social Programme 'The National Alliance for Reconstruction would adopt on a national scale, the Sou Sou land approach to the provision of land for housing, agriculture, industry, commerce, recreation, and social and cultural activities.'

On the assumption of public office the NAR government formally adopted the Sou Sou land approach to human settlement in Trinidad and Tobago. For example, the National Housing Authority document, *Towards a National Settlements Policy*, stated that the Sou Sou approach was intended to "provide land for the landless" (p. 1). To do so, the document states that: 'from the purchase of the land for settlement to its planning and development and finally to distribution to the settlers, (must be) financed by the participants themselves on the basis of the traditional Sou Sou.'

Laughlin explained that the term Sou Sou comes from the local patois dialect and means 'penny by penny', a traditional form of banking among village folk in Trinidad and Tobago. A fixed number of participants would pool savings, usually by fixed equal amounts on a regular basis, weekly or monthly depending on receipt of their pay packet. Each participant would then in turn, also at the same intervals as the deposits were made, draw their 'hand'. This is the lump sum of what their overall deposits would be, minus a small contribution for the Sou Sou organiser. This contribution is called the 'box'. Laughlin comments that: 'the process is democratically organised. There is no interest accruing to the participants and the fundamental ingredient for success is *trust* [my emphasis] in the promoters' (p. 2).

In applying the concept to the human settlement policy, the 'hand' would become the land. Laughlin further explained that the prospective settlers would deposit their money to the Sou Sou Land Company (which existed as the sole implementer of the concept before its adoption by the State in 1987) in affordable instalments. The company would purchase the estates for land allocation and develop them in a participatory management style by involving the settlers in all aspects of the decision-making. At the end of this exercise, the settlers would receive their parcels of land and proceed to organise their own shelter through self-help home construction.

In adopting the concept as part of state policy, the government sought to:

1. help break the back of the incredibly inflated land values that existed in the country by immediately increasing the supply of land to meet demand, at affordable prices;
2. spread the benefit of limited financial resources for the benefit of a greater number of people in need of shelter; and
3. take cognisance of the tremendous self-help energies which the populace has had traditionally, and provide a planned framework for these energies to be incrementally capitalised on in a legitimate and legally acceptable context. This is not only in terms of people housing themselves, but feeding themselves and optimising their inherent entrepreneurial skills (for example, in cottage and other service industries) (Settlements: Perspectives, Achievements, Projections, 1988 Budget Debate Summary Statement, p. 7).

In summing up the essence of the Sou Sou land concept as the basis of the settlement policy in Trinidad and Tobago, the board of the National Housing Authority noted:

> "We need to discover an internal dynamic for the process of national development by relying on our own exertions and the homegrown wisdom of indigenous approaches to self-help . . . in a situation of limited financial resources . . . We need to capture the needs and aspirations of a contemporary creative people in a development perspective appropriate to our own circumstances . . . [We must be careful] not to do for people what they can do for themselves" (pp. 2-3)

The attributes of the Sou Sou land concept in contrast to their antithesis, are set out as follows.

Attributes of Sou Sou concept	**Antithesis**
Resource limitations	Money no object
Value for money	Poor value for money
Decentralisation	Centralisation
Team work/coordination	Little coordination
Planning and implementation an indivisible process	Planning separated from implementation: no action planning
Self financing	State funded basis
Self help	Dependency
Smallness	Monumentality
Local solutions	Institutional solutions
Participatory democracy	Parliamentary democracy (mutually exclusive)
Appropriate standards	Metropolitan standards
Incremental development	'Everything one time'
Organic growth	Zoning
Self-contained and self Sustaining communities	Communities lacking in identity and spirit (no self-sustaining community dynamic)

A gender-aware policy framework

Caroline Moser, who worked in gender, planning and development for several years, provided a framework for devising land settlement and housing policies which reflect gender awareness in a systematic fashion as part of a Working Paper Series on Gender and Planning. She noted that it is necessary to lay bare the existing assumptions about land use and the utility of shelter in terms of family structure and lifestyles.

Settlement planning and management should attend to the technical considerations of land layout and house design; legislation concerning ownership rights and household activities; eligibility criteria; application and selection procedures; financing policies, including cost recovery strategies; home construction and maintenance activities, and infrastructural support service.

Efforts should also be made to ensure that the various criteria for human settlement planning and management do reflect the concerns of women in their socially expected triple roles of production, reproduction and home management and community action.

The framework provided by the working paper series is useful in order to determine the utility of the Sou Sou land concept in devising and institutionalising a gender-aware settlement policy for Trinidad and Tobago from 1986.

The Sou Sou land approach

The Sou Sou land concept has not directly addressed the issue of gender-sensitive settlement planning, but the approach does acknowledge some of the key concerns raised by development planners and administrators about meeting the needs of particularly poor women when promoting a settlement.

For example, the core issues of resource limitation particularly with respect to finance, incremental development, organic growth, self-help and local solutions, appropriate standards and participatory democracy are counted among the attributes of the Sou Sou concept outlined above. These attributes are said to be antithetical to the highly centralised, state-funded and formal policies which usually characterise housing based on metropolitan standards, as opposed to an integrated notion of settlement, land use and housing construction.

To the extent that the action planning orientation of Sou Sou land allows for participatory management of the settlements in Trinidad and Tobago, one can expect that the assumptions, principles, criteria and actual policy decisions of the settlements may be examined publicly in order to bring to the forefront gender-aware concerns about human settlement. The follow-up to this would be a reinforcement of those elements of the policy which are already gender-aware. There can also be a modification of elements which are contrary to gender-aware principles.

Sou Sou land policy assumptions

Gender-aware development planners often think that the traditional policy makers and technocrats involved in land development and housing plan for people as opposed to plan with them. Thus the class, status and cultural orientations of these public officials often infiltrate and undergird the planning process so that the definitions of needs with respect to land use and types of shelter do not reflect the concerns of the vast majority of women in the society.

Responsiveness to the populace on the whole and women in particular is low considering the varying economic and social conditions of the households. Moser points to the following as critical indicators of the woman's status in the society, community and home environment:

1. the woman's marital status;
2. the social context of female leadership;
3. the particulars of the woman's reproductive activities;
4. access to productive resources and income; and
5. household composition (p. 5).

The failure to acknowledge in a systematic way the variability of the social, economic and cultural circumstances of the beneficiaries of land and shelter, generally leads to settlement planning based on policy assumptions that are both metropolitan in origin and class-bound in context. For example, eligibility criteria for becoming a beneficiary are usually based on the assumption that the family household is male-headed.

Alternatively, policy assumptions which are democratic and participatory in character could lead to the realisation that the male-headed, nuclear family structure constitutes one type in the variety of households which exist among the differing social strata of Caribbean society. Consequently, existing eligibility criteria for access to land and housing should reflect an understanding of the multiplicity of family and household structures that exist. For example, in Jamaica, 40 per cent of households are headed by women. Unemployment rates are twice as high for women and the earning position of women is far less than that of men. This reality suggests the need for special consideration in the transaction with such women concerning their need for shelter.

The Sou Sou land concept, as a departure from the highly centralised, state-funded and bureaucratised system of settlement planning, offers an opportunity to open up a dialogue on the variability of the social and economic situation of women who seek land and shelter as a fundamental human right. This optimism that the Sou Sou land approach can make dialogue possible on the lower socio-economic status of many female heads of households who are seeking shelter is nurtured by the views expressed in the 'Sou Sou Land Story':

> the method of mobilization being pursued by Sou Sou Land is one being undertaken by the people themselves. The people are becoming part of the development process from the very beginning. Regular meetings are held . . . as a forum for an exchange of views . . . there is the growth of a rapport between the people who are planning and implementing the projects and those who are eventually to inhabit them. (p. 15)

The point is that while the Sou Sou land concept has not made explicit policy statements on the status of women in their bid for land and shelter, the philosophy of Sou Sou Land provides the opportunity for dialogue on the issue. The sensibilities of these 'grassroots' planners, many of whom assumed public office in Trinidad and Tobago from 1986, can be more easily attuned to the gender-aware dimension of development planning for settlement. For example, the Minister of Settlements in the Cabinet in 1986 had been a Sou Sou Land administrator from the very beginning of the project. Her commitment to its institutionalisation as an integral part of multisectoral state planning was widely acknowledged.

The multiple roles of women

Moser refers to the triple roles of women, particularly those who work mainly in the informal sector of the economy where self-help and self-employment activities are the mainstay of survival. These roles are those related to production, reproduction and the managing of both the domestic household and community action groups (p. 3). In order to reconcile these inter-related roles, the need for spatial arrangements which will allow women to function adequately in these three areas of endeavour should be taken into account. For example, women in the informal sector who head households and are involved directly in child-bearing and child-rearing activities usually want facilities for income-generating activities within the settlement area and more specifically, in the home itself. It can be seen that housing provisions which are zoned by legislation so that, for instance, no business activity can be done in high-rise residential areas, create undue hardship for many women. In zoned areas, there are also the burdens of inadequate infrastructural services like transport and business services needed to help child-rearing women to earn a living.

The Sou Sou land concept steers away from the dichotomy between home and work. It emphasises village revitalisation both in the urban and rural environments. The conceptual features of the settlement policy deal with the suggestion that the dichotomy between urban and rural is not as distinct as in large continental territories. The policy therefore supports: 'the need for mixed-use allotments catering for residential accompanied with commercial or light industrial usages under the same roof. Small scale farming . . . an essential part of any land reform . . . provides . . . land use between residential and farm steading' (p. 2).

The non-zoning approach to land use and the organisation of shelter in respect of the provision and use of space are cognisant of the triple role of women, particularly those in the informal sector of the economy. Home, work and community can be brought together under one roof so to speak, thereby alleviating the hardship for those women who must, of necessity, reconcile these triple roles. The national settlements policy document states:

> "Zoning runs totally counter to our way of thinking. In the first instance, we feel that zoning must be fought by democratic pressure that demands the reconstruction of urban communities where certain job opportunities and commercial community facilities are allowed to locate legally within each community and that a city should be viewed as a series of self-contained communities or small cities within the larger city.
>
> The focal point for planning and development should be the human settlement since most of the basic needs of people are met and their quality of life determined, not only in the case of the urban but also the rural settlements. These communities potentially possessed a self-sustaining dynamic governed by size and the existence of a range of symbiotic activities which reinforced community spirit and identity and in so doing have encouraged further community participation, thereby perpetuating the self-sustaining qualities of settlement life. It is not unlike the dynamic of an ecosystem." (p. 5)

Gender awareness is intuitively contained in the policy document, which says that self-reliance and self-help in an organisational structure of decentralisation could foster the growth and development of community cooperatives to ensure that village government would be able to manage, among other things, the communal areas set apart for village commerce and industry as well as those for recreational, educational and civic purposes (p. 30).

Ownership rights and access to funding

A key aspect of the eligibility criteria relates to the assumptions about ownership rights and the financial viability of the intended beneficiary. The Sou Sou land approach does not presume that the household of the beneficiary is male-headed. Financial viability is definitely not tied to the usual demand that there must be a strong collateral base linked to criteria such as: set income levels; proof and stability of employment; and credit rating (Moser, p. 9).

These income level and credit rating criteria often rule out women who earn their living in tenuous employment in urban areas or the informal sector. Gender awareness requires a sensitivity to the earning capacity and repayment patterns that can be realistically expected of such women.

The Sou Sou land approach, while putting the burden of responsibility for financing settlement on the beneficiaries, sustains the idea of state supportiveness by categorising beneficiaries (for example squatters and non-squatters); initiating the collection of 'hands' or partial payments from would-be beneficiaries; and making provisions for a government-arranged savings plan to be used later for land purchase.

With respect to the last, the national settlements policy refers to the floating of home savings bonds. These are expected to be a non-cash redeemable instrument whereby potential land or home-owners can purchase bonds as a means of saving towards the final purchase price. These bonds can only be redeemed when the holder is about to purchase either a serviced lot or house. Interest may be paid on the bonds at 3 per cent per year, and the feasibility of these bonds being tax-deductible with the interest exempt from tax is being envisaged. It is also noteworthy that there will be no restrictions on the transferability of the bonds. Special terms and conditions are being considered for mortgaged-funded home construction (pp. 13-14).

The support to improve the financial viability of the would-be beneficiaries of the settlement plan is integral to the Sou Sou land concept. This provides the opportunity to open up dialogue on the need to spell out the special provisions for women as part of the move towards an explicit state policy on gender-aware settlements provisions.

Sou Sou lands promotional strategies

Some complaints about gender-aware land and housing provision are access to information, the actual processing of application forms, and the style of communication during the financial transactions. Caught up in their triple roles, many women often do not find the time to seek out the information or to study the documents. Also, the use of print and electronic media, as well as the formalised mailing system can be intimidating to these prospective land and householders.

A gender-aware settlements policy requires a sensitivity and responsiveness to the social and functional literacy levels of the large numbers of working women who need shelter. The communication network must be user-friendly. This requires, for example, an end to what Moser (p. 22) calls the discriminatory interactive style of predominantly male bureaucrats which often results in communication distortions of language, language filtering and status barriers.

In the *Sou Sou Land Story*, reference is made to the community meetings which are conducted to alert people about the need to participate in the determination and resolution of the problems of settlement (pp. 6-7). Such meetings, which are held regularly in community centres or other suitable areas in the town or village, allow for greater face-to-face contact between the settlements administrators and the people.

In the late 1980s, for example, the Minister of Settlements and Public Utilities herself moved into many already established housing areas to communicate directly with the householders on the plans for further community development. She continually encouraged the board and management team of the national housing authority to demonstrate the Sou Sou land spirit by keeping in constant touch with those receiving the services. The minister actively participated in radio call-in programmes to respond to people's concerns. Given her strategic position as part of the political directorate and head of the settlements ministry, it was a demonstration that the state was serious about a grassroots, bottom-up approach to settlements planning. The views of all constituencies of interest, in this instance, women, could be heard. In a cooperative network which included the women themselves, there was a real opportunity for explaining the dimensions of a gender-aware settlements policy.

Discussion: Beyond the Rhetoric of Integration

The three case studies reveal the possibilities and constraints in the development of a gender lens in the development planning process. Each case study highlights in a positive way the growing awareness in the Caribbean policy environment of the need to devise cognitive analytical tools and plans of action for treating the concerns of women in policy planning and implementation. Slowly but surely, there is increasing respect, if not acceptance, of the view expressed by Mary Anderson, an economist at the Harvard University Graduate School of Education, that "without the gender variable, the development equation is undermined" (p. 3).

In the World Bank case study, the constraints of a gender-aware policy planning were reflected in the way in which the emphasis on the technical control function of planning, professional hegemony and sheer time pressure for delivering on projects dominated the process. Even more fundamental was the narrow interpretation of WID as largely pertaining to population management. This resulted in an approach to development planning, in which the project method predominates, that is essentially devoid of any systematically incorporated social analysis along the lines of gender at the stage of project identification and formulation and social impact analysis at the stage of review and evaluation. As a result, there has been missed opportunity for developing and using the gender lens in the planning process.

The second case study caused much optimism because two regional workshops were mounted specifically to address the issue of the social relations of gender in the management of change in Caribbean public- and private-sector organisations. Much was achieved in the cognitive and analytical and affective realms of the training process. For example, the issues of institutional development and organisational change as well as personnel management and human relations training were thoroughly aired and assessed.

However, the deficiencies of a gender-based methodology in the training process became very evident during the workshop activities. The difficulty lay in the translation, application and actual use of perspectives and concepts gained from the discussion in developing, training, designing cases and other practical activities. The search for grounded approaches and methods remained evident during the workshop sessions.

The last case study inadvertently provided the best prospects for gender sensitivity in development planning. It is significant that ideologically the Sou Sou land approach is based on participation democracy and community action. The policy planning framework for human settlements provided by Caroline Moser is useful in policy environments that are responsible to the demands of community-based development planning and participatory democracy.

The policy presentation on human settlement as encapsulated in the Sou Sou land concept has created the opportunity for a gender focus in the planning process.

At the time of writing, 1989, two years had elapsed since the state's adoption of the Sou Sou land concept. The institutionalisation of the policy was still a long way from fruition. One of the reasons has been the cognitive gap that is evident among the professional planners and administrators, who either remain sceptical of the concept and its viability or are still locked into the bureaucratic mode of centralised policy planning.

To the extent that there has been the reaffirmation of the Sou Sou land approach through mission statements, there is hope for participatory democracy in settlements planning and therefore gender sensitivity in the process.

The way forward

Gender sensitivity in development planning, particularly in the public sector, continues to present a formidable challenge to planners, policy-makers and development administrators. The three case studies presented show in varying degrees the kinds of advances made and constraints faced in the devising and use of the gender lens.

Progress has been made in the cognitive and intellectual area in terms of a conceptual and analytical framework for determining and assessing the issues of gender in the policy planning process. This is ably demonstrated in the case study on the espoused settlements policy in Trinidad and Tobago. The gender-related variables are clearly identified by Caroline Moser in the context of the triple roles of women in the home, workplace and the wider community. These are tested for their viability in a policy environment which seeks to emphasise popular participation in the public decision- making process and policy outcomes which are responsible to the needs of the population along democratic lines.

It is important to note that there is only a nexus between the community-based Sou Sou land approach to settlements planning and the gender lens created by Moser. The task that lies ahead requires that the nexus which is largely cognitive or analytical be translated and converted into viable policy instruments on settlements and housing provisions for the population. For example, community participation in public decision-making, financial viability criteria, promotional strategies and use of space in settlements programmes must become an empirical reality in order to facilitate the use of the gender lens.

In order for gender-aware management training to be effective, progress must be made beyond the cognitive and analytical dimensions. This is critical, so that the discussions on the impact of organisational hierarchy and the resultant top-down management styles could be quickly followed by practical strategies for social and political support. Additionally, organisational development strategies at individual, group and corporate levels must be devised in order to produce the behavioural changes that would reflect a human resource management philosophy and programmes that are gender-sensitive. This requires, for example, suitable types of affirmative action programmes that would bring gender equity to recruitment, selection, placement and career development paths.

The project method that constitutes the dominant mode of development planning in international and regional aid agencies must, as Cernea has said, put people first. To do this requires the timely injection of social analysis and social impact analysis data into the process of project management. The various stages of the project cycle—identification, preparation, appraisal, implementation, service delivery and evaluation—must be infused with the concerns of the project developers, client groups and the community at large. The efficiency of the technicians must be complemented by deliberations about the extent to which the project plans are culturally relevant and politically responsive to the various constituencies of interest, such as women.

Such an approach requires that social surveys be undertaken so that social data may be integrated into the technical database and used appropriately at the various stages of the project cycle. The clear call is for a multi- and inter-disciplinary approach to project development. The professional hegemony and technical control of the male-dominated organisational hierarchy at executive and managerial levels can be reduced if research on participation and action is undertaken and the outcome of this process results in a higher visibility for both social analysis issues. These include issues of gender both in the planning and in the social relations of organisational life in the policy environment.

References

Cernia, Michael M. (ed). *Putting People First: Sociological Variable in Rural Development*. World Bank. Washington, DC 1985.

Hewitt, Linda. "Some Dimensions of the Housing Problems in Trinidad and Tobago", Central Statistical Office. Government of Trinidad and Tobago.

Hogwood, Brian and Gunn, Lewis. *A Policy Analysis for the Real World.* : Oxford University Press, Oxford 1984.

Kardam, Nuket. "The World Bank and Development Policy", World Bank, Washington, DC 1986 (mimeo).

Ministry of Planning and Mobilization: Republic of Trinidad and Tobago. *A Macro Planning Framework: Outline of a Medium-Term Seven-Year Plan for Trinidad & Tobago, 1988-1994*. February 1988.

Moser, Caroline O.N. "Housing Policy and Women: Towards a Gender Aware Approach". Development Planning Unit, University College of London, 1985 (mimeo).

National Housing Authority. *Towards a National Settlements Policy*. Government of Trinidad and Tobago, 1987.

National Housing Authority. *Settlements - Perspectives, Achievements, Projections.* Summary Statement Prepared for the Minister of Settlements, re Budget Debate. Republic of Trinidad and Tobago, January 1988.

Staudt, Kathleen. "Gender Redistributive Policy and Practice: Theoretical Issues in Comparative Perspective". Association for Women in Development, Washington, DC, April 1987 (mimeo).

UNTIES, HABITAT. *Women and Human Settlements*. 1985.

Women in Development. "Gender Issues and Regional Policies—CARICOM Seminar for Senior Women Administrators". Report prepared by Administrative Staff College, Kingston, Jamaica, 1988.

Part TWO

Engendering Justice

The Challenge and Achievement of Feminist Law Reform

Engendering Justice

The Challenge and Achievement of Feminist Law Reform

Introduction

Defining "woman" in the Law

Christine Barrow

In most countries the law is very powerful. In contrast to other disciplines, such as the social sciences, which struggle for recognition and internal consistency, the law is viewed as unified, as an almost superhuman repository of the Truth. From a practical perspective also, the law is perceived as a force to be relied upon for the maintenance and restoration of the proper order in the face of social and political uncertainty and unrest. The law also asserts its authority to define people, men and women, and their rights and wrongs. In the process, however, while claiming neutrality, the legal definition of 'woman' continues to be plagued by ideological assumptions variously described as 'patriarchal', 'androcentric', even 'quasi-ecclesiastical', and the wrongs against women are disqualified or reduced to insignificance. Thus sexual harassment is labelled 'harmless teasing or flirtation' and domestic violence becomes a 'private matter'. A challenge to the authority of the law, whether from a feminist or other source, constitutes nothing less than subversion. The definition of 'woman' in the law and the feminist challenge to this definition constitutes a central theme addressed by the four papers in this section of the volume.

As the focus of these papers implies, the problem of defining 'woman' in the law centres primarily on the family and her roles as wife and mother. This is hardly surprising since the domains of kinship and domesticity are perceived as the woman's, although for many feminists they constitute a major source of her oppression. English common law, the foundation for Caribbean law, claimed that after marriage a woman lost her identity. As a 'wife', she became submerged into the person of her husband. The two became 'one flesh'; his flesh. Within the marital relationship, they were defined as different and unequal. As the superior partner, the male owned his wife—her property, her children and her person—and was responsible for providing economic support, security and protection. Conversely, as the subordinate, dependent partner, the wife was expected to freely provide domestic and sexual services. This structure of gender roles and relationships was justified by biology as 'natural' and by the law and the church as morally right and proper. As recently as 1980 the argument was still being used to justify legal interpretations of femininity by none other than the eminent Lord Denning:

> No matter how you may dispute and argue, you cannot alter the fact that women are quite different from men. The principal task in the life of women is to bear and rear children: ... He is physically the stronger and she the weaker. He is temperamentally the more aggressive and she the more submissive. It is he who takes the initiative and she who responds. These diversities of function and temperament lead to differences of outlook which cannot be ignored. But they are, none of them, any reason for putting women under the subjection of men. (Denning 1980:194, Quoted in Smart 1989:13)

While this last sentence may suggest cause for hope, it is difficult to see how it follows from the rest of the quote.

Furthermore, the family as a co-residential nuclear unit based on marriage was perceived as the norm and the ideal. If something went wrong with the structure of this family cornerstone, in particular if women objected to their status, they would be going against nature and the whole social and moral fabric of society would come under threat.

The feminist theoretical rejection of biological determinism and the notion of woman constructed as an organically fixed entity, opened the way for the reconstruction of 'woman' as a socio-cultural being, and specifically for a change in the legal definition. It is this issue that Carol Smart highlights in her paper. The grand debate on the redefinition of woman in the law has revolved around the issues of difference and equality, that is whether and in what respect women are different from men or whether and in what respect they are the same and therefore entitled to equal treatment under the law. Providing fuel for both sides of the argument is a mass of empirical information on women in various societies, the idea being that the law should acknowledge another Truth, that of women's reality. It was this debate also which prompted the recent surge of legal reform in the Caribbean, much of it from feminist perspectives. The papers which follow refer to reforms which extend the law to include women and others previously left out and those reforms which proclaim the equal rights of women.

Given that Caribbean law was inherited from England, not generated in response to local social and cultural circumstances, it is hardly surprising that many persons fell beyond its reach. They included common law "wives" and their illegitimate children. Recently, however, the laws of a few Caribbean countries have accorded recognition to the common law relationship as co-residential and stable, in other words as a sort of marriage. As Eileen Boxill points out, Succession Acts have given women in common law unions rights as beneficiaries to the estates of their deceased partners. But the equality between the two categories of "wife" remains incomplete. To qualify for legal recognition, common law women still have to satisfy a five-year co-residential requirement; not so their married sisters. Boxill notes, however, that full equality has been extended to children born out of wedlock by the abolition of the legal concept of 'illegitimacy' by Status of the Children Acts. In general though, legislation of this type merely brings into the scope and protection of the law those previously excluded. Gender definitions remain essentially unchanged.

On this note, however, the papers mention several legal reforms, for example, in the areas of guardianship, property, domicile and divorce, which have challenged the subordinate status of women, wives in particular, by promoting the principle of gender equality. Even so, it is important to acknowledge fully the tenacity of English common law interpretations of woman in Caribbean legislation. Although, for example, we may concede that through Married Women's Property Acts wives have acquired a *persona* and legal rights, persistent stereotypes present a barrier to complete gender equality in the law. Boxill acknowledges that a husband and wife may now have equal rights to acquire, control and dispose of property, but claims that women are disadvantaged in the distribution of property during divorce proceedings. She also refers to the continued assumption that a woman is her husband's dependent, which explains why he cannot claim citizenship in her country, although her brother's wife can. Additionally, as Ffolkes points out, her wifely obligation to give sexual services freely to her husband and his right to take, is interpreted to mean that she cannot be raped by him.

On this point also, Cherry Brady Clarke deals with persistent gender discrimination as regards the right of action against a third party for damages for loss of consortium, a right confined to the husband. Her paper examines the arguments presented to resist the extension of this right to wives. One of these, curiously, reconceptualises the law as a 'historical development', rather than a "logical whole" and on this basis justifies legal inconsistencies in terms of gender equality. Another sacrifices the principle of gender equality for expedient policy by referring to the unmanageable proliferation of lawsuits which would follow legal reform which enabled wives to bring cases for loss of consortium. Yet another argument, and perhaps the most significant for the theme of gender definition, reiterates the legal status of 'wife' as her husband's property and as the provider of services to him, while he owes no reciprocal services.

By narrowing the essence of a marital relationship and the grounds for legal action to the loss of 'services', the rights of a wife are denied in law. After all, isn't it the husband who loses the services and has to pay for a replacement to keep his household functioning? Paradoxically, in the process, domestic and child care services, unpaid and consistently undervalued, suddenly acquire an economic cost and legal significance. Amazing also is the case, identified by Brady Clarke, during which changes towards gender equality in the wider society were admitted, but, rather than extend the right to action for loss of consortium to the wife, the judge perceived the right of the husband as an anachronism and argued for its removal.

Clearly, the law must redraft the link between 'consortium' and a wife's 'services' to a more holistic perspective, taking into consideration the wide range of mutual exchanges which make up 'conjugal society' including assistance, companionship, affection and sex. It is only then that the law might be persuaded to adopt Brady Clarke's strong recommendation for the extension of consortium action to a wife and, within the cultural context of family in the Caribbean, one might add, to a common law 'wife'.

Although the emphasis of the papers is on the legal disabilities of women, the authors also recognise that men may be disadvantaged by the male stereotypes built into the law. As Boxill states, husbands carry the economic burden of support, even if their wives are financially able to support themselves, though she also notes a move towards recognising the mutual needs and responsibilities of both spouses. In addition, the process of registering paternity for an illegitimate child continues to be problematic.

Law reformers in those Caribbean territories that have begun the process of updating and restructuring their laws have much to celebrate. But even as their achievements are applauded, it is important to recognise limitations. For one thing, the assertion of equal rights for women has created additional conceptual problems. As Smart points out, one problem concerns just how women should be redefined in the law. One can well imagine members of the legal profession, accustomed to the tidy legal precision and moral certainty of 'natural woman', embarrassing feminist legal reformers for any ambiguity over what woman and her experience is. The response, more often than not, has been to adopt the simplistic and misconceived notion that all women are alike, and that this sameness is constituted in terms of a white skin, middle-class status and heterosexuality. Paradoxically, therefore, the assertion of equal rights with men ignores existing inequalities of race, class, age, nationality, and so on, and, while improving the position of those women defined according to this norm, in all probability has been detrimental to others. The other and perhaps more significant conceptual problem is that, whether women are perceived as being like or unlike men, it is the men that continue to be the central point of reference. As Smart puts it, women continue to be caught within the 'masculine signifying economy'. The dilemma is that, by defining women as other than men, thereby engaging in a discourse of hierarchical dualism, the legal language of gender, women affirm the definition of reality as determined by the law.

The law is an integral part of patriarchal society. Indeed, in claiming to represent the Truth, the law constitutes a central pillar in support of patriarchy. What this means is that in resorting to the law to solve their problems, women are simultaneously empowering the law and reinforcing patriarchy. As Smart explains elsewhere:

> In resorting to law, especially law structured on patriarchal precedents, women risk invoking a power that will work against them rather than for them. (Smart 1989:138)

> We need to consider that in exercising law we may produce effects that make conditions worse, and that in worsening conditions we make the mistake of assuming that we need to apply more doses of legislation. (Smart 1989:161)

Women therefore become entangled in a circular trap. By their misplaced faith in the law, they facilitate the further intrusion of patriarchy into their lives, especially into what was once perceived as the private domain of sex and family life. As Ffolkes explains, the legal solution to domestic violence by incarcerating the abuser may do more harm than good in circumstances of economic dependence.

The enormity of the task of feminist legal reform in the context of patriarchy is well illustrated by the backlash against women's rights achieved in Caribbean societies, loaded as they are with essentialist preconceptions of women's rightful place and roles in the family. Female as well as male voices have been heard to condemn as individualistic and selfish those women pressing for change. Their demands, it is claimed, work to the detriment of wholesome and stable family life, especially the welfare of the children they are supposed to nurture and socialise. By shirking their 'real' responsibilities they singlehandedly jeopardise the family unit and, as Ffolkes points out, the preservation of the family unit, that is the 'properly constructed' family unit, is another sacred principle enshrined in the law.

An important lesson to be learnt from the experience of feminist law reform is that the law cannot proceed alone, but must advance hand in hand with social change, especially as regards family values and gender ideology. As Ffolkes explains, if the social context of violence against women is not taken into account, legal changes will remain impotent. If the society continues to view women as 'wives' and 'mothers', biologically programmed to be emotional, submissive and at home, and men as leaders, strong, aggressive and dominant, and if society and the church continue to view common law women as immoral and illegitimate offspring as 'bastards' or 'outside children', then no matter how many laws are rewritten to remove discrimination and ensure gender equality, these will remain in the statute books, only occasionally seeing the light of day in court. Finally, another important message for the future is contained in Smart's insistence that we redesign the feminist challenge to the law. She notes both the advance of patriarchal law into women's existence and the near exhaustion of claims for equality before the law, but argues that this should not cause women to back off in frustration and preserve what they can of their lives from interference, on the one hand, or to sit back in complacency, on the other. The way forward must proceed by questioning the philosophical and procedural foundations of the law, by understanding and challenging the masculinity still embodied in legal logic and values, in the language and knowledge of the law.

Reference

Smart, C. *Feminism and the Power of Law*. London: Routledge, 1989.

Gender Issues in Law

A Feminist Perspective

Carol Smart

The main purpose of this paper is firstly to celebrate the achievement of feminist legal scholarship, and secondly to outline why feminist research in this field needs to be considering a range of new questions and problems which might well entail the conceptualisation of law, feminism and even the category of 'woman' differently. The argument is that, although feminist theories of law have produced of a great deal of critical knowledge in law and have been linked with important political and legal strategies, we may have reached a moment when we need to begin to reconceptualise some of the issues and reformulate some basic concepts. Concepts of equality and rights may well now be exhausted, at least in certain fields, quite simply because of the extension of formal equality or the power of countervailing rights claims. Moreover, it is necessary to take practical cognizance of the fact that to continue to demand special rights, in a context where it is held that women already have equal rights, may be counterproductive. This is especially important if we are already skeptical about rights claims.

There are two strands to feminism's achievements which go hand in hand. One is the practical achievement of changes in law, the other is the challenge to legal thought and knowledge. In terms of the former, we can look at what are often regarded as milestones of achievement. This would include married women's property acts, divorce legislation, guardianship rights, legal rights to abortion and contraception, equal pay and sex discrimination legislation and so on. The latter, which is the focus here, concerns the way in which law has been challenged to take women into account. Either relying on a form of feminist empiricism or on standpoint feminism, inroads have been made into legal research and teaching to challenge the masculine parameters of law as a system of knowledge. It is, therefore, worthwhile to consider the contribution of these approaches.

Feminist Empiricism

Feminist empiricism basically takes the approach of being a corrective to existing limited understandings of the social world, showing that most research has ignored the world of women and that the tools of research have been fitted to research men's lives rather than women's. Its aim is, therefore, to make the world of women visible and knowable. The best example in sociology is Anne Oakley's work on housework (1974). In law, this approach has operated to reveal the specific and special ways in which law affects the lives of women, or fails to protect or provide for women.

The best example of this work comes from Tove Stang Dahl (1987), who sets out a programme for the development of what she calls women's law. Her aim is to apply social scientific methods of enquiry to discover the reality of women's lives. This alternative reality can then be presented to challenge the structures and focus of law and to build a law geared to the relevances of women's lives rather than men's. Dahl's critique does not include social scientific or legal methods. These she perceives as a form of craft, neutral tools which can be applied objectively.

On the basis of this sort of work, Dahl has proposed radical changes to law in Norway, for example the reconfiguration of law into categories such as money law, housewives' law, birth law, equality law and so on. Her argument is that this organisation of law, in combination with a different order of values and principles, which are established from the ground up rather than imposed from above, will produce a more equitable social and legal system for women.

Standpoint Feminism

Standpoint feminism is most clearly articulated in the work of Dorothy Smith (1988) but in the field of law is perhaps most associated with Catharine Mackinnon (1987). Standpoint feminism, like feminist empiricism, asserts the central importance of experience. However, rather than being an assertion of women's experience as one that should be added to a partial picture to make it whole, standpoint feminism argues that a feminist perspective which is derived through consciousness-raising is a more correct truth, not half a truth which has to be added to the male half to get a whole. Derived from the work of Marx, standpoint feminists argue that only the most oppressed in a given society can see the workings of that society because they are the ones who make the system operate. However, the argument is not that all women have this vision, but only those who have collectivised their experiences through consciousness-raising. Consciousness raising therefore becomes the equivalent of a method for arriving at a true analysis. On the basis of knowledge thus formulated, it is argued that a more fitting policy can be developed, one which not only meets the real needs of women but is feminist in orientation.

It is not so much the intention here to criticise these approaches to law as to point out how they are constituted by a specific epistemological (and ontological) stance which is rarely expressly acknowledged in feminist legal scholarship. This stance is a form of realism in which it is taken for granted that we 'know' what law is, we know who or what 'women' are, and we only have to work on the relationship between these two givens.

Both feminist empiricism and standpoint feminism assume the possibility of a reality 'out there' which is discoverable;they may also assume the existence of a pre-social or supra-cultural infallible 'knower' (Hawkesworth, 1989). Both of these epistemological stances fit comfortably with the politics of the second-wave women's movement in Britain and North America although standpoint feminism more faithfully reproduces the political convictions of the Women's Movement at the epistemological level. It is, therefore, quite hard to abandon standpoint feminism because it feels like abandoning long-held assumptions, aspirations, truths and loyalties.

Moreover, the attraction of realist feminist scholarship in law is that it has had a purchase. Feminists have been able to engage in policy debates and have brought forward vital research findings to challenge developments which are harmful to some women. Empiricism research is being taken more and more seriously in law schools. Lawyers are becoming more interested in the social consequences of legal measures, sociologists are becoming respectable and, with this tide, empirical work on women has also found an entry. Even self-proclaimed feminist work like that of Mackinnon (1987) is finding a place. Work which questions the neutrality not just of legal practice but of legal principles, method and values is being taught. And the strength of these criticisms is that they are based on an alternative assertion of truth.

So why the skepticism concerning this sort of feminist approach to interrogating law? And should one begin to rock a boat which is at least recognised as epistemologically legitimate, even if it has far to go to achieve substantial changes? Why should we entertain theoretical work which challenges the epistemological basis of our fragile successes? Should we really flirt with anti-epistemology when it seems that: 'Should postmodernism's seductive text gain ascendancy, it will not be an accident that power remains in the hands of the white males who currently possess it.' (Hawkesworth, 1989: 557)

There are two elements to this cautionary tale. The first is that to think otherwise is to abandon the feminist project. The second is that if we continue as we are there is a guarantee of divesting these white males of their power. Neither of these reasons is compelling, as I shall try to show.

There are two main reasons why I think we should indeed begin to challenge realist thinking in feminist scholarship. One is the growing doubt that science (in the sense of modern, post-Enlightenment science, including the social sciences) can provide answers and solutions which, in turn, put us on the path to progress. In British social science there has been a strong commitment to the idea that further research (if only the sample size is large enough or as long as sufficient variables can be held constant) will lead to the solutions to social problems. In other words, it was assumed that studies were not merely descriptive, but that they held prescriptions for what was to be done to alter the situation for the better. Feminism, or at least some feminism, has almost started to share a kind of Fabian vision. The idea is that the research will tell us what to do and that this will lead to real improvements.

This link between research and policy, or sometimes between theory and strategy, has been challenged by writers often parcelled together and labelled post-modern. The point that can be taken from their writing is simply that we must question this link and the comfortable assumption that our research or our theorising tells us what should be done and that doing it will enhance progress. This does not mean that we give up doing research, nor that we cease to engage in policy debates. It does mean that when we make claims that research has shown this and therefore we need to do the following, we should recognise that we are deploying power and that we really do not know what the consequences of our proposals might be.

The second reason for skepticism about the realist approach is uncertainty over what women's experience is. Here this concept is deliberately framed in the singular because we can see immediately that, if we talk about women's experiences, we may have to acknowledge that they are different and that they do not point in one direction at all. Many feminists know this, not least because of the criticisms of black feminists about the orientations and concerns of the white women's movement. But it has taken a long time to take these criticisms seriously. An example from another sphere is the different conceptualisation of women in the sex industry and those campaigning against pornography or prostitution.

One solution to this problem has been seen as the standpoint approach, which basically gives priority to a feminist perspective over a woman's perspective. Hence, we can dismiss the women in the sex industry because they are falsely conscious and not feminists. The problem is, however, that not all feminists see the world in the same way either, so this just shifts the debate onto the dubious terrain of discussing who is a real feminist. It also operates a politics of exclusion in which some women must necessarily be silenced. Moreover, standpoint feminism operates under the assumption that there will ultimately be a discovered community of interests between all women, that difference will be eradicated at some level. This is a faith which can only be sustained if there is some adherence to an essentialism which remains unspoken.

This brings us to the fundamental point, which is the move to reject essentialism, which has been so central to much feminist work. In rejecting essentialism we become uncertain about what woman is. The pressure to reject essentialism has come from women who have been uncomfortable with a feminism which proclaimed it was talking about women in general when it was actually talking about white, middle-class, heterosexual women. So we are now faced with some very difficult questions about what makes a woman. To put this simply, feminists have always tended to argue that there are two sexes, but that the characteristics attributed to each are entirely cultural and could be swopped around if we tried hard enough.

But now the question has become why should we accept this binary division into two sexes. This division only reinforces the primacy of heterosexuality and we know that there are many women who never have sex with men, who never reproduce. Moreover, why should I, a white woman, assume that I am fundamentally the same as an Asian woman or a black woman, most particularly when in doing so I obscure the power inherent in the whiteness?

Once we recognise that the category of woman is constructed, that this category is not transhistorical, nor transcultural, we begin to realise that we can construct the category differently. This is what feminism has been doing for some time, but it has tended to see it in terms of revealing the real woman rather than constructing a different one. But we can go beyond this to ask why we should construct womanness at all when, in so doing, we make her in our own singular image, to the exclusion of others.

So what I am saying is that feminist discourse has brought a particular woman into being, but we should not presume that this category corresponds to all women. We can only force it into a correspondence by relying on a biological signifier and thereby becoming eternally wedded to a binary (and hierarchical) division between women and men which is, in turn, the very thing feminism wishes to overcome.

But what does all this mean for how we analyse law? Indeed, is not this all rather dangerous talk? Law, even less than sociology, wants to take feminism seriously. Having just started to be accepted as serious scholarship, will we now be easily dismissed if we say we can no longer speak for women and know what women want? The point is that law hears what we have to say about women as long as we are prepared to occupy the same epistemological and ontological space as law. In other words, as long as we collude with the woman that legal discourse has constituted, we can have some purchase, but we do this at the expense of silencing and alienating many actual women for whom we do not speak. We also do it at the expense of colluding in what has been called the masculine signifying economy.

This point needs some explanation. Feminist approaches to law have, by and large, been concerned with what law does to or for women. So the engagement has been very practical. Indeed, one of the main attractions of law is the appearance it gives that something is being done. But years of doing this have led feminists to start to ask different questions and, once we see law as discourse which constitutes a subject and deploys power, and not primarily an institution or practice, we begin to challenge the subject 'woman' that law has brought into being. At risk of repetition, we did this by saying: 'But real women are different to the mythical woman of law.'

In doing this we did not realise how much ground we were conceding. We entered into a debate which is interminable, namely the debate about whether women were more or less like men (otherwise known as the equality and difference debate). What an exquisite trap we are in. It does not matter if we are more or less like men, the point is that men remain the transcendental signifier. This is what is meant by the masculine signifying economy. As long as we remain inside this, all our struggles ironically confirm men as central. Law is one of the main vehicles in this economy.

To backtrack slightly, the argument is that in law, but also in other discourses, woman equals what man is not. Woman only exists in reference to man: we only understand what a woman is by reference to a man. To grasp this, we have to abandon the traditional idea that the sex difference exists in the real (that is unmediated, pre-cultural) world and also to reject the idea that language simply labels pre-existing differences. In other words, the suggestion is that we have to reject the idea that the signified precedes the signifier.

Language brings these differences into being and into significance and it does this partly through the construction of dualisms through which we construct meaning. Hence terms like rationality, objectivity, logic, active and culture gain their meaning by reference to terms like irrationality, subjectivity, emotion, passive, nature. But as many feminists have pointed out, these dualisms within language and meaning construction also constitute a hierarchy. So in learning the terms rationality, objectivity and logic we always already knew that they are superior to their counterparts. With the terms man and woman we always already knew that man is superior in symbolic terms. Some feminists have tried to re-evaluate the feminine, but that merely takes us straight into the heart of the never ending equality and difference dance.

Now law upholds this problematic dualism, a dualism which is, of course, our lived experience. The irony is, the more we assert our lived experience against law, the more we become entangled in the hierarchical dualism. Let me provide an example. Law has constructed the sexuated feminine subject, for example, everything that has ever been said about women who are raped. Feminism has countered this by saying that this is not the truth of women's sexuality. To put it in the words of Mackinnon (1983): 'Sexuality is to feminism what work is to Marxism; that which is most one's own yet most taken away.'

Thus, this form of feminism has constructed the feminine subjects as equally sexuated. That sexuality defines our beingness as woman is an ontological statement: we are our sex because it is only this that resides in nature (outside culture). This is how law and some feminisms construct us. We are our sex.

The problem is that neither discourse empowers; both retain man in the realm of culture, as disembodied mind, as the organising principle of culture. Women are constructed as corporeality and this corporeality is usually disavowed. We are back where we started.

There are no easy ways out of this dilemma. But at the moment we can argue that the struggle over meaning is one of the most vital that feminists in all fields are engaged in. This does not preclude engaging with law in various ways, but it does mean that we should be constantly aware of how we may be empowering the law's version of reality if we occupy the same epistemological and ontological space as law. In trying to overcome the hierarchy which is so central to law, we merely reaffirm it. This is, of course, not a dilemma which is peculiar to feminist work on law, it is reflected in a huge area of scholarship. But feminist work in this field should not become isolated from these developments. The challenge is, therefore, not only to law, but also to feminine legal scholarship.

References

Hawkesworth, (1989)
Mackinnon, C. *Feminism Unmodified: Discourses on Life and Law*. London: Harvard University Press.1987.
Oakley, A. *Housewife*. London: Allen Lane 1974.
Oakley, A. *The Captured Womb*. Oxford: Blackwell 1986.
Smith, D. 1988.
Stang Dahl, T. *Women's Law: An Introduction to Feminist Jurisprudence*. Oxford: Oxford University Press 1987.

The Reform of Family Law as it affects Women

Eileen Boxill

Introduction and Historical background

Family law in the Commonwealth Caribbean is founded on English law, which until the nineteenth century, was almost entirely common law. The common law rules relating to the family contained some of the most glaring examples of discrimination against women. These rules were strongly influenced by the doctrine of the unity of spouses and the concept of a wife as the property of her husband.

The doctrine of the unity of spouses was based on the scriptural injunction that upon marriage, the two shall become one flesh. The legal translation of the 'one flesh' was the husband. Upon marriage the legal being of a wife merged with and was incorporated into that of her husband. She assumed his nationality, his domicile and his name. Although the assumption of the name was dictated by custom it was also sanctioned by law. She lost the ability to own and control property, and also lacked capacity to enter into contract, or to sue or be sued in her own right.

The husband, on the other hand, acquired certain rights with respect to both the property and person of his wife. He became entitled to virtually all her property. He had a legal right to her services and companionship and was entitled to compensation for interference with or deprivation of this right. One of the actions for claiming compensation was 'criminal conversation' which was founded on trespass, a fact which illustrates the proprietary nature of the husband's rights. The superiority of the husband was visible also in the area of parental rights. As head of the household, the father had exclusive rights as regards the guardianship and custody of his legitimate children.

Over the years statutory reforms introduced in England and copied in the Caribbean, have removed some of the legal disabilities of married women. The most significant of the early reforms was the abolition of a wife's proprietary and civil disabilities in married women's legislation.[1] Also noteworthy was the recognition of a mother as having certain rights with respect to the guardianship and custody of her children.[2] Despite the improvement in the position of married women as a result of these statutory reforms, the male bias of the common law continues to overshadow family law.

Apart from the inferior status accorded to a wife, there is another sense in which family law has always been discriminatory against women in the context of Caribbean societies. The traditional focus of the law was the marriage-based family, that is, a husband, a wife and the children of the marriage. However, consensual unions and a high incidence of births occurring out of wedlock have remained characteristic features of Caribbean societies, despite the efforts of religious groups and other social reformers to induce conformity to a family lifestyle based on marriage.

Consensual unions had no legal status in common law. The child born out of wedlock or the illegitimate child, to use the nomenclature assigned to him, was *filius nullius*, meaning child of no one. The recognition of the mother for certain purposes, mainly custody, maintenance and succession, marked a retreat from this rigid stance. In this vein also were the statutory provisions for the legitimation of an illegitimate child where his parents marry after his birth, the registration of putative fathers and the maintenance of an illegitimate child by the putative father.[3]

Apart from these concessions made in respect of the illegitimate child, the non-marital family fell outside the ambit and protection of family law. In a situation where consensual unions, particularly those of the "common law" type, are prevalent, and roughly 70 per cent of all births in the Caribbean are illegitimate, this state of law in effect discriminates against a large proportion of women, as the mothers of illegitimate children and as common law wives.

The period from the late 1970s to the present has seen an unprecedented spate of new family legislation in some countries in the region, notably Barbados, Jamaica, and Trinidad and Tobago. The surge in legislative activity in this area of law is largely attributable to the concentration of attention on the status and affairs of women during International Women's Year 1975 and the ensuing Decade for Women. A number of countries in the region[4] have either signed, ratified or acceded to the UN Convention on the Elimination of all Forms of Discrimination Against Women. This convention imposes a general obligation on States Parties to accord to women equality with men before the Law.[5] Specifically, States Parties are required to take all appropriate measures to eliminate discrimination against women in all matters relating to marriage and family relations. This includes granting women and men the same rights to enter into marriage, the same rights and responsibilities during marriage and its dissolution, the same personal rights as husband and wife and the same parental rights and responsibilities irrespective of marital status.[6] States Parties are also required to grant to both sexes equal rights with respect to their own nationality and that of their children and the same freedom of choice in respect to residence and domicile.[7]

This paper reviews some of the more important family law reforms which have been introduced. It is based primarily on the Jamaican experience, but reference will be made to parallel developments elsewhere in the region for the purpose of illustrating differences and similarities in approach. It is not proposed to analyse the details of the various enactments, and indeed time would not permit such an analysis. The intention is to highlight those aspects which are of relevance to the status of rights of women.

The family law reform initiatives taken in Jamaica may be grouped conveniently under three heads:

1. Those relating to a child born out of wedlock;
2. Those relating to the property rights of spouses;
3. Those relating to divorce and other matrimonial causes.

1. Reforms relating to the child born out of wedlock

a. *The Status of Children Act 1976*

The most important legislation in this category is the Status of Children Act, 1976, of Jamaica. By 1976 some countries had in fact already enacted legislation which reflected a more liberal attitude towards the illegitimate child. There were two legislative models. One was the removal of the more serious consequences of illegitimacy which was the approach taken by the English Family Law Reform Act, 1969. The other was the abolition of the status of illegitimacy, as for example the New Zealand Status of Children Act, 1969. Legislators in the region favoured the more radical approach of the latter. The Jamaica Status of Children Act was the first of its kind to be enacted. Similar Acts have since been enacted in other parts of the region.[8] The provisions of these Acts vary in detail, but the overall effect is essentially the same.

The main changes which were effected by the Status of Children Act flow from the recognition of the relationship between a child born out of wedlock and his father. The most important consequence of this recognition is the reciprocal rights which the child and his father now enjoy with respect to succession. Succession rights are dependent on the admission or establishment of paternity, during the lifetime of the father if the child is to benefit or during the lifetime of the child if the father is to benefit.[9] This condition is a common feature of Status of Children legislation.[10]

Another common feature is the provision of evidential aids to the determination of paternity. The Jamaica Act lists certain matters as providing *prima facie* evidence of paternity; it introduces a new procedure for the declaration of paternity which constitutes conclusive proof of paternity and it provides for the use of blood tests in paternity suits.[11] A further evidential aid provided is a presumption of paternity which, like the common law presumption of legitimacy, applies where the mother was married to the father at the time of the birth or conception of the child.[12] The corresponding provisions in the Barbados Status of Children Reform Act, 1979, provide an interesting contrast.[13] Under that Act, the presumption of paternity is based on a number of factors. Some of these constitute *prima facie* evidence under the Jamaica Act. The significant point of difference is the treatment of the fact that the mother was cohabiting with a man at the time of the birth or conception of the child as giving rise to a presumption that the man with whom she was cohabiting is the father of the child. The Barbados Act is the only regional statute which includes this innovative provision. It is a practical approach to the determination of the paternity of a child born out of wedlock, which might usefully be adopted in other countries in the region.

b. The Registration (Births and Deaths Act) 1980

It has already been noted that the establishment of the paternity of a child born out of wedlock has assumed more importance as a result of the Status of Children Act. Registration of the father is one of the means by which paternity can be established. The Registration (Births and Deaths) Act of Jamaica was amended in 1976 and 1980 to extend the facilities for the registration of fathers.[14] The changes introduced by the 1976 amendments were relatively minor. The 1980 amendment deserves special treatment here because the provisions it introduced depart from the usual provisions which apply in the region.

Up until the 1980 amendment, the registration of the father of a child born out of wedlock could not be effected without his concurrence, except where a Declaration of Paternity had been obtained. The new provisions permit the registration of the father on the sole application of the mother. The procedure involves the filing of an allegation of paternity by the mother and the service of notice of the allegation on the person named. The Registrar is authorised to effect registration if satisfied that the prescribed notice has been served on the person named and that the person within the prescribed period has either admitted or has not denied paternity. Provisions are made for the cancellation of registration in certain circumstances and sanctions are imposed for securing false registration and the unreasonable refusal to surrender a certificate of registration for cancellation.[15]

The passage of the 1980 amendment marks the end of a long campaign for the enactment of provisions of this nature. There were two earlier abortive attempts, one in 1900 and another in 1904. It would seem that the battle is not yet won, since the provisions, although enacted, have not been implemented. It is not possible, therefore, to assess their usefulness in securing the registration of fathers.

The intention of the new procedure is to facilitate the registration of all fathers. In fact, the 1980 amendment and also the abortive previous attempts, are commonly referred to as providing for the compulsory registration of fathers, a description which is inaccurate as the initiation of the procedure depends on the voluntary action of the mother of the child. There is no sanction against the mother for refusal to disclose the identity of the father and it might well be argued that the imposition of such a sanction would be an undue restriction on her right to privacy. At best, the new provisions will assist where the father's attitude to registration is one of reluctance or indifference, but it will not assist the registration of the father where it is the mother who is indifferent or reluctant. To meet this case the father should be given a corresponding right to effect registration without the concurrence of the mother.

c. The Maintenance Orders (Facilities for Enforcement) Act 1987

The Maintenance Orders (Facilities for Enforcement) Act 1987 of Jamaica is included in this section because the provisions it makes are of particular benefit to children born out of wedlock. This Act repealed and replaced an earlier Act, similarly titled, which was modelled on an English Act which bore the same title. The provisions of the former Act had become outdated and inadequate. The main areas of inadequacy related to the limited geographical scope and the types of orders envisaged. They permitted reciprocal arrangements to be made with England, Northern Ireland and certain other designated Commonwealth countries. Affiliation orders were expressly excluded. The old Act, therefore, offered no assistance to women who were seeking support for themselves and their children from men who had migrated to non-Commonwealth countries, or to the mothers of children born out of wedlock who were seeking maintenance from fathers who had left the country.

The provisions of the 1987 Act have a much wider coverage. 'Maintenance Orders' is specifically defined to include 'an Affiliation Order or order consequent upon an Affiliation Order'.[16] They also permit arrangements for the reciprocal enforcement of maintenance orders to be made with any country that is willing to enter into such arrangements.[17]

Generally, the regional statutes which provide for the reciprocal enforcement of maintenance orders are based on the 1920 English Act and suffer from the same limitations as the old Jamaica Act.[18] It appears that Barbados is the only other country in the region which has replaced the old legislation with an updated Act.[19]

2. Reforms relating to the property rights of spouses

a. Succession rights

The distribution of the estate of a person who dies without leaving a will is governed by statutory rules. In Jamaica, these statutory rules are contained in the Intestates' Estates and Property Charges Act. An amendment to this Act in 1988 altered the rules for distribution in a number of respects, but the most significant changes are the substantially increased entitlement of a surviving spouse and the inclusion of a common law spouse among the categories of beneficiaries.[20]

The latter is the more dramatic of the two changes, as under the old law a common law spouse was not entitled to share in her deceased partner's estate on intestacy. The inclusion of a common law spouse as a beneficiary under the Act was achieved by the definition of spouse to include "a single woman who has lived and cohabited with a single man as if she were in law his wife for a period of not less than five years immediately preceding the date of his death".[21] A man who is similarly qualified is also treated as a spouse.

The recognition of a common law spouse for the purpose of intestate succession brings Jamaican law in line with the law in Barbados and in Trinidad and Tobago. In all three countries, the conditions for recognition are the same, namely, single status and cohabitation for a period of at least five years.[22] The Barbados Succession Act initially required cohabitation for a period of seven years or more, but this was subsequently reduced to five years.

As many Jamaicans, due to reluctance, ignorance or neglect, fail to make a will, the statutory rules of intestate succession are of much practical importance. The improvements effected by the amendment will ensure that a wife, legal or common law, is not left without reasonable provisions. However, there is no such guarantee in the case of testate succession. A husband, or indeed any person, may by will dispose of his property without making any provision for his spouse or family. The new Succession Acts which apply in Barbados and Trinidad and Tobago protect the interests of a surviving spouse by placing certain restrictions on the freedom of testamentary disposition.

The Trinidad and Tobago Succession Act, 1981, empowers the court to vary the terms of the will, or the distribution of the property on intestacy, so as to make financial provisions for certain dependants of a deceased person.[23] The dependants in respect of whom financial provisions may be made include a spouse, in the extended sense, and also "any person . . . who immediately before the death of the deceased was being maintained, either wholly or partly, by the deceased".[24] A cohabitee who does not qualify as a "spouse", and a woman with whom the deceased had a "visiting relationship" will fall into this latter category, provided the dependence test is satisfied.

The Barbados Succession Act, 1975 takes a different approach. Firstly, it entitles a surviving spouse to a fixed proportion of the estate as a "legal right" which takes priority over devises, bequests and shares on intestacy.[25] A surviving spouse is therefore not only protected from disinheritance, but is also guaranteed a minimum share of the estate. Secondly, it empowers the court in the case of intestacy to make maintenance provisions out of the deceased's estate for a dependant. Dependant is defined to include "any woman, other than his spouse, living together with a man as his wife immediately preceding the date of his death, and wholly or mainly maintained by him at that time".[26] This provision is directed at a cohabitee who does not qualify as a spouse for the purpose of succession rights.

In Jamaica, consideration is being given to the enactment of legislation to entitle the dependants of a deceased person to apply to the court for maintenance provisions out of the deceased's estate. The indications are that the proposed categories of dependants will include a spouse as defined for the purpose of succession rights, but will not include women who do not qualify as such.

b. Rights in matrimonial property upon breakdown of marriage

Reference was made earlier to the married women's property legislation, which put an end to the legal disabilities of a married woman with respect to property. The Jamaica Married Women's Property Act which was enacted in 1887 is representative of such legislation. It established the separate property regime upon which the present law relating to the property rights of a husband and wife is based. The present law recognises a husband and wife as having equal rights to acquire, control and dispose of property, but in practice it places women at a disadvantage as regards their rights to family property. One of the main criticisms of the present law is that it puts undue emphasis on the financial contribution, resulting in the disregard of the efforts of a housewife for the purpose of determining property rights upon the breakdown of marriage. Moreover, even in cases where the wife has made a financial contribution, it is difficult to prove this fact, or to trace the contribution to specific items of property.

The separate property regime was the subject of review in the 1970s and in some countries it has already been displaced by a new matrimonial property regime.[27] In Jamaica the government has been considering proposals made by the Family Law Committee for the reform of the law relating to matrimonial property.[28] The main proposal is that the court should be given a wide discretion to divide property between spouses upon the breakdown of marriage; and that the exercise of this discretion should be subject to statutory guidelines, which should require the court to take into account, among other things, the financial and non-financial contribution of the spouses, including the contribution made in the capacity of a homemaker.

The proposed Jamaican matrimonial property reform, in adopting the discretionary approach to matrimonial property division, follows the trend set by the Barbados Family Law Act, 1981.[29] The provisions of that Act apply not only to a husband and wife but also to the parties to a union. A union is defined as "the relationship that is established when a man and woman who, not being married to each other, have cohabited continuously for a period of five years or more".[30] The equation of long-term cohabitation with marriage in this instance is a recognition of the fact that the breakdown of a domestic relationship between a man and a woman gives rise to the same property considerations, whether the parties are married or are merely cohabiting. In fact, the judge-made rules regarding the division of family assets between husband and wife apply to a man and mistress.[31] In contemplating family law reform, thought should always be given to whether and to what extent special realities can be accommodated. Matrimonial property reform offers an obvious opportunity for the recognition of a common law spouse. The approach taken by the Barbados Act is commendable.

As a final note to this category of reforms, mention should be made of the Family Law Committee's proposal regarding maintenance, as this was complementary to the proposals relating to matrimonial property. Under the present law, a husband is under duty to maintain his wife irrespective of her being able to maintain herself.[32] There is no general duty on a wife to maintain her husband. The Family Law Committee has recommended a change in law to confer on both husband and wife equal rights to maintenance on the basis of financial need and ability.[33] The suggested change to the law is consistent with the mutuality of support rights and obligations enjoyed by spouses under modern maintenance legislation. The maintenance provisions of the Barbados Family Law Act reflect this approach and, as in the case of property rights, the parties to a union are accorded the rights of spouses.[34] The change proposed by the Family Law Committee represents a shift in the treatment of maintenance from a right flowing from the status of wife to a right based on need and factual dependence. The grant of maintenance rights to common law spouses seems to be the next logical step.

3. Divorce and other matrimonial causes

The main feature of modern divorce legislation is the replacement of the old fault grounds for divorce with the single ground of irretrievable breakdown of marriage. Such legislation also provides for the counselling of the parties with a view to achieving a reconciliation between them or the settlement of issues relating to the custody of children, maintenance and property. In 1989 Jamaica joined the other countries in the region in which such legislation exists by the enactment of the Matrimonial Causes Act.

With regard to the evidence required to establish the new ground, the Act followed the approach adopted in Australia and, closer to home, Barbados in requiring a period of separation of at least 12 months.[35] The other modern regional statutes follow the English approach of making irretrievable breakdown of marriage provable by certain facts. These briefly are: (a) the respondent's adultery plus the fact that the petitioner finds it intolerable to live with him or her; (b) the respondent's unreasonable behaviour; (c) the respondent's desertion for two years; (d) separation plus the respondent's consent to the divorce; and (e) separation for five years.[36] The Family Law Committee, on whose recommendations the Act is based, rejected the "facts approach" on the ground that it would perpetuate the fault emphasis of the old law. It is interesting to note that England is now contemplating a switch to separation as evidence of irretrievable breakdown.

The Matrimonial Causes Act, 1989, of Jamaica introduced other important changes, three of which have been selected for comment here because of the implications they have for women.

a. *The new injunction remedy*

The Act empowers the court to grant an injunction or other order for the personal protection of a party to the marriage or a child, for the protection of the property of a party to the marriage or in relation to the use and occupation of the matrimonial home.[37] Similar provisions are to be found in the Australia Family Law Act, 1975, and the similarly entitled Barbados Act of 1981.[38] This provision introduces the injunction as an independent remedy. Before the passage of the Act, an injunction could be obtained only as an ancillary relief where proceedings for one of the principal matrimonial remedies had been instituted.

The injunction is now popular as a remedy for abused women. In considering the usefulness of the new Jamaican provision in this regard, two points should be borne in mind. The first is that the main sanctions for the defiance of an injunction under the Matrimonial Causes Act, 1989, are fines and imprisonment. The Act does not authorise the attachment of a power of arrest to an injunction. There is a view that without the attachment of such a power the injunction lacks teeth. Criticism of the ineffectiveness of injunctions made under the Australian Act led its amendment to include a provision for the attachment of a power of arrest to an injunction.[39] It is still too early to assess the effectiveness of the Jamaican provision, but the Australian experience sounds a warning. The second point is that the injunction remedy is available only to 'a party to a marriage'. It will not, therefore, afford any protection to a cohabiting woman. This limitation is not fully applicable to the corresponding Barbados provision, as it applies to a party to a union, but a cohabitee with less than five years' cohabitation will not qualify. The limitation of the Jamaican injunction remedy to married couples is explained by the fact that it was conceived as a matrimonial remedy. It is directed at a spouse who is in need of immediate relief and protection, but who does not wish or is not entitled to institute divorce proceedings, and also in order to fill the gap left by the abolition of judicial separation.[40] Clearly, while the new injunction remedy under the Matrimonial Act, 1989, will offer some protection to abused wives, it does not dispense with the need for comprehensive legislation on domestic violence.

b. Domicile

Domicile, simply put, is the place where a person has his or her permanent home. The common law rule is that a wife takes her husband's domicile. Accordingly her domicile changes with his, even if they are living apart. Section 34 of the Act provides that for the purposes of the Act "the domicile of a woman who is, or has at any time been married shall be determined as if she had never been married". This has effectively reduced the importance of the common law rule, as it is in the area of matrimonial jurisdiction that its consequences were mainly felt. The retention of the rule, however, is contrary to the principle of the equality of the sexes. An English judge described the rule as "the last barbarous relic of a wife's servitude".[41] Some countries in the region, (notably Barbados), have taken the correct step in abolishing the rule altogether.[42]

Certain complementary changes were made to the rule for determining the domicile of a married minor. The common law rule is that a child born in wedlock takes his father's domicile, while a child born out of wedlock takes his mother's domicile. This rule was expressly preserved by the Status of Children Act, 1976.[43] This rule has combined with the rule relating to a wife's dependant to create complications where the minor is a married woman. The Act resolves the issue by providing that the domicile of a married minor shall be determined as if he or she had attained majority at the date of the marriage, or where the minor has been married more than once, at the date of the first such marriages.[44]

c. Damages for adultery

The Act abolished proceedings by a husband for damages against a person who committed adultery with his wife. Such proceedings were the statutory equivalent of the old common law action for criminal conversation of which mention was made earlier. The abolition of this remedy, which applied exclusively to a husband, marks the removal of one of the remaining vestiges of the common law's treatment of a wife as the property of her husband.

The recent family law reforms have improved the status of rights of women in many ways, but there are still some remaining areas of concern. Some of these have already been referred to. Mention was made earlier of the need for more comprehensive provisions for domestic violence, for the abolition of a wife's dependent domicile and for provisions to be made for a common law spouse in the proposed legislation on the division of property between, and the maintenance of, spouses upon family breakdown. I will now deal, briefly, with four other areas in which the unfavourable treatment of women by family law is evident.

4. The retention of the common law actions for enticement, harbouring and loss of consortium

These are essentially remedies for a husband who is deprived of his wife's services and companionship through the conduct of a third party.[45] They are a part of the common law which was received by the countries in the region. Although it appears that these actions have fallen into disuse, their retention as a part of the current law perpetuates the notion of a wife as property. The abolition of these actions requires specific legislation. It appears that Barbados is the only country in the region which has already enacted legislation to abolish these actions.[46]

5. Parental rights and responsibility

The Children (Guardianship and Custody) Act recognises the mother and father of a child as having equal rights to apply for custody, to assume guardianship as surviving parent and to appoint a guardian after his or her death to act jointly with the surviving parent.[47] The Act is based on the early English statutes on guardianship and custody which culminated with the Guardianship of Infants Act, 1925. While the provisions of the Act have removed the father's monopoly with respect to parental rights, they have not conferred on the mother equal rights with the father. This has a direct bearing on which parent has the decision-making power in respect of important matters pertaining to the child. For example, it is the father's consent that is still required to the marriage of a minor child born in wedlock.[48] The need for reform to this area of law is indicated.

The provisions on guardianship of children enacted in Barbados and in Trinidad and Tobago in 1975 and 1981, respectively, embody the principle of equality of the sexes with regard to parental rights.[49] These provisions apply to both married and unmarried parents, but take different approaches in relation to the putative father. The Barbados legislation treats the parties to a union as having equal parental rights: the putative father's entitlement to parental rights is, therefore, linked to long-term cohabitation with the mother. A putative father who is not living with the mother, or who has lived with the mother for less than five years, is not automatically entitled to parental rights, although he may be awarded custody of the child in certain circumstances.[50] The equality of parental rights conferred on the mother and father of a child by the Trinidad and Tobago legislation is qualified by the provision that the father of a child born out of wedlock is entitled to guardianship only if paternity has been registered or has been established by any of the modes specified in the Status of Children Act.[51] The modes specified in that Act include the establishment of paternity by judicial or administrative procedures.[52]

The wider basis for the recognition of the putative father provided by the Trinidad and Tobago legislation is to be preferred. Many fathers who do not share a common residence with the mother do in fact acknowledge and participate in the upbringing of the child. There is no reason for denying such fathers legal recognition. Equal responsibility is the corollary of equal rights. An important area of responsibility is maintenance. Accordingly, the legislation in the Barbados and Trinidad and Tobago Acts imposes on the mother and father equal support responsibility for the child.[53] Under Jamaican law, generally, it is the father who has the primary responsibility for child support, although the Maintenance Act requires a widow and an unmarried woman to maintain their children.[54] The need for a redefinition of parental rights and responsibilities is recognised.[55]

6. Acquisition of Jamaican nationality by marriage or descent

The acquisition of Jamaican nationality and citizenship is provided for in the constitution. These provisions are complemented by those in the Jamaican Nationality Act. With regard to the transmission of Jamaican nationality by marriage, the rule, simply put, is that the foreign wife of a Jamaican man is entitled to claim Jamaican [citizenship on the basis of the marriage, but the foreign husband of a Jamaican woman does not enjoy a corresponding right.][56] In the case of acquisition of citizenship by descent, the law recognises a distinction at two levels: (a) as between man and woman; and (b) as between married woman and unmarried woman. Basically, the rule is that a child born outside Jamaica acquires Jamaican citizenship through his father if he is born in wedlock and through his mother if he is born out of wedlock.[57] It should be noted that this rule was expressly preserved by the Status of Children Act, 1976.[58]

The preference shown for a husband and father of a child born in wedlock reflects the dependent status of the wife at common law and the recognition of the mother as the parent through whom nationality is transmitted to a child born out of wedlock is indicative of the non-status of the putative father at common law. These provisions, in addition to being echoes of the past, are in breach of Article 9 (2) of the Convention of the Elimination of all Forms of Discrimination Against Women, which requires States Parties to grant women equal rights with men with respect to their own nationality and that of their children. This made it necessary for a reservation to be entered in relation to this Article when Jamaica ratified the convention in 1984. The constitution and related Acts are soon to be amended to bring the law in line with the Convention's requirement.

7. A husband's immunity to prosecution for rape

This matter lies more in the realm of criminal law. Its relevance here is that it is derived from the marital rights to which a husband is entitled at common law. These include a right to sexual intercourse with his wife. Thus, at the time of marriage a wife is deemed to give her irrevocable consent to sexual intercourse with her husband during the subsistence of the marriage. He cannot, therefore, be guilty of raping his wife. The only recognised exception is where they are separated by virtue of a court order or a separation agreement which contains a non-molestation clause.

In modern times the husband's immunity has been the subject of review and legislation. The legislative approaches range from the abolition of the immunity to its modification to permit the prosecution of a husband in circumstances which suggest a breakdown of the marital relationship.[59] The indications are that it is the latter conservative approach that is favoured in the region. So far, only Trinidad and Tobago has enacted legislation on the subject, where the Sexual Offences Act, 1986, makes sexual intercourse by a husband with a wife without her consent punishable as a sexual assault in certain circumstances. These are where there is a decree nisi of divorce, a decree of judicial separation, a separation agreement or a non-molestation order, where the husband and wife are living apart or where matrimonial proceedings have been instituted by one of them.[60] Jamaica is at present reviewing the law relating to sexual offences and consideration is being given to a similar modification of the husband's immunity.

Conclusion

In Caribbean societies the realities of family structure and responsibilities make women the main victims of the inadequacies of family law. Consequently, any improvement in this area of law has a beneficial effect on women. In the recent spate of family law reforms women have benefited, not only in this general way but also from the specific improvement of their status and rights within the family.

Some general observations may be made about family law reforms in the region. The first is that the legislators have demonstrated a willingness to search for appropriate legislative models. Hitherto, the common pattern was the adoption of English statutes, often many years after their introduction in England. The influence of legislation enacted in countries other than England is visible in many of the recent reforms. For example, the regional statutes on the Status of Children incorporate features of the New Zealand Status of Children Act, 1969, and the Ontario Children's Law Reform Act, 1977, as well as the English Family Reform Act 1969. The new legislative provisions on divorce and the division of matrimonial property which now apply in Barbados, and those proposed for Jamaica, are based on the Australia Family Law Act, 1975.

The second observation is that the recent reforms represent a departure from the usual conservative approach to marriage and the family. There are two aspects to this. One aspect is the recognition of the husband and wife as equal partners. This approach is manifested in the new legislative provisions for divorce, maintenance and property rights. The other aspect is the more realistic approach taken to the family situation in the Caribbean. Of importance in this respect are the measures introduced in relation to a child born out of wedlock and the parties to a consensual union. The greater liberalisation has occurred in respect of the child born out of wedlock. With regard to consensual unions, the trend is to recognise stable common law relationships and the common indication is cohabitation for five years or more. The legislation enacted in Barbados with reference to the common law spouse is the most advanced.

The third observation is that the reforms mark a move towards the exorcism of the common law ghosts which have haunted this area of law, for instance those rules and remedies which are based on the doctrine of unity of spouses and the concept of a wife as property, such as a wife's dependent domicile and the old common law actions available to a husband.

These observations indicate the general direction of family law reform in the region. Some countries are at a more advanced stage than others in this respect. The review of the Jamaican situation highlights the main areas of concern.

While the ultimate responsibility for determining policy rests with the government, the public has a role in the determination of the considerations which inform the policy. Historically, law reforms relating to women have occurred largely in response to public opinion and agitation. This was true of the revolutionary reforms of the nineteenth century which resulted in the recognition of a woman as a legal entity. More recently, the debate on the status of women, both nationally and internationally, has acted as a catalyst for law reform. Public opinion serves not only to call attention to need for law reform, but can also influence the nature and content of new laws. In some countries it is the practice for family law reforms to be preceded by much public debate and discussion. In Caribbean countries public input is not only generally desirable but is also particularly vital in the case of reforms relating to women. Information on the social conditions of women cannot always be readily accessed from official records, as official data collection is not usually gender-based.

Public participation in law reform is a new experience in this part of the world, because generally the approach until recently was to adopt English statutes. Consequently, the opportunity to become involved in law reform exercise is sometimes not grasped. There is also a tendency to view the law relating to women as a thing apart from the social and economic conditions of women, the community and the entire society. There is a need for a new orientation in thinking: help to arouse a new awareness of the importance of research and investigation into the impact of the law on social and economic development of women and the need for collaboration between related disciplines with a view to shaping appropriate policy.

References

1. English Married Women's Property Act, 1925, provided the model for regional statutes, e.g. Married Women's Property Act (Ja.); Married Persons Act, Cap. 45:50 (T'dad & Tob.).
2. See e.g. Children (Guardianship and Custody) Act (Ja.).
3. See e.g. Legitimation Act (Ja.); Registration (Births and Deaths) Act, S. 19 (Ja.); Bastardy Act, renamed Affiliation Act (Ja.).
4. Barbados, Dominica, Guyana, Jamaica, St Christopher and Nevis, St Lucia, St Vincent and the Grenadines.
5. Article 15.1.
6. Article 16.1.
7. Article 9, Article 15.4.
8. Status of Children Reform Act, 1977 (B'dos.), Status of Children Act, 1980 (Belize); Status of Children Act, 1980 (St. Vincent); Status of Children Act, 1981 (T'dad & Tob.); Children Born out of Wedlock Act, 1983 (Guyana).
9. Status of Children Act, 1976, S. 7.
10. See e.g. Status of Children Act, 1980, S. 7 (Belize); Status of Children Act, 1981, S. 7 (T'dad & Tob.).
11. Status of Children Act, 1976, S. 8, S. 10, Ss. 11-15 (Ja.).
12. *Ibid.* S. 6.
13. Status of Children Reform Act, 1979, S. 7 (1) (B'dos).
14. Registration (Births and Deaths) Amendment Act, 1980, No. 17/1980.
15. Registration (Births and Deaths) Act, S. 19A (Ja.).
16. Maintenance (Facilities for Enforcement) Act, 1987, S. 2 (Ja.).
17. *Ibid.*, S. 20.
18. E.g. Maintenance Orders (Facilities for Enforcement) Act, 1921, Cap. 50 (Antigua and Barbuda); Maintenance Orders Facilities for Enforcement Act, 1923 Cap. 45 (Bahamas.); Maintenance Orders (Facilities for Enforcement) Act, 1921, Cap. 46 (British Virgin Islands); Maintenance Orders (Enforcement) Act, 1922, Cap. 45:53 (Trinidad & Tobago.).
19. Maintenance Orders (Reciprocal Enforcement) Act, 1974 (B'dos).
20. Intestates' Estates and Property Charges (Amendment) Act, 1988 (Ja.).
21. Intestates' Estates and Property Charges Act, S. 2 (Ja.).
22. Succession Act 1975, S. 2(3) (B'dos.); Succession Act, 1981, S.2(3) (T'dad & Tob.).
23. Succession Act, 1981, Ss. 95-96.
24. *Ibid.*, S. 95 (e).
25. Succession Act, 1975, S. 94 (B'dos).

26. *Ibid.*, S. 57.
27. New matrimonial property regimes are of two basic types. One leaves the division of matrimonial property to the court (e.g. Matrimonial Causes Act, 1973, S. 24 (e.g.); Family Law Act, 1975, S. 79 (Aus.). The other entitles the spouses to equal shares in matrimonial property upon the breakdown of marriage (e.g. Matrimonial Property Act, 1976 (N.Z.); Family Law Reform Act, 1978 (Ont.).
28. Family Law Committee: Report on Matrimonial Property Reform, March 1990.
29. Family Law Act, 1975, S. 57 (B'dos).
30. Family Law Act, 1981, S. 39 (B'dos).
31. Cooke v. Head [1972] 1 W.L.R. S. 18.
32. Maintenance Act, S. 12 (Ja.).
33. Family Law Committee: Report on Matrimonial Property Reform; para. 7.9.
34. Family Law Act, 1975, S. 50 (B'dos).
35. Matrimonial Causes Act, 1989, S. 5(2) (Ja.); Family Law Act, 1975, S. 48(2) (Aus.); Family Law Act, 1975, S. 27 (B'dos).
36. See e.g. Matrimonial Property and Proceedings Act (T'dad & Tob.); Matrimonial Causes Act (Cayman Is.); Divorce Act, 1973 (St Lucia).
37. Matrimonial Causes Act, 1989, S. 10.
38. Family Law Act, 1975, S. 114 (Aus.); Family Law Act, 1981, S. 91 (B'dos).
39. Family Law Act, 1975, S. 114A (Aus.).
40. Family Law Committee: Report No. 1, para. 39.11.
41. Lord Denning in *Gray (Orse Formosa) v. Formosa* (1963), P. 259 at 267.
42. Domicile Reform Act, 1979 S. 5 (B'dos).
43. Status of Children Act, 1976 S. 4(a) (Ja.).
44. Matrimonial Causes Act, 1989, S. 34(1) (b) (Ja.).
45. An action for enticement may be brought by a wife: *Best v .Samuel Fox & Co .Ltd.* [1950] A.C. 716.
46. Accident Compensation (Reforms) Act (B'dos).
47. Children (Guardianship and Custody) Act, S. 3, S. 4 (Ja.).
48. Marriage Act, S. 24 (Ja.).
49. Family Law Act, 1975, S. 40 (B'dos); Family Law (Guardianship of Minors, Domicile and Maintenance) Act, 1981, S. 4 (Trinidad & Tobago).
50. Maintenance Act, 1981, S. 20 (2).
51. Family Law (Guardianship of Minors, Domicile and Maintenance) Act, 1981, S. 6 (Trinidad & Tobago).
52. Status of Children Act, 1981, S. 8 (T'dad & Tob.).
53. Family Law Act, 1975, S. 57 (Barbados); The Maintenance Act, S. 4, 1981 (Barbados); Family Law (Guardianship of Minors, Domicile and Maintenance) Act, 1981, S. 13 (5) (Trinidad & Tobago).
54. Maintenance Act, S. 3 (Ja.).
55. The law relating to children in Jamaica is under review, and guardianship and custody are areas in respect of which a report has already been made. See Leighton Jackson: *The Law Relating to Children in Jamaica*, Part I.
56. The Constitution of Jamaica, S. 4 (1), S. 4 (3). S. 7.
57. *Ibid.*, S. 3 (2), S. 6, S. 12 (2).
58. Status of Children Act, 1976, S. 3 (4) (b).
59. The husband's immunity has been abolished in some countries, e.g. Australia, Canada and New Zealand.
60. Sexual Offences Act, 1986, S. 5 (Trinidad & Tobago).

A Controversial Revisiting of the Right to Consortium

Cherry Brady Clarke

Introduction: The action for loss of consortium

This chapter is part of a longer study of gender issues in the law of personal injuries.[1] This part examines the action for loss of consortium. At common law a husband has the right of action against a third party for injuries arising from the tort committed against his wife. This is independent of the wife's cause of action and there is no reciprocal right of the wife in the case of an injured husband.

Historically,[2] the husband's right to an action for loss of consortium developed by analogy to the master-servant relationship in which the master could bring an action *per quod servitium amisit* against a defendant who had taken away, imprisoned or done physical harm to his servant, always provided that the wrong was also a tort to the servant and that the master was deprived of the servant's services as a result. The action *per quod consortium amisit* was available in similar circumstances when the person taken away, imprisoned or harmed was the master's wife. Both servant and wife enjoyed the same status in the eyes of the law: that of a chattel in which the husband's interest was proprietary.[3] A recovery of damages in either action was entirely the property of the husband.[4]

In *Guy v. Livesey*[5] the plaintiff husband brought an action in trespass against the defendant for beating his wife. The action was separate from another action in which he was joined with his wife as plaintiff for the same assault. The court rejected the argument that to allow the husband to succeed would be, in effect, punishing the defendant twice. The court found for the husband, noting that: 'the action is not brought in respect of the harm done to the wife, but it is brought for the particular loss of the husband, for that he lost the company of his wife, which is only a damage and loss to himself, for which he shall have this action, as the master shall have for the loss of his servant's service'.

The philosophical basis of the action for loss of consortium was the extinction of the legal personality of the *feme covert* who, on marriage, lost the right to own property, to sue and be sued in her own name without her husband being joined, and who owed to her husband her "services", none being reciprocally owed by him. In exchange for the *mund,* the profitable guardianship of the husband over his wife, he had a legal duty to maintain her (actually provide food and board) while she remained in his house and on her good behaviour. His remedy for an injury to his rights over his wife lay also in the old common law actions for criminal conversation against the male adulterer,[6] enticement and harbouring.[7] This was clothed in the quasi-ecclesiastical notion that on marriage a husband and wife became one person and that person was the husband. Remnants of this legal fiction persist even to today.[8]

The consequence of the legal unity of husband and wife was the denial of a cause of action on the part of the wife for tortious interference with the marital relationship as the wife thus had a procedural disability at common law which the Married Women's Property Acts[9] were designed to remove. The effect of these Acts was to enable a married woman to own property and to sue and be sued in her own right as if she were a *feme sole*. Notwithstanding the removal of the procedural difficulty, the courts still held that a wife had no cause of action to sue for loss of consortium.

Consortium defined

A major difficulty lies in the delineation of the interest which is harmed as a result of the tortious interference with consortium, and indeed, with the definition of the word itself. In *Best v. Samuel Fox* [10] Lord Reid observed:

> In the old cases a number of words are used to describe the Husband's loss or damage. He has by the act of the wrongdoer lost his wife's service, assistance, comfort, society, etc.... Sometimes the word 'consortium' is used in conjunction with one or more of these words. Sometimes it appears to be intended to include them. I doubt whether there was any fixed practice.[11]

Lord Reid distilled the essence of consortium to a "bundle of rights some hardly capable of precise definition", but including the right to a wife's society as well as her services.[12] In the same case, Lord Porter did not define consortium, but said that today the measure of damages is determined by the husband's expenses, and "little, if any, attention is paid to a loss of consortium which involves consideration beyond [expenses]".[13] Decided cases support the view that the husband is compensated for the loss of the wife's *services (servitium)* and damages are seldom awarded for the loss of the wife's society and comfort (*solatium*), damages usually being nominal in those cases. However, older cases have held that the action is "for the loss and damage of the husband, for want of her company and aid".[14] In *Lynch v. Knight*,[5] (a decision on which the House of Lords in deciding *Best v. Samuel Fox* placed great reliance), Lord Wensleydale stressed the material value of the wife's services capable of being estimated in money which "resemble the services of a hired domestic, tutor or governess".[16] Thornton[17] argued:

> This lowly perception of the value of the full-time home-maker tends to emanate from a judicial and societal inability to evaluate the contributions of unpaid work in a capitalist structure concerned with the acquisition of wealth and monetary reward. No margin is allowed for the intellect of the woman, of her academic ability in educating the children or critically examining the husband's work, the proficiency in entertaining his colleagues, or for any other particular talents or skills she might have. The judiciary have adopted the view that the loss of all these skills is compensable at the lowest market rate for a replacement of domestic worker or servant.

Other jurisdictions have, however, achieved more satisfactory definitions of consortium and have thus enlarged the scope of compensable injuries in the action for loss of consortium. In *Hittafer v. Argonne Co.*[18] an American court defined consortium thus: 'although it embraces within its ambit the meaning of the wife's marital services, [it] also includes love, affection, companionship, sexual relations, etc., all welded into a conceptual unity".[19]

An Australian court has stated that although consortium has been defined as a partnership or association,[20] in the matrimonial sense "it implies much more than these cold words suggest".

> It involves a sharing of two lives, a sharing of the joys and sorrows of each party, of their successes and disappointments. In its fullest sense it implies a companionship between each of them, entertainment of mutual friends, sexual intercourse - all those elements which, when combined, justify the old common law dictum that a man and his wife are one person.[21]

In that jurisdiction also, in the context of a matrimonial cause, Justice Watson defined 'the marriage relationship', which he also termed "the *consortium vitae*", as including sexual intercourse, mutual society and protection, determining that "[w]hat comprises the marital relationship for each couple will vary".[22]

Inequality under the law

The action for loss of consortium is a gross and obvious example of the law's unequal treatment of men and women and, as such, is inconsistent with justice and the rule of law. There is no doubt that the action is part of the received law of the Commonwealth Caribbean jurisdictions and it is a matter which should be addressed.

In the absence of binding precedent, it is the general practice of the courts in the region to follow English decisions, decisions of the House of Lords being most highly persuasive or binding in practice, if not as a matter of law.[23] We can therefore safely assume that since *Best v. Samuel Fox*[34] is the last word of the House of Lords on the matter of consortium, in the absence of decided cases it would be followed by a Caribbean court. Indeed, Forde[25] assumes that that case is part of the law of the Caribbean, except for Barbados where the action has been abolished by statute.[26]

In *Best v. Samuel Fox*, the plaintiff wife brought an action against the defendant for damages for the loss of her husband's consortium. The husband, a 30-year-old steel erector, had become incapable of sexual intercourse as a result of the negligent action of the defendant and as a consequence his wife's health suffered. The basis of the wife's claim was that she had been deprived of the opportunity of having further children and of enjoying normal marital relations.

At first instance, Justice Croom-Johnson held that no such right existed. The wife appealed and the Court of Appeal dismissed the appeal, holding that a wife could only succeed if she could prove total loss of consortium as distinct from impairment of consortium.[27] The court was divided on the question of whether the wife had a right to bring an action for loss of consortium occasioned by the wrongful act of the defendant in respect of her husband. On appeal, the House of Lords dismissed the appeal, deciding, *per curiam*, that there was no such right and that the right of the husband to such an action is an anomaly at the present day which only Parliament can abolish and which should not be extended in respect of a wife's claim.

The House of Lords missed a golden opportunity to decide the matter on principle, there being admittedly no authority on the point. Argument before the House proceeded on the basis of an analogy to the enticement cases in which it was acknowledged that a wife have a cause of action.[28] The House of Lords refused to allow the principle to be extended to the wife's action for the loss of consortium. Lord Porter stated his views as follows: 'Even, however, if it be assumed that in enticement cases the husband and wife have equal rights, it does not follow that today they have equal rights and liabilities one towards the other in all respects'.

Acknowledging that certain differences between the position of husband and wife 'undoubtedly' had been extinguished or modified by Parliament and that the general opinion of the relationship which exists between the spouses has changed, he said:

> I do not think it is possible to say that a change in the outlook of the public, however great, must inevitably be followed by a change in the law of this country. The common law is a historical development rather than a logical

> whole, and the fact that a particular doctrine does not logically accord with another or others is no ground for its rejection.[29]

Lord Porter's speech betrays a narrowly conservative point of view on the question of gender equality. He grudgingly states: "Even if it be conceded that the rights of husband and wife ought to be equalised." Yet he would prefer to abolish the husband's right of action rather than grant the equal right to the wife. If the injuries were reversed, the husband would be liable for the wife's medical treatment and for payment of a replacement for the household services which, by virtue of her injury she is unable to perform: 'The expenses so recovered by the husband fall on him whereas the wife does not incur any similar liability, and, therefore, it is natural that he should recover and she should not'.[20] One can hardly see anything 'natural' about Lord Porter's proposition.

Be that as it may, their lordships were firm in their view that the right should not be extended to wives and that the action could only be (not should be) abolished by statute. The reasons given by their lordships for not extending the right of action can all be defeated by logical argument.[31] The main reasons advanced were: the proliferation of suits which might follow; that no duty was owed to the wife and the injury was too remote; that the husband's action was obsolete, being founded on the proprietary right 'which, from ancient times it was considered the husband has in his wife'; and that to allow a wife to recover would in effect be a double recovery.

It is submitted that once the House conceded that no action for damages for enticement was brought by a married woman until the procedural fetters were removed by the Married Women's Property Act, 1882, it was open to them to accept that similar proceedings in an action for loss of consortium were indeed possible since 1882. Additionally, there is no conceptual difference between loss of consortium by enticement[32] and loss of consortium by negligent injury. Nevertheless, Lord Porter distinguished the former on the basis that, in enticement actions, the wrong was a deliberate act taken by a third party to persuade the errant spouse not to fulfil the mutual duty of consortium which one spouse owed to the other. The House of Lords appears to have taken support from a decision of the High Court of Australia in *Wright v. Cedzich*[33], an enticement action by the wife, in which the majority (Chief Justice Knox, Gavan Duffy, Justices Rich and Starke) held that a wife has no cause of action for the loss of consortium by her husband, a view vigorously opposed by Justice Isaacs. After a review of the history of the action at common law, the court made its decision on the ground that the common law had always recognised the *dominium*[34] exercised by the husband over the wife. The wife never had any such *dominium* over the husband.

The House of Lords, deciding *Best v. Samuel Fox* in 1952, would have done better service to the principle of equality under the law had they accepted the reasoning of Justice Isaacs, who attacked the legal fiction at the basis of the medieval doctrine that a woman lost her identity on marriage and became subsumed within the *persona* of her husband. He urged that it was time the law abandoned the notion that women were 'merely adjuncts or property or the servants of their husbands' and took cognisance of the formal changes in women's status and their actual role in society.[35]

Lord Porter advanced the floodgates argument in *Best* that an extension of the right to an action would result in the proliferation of suits. But this is best answered by Professor Ronald Dworkin's thesis that in hard cases justice requires that judges choose principle over policy.[36]

Where the House of Lords was of the view that there was no duty owed to the wife or that the injury was indirect and therefore not sufficiently proximate, the very existence of the husband's action makes this argument less persuasive. Further, the modern development of the law of tort in relation to nervous shock supports the view that an action done to one person may result in a tort being committed to a third party in certain circumstances, the only qualification being the requirement of foreseeability.

Indeed, the nervous shock cases present a good illustration of the willingness of the judges to adapt and mould the law when they choose to do so. Less than a 100 years had passed since the decision in *Victorian Railway Commissioners v. Coultas*,[37] in which the Privy Council held that losses for nervous shock were not recoverable, to the decision of the House of Lords in *McLoughlin v. O'Brian*[38] which extended the category of persons to whom a duty of care is owed beyond persons at or near the scene of an accident. In tracing the development of this area of law, Lord Wilberforce noted: 'throughout these developments, ... the courts have proceeded in the traditional manner of the common law from case to case upon a basis of logical necessity'.[39]

Finally, one cannot help but think that their Lordships' reluctance was based on their overwhelming fixation with the wife's services rather than on the intangible (and some tangible) aspects of consortium which arise out of the marital relationship. Furthermore, the emphasis on the wife's services is demeaning to women. This emphasis persists in recent decisions in that, even where a woman is employed outside the home, housework is the province of women.[40]

Abolish the action or extend it?

Admitting that the action for loss of consortium is an overt discrimination against women, jurists in the Commonwealth Caribbean must ask themselves whether *Best v. Samuel Fox* is really the last word, or whether the right to sue for loss of consortium should be extended to the wife. The question has been decided for England by Parliament. Section 2 of the Administration of Justice Act 1982, cap. 53 abolished the action. It is clear that the law, as it stands, is in need of rectification, particularly in the light of the independence constitutions which either expressly[41] or impliedly[42] guarantee freedom from discrimination on the basis of sex.

But what has been the experience of other jurisdictions with a similar common law background? Two years before the House of Lords decision in *Best v. Samuel Fox*, the US Court of Appeals (District of Columbia Circuit), in a landmark decision extended the right of action for loss of consortium to the wife for loss of her injured husband's "aid, assistance, and enjoyment, specifically sexual relations".[43]

In this case, the husband was injured while in the appellant's employ and as a result suffered injuries about his body and particularly about the abdomen, the result of these injuries being his loss of sexual ability. At first instance, the complaint was dismissed when the defendant moved for a summary judgment on the grounds that the court lacked jurisdiction and the complaint failed to state a cause of action. On appeal to the Court of Appeals, Justice Clark admitted the "unanimity of authority elsewhere denying the wife recovery under these circumstances".[44] Thus flying in the face of the doctrine of *stare decisis*, the court stated the modern rule as follows:

> The actual injury to the wife from loss of *consortium*, which is the basis of the action, is the same as the actual injury to the husband from that cause. His right to the conjugal society of his wife is no greater than her right to the conjugal society of her husband. Marriage gives each the same rights in that regard. Each is entitled to the comfort, companionship, and affection of the other. The rights of the one and the obligations of the other spring from the marriage contract, are mutual in character, and attach to the husband as husband and to the wife as wife. Any interference with these rights, whether of the husband or of the wife, is a violation, not only of a natural right, but also of a legal right arising out of the marriage relation . . . As the wrongs of the wife are the same in principle, and are caused by the acts of the same nature, as those of the husband, the remedy should be the same.[45]

The judgment, which reviewed and disposed of previous arguments against extending the right of action to the wife, was based solely on the principle of equality of husband and wife. The decision was met by both approval and ire. Jaffe described *Hitaffer v. Argonne Co.* as "another instance where the decision is made to turn on a series of fashionable propositions quite divorced from their function in the current scene". Jaffe argued for the abolition of this "fossil from an earlier era".[46] The decision in *Hitaffer v. Argonne Co.* is now vindicated, as in most of the states of the USA, a wife has a right of action for wrongful injury to her husband which results in the loss of consortium.[47]

In Canada, a jurisdiction with historical and constitutional ties to the Commonwealth Caribbean, the courts have not extended the action to the wife.[48] Nevertheless, the Ontario Law Commission has recommended it: "It is generally recognised today that the societal and political forces have changed the relationship between the sexes and lent to the establishment of greater equality. Such being the case, the common law which is founded upon the assumption of a by-gone inequality should be superseded."[49]

In a recent Canadian case, however, the Saskatchewan Court of Queen's Bench rejected a claim by a husband by reason of injuries sustained by his wife in an accident in which he, his wife and daughter were each injured by the defendant's negligent driving. All three plaintiffs were awarded damages in respect of their own injuries.

The court (Justice MacLeod) carefully distinguished between servitium ("the duties of a wife as a worker and manager of [the husband's] domestic establishment") and consortium, which he said has a "more intimate meaning". The learned judge cited, but did not comment directly on, the definition of consortium in *Halsbury*, that is her society and services and the definition given by Lord Reid in *Best v. Samuel Fox*, "companionship, love, affection, comfort, mutual services, sexual intercourse". In his own view: "Consortium includes (although it is not limited to) the benefits with which a *man* has historically associated the marriage bed. Consortium is what marriage is all about."[50] (Emphasis added)

The court stated that an essential characteristic of this claim is that it is one-sided. It is the husband's claim and there is no equivalent right of action for loss of a husband's consortium. Justice MacLeod concluded that this historical anomaly is in violation of s. 15 (1) of the Canadian Charter of Rights and Freedoms[51] and must cease to exist. Noting that the anomaly might be erased either by abolition of the action entirely, or by extending it to the wife, he declared that he was satisfied that in 1984 in Canada abolition of the action was preferable.

This decision, however, must be approached with caution. It is a first instance decision and, other than citing *Charlesworth on Negligence* as authority for the proposition that the action for loss of consortium is a historical anomaly which should not be extended to the wife, the learned judge advanced no reasons. He further obfuscated the decision by stating: "I emphasize that I refer only to consortium. Servitium is a different matter. It may be that the right of servitium is one which should apply equally to a husband and a wife, and that each should be entitled to make a claim for its loss in the other. But that is not the question before me now."[52]

Justice MacLeod's statement is in direct contradiction to Lord Reid's statement of clarification in *Best v. Samuel Fox*: 'There was not one action for loss of consortium and another for loss of servitium, and in the same cause of action loss or damage under any of these heads could properly be taken into account though often the main emphasis might be on the value of the services or assistance which the husband has lost'.[53] For these reasons, *Shwarchuk v. Hansen* is but weak authority.[54]

Conclusion

It is submitted that both justice and good sense require the extension of the common law action to a wife. The law should recognise the modern concept of marriage as a partnership of equals in which husband and wife are mutually dependent and give to each other household services, mutual support, comfort, affection, sex and all of the appurtenances of the marriage relationship.[55] The action is only an anachronism when it is linked to the idea that consortium means the wife's services. Indeed, this view may well be a perversion. In *Guy v. Livesey*[56] the injury to the plaintiff was "for that he lost the *company* of his wife, while in *Hyde v. Scyssor*[57] the action is "for want of her *company and aid*" (emphasis added).

Whatever the historical origins of the action, it is clear that the wife's interest in the marital relationship is an interest worthy of protection and negligent interference with it should be actionable on the principle of the foreseeability of the harm. The abolition of the old common law actions for enticement, harbouring and criminal conversation by some jurisdictions is not good and sufficient reason for abolishing the consortium action. The true reason why enticement, harbouring and criminal conversation are no longer tenable is that in each there is the element of consent of the party which should absolve the wrong-doer from liability in damages. An extension of the consortium action to wives is not without precedent in the Commonwealth, for in 1970, the legislature of Southern Australia followed the recommendation of the South Australia Law Commission[58] and extended the right of action for loss of consortium so that now it applies equally between the sexes.

Generally, *Best v. Samuel Fox* is not binding on the courts of the Commonwealth Caribbean, it being merely declaratory of the common law of England.[59] The abolition of the action in Barbados[60] seems to have been influenced by the vehemence of the speeches of the lordships in the House of Lords as much as by the traditional Barbadian affinity with things English. It is submitted that this is an appropriate case in which to depart from English precedent. In the words of Chief Justice Bollers of Guyana: 'as [our countries have] now achieved the status of complete independence, we judges will no longer consider ourselves hide-bound by English decisions, but with mature judgment in appropriate cases will strike out on our own and mould the common law to suit the needs of our ever changing society.'[61]

References

1. I am grateful to the Institute of Social Studies, through the Women and Development Studies Group at Cave Hill, for a research grant which has made this work possible, to Linda Abbensatts for her diligent research and to Dennis Morrison, attorney-at-law, for his helpful comments.

2. A good historical review of the action is that by M.D. Popescul, "Action *Per Quod Consortium Amisit*", 43 Sask. L.R. 27 (1979).
3. See generally, Holdsworth, *A History of English Law* (3rd 1966), Vol. III, at pp. 381-83; 421-33; 459-63.
4. The action was not available if the injury to his wife resulted in her death: *Baker v. Boulton* (1808) 1 Camp. 493; 170 E.R. 1033.
5. (1618), 79 E.R. 428. This case cited as authority *Chomley and Conge's Case* (1585), 74 E.R. 748, which is the first reported decision on the question of the existence of a cause of action based on injury to a wife.
6. See *Duke of Norforlk v. Germaine* (1692), 12 S. Tr. 927.
7. This action later became available to the wife also.
8. See *Midland Bank Trust Co. Ltd. v. Green (No. 3)* [1981] 3 All E.R. 744; [1982] 2 W.L.R. 1; 125 Sol. Jo. 544 (CA) in which Justice Oliver (as he then was) discusses

the fiction of the unity of husband and wife in a modern context. Affirmed [1981] 3 All E.R. 744 (C.A.).

9. These Acts were re-enacted in the then British Colonies in the Caribbean. See, e.g., Married Women's Property Act, 1887, Laws of Jamaica. See also *Marri v. Stamford Street Rwy. Co.* 78 All 582 (Conn.) 1911 in which the court considered the effect of the Married Women's Property Act. Noted 24 Harv. L. Rev. 501 (1911).
10. [1952] 2 All E.R. 394.
11. *Ibid.*, at p. 401.
12. Note that *Guy v. Livesey* (1618), 79 E.R. 428 states the injury as "for that he lost the company of his wife".
13. [1952] 2 All E.R. 394, at p. 396.
14. *Hyde v. Scyssor* (1619), 79 E.R. 462.
15. [1861] IX H.L.C. 576.
16. Ibid., at p. 598. See also *Cutts v. Chumley* [1967] 1 W.L.R. 742. The wife was hospitalised for nearly three years after an accident in which she suffered serious brain damage which reduced her intellectual capacity to that of a three year old child. The husband was awarded £5,000 for the loss of her services and £200 for the loss of her society.
17. M. Thornton, "Loss of Consortium: Inequality Before the Law", 10 Sydney L. Rev. 259 (1983).
18. (1950), 87 App. D.C. 57; 183 F. 2d. 811; (1952), 23 A.L.R. 2d. 1366.
19. *Ibid.*, at p. 1370.
20. The literal translation of the word is 'friendship'.
21. *Crabtree v. Crabtree (No. 2)*, [1964] A.L.R. 820.
22. *In the Marriage of Todd (No. 2)*, 9 A.L.R. 401. This definition was adopted by Chief Justice Douglas in *Marconi v. Marconi*, H.Ct. Barbados, No. 12 of 1986, 24.6 1986 (unreported).
23. See generally A.D. Burgess (1978), 'Judicial Precedent in the West Indies', W.I.L.J., pp. 27-36.
24. [1952] 2 All E.R. 394.
25. N.M. Forde, *Women and the Law* (1981), ISER, University of the West Indies, p. 21.
26. Accident Compensation (Reform) Act, 1980.
27. [1951] 2 K.B. 639.
28. *Gray v. Gee* (1923), 39 T.L.R. 429; *Place v. Searle* [1932] 2 K.B. 497; 101 L.J.K.B. 465; 147 L.T. 188.
29. [1952] 2 All E.R. 394. at p.
30. *Ibid.*, at p. 396.
31. See e.g. G.H.L. Fridman, "Consortium as an 'Interest' in the Law of Torts" 32 Can. Bar Rev. 1065 (1986); M.R. Little, "Consortium: A Survey of the Present Law", 19 *Journal of Family Law* (1980 -81); M. Popescul, "Action *Per Quod Consortium Amisit*", 43 Sask. L.R. 27 (1979).
32. *Gray v. Gee* (1923), 29 T.L.R. 429 failed on its facts. In *Place v. Searle* [1932] 2 K.B. 497, the statement that the wife had the same right as the husband was *obiter*.
33. (1930) 43 C.L.R. 493.
34. *Dominium*, a term in Roman law used to signify ownership of a thing.
35. (1930) 43 C.L.R. 493 at p. 505. Cited in M. Thornton, "Loss of Consortium: Inequality Before the Law", 10 Sydney L.Rev 259.
36. R. Dworkin, *Taking Rights Seriously*, London, Duckworth, 1977.
37. (1888) 13 App. Cas. 222.

38. [1983] 1 A.C. 410.
39. *Ibid.*, at p. 419. Sir George Baker, P. in *Midland Bank Trust Co. Ltd. v. Green (No. 3)* stated that "[T]he law is a living thing; it adapts and develops to fulfil the needs of living people whom it governs and serves. Like clothes it should be made to fit people". [1981] 3 All E.R. 744 at p. 751.
40. See e.g. *Lawrence v. Biddle* [1966] 1 Q.B. 504. The husband was compensated for having to perform his own household services where these had been done for him by his wife before her injury. See also *Bagias v. Smith* [1979] F.L.C. 78. The decision is preoccupied with the husband's loss notwithstanding that it was the wife who did the housework while maintaining a full-time job and looking after two young children. The examples are legion.
41. See e.g. *The Commonwealth of Dominica Constitution Order*, 1978, art. 13; *The St. Lucia Constitution Order*, 1978, art. 13; *The St. Vincent Constitution Order*, 1979, art. 13; *The Constitution of the Cooperative Republic of Guyana Act*, 1980, art. 29 and art. 40.
42. See e.g. *The Anguilla (Constitution) Order*, 1977, art. 13; *The Antigua Constitution Order*, 1967 (amended 1972 and 1978) art. 12; *The Constitution of the Commonwealth of the Bahamas* 1973, art. 26; *The Barbados Independence Order* (amended 1974) art. 26; *St. Christopher and Nevis Constitution Order*, 1967, art. 13; *The Jamaica (Constitution) Order* in Council 1962, art. 13; *The Constitution of the Republic of Trinidad and Tobago*, 1976, (amended 1978) arts. 2 and 15.
43. (1950) 23 A.L.R. 2d. 1366.
44. *Ibid.*, at p. 1368.
45. *Ibid.*, at p. 1368.
46. R.L. Jaffe, "Damages for Personal Injury: The Impact of Insurance", 18 *Law and Contemporary Legal Problems* at pp. 230-31 (1953). Cf. Note, 64 Harv. L. Rev. 672 (1951) which heartily approves of the decision.
47. See M.R. Little, "Consortium: A Survey of the Present Law", 19 *J. Family Law* 707 (1980-81).
48. See e.g. *Honey v. Sykes*, 37 D.L.R. 2 d. 225 (Sask. C.A.), a husband's action in which the observation was made *obiter*.
49. Study of the Family Law Project, Torts, Vol VI Ont. 1968, 203-04.
50. *Shwarchuk v. Hansen* (1984) 30 C.C.L.T. 121 at p. 126.
51. Constitution Act, 1982, Canada Act, 1982(U.K.)cc. 11, s. 1 - Pt 1 (Canadian Charter of Rights and Freedoms)S. 15(1).
52. (1984) 30 C.C.L.T. 121 at p. 127.
53. [1952] 2 All E.R. 394 at p. 401. See also *MacGregor on Damages*, (12th ed.) at para. 1233: The action is fully entitled: "An action *per quod consortium et servitium amisit*".
54. Cf. *State Rail Authority of New South Wales v. Sharp* [1981] 1 N.S.W.L.R. 240, in which the mother of a victim of a railway crash suffered nervous shock on hearing of the death of her daughter and was awarded substantial damages. The father of the girl brought a successful action against the defendant for loss of consortium arising from his wife's injury. This seems to be a further extension of the action.
55. It is possible to further argue that the right of the action should be extended to qualifying cohabiting relationships but it is not proposed to do so here. See *Bulloch v. United States*, D. New Jersey, 1980, 487 F. Supp. 1078. The court held that an unmarried woman could in those circumstances sue for loss of consortium of her live-in companion. See also D. Meade, "Consortium Rights of the Unmarried: Time for a Reappraisal", 15 3 F.L.Q. 223 (1981). See also Bromley & Lowe, *Bromley's Family*, 7th edn, at p. 120. The authors take the opposite view.

56. *Guy v. Livesey* (1618), 79 E.R. 428.
57. *Hyde v. Scyssor* (1619), 79 E.R. 462.
58. *11th Report of the Law Reform Commission of Southern Australia*, 1970.
59. The situation is complicated by those Caribbean jurisdictions whose statute law includes an open reception provision, enacting that "the law of England (in a particular area of law) from time to time in force shall be the law of X". See generally, K.W. Patchett (1973), Reception of Law in the West Indies, Jamaica Law Journal, April 17-35; October 55-67.
60. Accident Compensation (Reform) Act, No. 60 of 1980.
61. *Persaud v. Plantation Versailles Ltd.* (1971) 17 W.I.R. 107 at p. 118.

Violence against Women

Some Legal Responses

Suzanne Ffolkes

Introduction

Women in the Caribbean are particularly susceptible to many forms of violence, both mental and physical. There are many theories explaining this acute problem, ranging from colonialism to masochism. Whatever the causes, it is a fact that domestic violence, rape and incest are the most prevalent forms of violence perpetrated against women, although reported cases of other forms of violence related to these categories are on the increase. These related problems are domestic violence resulting in death or maiming, rape of wives, abuse of the elderly (particularly women), violence by and among women and increasing suicide among women. Apart from women charged with drug-trafficking, usually for men, women charged with crimes of passion constitute the largest number of women in prisons (Morgan, 1991).

The legislative bodies have been slow to respond to both the causes and effects of the unique problems which arise as a result of violence against women. It may be argued that the slow responses to this form of violence has been partly due to societal tolerance, at one end, and the fact that it is largely hidden, at the other. The lack of statistical data related to violence against women and the paucity of literature dealing with the problem in the Caribbean support this. It cannot be denied, however, that the lobbying of the many women's groups and organisations has resulted in a move in the Caribbean to reform laws or to create new ones to deal specifically with the protection of women against violence.

Nevertheless, it is not sufficient to focus on legal issues alone. Medical and sociological issues need also to be taken into account in any reform initiative. To ignore the physical, psychological and social impact which violence has on a woman and the context in which it occurs is to defeat the whole purpose of granting legal action. Without a holistic approach, legal change will make no difference.

It was once thought that violence consisted only of the unlawful exercise of physical force. This legal definition, however, does not reflect the modern approach to violence, particularly as it affects women. The current approach which the law takes in certain circumstances is that violence includes physical, emotional and mental abuse, including sexual or other types of harassment. Indeed, under the Barbados Domestic Violence (Protection Orders) Act, 1992, "harassment", which is considered a form of domestic violence, includes the intimidation of a person by persistent verbal abuse, threats of physical violence, etc.[1] Violence, therefore, can be seen as actual or threatened, physical, mental or emotional, but always having as its basis the use of power.

This paper will focus on four main categories of violence, highlighting their legal responses. These categories are: domestic violence, rape and incest, along with other social sexual offences. Whether the legal responses adequately take into account medical and social considerations will be questioned.

1. Domestic violence

"Wife" beating is the most common form of domestic violence in the Caribbean. The reasons for this form of violence against women in the home, whether in a marital situation or not, have been subject to very little research. The causes suggested by various sources, however, can be narrowed down to the following:

a. Pathological (i.e. a mental illness suggesting that the answer to the problem is medical treatment).

b. Psychological predisposition on the part of both the abuser as well as the victim.

c. Tradition and behaviourism (i.e. violence begets violence in the home, generation after generation).

d. Structural, e.g. the pressures of society, dehumanising conditions and the economy, thus men use violence as a means of relieving their social frustrations.

e. Male supremacy based on culture and accepted as a part of life.

f. Substance abuse.

g. Media portrayal of relationships which include violent scenes, often related to sex, on screen or on the television. Some songs, dance hall and calypso in particular, support woman beating.

All these theories seem to have a good measure of validity and the better view seems to be that it may be any of these factors or a combination of them (Seebaran-Suite 1990).

Unfortunately, most of the legislative bodies in the Commonwealth Caribbean have been slow to respond in terms of deterrence and punishment. Where they have responded, the causes are not addressed. This may be explained by the fact that the problem has in the past been largely hidden due to societal attitudes which result in shame or acceptance on the part of the victims. A further problem is the police's reluctance to interfere in domestic disputes. Caribbean society tends to tolerate such abuses mainly because traditionally the vast majority of women either feel that the man has the right to behave that way or that it shows that he loves them or that they are so dependent that they cannot "afford" to report it. It cannot be denied, however, that there is now a growing awareness of the severity and prevalence of the problem because of the effects that domestic violence has both physically and mentally not only on the women, but on the entire family.

Effects of domestic violence

Medical evidence suggests that the pattern of injuries inflicted on women who are victims of chronic battering include broken limbs, injuries to the head, abdomen and rib area, permanent injury to the eyesight and hearing, broken noses and knocked-out teeth. Extreme cases may result in complications in a woman's reproductive organs or death (Seebaran-Suite 1990). This is not to discount the mental and emotional effects of battering in the home. Limited evidence suggests that the mental effects of physical violence on the victims are isolation and insecurity. Extreme cases may lead to suicide. It also may affect the children, in that the girls may have difficulty in their relationships with men either by becoming victims themselves or being non-committal. The boys may repeat what they see at home on becoming adults and in a sense may be considered to be victims as well. One need only imagine the negative impact this has on society as a whole.

Legal responses to domestic violence

It is important to note that redress for victims of domestic violence in most Commonwealth Caribbean territories can only be found under the heading of assault and battery. These charges may be laid under criminal law or civil law. Assault is defined as an attempt or offer to beat another without touching him, and though no actual suffering is proved, the party injured may have redress by action for damages as a compensation for the injury, or nominally by criminal prosecution. Battery is defined as the unlawful beating of another and includes the least touching of another's person willfully or in anger.

A criminal charge of assault and battery may be brought by police or as a private complaint. As mentioned earlier, however, there are many deterrents against charges being laid by either the victim or the police. Victims may be afraid, insecure or so economically dependent that they will not readily report abuse, as incarceration of the abuser may do more harm than good. Police officers are reluctant due to the nature of the crime, because victims retract their stories as readily as they give them or because they are "wife" beaters themselves.

Alternatively, a civil charge of assault and battery may be made. However, the main deterrent is the high cost of bringing the action. It is also very time-consuming and technical. Enforcement in terms of injunctive relief may prove difficult since, if there is a breach of the injunction, the victim will have to return to court for the purpose of charging the abuser with contempt of court. Even if this ordeal is undertaken, the result will be that the offender/abuser will be imprisoned which may not be desirable, especially in cases where the victim and her family depend economically on the offender.

One answer to the inadequate legal response has been the institution of legislation which deals specifically with domestic violence as an offence. This approach has been attempted recently in Trinidad and Tobago and in Barbados by the enactment of the Domestic Violence Act, 1991, and the Domestic Violence (Protection Orders) Act, 1992, respectively. These Acts attempt to strike a balance between the competing ethics of protecting persons against abuse and preserving the family unit.

These domestic violence Acts are not punitive in nature, in terms of the criminal sanctions which flow from a criminal charge of assault and battery. They are preventative in that they grant personal protection orders to the victim. A protection order restrains a person who has engaged in or threatens to engage in conduct which is capable of constituting a criminal offence or an attempt to commit a criminal offence. The respective domestic violence Acts refer specifically to the protection of spouses and former spouses (a term which includes couples living together as husband and wife), a child of that person or some other member of the household under any law.[2] Harassment is included as grounds for an application for this Order, which includes intimidation by the use of, *inter alia,* persistent verbal abuse and threats of physical damage.[3]

The court must be satisfied that the person against whom the protection order is requested, has done the above and that, unless restrained, is likely to engage in further conduct that would constitute that or another offence. The standard of proof that is required under civil law, that is on a balance of probabilities, is a much less onerous standard than that required under the criminal law, which is beyond a reasonable doubt. The granting of the protection order is discretionary, and the court takes into account a number of factors including the preservation of the family unit and any hardship that will be caused to the abuser.[4] The wide range of possible applicants addresses the problem of victims who are reluctant to report the violence. In Barbados, these include a spouse, former spouse, any other member of the household, child care officer and commissioner of police. In Trinidad and Tobago, the list of possible applicants includes, *inter alia* , a police officer and a partner of a spouse.[5]

Other sociological considerations are reflected in the flexibility of the Order. For example, the Order may restrain the abuser from being on the premises on which the complainant for the protection order resides or works or where the child in respect of whom the order was made resides or goes to school. It may also restrain the abuser from entering or remaining at the said premises of residence while intoxicated or under the influence of drugs. In Barbados the Order may also require the abuser to pay the rent, mortgage or utilities even though he may be required to leave the premises.[6] This too, takes into account the reality of dependence on the part of many victims as a deterrent to reporting domestic violence.

Police intervention is encouraged by the Acts due to provisions which allow the police to enter premises without a warrant where the officer's assistance has been requested by the victim. He may also make an arrest without a warrant where he believes, on reasonable grounds, that the offence is threatened or has been committed.[7]

There is a general prohibition of the publication of the identity of the parties to proceedings in connection with a protection order. This also serves to encourage complaints and therefore effective protection.

Despite the many criticisms levelled at this novel legislative attempt to combat family violence, the fact that many sociological issues are addressed in the legislation is commendable. In Puerto Rico where an even more daring approach in terms of domestic violence legislation has been taken, the protective order has been widely used and the number of reported cases of domestic violence has sky-rocketed.[8]

Lamentably, these new laws do not address the medical problems associated with domestic violence. These initiatives need to be married to a network of protection through social agencies, the police and medical centres to address the problem. Although women may have more opportunity under the law to address domestic violence, if there is no support from the medical community in terms of treatment for both the abuser and the victim, society as a whole is no better off.

2. Rape

The most devastating sexual offence perpetrated against women is the crime of rape. The legal definition of rape is sexual intercourse with another person without the consent of that person and knowing that that person does not consent to the intercourse or is reckless as to whether that person consents to the intercourse.[9] Rape is a common occurrence in the Caribbean. For example, in Jamaica, statistics show that a woman is raped every eight hours.

There is no acceped explanation for this crime, nor are there any wholly satisfactory ones. Indeed, there is a grave need for sociological research on the phenomenon of sexual offences against women, and in particular rape. What must be emphasised, however, is that rape is a form of violence and not, as many believe, an act motivated by lust.

Treatment of rape victims: From the police station to the courts

The many misunderstandings surrounding the motive for rape are reflected in the legal system. Often a woman who has been raped, is treated with a great degree of insensitivity, from the interview with the police, to the medical examination, to the court room. To begin with, no special police rape unit exists in most of the territories, save for Jamaica. The results of this is that most victims are first interviewed by a male police officer, who may be insensitive towards the victim and may even add to the trauma by blaming her or making snide remarks, reflecting general societal attitudes towards victims. Identification parades may cause further emotional trauma for the victim who has to face and in some cases even touch the offender. A one-way mirror could solve the problem. Medical examinations may also add to the trauma, in that in many territories there is no specialised treatment from sensitised medical practitioners. The victim needs both a psychological as well as a physical examination along with counselling. A victim needs also to be informed of her right to demand her choice of doctor and, indeed, a lawyer.

In Jamaica, the problem has been addressed by the implementation of the Police Rape Unit, in which police officers, most of whom are women, are trained to counsel and refer the victims to special doctors. The success of the Unit is reflected by the increased number of reported cases of rape since its inception.

Legal responses to rape

Rape is dealt with in most Caribbean territories as a criminal offence under the Offences Against the Person Act. This is an Act derived from English statute law. There is, regrettably, no definition of rape in these Acts. However, the common definition that is derived from cases and precedent, not statute, is adopted. The only difference between the definition of rape at common law and that provided for above under the Barbados Sexual Offences Act, 1992, is that at common law the offence is limited to a man as the offender and a woman as the victim whereas under the Barbados legislation the word "person" is used for both. The Barbados legislation therefore recognises the possibility of a woman raping a man and a man raping a man.[10] The punishment in most jurisdictions is life imprisonment.

The main problem with the prosecution of rape lies not in the definition, but in proving lack of consent. Proof of lack of consent is notoriously difficult as the nature of the crime is such that it does not admit of witnesses. Further, a man may very well plead that he believed that the woman was consenting, as all that the law requires is that he knew or was reckless. This indicates a very subjective view of the act and, indeed, the common law affirms this view by stating that the offender is not guilty as long as he believed there was consent, no matter how unreasonable.[11]

Does this mean that medical evidence to the contrary is of no effect once the accused states his "honest" belief that the victim was consenting? The Barbados Sexual Offences Act, 1992, states instances in which the victim is deemed not to have given consent. These include intimidation or force and threats, not only to the complainant but to a person other than the complainant, fear of bodily harm, fraudulent representations as to the nature and quality of the act or, in the case of a married woman, by impersonating her husband.[12]

Another sore point with the common law as it relates to rape is that of the immunity of husbands from a prosecution for rape of their wives. Indeed, most reform initiatives maintain this except where the husband and wife are separated. Separated as defined in the Barbados Sexual Offences Act, 1992, is having a decree *nisi* of divorce, a separation order, a separation agreement or an order for the husband not to molest or have sexual intercourse with his wife.[13] The view seems to be that if sexual offences bills establish that a husband may be prosecuted for raping his wife, this will not be passed by Parliament. This fear suggests three things:

a. that most parliamentarians are men;

b. that there is still the belief that a wife is her husband's property; and

c. that rape is not an act of violence.

Indeed, many acts of domestic violence culminate in what would be considered rape, were the persons involved not married.

However, an encouraging case from the United Kingdom suggests the possibility of a husband raping his wife at common law. The House of Lords decided in the case of *R v. R14* that a husband could in fact rape his wife. The learned law lords there stated that where the United Kingdom Sexual Offences (Amendment) Act 1976, which restates the common law, defines rape as having "unlawful" intercourse with a woman without her consent, it does not mean "outside marriage". This is highly persuasive authority, although our region is not bound by the decision.

The issue of rape within marriage is crucial particularly as the implications of rape, whether by a stranger or a husband, now go far beyond emotional and psychological destruction of a woman to include the fear of AIDS, which is fatal.

Additionally, the judge in a rape trial is required by law to warn a jury against conviction where there is no corroboration of the complainant's story. In the peculiar circumstance of rape, it is unlikely that there would be any witnesses, yet in most jurisdictions this warning serves only to prejudice the trial in favour of the accused. The corroboration warning should be abolished for rape cases.[15]

It is also possible that defence counsel may be insensitive to a victim's feelings so that cross-examination may be so fierce as, in effect, to put the victim on trial. Indeed, a victim's sexual history may be brought into evidence. However, the Barbados Sexual Offences Act, 1992, states that a complainant's sexual history is inadmissible, save in certain specified circumstances.[16] The ordeal is heightened with respect to children who are victims of rape. Due to time lapses and numerous court appearances, they may have to repeat details. The negative psychological effect on such victims cannot be over-emphasised.

A further problem is lack of anonymity which is the norm, save in Trinidad and Tobago, Barbados and St Lucia. This can only deter a complainant from prosecuting. The risk of losing the case is high, and the only result may be that she is ostracised by her community and possibly the public at large. Recent legislative reform therefore guarantees anonymity for both parties during the fraudulent representations as to the nature and quality of the act or, in the case of a married woman, by impersonating her husband.[12]

Another sore point with the common law as it relates to rape is that of the immunity of husbands from a prosecution for rape of their wives. Indeed, most reform initiatives maintain this except where the husband and wife are separated. Separated as defined in the Barbados Sexual Offences Act, 1992, is having a decree nisi of divorce, a separation order, a separation agreement or an order for the husband not to molest or have sexual intercourse with his wife.[13] The view seems to be that if sexual offences bills establish that a husband may be prosecuted for raping his wife, this will not be passed by Parliament. This fear suggests three things:

a. that most parliamentarians are men;

b. that there is still the belief that a wife is her husband's property; and

c. that rape is not an act of violence.

Indeed, many acts of domestic violence culminate in what would be considered rape, were the persons involved not married.

However, an encouraging case from the United Kingdom suggests the possibility of a husband raping his wife at common law. The House of Lords decided in the case of *R v. R14* that a husband could in fact rape his wife. The learned law lords there stated that where the United Kingdom Sexual Offences (Amendment) Act 1976, which restates the common law, defines rape as having "unlawful" intercourse with a woman without her consent, it does not mean "outside marriage". This is highly persuasive authority, although our region is not bound by the decision.

The issue of rape within marriage is crucial particularly as the implications of rape, whether by a stranger or a husband, now go far beyond emotional and psychological destruction of a woman to include the fear of AIDS, which is fatal.

Additionally, the judge in a rape trial is required by law to warn a jury against conviction where there is no corroboration of the complainant's story. In the peculiar circumstance of rape, it is unlikely that there would be any witnesses, yet in most jurisdictions this warning serves only to prejudice the trial in favour of the accused. The corroboration warning should be abolished for rape cases.[15]

It is also possible that defence counsel may be insensitive to a victim's feelings so that cross-examination may be so fierce as, in effect, to put the victim on trial. Indeed, a victim's sexual history may be brought into evidence. However, the Barbados Sexual Offences Act, 1992, states that a complainant's sexual history is inadmissible, save in certain specified circumstances.[16] The ordeal is heightened with respect to children who are victims of rape. Due to time lapses and numerous court appearances, they may have to repeat details. The negative psychological effect on such victims cannot be over-emphasised.

A further problem is lack of anonymity which is the norm, save in Trinidad and Tobago, Barbados and St Lucia. This can only deter a complainant from prosecuting. The risk of losing the case is high, and the only result may be that *c. Indecent assault*

Indecent assault means an assault accompanied by words or circumstances indicating an indecent intention. In most Caribbean territories this is a crime. However, consent may be open to the offender as a defence, once the victim is over 16 years of age. If a male is under 24 years of age and his defence is that he honestly believed the girl to be 16 years of age, he may walk away free. "Protection" is therefore afforded to males under 24, but not to women over sixteen. More recent legislation, however, does away with this "protection" for males, although 16 is maintained as the age at which a woman can give 'consent'.[23]

d. Serious indecency

Serious indecency is an act, whether natural or unnatural, by a person involving the use of the genital organs for the purpose of arousing or gratifying sexual desire. This is a new offence and the level of punishment depends on whether the victim is under or over 16 years of age. Inciting another to commit this act is also an offence.[24]

Conclusion

The legal response to violence against women in all its destructive forms is becoming more creative. This is true particularly in the light of recent legislative developments which take into account a woman's psychological distress upon becoming a victim. This is not to say, however, that the responses do not still have a long way to go.

a. Only a few Caribbean territories have passed legislation specifically dealing with the problem of violence against women.

b. These Acts, although progressive, still do not address all the effects of violence against women, whether physical or social.

c. The police system dealing with such acts of violence is highly inadequate in that in most territories police are not trained specifically to deal with such cases.

d. Doctors to whom these victims are referred by the police are not necessarily sensitive to the circumstances of the victim.

e. The court system is also unsympathetic to victims, particularly of rape.

f. The medical and legal responses often ignore the needs of the offenders.

g. Caribbean society as a whole tolerates to a great degree violence against women.

References

1. See also the Domestic Violence Act, 1991, Trinidad and Tobago.
2. See for example S. 4, Domestic Violence (Protection Orders) Act, 1992, Barbados.
3. See for example S. 3, Domestic Violence (Protection Orders) Act, 1992, Barbados.
4. See S. 7, Domestic Violence (Protection Orders) Act, 1992, Barbados, and S. 6 Domestic Violence Act, 1991, Trinidad and Tobago.
5. See, for example, S. 7, Domestic Violence (Protection Orders) Act, 1992, Barbados.
6. S4, Domestic Violence (Protection Orders) Act, 1992, Barbados.
7. See for example S. 4, Domestic Violence (Protection Orders) Act, 1992, Barbados.
8. The Domestic Violence and Matrimonial Proceedings Act 1984, St Vincent and the Grenadines, seeks to protect victims of domestic violence in a marital situation by issuing an injunction to restrain the other party or against a child, or excluding the violent part from the matrimonial home.
9. S.3 (1), Sexual Offences Act, 1992, Barbados.
10. In fact, "rape" is redefined in S. 3 (6) of the Barbados Sexual Offences Act, 1992, to include oral or anal penetration.
11. *Morgan v. Director of Public Prosecutions* (1975), 2 All E.R. 347.
12. S. 3 (2).
13. S. 3 (4).
14. (1991) 4 All E.R. 481.
15. As has been done by the Sexual Offences Act, 1992, Barbados.
16. S. 26.
17. See for example, S. 35, Sexual Offences Act, 1992, Barbados.
18. See S. 30, Sexual Offences Act, 1992, Barbados.
19. *Dimes* (1911) 7 Cr. App. Rep. 43.
20. S. 6(3), Sexual Offences Act, 1992, Barbados.
21. S. 7, Sexual Offences Act, 1992, Barbados.
22. S. 7, Sexual Offences Act, 1992 Barbados.
23. Compare S. 53, Offences Against the Person Act, Jamaica, with S. 11, Sexual Offences Act, 1992 Barbados.
24. S. 12, Sexual Offences Act, 1992 Barbados.

Books/ Papers

Morgan, V. *Violence against Women in Jamaica. The Situation and Who is Addressing it.* Jamaica, Bureau of Women's Affairs 1991.

Seebaran-Suite, L. "Legal and Other Strategies to Combat Family Violence in Trinidad and Tobago", paper presented to Women and Development Studies, Faculty of Law Seminar, Barbados 1990.

Part THREE

Gender Perspectives in Education

Gender Perspectives in Education

Introduction

Barbara Bailey

The papers included in this part are drawn from those presented at two of the seminars associated with the Women and Development Studies Project: the Interdisciplinary Seminar and the Gender and Education Seminar held in Jamaica in 1987 and 1989 respectively. These seminars provided a platform for exploring some gender issues that have some considerable impact on the educational process at all levels.

Marlene Hamilton reports on a historical review of the extent to which opportunities for education were made available to female students in Jamaica for three periods during the time of British rule: pre-emancipation (1655-1833); post-emancipation (1834-99); and pre-independence (1900-61). The content of the curriculum offered to girls at these periods is examined and assessed in terms of the changing roles of women in society over those years.

The information provided in this paper points to the fact that in the early years the opportunity for education discriminated in favour of the white elite population, and boys. The few opportunities that existed for girls prepared them for domestic roles or for a limited range of gender-appropriate occupations.

Provision of education for the slave population coincided with emancipation in 1834. In the years following, the opportunity for secondary education increased but continued to be the preserve of the white population. The curriculum at both levels was clearly segregated along sex lines and prepared girls and boys from the two social strata for gender-linked occupations related to their social status.

These trends, established at the elementary and secondary levels, were perpetuated in the first half of the twentieth century. By 1948 the University College of the West Indies had been established; although initially the student population was mainly male, females rapidly took advantage of it for professional development. This signalled the start of the limited entry of females into previously male-dominated areas such as the civil service and professions such as medicine and law.

Barbara Bailey's paper picks up on the analysis started by Hamilton and focuses on the current situation and the continuing sex segregation of the curriculum at the secondary level. The discussion is extended to the subsequent under-representation of girls in the technical areas of a post-secondary training programme and the implications for employment opportunities for girls.

The consequences of these patterns of education and training for both sexes are presented. The situation of girls is highlighted in relation to the fact that labour market statistics for Jamaica indicate that feminised occupational areas are over-subscribed. The preparation of girls in schools along traditional lines therefore not only perpetuates sex-stereotyping but is self-defeating. Suggestions of initiatives that could be introduced to break this cycle are made by the author.

Kathleen Drayton's paper, "White Man's Knowledge: Sex, Race and Class in Caribbean English-language Textbooks", focuses on another important curriculum issue: the power of textbooks to perpetuate eurocentric and patriarchal biases in contemporary Caribbean society. The Marxist theories of capitalism and the sexual division of labour are presented, providing the framework for examining the intersection of race, class and gender in both the textual and non-textual elements of the texts.

Drayton argues that, in spite of the demise of colonialism, Caribbean society is dominated by the few in powerful positions and that this is perpetuated through social institutions such as the school. Textbooks are a universal vehicle and tool in the socialisation process, which is confirmed by the results of the analyses presented.

The concern of Ewart Taylor's paper is the under-representation of women at all levels of school administration. A review of worldwide literature and survey data undertaken by the author shows that there was a strong tendency, especially before the mid-1980s, for women to be under-represented in practical educational administration and related research publications. The data presented for Trinidad and Tobago substantiate these trends.

Two associated concepts are used to explain this phenomenon. The first of these is the fact of exclusion, which prohibits women access to administrative posts. The second is isolation, that is, the reduction of substantive decision-making functions by women relative to men in similar positions.

In the final section of the paper, the author examines theories that purport to explain gender bias. Recommendations are made for how women may work to improve their numbers and make substantive contributions to the theory and practice of educational administration.

The Availability and Suitability of Educational Opportunities for Jamaican Female Students

An Historical Overview

Marlene Hamilton

Pre-emancipation Provisions

According to the historian Frank Cundall[1], the earliest reference to education in Jamaica is in 1663, eight years after the English conquest of the island, when a warrant was issued for a bill to be prepared authorising the Treasurer of the Exchequer to pay the sum of £500 annually to five ministers of religion and one schoolmaster serving in the new colony. Such records as are available suggest that there were for most of the remaining years of the 17th century few children of school age in Jamaica, and little interest in their education was being demonstrated on the island. Those parents who could afford it, sent their sons back to the "mother country" for their schooling[2], and others hired private tutors or else (as was the case for the less affluent) sent them to one of the few free schools erected from the various educational bequests made by local notables.[3]

There is ample evidence that the few provisions made for education at that time were reserved for whites (largely children of poor parentage) and mostly white boys specifically, although one or two bequests did mention the education of girls. Charles Drax's will, for example, dated 1721 directed that: "A charitable school should be established in the said parish of St. Ann for maintaining and educating eight poor boys and four poor girls belonging to the said parish as well as for other charitable purposes."[4]

However, funds from such bequests or trusts were allowed to lie dormant, were misappropriated or mismanaged; and as Cundall pointed out: "By the end of the 17th century, the need of education for the sons and daughters of the colonists must have become pressing."[5]

Leslie's review of education during the first half of the eighteenth century is enlightening.[6] In his words: "Learning is here at the lowest Ebb; there is no public School in the whole Island, neither do they seem fond of the thing; several large Donations have been made for such Uses, but have never taken Effect."[7]

According to Leslie, the young white boy until the age of seven or eight: "diverts himself with the Negroes, acquires their broken way of talking, their Manner of Behaviour, and all the Vices which these unthinking Creatures can teach: Then perhaps he goes to School; but young Master must not be converted; if he learns, 'tis well; if not, it can't be helped."[8]

The same author writes about young white girls:

> Some of the Ladies read, they all dance a great deal, coquet much, dress for Admirers, and at last, for the most part, run away with the most insignificant of their humble Servants. Their Education consists entirely in acquiring these little Arts. 'Tis a thousand Pities they do not improve their Minds, as well as their Bodies; they would be charming Creatures indeed.[9]

One of the few endowed schools of the era which was to survive was Wolmer's Free School, established in 1736 from a bequest made in John Wolmer's will, dated 1729, for "the foundation of a Free School in the Parish where I shall happen to Dye".[10] There was no mention in Wolmer's will of the exclusion of any class or sex of student, yet not unexpectedly during the first 34 years of its existence only boys were admitted. At the time in fact, for perhaps the first century of its operation (at least) the aim of Wolmer's Free School was to offer a classical education to young gentlemen so that they would be properly fitted to take their place in society.[11]

It was only in 1770 that girls were accepted as scholars at Wolmer's for the first time, and even then a modified curriculum was designed on their behalf. It was felt that many of the subjects taught boys (for example, navigation) would bear no relevance to the future life of the "weaker sex": instead, while they were offered "instruction in Reading, Writing and [surprisingly] Accounts",[12] they were also taught the more feminine skills of needlework and the like in preparation for running a home (some could, as a result, marry respectably), or to enable them to gain employment as seamstresses and mantuamakers. The Kingston Common Council's Minutes of 10 August 1818 actually state that "girls are not to return to the afternoon session since they must go elsewhere to learn needlework".

Whereas no records have been located to indicate whether, indeed, girls were actually able to marry respectably or find work as seamstresses and mantuamakers, it documented that the boys were "generally sought after by storekeepers in Kingston"[13] as well as in great demand as tradesmen, schoolmasters and recruits for the Royal Navy. There is the suggestion that some girls secured teaching jobs at Wolmer's and elsewhere, their training being derived from the monitorial system inaugurated around 1820 at the school, whereby monitors assisted in teaching some of the younger children.

Interestingly, one of the earliest references to formal teacher training in Jamaica is of a "training place for female teachers" started in 1829 at New Carmel. In 1833 the Moravians opened a college in Refuge to train "brown women as teachers". Both of these ventures were, however, short-lived.

The period, 1834 – 1900

It is a general view that "until Emancipation Day in 1834, there was no question of an education system" in Jamaica.[14] However, a type of elementary education for the newly freed gradually evolved in the years following emancipation, managed initially by the missionary societies, and taken over by the state by the 1860s. The curriculum centred on the three Rs, together with religious education, for it was felt that this represented an "appropriate form of schooling for children whom the legislators hoped would become estate labourers".[15] Sometimes other subjects such as geography and history were added, but the content of these was learnt by rote. The main curricular differences which evolved in the training of the sexes were related to the introduction of agriculture and other forms of manual (industrial) instructions for boys, and, for girls, sewing and the domestic sciences.

The Lumb Report of 1898 formalised this in the recommendation that: "Domestic economy and household duties should be taught to girls from the three upper classes (of elementary schools)."[16] It also suggested that women teachers should: "take part and receive instruction in . . . cooking, laundry work and domestic arrangements".[17] The Report called for sewing to be confined to: "plain sewing, cutting and repair of garments and knitting of useful articles. [Further] all women teachers should teach it without addition to their ordinary salaries."[18]

The recommendation for agricultural instruction to be given to both boys and girls, was important; it should be taught in "such a manner as to overcome the prevalent distaste for these pursuits so essential to the economic standards of Jamaica and its citizens".[19] This was felt to be particularly necessary, since, according to Lumb: "the present system of education tends to encourage a distaste for manual labour in favour of clerkship and such occupations, and to create an exodus from the country into towns".[20]

During the post-emancipation period the type of secondary education offered at schools such as Wolmer's continued to discriminate between boys and girls, although both sexes were felt to be getting a "plain, but sound English education".[21] The boys were exposed to a classical education of sorts, and the emphasis for girls was still on domestic duties, although there is mention of those in the upper class of Wolmer's being taught French in 1837, and music and drill in 1887,[22] no doubt these were subjects considered as accomplishments suited for young ladies of the day.

In 1879 Wolmer's was put on a much firmer footing as a secondary-level institution after the establishment of the Jamaica Schools Commission. In 1894 it was reorganised to provide two sides of training—classical and commercial—the latter including "in addition to the usual subjects, typewriting and shorthand, or such other similar subjects" for girls.[23] This served to emphasise the differences in the vocations which Wolmer's graduates were expected to engage in, girls being trained now for secretarial work in addition to homemaking skills.

There seems to have been some effort to do away with such discriminatory practices at the turn of the century, for, in 1900, the by-laws of Wolmer's state that: "The school shall be so worked as to give the girls access to teaching of the same kind given to the boys, in cases where it is desired or thought likely to help the future career of such girls, while at the same time, special subjects suitable to the girls shall also be taught."[24]

Nonetheless, these by-laws reveal a prevailing, condescending attitude to girls in the statement that: "Girls who are candidates for election as Foundationers or Exhibitioners shall be required to pass the same examinations (as boys) with the omission of Latin, Algebra and Geometry, and for girls over 11, the alteration of the standard in Arithmetic to that for boys a year younger."[25]

When the Cambridge Local Examinations were introduced in Jamaica in 1882, the candidates were all male. In 1890, however, 12 girls entered, in addition to 38 boys, with seven girls and 30 boys passing.[26] However, for all of the closing years of the nineteenth century the Jamaica Scholarship, which was first offered in 1881, was awarded to boys. (In fact, it was not until 1903 that a girl won this scholarship for the first time.)[27]

The Higher Schools' Examination was first held in 1892, and the first female entered in 1896. The government made a special grant towards the expenses of her examination, and was duly rewarded when she passed in the third class in mathematics, psychology, English history and constitutional history.[28]

Any references to post-emancipation education must include the teachers needed to work the system. Shortly after 1834, the importance of training native teachers was recognised,[29] and in 1836 the Mico Charity established a normal school (teachers' college) for this purpose. In its first year Mico was co-educational, with 21 men and seven women registered, but shortly afterwards, only men were accepted. In 1861 the Bethabara (Bethlehem) Training College was opened to train female teachers for the infant school, and in 1885, as a result of recommendations from the *Report upon the Condition of the Juvenile Population in Jamaica*, 1879, Shortwood Training College was started, also to train women. In 1897, another teachers' college for women, St Joseph's, was opened.

As a result the proportion of women to men in the teaching profession rose considerably towards the end of the nineteenth century. An indication of the shift in numbers is shown below.[30]

Year	MALES		FEMALES	
	No.	%	No.	%
1875	89	93.7	6	6.3
1880	75	90.4	8	9.6
1885	112	75.5	36	24.3
1890	81	65.9	42	34.1
1895	137	70.3	58	29.7
1900	76	58.0	55	42.0

There were disparities in the salaries given to male and female teachers; and even when the recommendation was put forward for fixed salaries to be paid teachers in the Lumb Report[31], the scales suggested for each sex were different, as shown below.

Size of School Population	Recommended Salaries for Heads	
	Males	Females
50 - 80	£50	£36
301 - 400	£120	£80
Recommended salaries for assistants	£35 – 45	£25 – 30

The Twentieth century up to Independence

Schooling in this period in the main perpetuated nineteenth century aims, reflected in the statement: "Let them receive such an education as would benefit their station in life."[32]

This held true particularly for the elementary school, where, in addition to reading and recitation, writing and English, arithmetic and Scripture, provisions at the turn of the century named manual training and agriculture (which was "open to girls").[33] The emphasis placed on agricultural education was because thinkers of the day believed that:

> Absolutely nothing was done in most instances here to help boys and girls while at school to prepare directly for their future work in life . . . (Hence, plans were put afoot to) . . . combine a fair amount of intellectual training in the primary schools of Jamaica, with such training, both theoretical and practical, as will directly help to fit children for taking an increasingly intelligent interest in agriculture and handicrafts.[34]

There was, however, strong resistance to any form of agricultural training (a feature which was carried over from the nineteenth century view that agricultural work was synonymous with slavery). The elementary schools' syllabuses for the period from 1910 to the 1950s reveal the efforts made to include agricultural education in the elementary science curriculum and to devise a special science course for elementary schoolgirls in the upper division, which strongly reflected homemaking skills.

This so-called science course was, in fact, intended to provide preliminary training for household help, which could be upgraded at institutions such as the Girls' Industrial School at Shortwood or the Practical Training Centre for Girls at Carron Hall (originally designed as a centre to train girls as the future wives of farmers). The Kandel Report of 1943 pointed out that the latter: "has a great opportunity for training young women as intelligent homemakers, as district visitors, as assistants to social welfare visitors, and, with further preparation, as teachers of housecraft. Unfortunately, the school has come to be regarded as an institution for training superior domestic servants."[35]

As a result it was suggested that the term "domestic science" be changed to "household arts" or "housecraft" both at Carron Hall and in the other schools offering the subject.

The Kandel Report further called the senior schools or departments (which evolved out of the higher grades of the elementary schools) to: "add a variety of types of practical work—wood and metal work for boys, handicrafts and housecraft for girls, and in rural areas some agriculture for both. On the senior school would be built the practical training centres and vocational schools (industrial and commercial schools) for boys and girls."[36]

The West India Royal Commission of 1938-39[37] had already recommended formalised training in domestic science and child welfare for elementary schoolgirls and that, although the literary curriculum should be the same for boys and girls, vocational subjects (such as domestic science) should be taught to girls from an earlier age. The Stockdale Report of 1940-42[38], along similar lines, strongly supported the need for girls to be trained to take part in the tasks that should normally fall to a woman in a household.

In 1944 another report, *A Plan for Post-Primary Education in Jamaica*,[39] attempted to translate the principles laid down by Kandel into concrete plans. The relevant recommendations were, for domestic subjects to be taught to elementary schoolgirls, and for all post-primary institutions to follow a "common core" curriculum, which should include practical activities (gardening for boys, and handicrafts and homecrafts for girls).

A number of secondary girls' schools such as Wolmer's had already institutionalised the teaching of domestic subjects before the 1944 Plan. In the early years of the twentieth century such subjects were apparently offered as options to be taken during out-of-school hours. After being inspected by H. H. Piggott, Visiting Inspector for Schools, UK, in 1911,[40] and in response to his recommendation that domestic science should be made compulsory in the middle and lower sections of all girls' schools, Wolmer's Girls' School set about including the subject, along with needlework, in its regular curriculum. In succeeding years, funds were collected for the erection of a domestic science building which was eventually completed and opened in 1942.

Along with its early and continued emphasis on the domestic arts and later, on commercial subjects (long before Wolmer's Boys' School introduced a technical stream in its curriculum[41]), it must be acknowledged that Wolmer's Girls' School also offered training in the sciences, including chemistry, from the 1900s. In this respect, the school was remarkably forward-looking, since for most of the period 1900-60 the only science subjects which girls were taught at most of the other secondary schools were biology and health science. It is not surprising, therefore, that more and more girls from Wolmer's (and from some other schools), began entering for subjects such as chemistry, which were at one time considered the domain of men rather than women in external examinations. Despite this trend, however, up to independence generally Jamaican girls entered for, and passed, more arts subjects at Senior Cambridge and Higher Schools, than boys, who continued to dominate the field in the sciences.

When the region eventually obtained its own university, the University College of the West Indies (UCWI), situated at Mona, Jamaica, this trend was perpetuated right up to independence, and afterwards. At the outset, in 1948, the UCWI's student enrolment was largely male in all faculties, since at that time university education was considered the privilege of men rather than women. In time, the numerical composition sorted itself out, revealing that women represented the majority in non-science-based faculties, while men predominated in the science-based ones.

This was the converse of what was happening in the teachers' colleges: the trend at the end of the nineteenth century for more and more women to enter teaching was to escalate in the twentieth century. Although all new teacher training colleges built since the 1950s have been co-educational, the enrolment has been very strongly weighted in the direction of females. Thus, the 1900 percentage enrolment of 58 per cent males to 42 per cent females, was by independence in 1962, unequivocally replaced, the 1963 enrolment figures being 25.1 per cent males to 74.9 per cent females.[42] According to Miller,[43] "After 1900, more females were employed as pupil-teachers and enrolled in colleges for training as teachers (than were males). It would appear that increased opportunities for women to enter teachers' colleges also brought with (them) increased employment opportunities both as pupil-teachers and as trained teachers."

Perhaps these 1900 figures reflect the use of teacher training certification by males in particular to move out of the profession into better paid employment as policemen, clerks and extension officers, despite the fact that male teachers continued to be paid more than females.[44]

No doubt the two world wars affected the male/female ratio of the teaching force. Unfortunately, college enrolment data are significantly absent for most of these years, except for 1938, when there were nine men and 128 women in training. Figures for the decade preceding independence reveal the trend, which was well established by that time.[45]

Year	MALE		FEMALES	
	No.	%	No.	%
1954	109	32.1	231	67.9
1963	244	25.1	729	74.9

Although by 1963 the salary scales were the same for both sexes, teaching had come to be regarded as women's work, men's excuse being that they could not support a family on a teacher's salary.

In like manner, another "nurturing" profession, nursing, had similarly been established, along with teaching and secretarial work, as an appropriate vocation for women. It is important to note that each of these vocations carried with it a lower salary than those which were pursued by men requiring a comparable level of training. Thus, while women were by this time making their contribution to the island's labour force, their remuneration was markedly below that accorded men.

Conclusions

These conclusions are drawn against the cautionary note that this paper has attempted to provide an outline only, of educational provisions and their suitability for the Jamaican female over the years.

1655-1833

There was little by way of educational provision in Jamaica in the pre-emancipation period. Such that did exist (largely arising out of endowments) were intended to cater for white boys of the society. White girls were not expected to receive much by way of schooling; instead, they were to concentrate on learning the little arts of coquetry in the hope of attracting a husband. One assumes that this would apply to the more affluent ones. Even when girls started attending endowed schools such as Wolmer's in 1770—and these would have been white girls of poor parentage—theirs was a simplified curriculum (reading, writing, needlework and the like), largely devoted to preparing them to be good homemakers and so to marry respectably, or for employment as seamstresses and mantuamakers. Some were also allowed to become monitors at school and help with teaching younger children. This no doubt paved the way for women's (in time, "brown women", in addition to poor whites) entry into the teaching professionin the 1820s and 1830s, mainly as infant schoolteachers. There were no provisions at all for educating negro slave girls during this era, except when in isolated instances missionaries attempted to offer religious indoctrination.

1834-1899

After emancipation in 1834 a type of elementary education gradually evolved for the newly freed. The curriculum for Negro boys and girls centred on the "three Rs" and religious education, since this was felt to represent an "appropriate form of schooling for children whom the legislators hoped would become estate labourers". Once this basic curriculum had been placed on a firm footing, domestic science subjects (plain sewing, cooking and household duties), were introduced for girls in the upper classes of elementary school. This no doubt provided some preparation for them to gain employment as servants of the wealthy, as cooks, laundresses and maids. On the other hand, secondary education still catered mainly for white children and continued to discriminate between the sexes. Girls were rarely taught the classics or sciences, but were taught less taxing subjects, receiving instruction in subjects such as music, needlework and French, which were considered appropriate accomplishments for young ladies of the day. By the 1890s, commercial subjects (shorthand and typewriting) were included in the curriculum, thereby enabling girls to enter the secretarial field. Entry into the teaching profession escalated, especially with the establishment of Bethlehem, Shortwood and St Joseph's training colleges for women. Women teachers, however, received a much lower salary than did men.

Girls started entering for the Cambridge Local Examinations some years after they were introduced in Jamaica in 1882 although not with the same frequency as boys. They failed, however, to win the Jamaica Scholarship during the closing years of the nineteenth century.

1900-1961

Many of the educational trends established by the close of the 19th. century were perpetuated during the first half of the 20th. century. Elementary schools (and later, senior and industrial schools) continued to emphasise training in housecraft for girls, their graduates very often securing employment as domestic servants, although some from the industrial schools did, admittedly, become assistants to social welfare visitors and district visitors. Secondary education likewise emphasised the teaching of homemaking subjects along with secretarial skills for girls, the intention being to prepare them as wives, rather than domestic servants. A few secondary schools began offering girls subjects traditionally taught boys, for example, physics and chemistry, but they were in the minority. Post-secondary education continued to centre on teacher training, although secondary high school graduates generally had no problems gaining employment as teachers without any further training. Such graduates could also find employment in banks, if they were the "right" colour, and as clerks in stores, but rarely in any managerial position; nursing rapidly became a sought-after profession for women because of its call for a nurturing disposition. When the University College of the West Indies opened in 1948, the student population was mainly male. Females, however, rapidly took advantage of the educational opportunities there, although they were usually in non-science fields. A Bachelor of Arts degree gained them greater access to certain areas of the Civil Service, as well as social work, teaching, librarianship and, to a lesser extent, business and commerce. Their representation in the traditionally masculine fields of medicine, engineering and law continued, however, to be very limited, although a few progressive women began to make their mark, even if they were not always accepted by society at large.

References

1. Frank Cundall *Some Notes on the History of Secondary Education in Jamaica.* Pamphlet prepared for the information of H. H. Piggott, HM Inspector of Schools, sent to Jamaica in 1911 to inspect the endowed secondary schools of the island at the request of the Jamaica Schools' Commission. Education Department, Jamaica. 1911.
2. Cundall, p. 2. Also, Gordon, Shirley. *A Century of West Indian Education.* London: Longmans 1963. p. 4.
3. *Report on Negro Education in Jamaica, 1837* (Latrobe Report), p. 74. Report received 19th. October, 1837—House of Commons Paper No. 113, published in 1838. See also *Report of the Charity Commissioners to the House of Assembly,* October 1844, Appendix (p. 177).
4. Cundall, p. 3.
5. *Ibid.* p. 2.
6. See Leslie, C. *A new history of Jamaica.* London: Hodges. 1740.
7. Cundall, p. 2.
8. *Ibid.,* p. 3.
9. *Ibid.*
10. This is Will 17 of 1729, Jamaica.
11. See Hamilton, Marlene. *The social implications of Wolmer's role in Jamaica over the years.* Mimeo 1978(mimeo). p. 2.
12. See *Minute Book 1* (1736-87) of the Wolmer's Corporation: entry for the year, 1782.
13. Hamilton, *op. cit.,* p. 14.
14. Gordon, Shirley. *Reports and repercussions in West Indian education, 1835-1933.* London: Ginn 1968. p. ix.
15. Gordon (1963), p. 44.
16. Gordon (1968), p. 123.
17. *Ibid.,* p. 127
18. *Ibid.,* p. 122.
19. *Ibid.,* p. 21.
20. *Ibid.,* p. 125.
21. *Handbook of Jamaica.* 1882.
22. *Handbook of Jamaica.* 1887-1888. p. 393.
23. *By-Laws for the Management of Wolmer's Free School.* 1894.
24. *By-Laws and Scheme for the Management of Wolmer's School.* 1900.
25. *Ibid.,* p. 9.
26. See *Jamaica Minutes Book,* 22 November, 1890 and 18 April 1891.
27. Cundall, p. 12.
28. *Jamaica Minutes Book,* 19 October 1895, 18 January 1896, 11 April 1896 and 3 October 1896.
29. Gordon (1963), p. 23.
30. See Miller, Errol. *Marginalization of the Black Male.* Kingston: Institute of Social & Economic Studies, University of the West Indies. 1986. pp. 13-14.
31. Gordon (1968), p. 120.
32. *Proceedings of the Jamaica Legislative Council:* Debate on the Montego Bay High School for Boys, 1893-94 (p. 93). Cited in Miller, p. 32.
33. See Enos Nuttall's chapter on "Education in Jamaica in its Relation to Skilled Handicraft and Agricultural Work" (1902); in *Special reports on educational subjects,* Vol. 12. Board of Education, Great Britian. London: HMSO. 1905. p. 282.

34. *Ibid.*
35. *Report of the Committee Appointed to Enquire into the System of Secondary Education in Jamaica, 1943* (Kandel Report). (p. 16).
36. *Ibid.*
37. "Statement of actions taken on the recommendations of the West Indian Royal Commission, 1938-1939" (Section 7: Education). In *State papers-Accounts and papers* Vol. 4. London: HMSO. 1944-49.
38. Development and Welfare in the West Indies, 1940-42 (Stockdale Report). In the 1944 *Plan*, p. 10.
39. *A Plan for Post-Primary Education in Jamaica—Being the Report of the Secondary Education Continuation Committee*, 1944. Kingston: The Government Printers. Published for general information, but, at time of publication, not yet considered by government.
40. See Cundall. Piggott visited Jamaican secondary schools during the period January-March 1911.
41. It was not until the 1970s that Wolmer's Boys' School built a technical block.
42. Miller, p. 15.
43. *Ibid.*, pp. 17-18.
44. As late as 1944 it was recommended in the *Plan* that the basic salary for headmasters should be £800, as against a basic salary for headmistresses of £650.
45. Miller, pp. 14-15.

Sexist Patterns of Formal and Non-formal Education Programmes

The Case of Jamaica

Barbara Bailey

Historical background

Jamaica is quite a young independent nation, having ceased to be a political dependent of Great Britain in 1962 after some 300 years of colonisation. Although educational institutions existed during that time, legislative enactment concerning the provision of formal schooling on a national level did not appear until after emancipation.[1] In the case of the white ruling population, Gordon[2] records that 'all who could afford to, sent their sons "home" for their education'. Missionaries of various denominations established private schools to serve the needs of the poorer free coloured and white children. Wealthy planters and merchants made bequests to establish endowed schools, such as Wolmer's Free School, to provide a superior type of education for wealthy white boys. The 'imported' curriculum of these schools was classical and mirrored that offered in similar schools in Great Britain.

Only in exceptional cases were slave children educated and this usually took the form of 'catechetical exchanges of the religious bodies conducted at long intervals'[3]. Such instruction was offered to both sexes. This is confirmed by a report made by a Moravian missionary to Jamaica: 'I hope that they will soon have more time allowed them to come to instruction, not only the little children, but the boys and girls from 13-15 years of age.'[4]

The few provisions made for education at that time were predominantly for white boys, although one or two bequests made special mention of provision for girls. Hamilton[5] notes that although girls were finally accepted at Wolmer's in 1777, a modified curriculum, based on literacy, numeracy and feminised homemaking skills was designed for them. In 1894 commercial subjects were made available to girls.

With the granting of emancipation in 1834, elementary schools were set up under the Negro Education Grant to provide opportunities for the basic education of the children of the ex-slave population.[6] The number of grammar-type schools also increased and many denominations were active in setting up new schools, especially for girls, who had hitherto been for the most part denied access to such schools.[7]

Thus, the beginnings of a dual system of education, differing in structure, administration and financing, was founded and maintained: grammar schools were modelled on those of the metropole for the colonisers who could afford them and an inferior elementary system for the colonised slave population.

Cole[8] notes that there was no discernible policy of discrimination against the participation of girls in primary education, but that the same could not be said with respect to the curriculum. From its inception the curriculum of the elementary school was differentiated along gender lines. The Lumb Report of 1898[9] describes the curriculum as centring on the three Rs but with additional subjects such as geography, history, grammar and Scripture and morals forming a core for all students. Specific reference was made to the sex of individuals in relation to certain subjects. Sewing was to be taught, presumably to girls, by all female teachers. It was recommended that domestic economy and household duties be taught to girls in the three upper classes. General manual skills were to be taught to boys; and, not unexpectedly, given the dominance of the plantation economy, it was further recommended that agricultural instruction should be given to both boys and girls to help to prepare them to earn a living.

The consequences of the education of girls from the two social strata, for employment, are self-evident. Lower-class girls were trained for domestic work, which was crucial for the supportive role they were required to play in the wider society as mothers or as low-paid servants in upper-class homes.[10] The education of white girls prepared them to be good wives, clerical workers and, eventually, with the establishment of teacher training colleges for women, teachers.

This pattern of schooling and employment illustrates the intersection of two factors, class and gender. Not only was schooling generally differentiated on the basis of social class assignment, but the curricula of the elementary and secondary schools were further segregated on the basis of gender, both of which determined occupational options. Gender biases in terms of access to schooling and curriculum differentiation, resulting in occupational segregation, are therefore historical phenomena.

The Post-independence Period

Hamilton's[11] analysis of schooling from the pre- and post-emancipation periods through to 1961 notes: 'The educational trends established by the close of the 19th century were perpetuated during the first half or so of the 20th century.'

But what of the second half of the century? With the gaining of independence in 1962 the need to expand opportunities for education, particularly at the secondary level, was seen as an imperative to sustain and accelerate developmental initiatives.

In nearly all societies education is viewed as the primary tool in the overall development of society (Cogan).[12] Societies therefore depend on the education system to provide an efficient and educated workforce, trained in the skills required by the various sectors contributing to economic development. Secondary education is particularly critical in this respect, since opportunities for higher education are available for only a negligible proportion of the population of developing countries. It is therefore important to examine what obtains at the secondary level in relation to gender inequities, if girls who have been historically disadvantaged, and who constitute approximately 50 per cent of the country's human resource, are to be equipped to contribute to national development.

Over the past four decades, there have been several educational reforms, including the 70/30 plan, the 1967 New Deal for Education, the Educational Thrust of the 70s[13] and the introduction of a programme to rationalise education at the secondary level in the 1990's. These reforms have been attempts to reverse the historical reality of secondary education and to make it less elitist, less divisive, more accessible to all social groups of the population and therefore, more unified and egalitarian.

The statistics state that 238,950 secondary-level places were provided in 700 public and private schools in 1991,[14] which represents a 73 per cent enrolment rate for the 12-17 age cohort. The ratio of boys to girls was 51.4 to 48.6, which indicates a slightly higher male population, but which also closely reflects the ratio of the general population in that age range.

Enrolment figures for this level would therefore suggest fairly equitable access for both sexes. Leo-Rhynie,[15] however, points to the fact that the selection process applied at the end of the primary cycle to determine access to the more limited number of places in the different school types at the secondary level has definite built-in gender biases in favour of boys.

In the 11+ Common Entrance Examination (CEE), although boys get a smaller number of the total awards, they receive a higher percentage award than girls. This is only possible because lower-scoring boys are awarded places over higher-scoring girls. Girls have, therefore, been consistently awarded places which constitute a lower percentage of their entry. This deliberate strategy is used to accommodate the later development and maturation of boys, and so retain an approximate 1:1 sex ratio in the traditional high schools.

Although the sex balance is maintained, higher-scoring girls are deprived of the opportunity of a high school education and are relegated to either a new secondary or an all-age school. In the case of the latter, there is a slim chance for such girls to secure a place in a technical or traditional high school a year later through further selection processes.[16] The majority, however, will have to complete the secondary cycle in these types of schools, both of which offer an education which carries less social currency and prestige and confers fewer life chances on graduates than those of the traditional high schools.

Access to education is only half the picture. Differentiated life chances for boys and girls are further determined by the curriculum options available to both sexes at the secondary level. Strong gender divisions are evident, which are encouraged and reinforced through both explicit and implicit practices in schools. These factors ensure differential access to various subject areas based on gender stereotyping and biases that affect both sexes.

In terms of explicit policy and practice, Bryne[17] observes that in single-sex schools (like many Jamaican traditional high schools), the curriculum is designed to accommodate only half of the possible curriculum areas. Girls' schools, for the most part, offer no technical skills such as woodwork or metalwork. Conversely, boys' schools offer no domestic skills (food and nutrition, clothing and textiles) and no commercial skills such as typewriting, shorthand and office procedures.

On the other hand, although the co-educational schools offer a fuller range of subjects, explicit practices such as cross-timetabling, as well as implicit teacher and societal expectations and parental and peer pressure, ensure that the gender divisions of the single-sex school are retained.

This sharp gender segregation of the curriculum is reflected in entries to the two major certifying examinations made available to students after five years of secondary schooling, the Basic and General Proficiency Level examinations of the Caribbean Examinations Council (CXC) and the Secondary School Certificate (SSC) examination administered by the Ministry of Education.

Entrants for the CXC examinations are drawn primarily from the traditional and technical high schools, while those for the SSC are mainly from the new secondary schools. Students attending traditional high schools are those who were awarded places through the CEE, while those in the new secondary schools either failed to qualify for such places or were not entered for the CEE. Although both sorts of schools offer a range of subjects, there is greater emphasis on the academic options in the former and on vocational options in the latter. The new secondary schools were, in fact, established as vocation-oriented schools for those whom it was felt would not benefit from the academic curriculum of the high school.

Data on the June 1992 entries for the SSC and CXC examinations are presented in Tables 1 and 2 respectively. These data indicate two intersecting and related phenomena. Firstly, a unidimensional vertical axis, which can be divided into two tracks, is recognisable. A distinction can be made in both sets of data between entries for academic and vocational subjects. The common practice is for schools to assign students to these tracks on the basis of ability, with the more intellectually able students channelled into the academic track and the less able into the vocational track. Although no data are presented to substantiate this claim, this dichotomy is often associated with social class differences.

Tables 1 and 2 illustrate this. For both the SSC (Table 1) and the CXC (Table 2) examinations, the two tracks along the vertical axis are identifiable. In both cases -- and particularly in the case of the SSC, as is expected -- there are fewer academic offerings, confirming that the first dichotomy is, in fact, on the basis of school type (as previously discussed). Of the 24 subject offerings in the SSC examinations, only five (20.8 per cent) can be regarded as academic, while the remaining 19 (79.2 per cent) are vocational. In the CXC there is a more equal distribution, with 14 (43.75 per cent) of the 32 offerings academic and 18 (50.25 per cent) vocational areas.

This unidimensional vertical ranking of courses into high and low ability tends to mask gender distinctions, which in fact appear as horizontal divisions in each track (Gaskell).[18] To establish this horizontal axis within each of the two tracks, the criterion of 66 per cent or more of the entry being male or female was used to identify male- and female-dominated curriculum areas. When this criterion is applied, no gender segregation is evident in the academic track for the SSC examinations. In the case of the CXC, however, some aspects of the typical gender segregation pattern of academic courses are evident.

English B (Literature) and the modern languages (French and Spanish) are female-dominated, as are integrated science and social studies. On the other hand, physics is male-dominated. This pattern conforms with the typical sex-linked dichotomy between language and the physical sciences that has been well documented by other researchers (Hamilton,[19] Stanworth,[20] Murphy,[21] Bryne[22]). Although integrated science includes aspects of the physical sciences, it is regarded as a softer subject than physics and chemistry. It is therefore not surprising that it is included in the female-dominated cluster of subjects.

However, some subjects which usually fit neatly into such a dichotomy are categorised on the basis of the criterion applied, as being 'neutral' (Items 6-13). The higher female entry for mathematics, an area which has been traditionally regarded as belonging to the male domain is to be noted. Males have only a slight margin over females in chemistry, suggesting that the male stereotype is breaking down in these two subject areas. Entries for English A (Language) are almost equally divided, reflecting the fact that schools require all students to enter for this subject.

In the case of the vocational curriculum areas, in both instances there is a much sharper line of demarcation along extremely gender-stereotypic lines. In both the SSC (Table 1) and the CXC (Table 2) a clear horizontal axis is discernible, with the typical female choices being the domestic and business subjects (Items 6-14 for SSC and 15-22 for CXC), and the male choices include the range of technical subjects (Items 17-24 for SSC and 26-32 for CXC).

For the most part the pattern of sex segregation of courses is very typical. A point of departure, however, is accounting which has been traditionally a masculinised area. In the case of the SSC (Table 1), this subject is classified as 'neutral', but with a high female participation, while in the case of the CXC (Table 2), it falls into the 'female-dominated' category. This, again, indicates a shift in the accepted pattern of curriculum segregation.

This pattern of segregation of courses in schools has always been attributed to the effect of ability streaming, but it is now recognised that there is an interplay of two variables and that gender is an even more powerful determinant. This segregation not only has the effect of reproducing and reinforcing the division of gender roles in the home and workplace but, as Bryne[23] claims, the deprivation of exposure to the technical areas of the curriculum is far more disadvantageous to girls than the reverse of denying boys exposure to domestic crafts. She cites three reasons.

1. Technical work, machines, tools and draughtsmanship are labelled as "masculine" with all the resulting implications.
2. The technical crafts underpin mechanical and spatial understanding which forms the basis for mathematics, an area in which girls are regarded as under-achievers.
3. The technical crafts are an excellent base for leisure pursuits and non-vocational skills which are essential for personal living.

She argues that the deprivation of boys from exposure to domestic crafts is less detrimental, since the likelihood is that some female will carry out related tasks on their behalf. She proposes that the education of boys should include these areas and so prepare them for shared domestic roles, which is essential for women's freedom and mobility.

Of even greater significance is the fact that these gender divisions in the school's curriculum correspond to similar gender divisions in the labour force. It is difficult to determine which exerts the stronger influence, but what is evident is the inextricable link between curricular options and occupational choices. Gaskell[24] opines that the gender segregation of occupations has influenced the way curriculum options are defined at school, but that the organisation of school training has also affected the shape of occupational segregation.

This claim is supported by data (see Tables 3 and 4) showing enrolment by sex in the different occupational categories of training programmes pursued by graduates of the secondary level of the school system. These programmes are offered by the Human Employment and Resource Training (HEART) Trust in collaboration with the National Training Agency (NTA), which has been established to coordinate, monitor, fund, standardise and evaluate the activities within the Technical Vocational Education and Training (TVET) system in Jamaica.[25]

Data collected for enrolment in the School Leavers Opportunities Programme (SLOP) for April-September 1992 (see Table 3) show that for 30 main occupational areas, there were 1,069 trainees, with the majority (775 or 72.5 per cent) being female.

As with analysing the pattern of subject choice in the SSC and CXC examinations, occupations were categorised as being male- or female-dominated on the basis of there being more than a 66 per cent level of enrolment of either sex in a particular area. On the basis of this criterion, 15 occupational areas were classified as feminised (1-15), 10 as masculinised (20-30), while 4 areas were neutral (16-19).

These categories were divided along very traditional sex-segregated lines, with the dominant female occupations being service, clerical and business-related, while the more technically skilled jobs were restricted to the male domain. The inclusion of accounts (Item 14) in the 'female-dominated' category mirrors the pattern observed in the examination entries (Tables 1 and 2) and as before appears to be a departure from the norm. However, in this particular programme of on-the-job training, the nature of the required tasks would be routine and clerical rather than technical. It is therefore not surprising that there is a higher female participation.

A similar picture emerges when enrolment in two of the six training academies is examined. Table 4 includes data for the Stony Hill and Portmore Academies, which, by the nature of their emphases on commercial skills and construction skills respectively, have corresponding female- and male-dominated participation. The typical gender segregation is very evident in the complete reversal of the ratio of females to males in the two programmes (91:9 and 9:91). Of the few males (59) pursuing courses at the commercial skills academy, 30 (50.84 per cent) opted to specialize in sales, and 19 (32.2 per cent) in sales and accounts, areas perceived as being more masculine than feminine. In the case of the construction skills academy, all 23 females were in non-traditional areas, with the majority opting for the subject of electrical installation. This suggests that more females seem willing to challenge and break into male-dominated occupations than is the reverse.

Entry to these programmes require stated levels of passes in the two examinations under consideration. Although no attempt was made to establish any correspondence, the participants reflected in these data would have been drawn from a pool of secondary school graduates who would have been candidates of the SSC and CXC examinations in the previous year or earlier. It is therefore not surprising that when these data are compared with the segregated pattern of subject choices, as reflected in Tables 1 and 2, certain parallels are recognisable.

The vocational curriculum options pursued by males and females (see Tables 1 and 2) would predispose and even dictate the gender segregated occupational pattern of training reflected in Tables 3 and 4. Girls who pursue domestic crafts and business subjects in school seek training in service, clerical and business-related occupations, whereas boys who take the technical subjects would opt for occupations with a technical background. Based on the general pattern of school training, if either sex wished to cross the gender barrier and select non-traditional occupations, it would require a reorientation and exposure to completely new concepts and skills.

It can therefore be hypothesised that the more rather than less rigid occupational segregation of trainees, as shown by the data, is an extension of the sex segregation and stereotyping evident in subject choices made by both sexes at the secondary level. These gender-linked biases in training are further reinforced by factors such as socialisation and parental, peer and teacher expectations, accessibility to programmes, entry requirements and other inherent factors of the system such as residency facilities in some training institutions. To date, the academies for commercial and construction skills have offered residential facilities for women only, and men only, respectively.

This sex-segregated occupational training pattern mirrors divisions in the labour force. The report of the Sub-Committee on Employment prepared for the United Nations End of Decade Conference in 1985[26] noted that Jamaica experiences a persistence of concentration of female workers in a limited number of occupations. The two main groups of feminised occupations identified were services and clerical, and sales workers.

Data for 1991 indicate that this trend has not changed. The employment sectors in the labour force[27] with the highest female participation are clerical and sales, and services, with 19 per cent and 24 per cent respectively of the total female force. The sector with the highest male representation is craftsmen production process and operating occupations, with 23 per cent of the total male labour force. It is therefore not surprising that the highest levels of female and male involvement in SLOP (see Table 3) are in corresponding training categories.

These observations of the gender segregation of employment sectors need to be contrasted with two other factors, the disparity in wages in the female- and male-dominated sectors and the unemployment situation of women, particularly those in the 14-24 age group, who form a pool from which recruits for training in these programmes would be drawn.

Both Wickham[28] and Gaskell[29] contend that labour market skills are socially constructed; the latter points out that this is of particular concern to women because the fact that women earn less than men has been attributed to women's lack of skill. Skilled work has become, by definition almost, that work which women do not do (Phillip and Taylor[30]). Gaskell[31] opines that this inability of women to define their work as skilled has institutional consequences in relation to educational qualifications and opportunities for vocational training, as well as in relation to wages. Wickham[32] agrees, arguing that whilst the concept of skilled work is used for the benefit of working-class men, it has been used against women, whose work is often defined as low-skilled and therefore is low-paid. She claims that feminists argue that it is in the male interest to exclude women from masculinised jobs and confine them to the female ghettos of low-level, low-paid jobs in feminised work sectors, thus reproducing the segregated patterns of employment.

The pattern of unemployment of both sexes also needs to be considered in a discussion of the sex segregation of the labour market. Unemployment has always been a chronic problem in Jamaica, but the plight of women has been more pronounced because they account for a disproportionate share of total unemployment.

In October 1991,[33] there were 168,700 unemployed persons, of which 114,500 (67.9 per cent) were female and 54,200 (32.1 per cent) were male, indicating a ratio of slightly more than 2:1. Of these numbers, 34,400 of the females and 16,100 of the males were in the 20-24 age group, figures which also represent a

2:1 ratio. The unemployment data further show that many unemployed females have service, clerical and sales skills.

The establishment of the HEART programme[34] was a direct response to the unemployment situation among young people and the need to equip them with employable skills. It was envisaged that the programme would provide a pool of skilled persons to meet the projected training needs of the economy.

The training of women along traditional gender-linked lines to function only in feminised occupations is therefore self-defeating and only serves to perpetuate the sex segregation illustrated by these data. To continue this approach to the training of women will prepare them for unemployment rather than employment and so constantly swell the ranks of the unemployed, since these traditional feminised occupational sectors are already over-supplied.

Conclusion

The sex-segregation of the curriculum and the under-representation of girls from the technical areas of the training programmes identified in this paper confirm the subordinate position of girls in the formal and non-formal education sectors. The result, as confirmed by labour market data, is the continuing low level of participation of women in areas that are perceived to be skilled and high-status and therefore higher-paying.

The data indicate that for the most part the curriculum options pursued by girls predispose them to seek training in clerical and service-related occupations. In so doing, girls are in fact acquiescing to dominant societal expectations. In school these gender categories are reproduced through explicit and implicit practices associated with the hidden curriculum. Gaskell[35] is of the opinion that girls are so habituated to the principles of this dominant ideology that they happily behave in ways which contradict their experience of the world and operate against their best interest.

This observation is of particular significance. Previous reference to labour market statistics indicates that feminised occupational categories are oversubscribed. In addition, in Jamaica as elsewhere it is likely that the demand for clerical workers will decline as new technology is introduced at the workplace. The preparation of girls along traditional lines, to function only in the feminised occupations, not only perpetuates the sex stereotyping syndrome described here but is also self-defeating.

If this cycle is to be broken, intervention is required at both the school level and in formal and non-formal training initiatives. First, the sex-segregated pattern of curriculum choice will have to change. Both sexes should be actively encouraged to cross the sex-linked boundaries and progress towards non-traditional options, particularly in vocational areas.

All barriers that prevent the participation of either sex in the full range of curriculum and training offerings must be eliminated. This means attention must be given to both overt and covert practices which are in any way discriminatory. Several initiatives are possible.

1. Textbooks and other educational material should be evaluated for evidence of bias and stereotypic sex representation of the sexes which could help to reinforce and perpetuate socially expected behaviours and roles.
2. In single-sex schools where virtually only one half of the possible range of vocational options are offered, efforts should be made to introduce at least one non-traditional area to begin to break down the sex-linked attitudes to certain occupations. Initially, this could be provided as a co-curricular activity geared to prepare individuals for life, e.g. basic auto mechanics for girls and basic food and nutrition for boys.
3. In co-educational schools, where a fuller range of vocational options are available, a guidance and counselling programme should be mounted to encourage actively both sexes to move towards non-traditional vocational areas. Additionally, any barriers that prevent the full participation of either sex in any curriculum area should be eliminated, e.g. cross-timetabling practices.
4. Since teachers often inadvertently contribute to the reinforcement of expected sex roles and behaviours, a course on gender issues in education should be introduced and made mandatory in all teacher training institutions.
5. Where established training programmes in traditional sex-linked areas exist, practices which exclude the opposite sex should be discontinued, e.g. residency restrictions.
6. Traditional strategies utilised to provide skills training exclude some individuals and is usually long-term. These factors militate against young unemployed women of a low educational level. Alternative innovative strategies should be devised, e.g. a mentorship or apprenticeship approach to training.
7. Skills training policies for women should be articulated on the basis of an analysis of labour market needs to ensure that on completion of training individuals can be absorbed into the work force.

Implementation of these recommendations is only a starting point. Attitudinal change is also an imperative. The above initiatives would provide greater opportunity for some women to move into male-dominated areas where employment opportunities exist. Gaskell,[36] however, points to the fact that this merely juggles numbers within an existing situation where the majority of women workers will continue to provide a cheap source of labour. She postulates that, if there were to be an influx of women into male-dominated occupations, it is likely that these areas would be transformed into feminised occupations, with the associated problems of low pay and low status. Women would therefore not have made any major gain in the long run.

It seems that this type of entrenched response and the persistence of sex-based inequalities can only be averted if there is accompanying attitudinal change. Sex-linked skill hierarchies will have to be deconstructed and the value placed on skilled work will have to be determined not on the basis of which sex does the work, but rather on the basis of how well the job is done.

TABLE 1 *Entries in the Secondary School Certificate (SSC) Examination by Subject and Sex, June 1992*

		Subject	No. females	% females	No. males	% males	Total
TRACK A	N	1. Science	3712	61.74	2300	38.26	6012
		2. Social Studies	4532	59.69	3060	40.31	7592
		3. Language Communications	8494	51.03	8150	48.97	16644
		4. Mathematics	7927	47.83	8647	52.17	7592
		5. Art	200	36.83	343	63.17	543
TRACK B	FD	6. Shorthand	27	100.00	–	–	027
		7. Beauty Culture	512	94.29	31	5.71	543
		8. Child Care	695	91.45	65	8.55	760
		9. Typewriting	1083	77.75	310	22.25	1393
		10. Prin. of Business	1050	77.09	312	22.91	1362
		11. Business Comm.	872	74.91	292	25.09	1164
		12. Clothing & Textile	1400	70.14	596	29.86	1996
		13. Food & Nutrition	1718	68.47	791	31.53	2509
		14. Principles of Mktg.	350	67.56	168	32.43	518
	N	15. Accounting	980	64.09	549	35.91	1529
		16. Office Procedure	910	64.08	510	35.92	1420
	MD	17. Auto Mechanics	176	23.31	579	76.69	755
		18. Electrical Install.	411	22.08	1450	77.92	1861
		19. Plumbing	54	16.67	270	83.33	324
		20. Drafting	20	16.39	102	83.61	122
		21. Welding/Machine Shop	207	12.80	1401	87.20	1617
		22. Agriculture	80	11.76	600	88.24	680
		23. Carpentry/Cabinet Mkg.	18	0.93	1910	99.07	1928
		24. Farm Mechanics			023	100.00	023

Source: Ministry of Education, Kingston, Jamaica

Key:

FD	=	Female - dominated
MD	=	Male - dominated
N	=	Neutral

TABLE 2 *Entries in the Caribbean Examinations Council (CXC) Examination by Subject and Sex, June 1992 (Jamaica)*

		Subject	No. females	% females	No. males	% males	TOTAL
TRACK A		1. French	268	82.46	057	17.54	325
		2. Spanish	978	75.52	317	24.48	1295
		3. Int. Science	425	73.28	155	26.72	580
		4. Social Studies	1864	72.64	702	27.36	2566
		5. English B	3477	67.03	1710	32.97	5187
		6. Biology	1503	64.31	834	35.69	2337
		7. Carib. History	2635	63.63	1506	36.37	4141
		8. Mathematics	10942	61.97	6716	38.03	17658
		9. Ag. Science	290	61.44	182	38.56	472
		10. English A	6488	50.20	6436	49.80	12924
		11. Chemistry	847	48.29	907	51.71	1754
		12. Geography	1767	46.91	2000	53.09	37.67
		13. Art	168	41.38	238	58.62	406
		14. Physics	548	32.45	1141	67.55	1689
	FD	15. Clothing & Textile	532	99.25	004	0.75	536
		16. Shorthand	335	99.11	003	0.89	338
		17. Home Management	725	97.71	017	2.29	742
		18. Food and Nutrition	1150	94.49	067	5.51	1217
		19. Typewriting	2395	91.69	217	8.31	2612
		20. Office Procedures	3305	83.33	661	16.67	3966
		21. Craft	041	74.55	014	25.45	055
		22. Prin. of Business	5070	67.31	2462	32.69	7532
		23. Prin. of Accounts	5469	66.96	2089	33.04	8167
		24. Book-keeping	187	65.84	097	34.15	284
		25. Art & Craft	076	59.84	051	40.12	127
	MD	26. Electrical Tech.	024	7.67	289	92.33	313
		27. Electrical Elect.	020	5.68	332	94.32	352
		28. Mechanical Tech.	009	5.52	154	94.48	163
		29. Technical Drawing	086	5.37	1515	94.63	1601
		30. Building	007	4.00	168	96.00	175
		31. Woods	005	1.51	325	98.48	330
		32. Metals	002	0.80	247	99.20	249

Source: Caribbean Examination Council, Kingston, Jamaica

Key:

FD=Female - dominated MD=Male - dominated N=Neutral

TABLE 3 *School Leavers' Opportunities Programme: Trainee Placements, April - September 1992*

Skill	No. females	% females	No. males	% males	Total
1. Reception Skills	35	100	—	—	35
2. Typing Skills	29	100.00			29
3. Cashing	13	100.00			13
4. Medical Records	12	100			12
5. Telephone Operating	6	100			6
6. Cookery	2	100.00			2
7. General Office Practice	28	96.55	1	3.45	29
8. Counter Clerk	48	96.00	2	4.00	50
9. Secretarial Skills	30	93.75	3	6.38	47
10. Teachers' Aide	44	93.61	3	6.38	47
11. Clerical Skills	279	87.74	39	12.26	318
12. Sales	68	71.59	27	28.42	95
13. Librarian/Audio-Visual	5	71.42	2	28.57	7
14. Accounts	94	69.12	42	30.88	136
15. Bank Related Services	21	67.74	10	32.26	31
16. Lab Technology	9	60.00	6	40.00	15
17. Resort Skills	31	50.00	31	50.00	62
18. Computer Operation	6	46.15	7	53.85	13
19. Inventory/Stock Control	6	37.50	10	62.50	16
20. Printing	6	31.58	13	68.42	19
21. Factory Worker/Prod	3	21.43	11	78.57	14
22. Carpentry/Joinery			3	100.00	3
23. Chef			3	100.00	3
24. Auto Mechanic			4	100.00	4
25. Woodwork			4	100.00	4
26. Technical Drawing			5	100.00	5
27. Technician			10	100.00	10
28. Motor			13	100.00	13
29. Mechanics/Rewinding			22	100.00	22
30. Machine Shop			24	100.00	24
Total	775		294		1069

TABLE 4 *Enrolment by Area of Specialization and Gender in Academies* September 1992 (Jamaica)

A. Stony Hill - commercial skills

Specialist area	No. females	% females	No. males	% males	Total
1. Accounts	168	84.85	30	15.15	198
2. Sales/Accounts	80	80.81	19	19.19	99
3. Secretarial Skills	69	100.00	—	—	69
4. Clerk/Typist/Receptionist	227	99.56	1	0.44	228
5. Data Entry	35	79.55	9	20.45	44
Total	579	—	59	—	638

B. Portmore - construction skills

Specialist area	No. females	% females	No. males	% males	Total
1. Electrical Installation	16	11.43	124	88.57	140
2. Masonry	5	8.93	51	91.07	56
3. Plumbing/Pipefitting	1	3.03	32	96.97	33
4. Welding/Fabrication	1	2.94	33	97.05	34
Total	23		240		263

References

1. Cole, Joyce. "Official Ideology and the Education of Women in the English-Speaking Caribbean 1835-1945, with Special Reference to Barbados". *Women and Education*. Institute of Social and Economic Research, University of the West Indies, Cave Hill, Barbados. 1982.
2. Gordon, Shirley. *A Century of West Indian Education*, London: Longmans. 1963.
3. *Ibid.*
4. *Ibid.*, p. 11.
5. Hamilton, Marlene (1987). 'The Availability of Educational Opportunities for Jamaican Female Students: An Historical Overview'. Paper prepared for first interdisciplinary seminar on Women and Development Studies - "Gender, Culture, and Caribbean Development". UWI, Mona, Jamaica. 1987 (mimeo).
6. Gordon, Shirley (1963), *loc. cit.*
7. ______. *Reports and Repercussions in West Indian Education 1835-1933.* London: Ginn. 1968.
8. Cole, Joyce, *op. cit.*
9. Lumb Report, Jamaica, 1989. In: Gordon, Shirley (1968).
10. Cole, Joyce, *op. cit.*

11. Hamilton, Marlene, *op. cit.*, p. 12.
12. Cogan, John J. "Jamaica: Education and the Maintenance of Social Class System". In Murray Thomas, R. (ed.), *Politics and Education*, Oxford:Pergamon Press. 1983.
13. *Ibid.*
14. *Economic and Social Survey of Jamaica, 1991* Kingston: Planning Institute of Jamaica.
15. Leo-Rhynie, Elsa. "Gender in Education: Labour Force Implications". In Hart, Keith (ed.). *Women and the Sexual Division of Labour in the Caribbean*. Kingston: Consortium Graduate School of the Social Sciences, UWI, Mona. 1989.
16. *Ibid.* See page 82 for structure of the education system in Jamaica.
17. Bryne, Eileen M. *Women and Education*. London: Tavistock Publications 1978.
18. Gaskell, Jane. *Gender Matters from School to Work*. Toronto, Ontario: Oise Press. 1992.
19. Hamilton, Marlene. "Performance Levels in Science and Other Subjects for Jamaican Adolescents Attending Single Sex and Co-educational High Schools". In: Science Education, Vol. 64, No. 4, 1985, pp. 535-47.
20. Stanworth, Michele. *Gender and Schooling, a Study of Sexual Divisions in the Classroom*. London: Unwin, Hyman. 1981.
21. Murphy, Roger J.L. "Sex Differences in Examination Performance: Do these Reflect Differences in Ability or Sex Role Stereotyping?" In Hartnett, O., Boden, G., and Fuller, M. (eds). *Women Sex Role Stereotyping*. Tavistock Publications 1979.
22. Bryne, Eileen M. (1978).
23. *Ibid.*
24. Gaskell, Jane (1992).
25. *Economic and Social Survey of Jamaica 1991*. Kingston: Planning Institute of Jamaica.
26. *Employment Report 1985*. Jamaica's Report to the UN End-of-Decade Conference for Women, prepared by the Bureau of Women's Affairs, Kingston, Jamaica.
27. *Labour Force Report 1991*. Kingston: Statistical Institute of Jamaica.
28. Wickham, Ann. "Gender Divisions, Training and the State". In (ed) R. Dale, *Education, Training and Employment*. London: Open University and Pergamon Press. 1985.
29. Gaskell, Jane (1992).
30. Phillips, A. and Taylor, B. "Sex and Skill: Notes towards a Feminist Economics". *Feminist Review*, 30, 1980, pp.79-88.
31. Gaskell, Jane (1992).
32. Wickham, Ann (1985).
33. *Labour Force Report*, 1991.
34. *Social and Economic Survey of Jamaica*,. Kingston: National Planning Agency 1982.
35. Gaskell, Jane (1992).
36. *Ibid.*

White Man's Knowledge

Sex, Race and Class in Caribbean English Language Textbooks

Kathleen B. Drayton

Although the Caribbean has struggled through the long night of slavery and direct colonial domination to political independence, the economic system has remained part of the international capitalist system. The control of the economic system remains in the hands of a few native and a large number of foreign capitalists.

Groups exercising Domination, Control, Knowledge

A major concern of this paper is the process by which some groups in society exercise domination over other groups. Classical Marxist theory advances the valuable concept of class struggle, and there is a large and important body of work which examines racial domination and discrimination, but neither of those contributes much to our understanding of the subordination of women. Indeed, it has been left to female Marxist scholars to show that the class struggle and the way capitalism itself functions cannot be adequately explained unless the struggles for human liberation are seen as struggles against class, race and sex exploitation. The monster we fight has three heads, each with its contradictions and strategies of control, and to aim the axe at one head will not destroy it.

The major national liberation struggles of the nineteenth and twentieth centuries in the Caribbean and elsewhere all had layers of class, race and sex. A victory at one level often appeared to be an overall victory. There was a persistent belief that the interests of all workers, regardless of sex and race, were the same. We can easily see that this is false consciousness if we contrast the interests of poor with those of rich women, or the interests of women in the Caribbean with those of North American women, or if we contrast the interests of black and white workers, whether they be in South Africa, the USA, the UK or the Caribbean. The class struggle has several facets. Gender and race are not separate struggles; Selma James illustrates this clearly. She argues that black struggle is often wrongly perceived as a race and not a class struggle and therefore "When black workers burn the centre of a city white eyes see race not class" (James 1986:8).

Similarly, the women's struggle is not a battle of the sexes; it is a fundamental part of what is often called the class struggle, but it has its own characteristics and specific goals. When Rosa Parks got on to an Alabama bus and sat in the whites-only section, she was both a black woman and a worker, tired after a day's work. Her challenge of the social and economic relationship of powerful white America was a crucial incident in the civil rights struggle and it was a consequence of her being black, poor and female. Rosa Parks' act symbolises what I mean by the integration of sex, race and class in a liberation struggle. Bell Hooks (1981:3) says that black women linked women's liberation with the mass struggles for social emancipation in the USA. James (1986) suggests that the work that white women did, both in helping to organise the underground railway as well as during the civil rights' crisis period, gave them an "occasion to transcend the limitations in which the female personality is imprisoned" and had a direct connection with the nineteenth-century American women's movement, and with the Women's liberation movement from the late 1960s. The experience of class and race struggle was a preparation for the struggle for women's rights. In passing we must also note that if you ask a class of children who Martin Luther King is, all hands will be raised, but, if you ask who Rosa Parks is, there will be silence. We are living witnesses to the process by which knowledge itself is a product of a dominant male culture, so that "the cultural imagery of gender in our society has been incorporated into the very framework in which we receive and assess all forms of knowledge" (Barrett 1980:149).

The Importance of Gender Analysis

Gender analysis, applied to the categories of class and race, therefore brings into focus the invisible 50 per cent of the human race and raises the whole question of legitimate knowledge, a present-day concern in both Marxist and Weberian sociology. Gender analysis begins from the assumption that "women's place is not a separate sphere but a position within social existence" (Kelly 1984:57). It therefore seeks the "link between the socio-economic order and the organisation of capitalist production in and out of the home" (*ibid*.:4). In an analysis of state policies it is not enough to ask how policies will affect rich and poor, or black and white, but how they will affect men and women. Gender analysis is not sexist. It is not simply about women. It examines the many, varied and complex relationships between women and men in society.

A central and relevant issue in the debate is the sexual division of labour. It used to be put about that, as Freud said, "anatomy is destiny", and that the functions performed by men and women in society were biologically determined. Recent work, including that of our Caribbean historians Beckles (1988 and 1989), Mair (1987) and Reddock (1984), has effectively demonstrated that functions in society are socially determined. While at one level women were said to be weak, frail, helpless and dependent, at the plantation level they did the same heavy work as men.

In discussing the origins of this "asymmetric, hierarchical and exploitative" division of labour, Mies (1988) points to the difference in the way women's productive activities are defined as compared with men's. Women's productive activities are described as natural or out of nature. Men's productive activities are called work. Mies accepts Marx's premise that man finds his humanity in his mastery of nature to produce the means to satisfy his needs, but she points to the biased use of the concept of nature. She argues that men and women differ in a material way in their interaction with nature. Men can only use their hands but women can use their uterus and breasts. The production of life, of babies, is an essential social task that women perform; it is not simply a natural function. In the same way all the tasks connected with child care are essential social tasks. The reassessment of the labour process, a central issue in feminist research, provides a new way of looking at what is called work in society.

The reassessment of work has led to the issue of family and household organisation. Engel's view that the patriarchal nuclear family is the site of female subordination remains important, although there is criticism of his work (see Beechey 1987:53-56). His famous argument that monogamous marriage resulted from the male need to be certain of the paternity of heirs to his property, and his tracing of the historical process through which women became more subordinate to men, informs feminist views about the family. Nowadays the importance of the family to capitalism is our concern. Both church and state joined in the promotion of the ideal of the nuclear family with its patriarchal structure. What is becoming clear is that it is also an important vehicle for providing a cheap reservoir of labour for capitalism (Boserup 1970; Rogers 1980). These essential unpaid tasks performed in the home are important not only to the individual's well-being but also to production outside the home. The wage that is paid for one person's work within a given span of time actually represents either the work of more than one person, or work done by the same person outside the work time span to enable the worker to carry out the work for which the wage is paid—one wage for two jobs.

Ideological control through Education

Domination in society is therefore effected initially by control of the means of production, but it is sustained, consolidated and perpetuated by social institutions. To prevent confrontation with the social order, "social norms and models of behaviour" must be diffused for imitation. In the process of imitating or learning to be like, of internalising ruling class values, "self-awareness among the people must be cultivated" (Falcon 1980:3). Ideological control through social institutions is thus a prerequisite for the continuance of power in the hands of those who have it. A major social institution contributing to this ideological control is the school (Bowles and Gintis 1976; Carnoy 1974; King 1979; O'Jon 1979; Turner 1979). Its socialising processes operate through organisational structures which create its social hierarchies as well as through the curriculum. School textbooks are a universal vehicle and tool. They are aimed at the minds of the youngest and most impressionable in the population who are taught to internalise dominant social values. An analysis of school texts is therefore essential to an understanding of the process by which social values and ideologies are transmitted.

That textbooks influence the shaping of children's ideas is supported by the findings of 32 studies done in the USA and cited by Witenberg and Campbell in separate reports (Council on Interracial Books for Children: 68) as well as by Zimet (1980: 18-22). In one of these studies (Jackson 1944), the gain in positive attitude to blacks disappeared after two weeks (Zimet 1976:20) suggesting the need for follow-up study on the long-term effects of changed attitudes resulting from reading. Jackson's finding may, however, be explained by Purves and Beach (1972), who found that when reading material conflicts with readers' world views, readers misinterpret, select what they agree with or reject what they read.

The importance of the work cited in the previous paragraph is that it reports not what is believed about the effects of reading textbooks, but what is actually known. One rationale for textbook analysis is therefore that we know that textbooks reflect, consolidate and perpetuate dominant values: 'children's attitudes towards another person's race, ethnicity, gender, social class, or age can be influenced by books . . . the development of a child's self-esteem, values, inspiration and fears may be either assisted or inhibited by the content of textbooks.' (Council on Interracial Books for Children: 68)

It is against the background of these theoretical issues that the analysis of selected English-language textbooks used in Barbados was undertaken.

Secondary–level Enrolment and Language Textbooks in use

Barbados has free and compulsory education to age 16 offered in six private and 21 government schools. The latter not only include the most prestigious schools in the island but the bulk of the secondary school enrolment.

Table 1 *Enrolment in Barbados Secondary schools, 1988-89*

Type of school	No. of Students	%
Government secondary schools	50,119	89.93
Private Approved Schools	5,611	19.06
	55,730	

Source: Barbados: Ministry of Education, October 1989.

The six private approved schools surveyed together contain about half of those enrolled in that category of school. Thus in all the schools reporting contained approximately 93 per cent of the secondary age cohort. Also relevant is that the island has had a free textbook scheme which has been in operation since 1975. Each year teachers select the texts they want ordered and the Ministry of Education provides them. What this means is that there are English-language texts for every child in every secondary school; each child in the system is using or has used the textbooks listed. The 1989-90 text book budget was BDS$1.6 million (Barbados Ministry of Education).

A large variety of different texts is being used in schools but each of the 26 schools used one or more of the following series which are listed in order of their popularity.

Table 2 *English-language series in use in Barbadian secondary schools, October 1989*

Title	No. of school	%
English for Life 1–4 (EL)	20	76.9
Language for Living 1–5 (LL)	12	46.1
Growing with Language 1–4 (GL)	11	42
New English for the Caribbean 1–4 (NEC)	11	42
New World English 1–4 (NWE)	10	38
Exploring English in the Caribbean 1–4 (EE)	9	34
Black & Wood's English	3	11.5
Graded Secondary School English	3	11.5
Mastery of English	3	11.5

English for Life, used by 76.9 per cent of these schools, is obviously the most popular, but a striking fact is that 23 (88.6 per cent) of schools use several textbook series. One school uses seven sets and several use three, four or five series. Only four schools reported using one textbook series. The last three series in the table date back to the 1960s and are by UK authors. The 24 books in the first six series were all written between 1978 and 1985 and all have Caribbean authors, the majority of whom are male. These were the ones selected for analysis. Two other texts used by five schools were added to the list. These texts are: *Comprehension for Caribbean Examinations* (CC) *and English for CXC* (EC).

The total number of texts analysed was 27. The textbooks selected for analysis were all produced to meet the needs of the new English syllabus introduced into Caribbean schools in 1978 by the new Caribbean examination system. Most also incorporate some of the new ideas of Caribbean language scholars about teaching language structures to a population that is mainly creole-speaking.

The Collection and Method of Analysis of Data

Quantitative and qualitative content analysis methods were used. The written body and illustrations of each text were analysed to find answers to the following questions.

1. How many males and females are principal characters?
2. What are the occupations of males and females?
3. In what kinds of social reproductive activities are males and females engaged?
4. In what types of leisure activities do males participate?
5. What kinds of families appear and what sort of relationships of males and females are portrayed in the text?
6. How does the language used in the texts communicate bias?

The activities of males and females were then categorised under these headings.

1. Work: those occupations from which wages, salaries or other material reward are to be gained.
2. Social reproduction: those tasks performed by males and females in and around homes and usually connected with family. This work is unpaid and reaps no material gain but it comprises all those tasks which enable the worker to go out to work and thus they make capitalist production possible.
3. Leisure: those activities engaged in by males and females for recreation and relaxation.

In order to collect data for questions 2, 3 and 4 the occurrence of activities for each category for each text and for each series was prepared and totals of each group of activities were obtained. From these it was possible to compare the textbook images of how males and females functioned in society.

In order to gather data for question 5, kinds of families were listed as they appeared. Patriarchal ideology has long taught that a woman's major responsibility in life is to get married and look after a husband and children. The nuclear family, which is not a Caribbean norm, is held up as the ideal model and women are frequently defined solely in terms of their family.

Since the choice of vocabulary and supposedly innocuous insinuations often conceal a sexist message (Michel 1982:53), to address question 6, adjectives describing males and females and statements from either male or female characters illustrating male or female attitudes were noted as were the themes around which material was grouped in each text.

The findings are discussed below under ten headings. This analysis does not, however, address the quality of questions, exercises and tests designed to teach the language skills of listening, speaking, reading and writing, although judgements have been made about the intrinsic interest of texts for the levels for which they have been designed and about their artistic and graphic value.

The Findings

1. Principal Characters

Of the 401 principal characters in the texts, 78 per cent were males compared with 22.5 per cent females. Since in our society, as in virtually all others, women are half or more than half the population, their under-representation clearly indicates the sexist bias of all the texts.

Table 3 *Principal characters*

Series	EL	EE	GL	LL	NWE	NEC	CC	EC	Average
No in Series	4	3	4	5	4	4	1	1	
% males	74.6	80	92.2	69.8	75.8	77.7	66.6	92.3	78
% females	25.3	20	77	30	24.4	22.2	33.3	7.6	22.5

2. Occupations

The workforce is defined as those who work for pay or profit, the wage and salary earners and owners of businesses. This group and all those seeking work, a euphemism for the unemployed, comprise the labour force. Students and housewives are defined as outside the labour force. This creates the impression that these groups are outside the capitalist wage labour system. Although these groups do not receive wages, they are in fact part of the division of labour in society. "The rule of capital through the wage compels every able-bodied person to function under the law of the division of labour . . . in ways that are if not immediately profitable, then ultimately profitable to the expansion and extension of the rule of capital. That fundamentally is the meaning of the school." (Dalla Costa and James 1972)

The work of 'housewife' was picked up in the social reproduction category; 'student' was recorded among occupations. Also included were non-human personae such as gods and goddesses, archangels and angels, and two female bloodsuckers, Ol' Higue and La Diablesse. The proportions of male to female occupations were calculated first for traditional workforce occupations, secondly with students included, and thirdly with non-human personae.

Table 4 *Proportion of male to female occupations in texts*

Occupations	% males	% females
Traditional workforce	95	4.9
With students	94.9	5.07
With students and non-humans	87.5	12.48

The proportions bore no relation to the social reality. Commonwealth Caribbean census data tabulated by Massiah show general worker rates by sex from 1891 to 1980. Of the 13 countries only Belize, the Virgin Islands (BVI) and Guyana have ever fallen below a 20 per cent female worker rate; Belize recorded 14 per cent in 1921, 16.6 per cent in 1946 and 18.4 per cent in 1970. The BVI recorded 12 per cent in 1956 and 17.4 per cent in 1960 and Guyana recorded 18.4 per cent in 1970. The proportion of women in the working population has never fallen below 14.1 per cent between 1891 and 1980 (Massiah 1989).

The variety of male occupations in the texts is significantly greater than females, with males in 105 occupations compared with females in 42 (71 per cent compared with 28.57 per cent). This gross distortion of reality discriminates against women by suggesting that their social contributions are inferior to those of males. The stereotype contributes to maintaining women in an inferior social position (Blumer 1958, in Michel 1986).

Occupations were coded into five levels. Level 1 includes administrative executive and managerial, the top people, those who own and control power and wealth. Gods, goddesses and super-heroes were placed in this category. Level 2 is the higher professional and related occupations. People in this category generally have a high level of education and professional training. Their positions are regarded as high-status in the Caribbean, and generally their earnings are at the upper end of the scale. Level 3 contains lower-level professionals. They too are generally regarded as lower in status than those people in level 2. Level 4 are the skilled and includes artisans, small farmers and small-scale landlords and landladies. The greatest number of occupations and the largest number of people fall into this category. Level 5 are the unskilled and the second largest number of occupations and people were included in this category (Table 5). Students and the two female bloodsuckers were placed in level 5. The reasons for this are that the two latter are figures of evil who do not have the power that gods or goddesses have, and students are going through a process of learning skills. Table 5 summarises the occupations found at the five levels.

Table 5 *Proportion of male and female occupations in texts*

Occupational level	Totals	Males		Females	
		No	%	No	%
Level 1	141	139	98.58	2	1.45
Level 2	147	138	93.8	9	6.1
Level 3	259	169	65.2	90	34.7
Level 4	1597	1570	98.3	27	1.69
Level 5	563	335	62.69	210	37.3
	2707	2351	87.5	338	12.48

It is immediately obvious that there are few females in the two top levels and that the highest percentage of female figures is in Level 5, the unskilled. The two females in the top are a politician and a Goddess. Males occupy all the other top-level occupations. In higher professional and related occupations the nine females are two scientists, two writers (one is Charlotte Bronte, the other is unspecified) and two are lawyers (one of these is Portia with her "quality of mercy" from Shakespeare's *Merchant of Venice*). In the explorer/discoverer category related to Level 2, there is the story of Kwailan La Borde who with her husband and son completed crossings of the Atlantic and a journey round the world in their sailing boat, and there is one artist. Again men are represented in every occupation. In Level 3 lower professionals, traditional female occupations appear with teachers (43), nurses (14), clerks (11) and cashiers (3). There are only two females in non-traditional positions, a female clerk of court and a female builder. It is noteworthy that the apparently large number of female teachers is outnumbered by males (54), a contradiction of what actually obtains today.

Among the skilled in Level 4 the largest number are soldiers (1,386). While this figure is skewed by the reporting of the actual numbers in one particular battle, the numbers reflect textbook writers' interest in the recurring theme of war.

The highest numbers of females in Level 3 are shopkeepers (8) and landladies (6), occupations which, according to Beckles (1988) and Mair (*ibid.*), women went into during the slavery and immediate post-slavery periods. These are therefore traditional Caribbean female occupations.

Although males continue to outnumber females at Level 5 (the unskilled), this is the level of occupation where the majority of females appear. Of the 113 females, 89 are students, 60 are vendors and 32 are domestics. It is interesting that all vendors, male and female, sell food and are traditional market and roadside vendors or higglers. None of the modern-day higglers we have come to know since the early 1970s in the bend down plazas or thronging airports as they enter or leave countries with their goods appears in these texts.

The 12 male and female occupations in which the largest numbers were clustered was compared and the data are presented in Table 6.

Table 6 *12 male and female occupations with largest numbers*

Male	No	Level	Female	No	Level
Soldier	1386	5	Student	89	5
Student	104	5	Vendor	60	5
Labourer	69	5	Teacher	43	3
Teacher	54	3	Domestic	32	5
Politician	52	1	Nurse	14	3
Police	49	3	Clerical/Sales	11	3
Fisherman	45	5	Labourer	9	5
Entertainer	32	3	Shopkeeper	8	4
Priest	31	2	Entertainer	6	3
Criminal	25	5	Landlady	6	4
Scientist/Inventor	23	2	Factory/Worker	5	5
Shopkeeper	20	4	Cashier/Bank teller	4	3

This ranking permits us to see that the majority of females is all at Levels 3, 4 and 5, while the majority of males is spread from Levels 1-5, or represented at all occupation levels. Males not only occupy all but two of the Level 1 occupations and all but 9 of the Level 2 occupations, but also they alone possess the means to control by force. It is notable that in this ranking the tenth largest number of males are criminals. They are burglars, pickpockets, murderers and one assassin (one is Magwich from *Great Expectations*).

The texts not only suggest an almost limitless variety of occupations for males on both sides of the law, but present males as "more intelligent, more creative, more inventive and more adventurous than women". The textbook world our children enter presents it as natural that males should rule, controlling all the leadership positions in the economic and political structure and in the professions. Girls, as well as boys, are exposed to this patriarchal ideology of male domination.

Again, as a comparison with the percentage distribution of the working population by occupational group will show, the textbooks distort reality (see Table 7).

Table 7 *Comparison of actual and textbook proportion distribution of working population by occupational group*

Occupational groups	Male		Female	
	Actual	Texts	Actual	Texts
Administrative & Executive	2.6	5.1	0.8	0.07
Professional & Technical	9.6	10.89	11.4	3.1
Clerical	8.7	—	20.8	—
Sales	7.1	0.44	11.5	0.55
Agriculture	10.7	3.28	8.3	0.36
Production & related	49.4	4.5	20.1	2.7
Service	10.5	0.33	25.9	1.25

Source for actual figures: 1980 Census.

3. Social reproduction work

The work or activities that have been coded as social reproduction work is excluded from conventional definitions of active labour, since orthodox economics focuses on the market. Marx concentrated on the capitalist mode of production and on the process of accumulation, but ignored the household economy and subsistence production in and for the family and society. The household economy and social reproduction work is, however, essential to capitalist production and it recreates and reinforces the male and female social relationship of domination and subordination which the market place creates. The categories identified as social reproduction work included indoor and outdoor household activities, subsistence work, household production, household consumption activities and child care and social care activities. All these categories, except perhaps for subsistence work, are self-explanatory. This term, suggested by an article by Beneria (1981), is used for all those activities which may require long hours of work and which are necessary for the maintenance of life or of household possessions. The persistent undervaluation of these types of work is probably because it is mainly done by women. It must also be emphasised that social reproduction work enables the capitalist to pay all workers one wage for two jobs.

In addition to household work, child care, home production and consumption and subsistence work, people in society are called upon to perform for others a variety of caring services essential to emotional happiness and well-being. These activities include listening to the troubles and concerns of others, providing comfort and reassurance, remembering and organising celebrations important in peoples' lives, such as birthdays, anniversaries and visiting the sick and the lonely. The importance of these activities, performed out of care and love, is often ignored but they form an essential part of social reproduction. They have been classified as social care acts.

Predictably females predominate in social reproduction labour, which is unwaged. The totals for the different categories are set out in Table 8.

Table 8 *Summary of male and female social reproduction work*

Category	Total	Male		Female	
		No	%	No	%
Household work	50	23	15.3	27	84.6
Subsistence work	15	10	66.6	5	33.3
Household production	7	1	14.28	6	85.7
Household consumption	117	27	23.0	90	76.9
Child care activity	127	18	14.0	109	85.8
Social care acts	108	38	35.1	70	64.8
	424	117	27.6	307	72.4

The largest numbers of representations are in household work and child care activities, followed closely by household consumption tasks and social care acts. The smallest numbers are in household production. Males predominate in one category: subsistence work. The stereotype of women working in the house and men working outdoors or in the yard is replicated.

A clearer view of the picture can be gained by looking at the domestic tasks done by the 20 or more persons in rank order (see Table 9).

Table 9 *Rank order of social reproduction tasks done by 20 or more males and females*

Category	Total	Males		Females	
		No	%	No	%
Shopping	108	19	17.59	89	82.4
Minding child at home	77	4	5.19	73	94.0
Cooking	53	5	9.4	48	90.5
Giving advice/care/comfort	42	5	11.9	37	88.0
Participating in religious ceremony for someone	38	20	52.6	18	47.3
Unspecified household chores	31	2	6.4	29	93.5
Taking child out	29	5	17.22	24	82.7
	378	60	15.8	318	84.1

The largest number of males and females shop for food for families, which is not surprising considering that the smallest numbers are involved in the household production of food. The family as a consumer of capitalist production is thus revealed, with females having the major responsibility for expenditure on food. Females also have the major responsibility for all child care functions. The second category of interest is that of giving advice, counselling and comforting. Both males and females engage in this activity but the proportion is 37 females compared with 5 males. The third category worthy of comment is related to the participation in religious ceremonies to heal an individual or the community. Here males predominate 20:18. This category was developed from extracts of accounts of what the writers called *obeah* ceremonies. As we know, these forms of African religion are part of Caribbean cultural life and experience and represent a form of struggle against European cultural domination. In the texts they are generally referred to in disparaging ways. Priests are called witchdoctors and are categorised as uncivilised. These religious practices, however, have social interaction patterns important in the lives of the community and this is particularly revealed in one extract from De Lisser's racist and sexist novel *The White Witch of Rosehall* (NEC 3). If the writer's bias in interpreting social events is ignored, it can be seen that large numbers of both males and females take part in these ceremonies, not to benefit themselves but to help an individual or the community. Often the participation by people means risking their lives. Gender analysis thus permits us not only to analyse male and female participation but in this instance to see the hidden sexist, racist and class ideology of the dominant group, operating at a level where we are barely conscious of it.

Another interesting observation can be made about the teaching that is part of child care. Females teach girls to do household tasks and males teach boys to do carpentry. From this we gain an insight into how stereotypical behaviour is reproduced in males and in females and also (to stretch the analysis), how families reproduce themselves, with the young being trained in the interests and occupations of the particular family.

There are no statistics available with which to compare the textbook reality. We know that females carry the major burden of social reproduction work. We are aware that males have always performed some of these tasks and that more and more males are now performing more and more of these tasks. What we hope is that this way of looking at what I have called social reproduction labour will fundamentally change the concepts and definitions of work and labour; that the integral relationship of home and the market will be acknowledged so that wages will permit workers, especially female workers, to pay for the services they must all now perform free. Until women can be offered some form of release from one of the two full-time jobs they now do their activities in the major public areas of social life will be severely curtailed, and, more than this, the social relations between men and women will never rest on a basis of equality.

4. *Leisure activities*

The wide range of leisure activities (89) were coded into seven categories: (1) competitive outdoor sports; (2) outdoor games and activities; (3) hunting and gathering; (4) pranks and antisocial acts, the latter category included stealing, playing truant and provoking and stoning passers-by and several texts presented these acts as acceptable boyish behaviour. The fifth category included personal entertainment and attendance at ceremonies, church and weddings. In the sixth category came creative and reflective pastimes such as reading, stamp-collecting, imaginative play and the like, and the seventh category brought together inactive and reactive behaviours. Table 10 shows the proportion of males and females engaged in different types of leisure activities.

Table 10 *Proportion of males and females engaged in different types of leisure*

Type of leisure activity	Total	Male		Female	
		No	%	No	%
Sports, outdoor/competitive	133	124	93.2	9	6.7
Outdoor games & activities	242	193	79.7	49	20.2
Hunting & gathering	41	37	90.2	4	9.7
Pranks & anti-social acts	36	34	94.4	2	5.5
Personal entertainmnt	165	113	68.48	52	31.5
Creative/reflective	46	32	69.5	14	30.4
Inactive/reactive	274	212	77.3	62	22.6
	937	745	79.5	192	20.4

Few females (20 per cent) engage in leisure activities compared with males (80 per cent). This may be because of the high level of female involvement in social reproductive labour. Males score over 90 per cent in three of the categories and 70 per cent in two. The highest proportion of females to males is in the creative and reflective category. If we rank male and female activities we find that the majority of females is in the inactive and reactive. The next category for females is entertainment, while for males it is outdoor games and activities.

Not only is the number of males much greater than females overall but leisure activities are stereotyped: girls only play netball, for example, and overall women are presented with the "passive girl" stereotype. What the figures also show is that the majority of males are also in the inactive and reactive category.

The largest numbers of males and females simply look on or watch a variety of events such as riots, fires, games or carnival bands. 'Watchers' were separated from 'limers'. Limers also watch but they may react and sometimes provoke as well (see LL2). The only persons taking a siesta or lying in a hammock were males. Males also talk politics. The extract that depicted this was from Tressal's *Ragged Trousered Philanthropists* (NEC 4) and the discussion concerns the exploitation of the capitalist system. More men than women are also shown sunbathing on the beach. In this category waiting appears. It is all females waiting for lovers to call or to arrive. In one extract from Beverly Clarke's *Fifteen* (EL 3) the American tribal custom of dating is introduced. The girl is nervous and behaves foolishly, the boy is manly and in charge of the situation. The concept of dating probably comes from America, and its rules and conventions have always been culturally foreign, as is the word itself, used to suggest a male and female relationship. Finally, attention should be drawn to the implicit approval of stealing and other illicit behaviour by boys. Male writers, it would seem, glorify and find these illicit boys' behaviour amusing. If the same acts were performed by men they would be recognisably criminal. This male attitude has been seen by the present author in several classrooms, where teachers have set compositions to students on topics such as "Tell what happened when you were stealing mangoes, etc, one day."

5. Images of families and of dominant groups

The actual selections of texts were analysed to determine the images of males and females and the relationships between males and females. All of this is communicated by the language of writers, hence some quotations are used to illustrate the point and some actual examples of words used in description are given. The results illustrate the process by which, perhaps unintentionally, the texts expose children to the value that social domination by one group over another is "natural". Domination by class, race and sex is illustrated in all the texts. The message is that the rich, as of right, have power over the poor, that white is naturally superior to black, and males should have power over women.

Families

Families were categorised as nuclear if it was clear beyond doubt that they comprised mother, father and children living in one household; or were one-parent if this was also indisputably clear. Surprisingly there were few one-parent families except in extracts from *In the Castle of my Skin* (Lamming). *Alleluia Morning* (Wickham), *Jane's Career* (De Lisser), *Miguel Street* (Naipaul) and *He Who Say No* (Brecht). Overwhelmingly children in the text lived in nuclear families, which in the majority of cases were poor. The variety of extracts illustrating this is too long to list but they came from English, American and West Indian literature. An extract from the *Intelligent Parents' Manual* (EL 3) also reminds us that intelligent parents have nuclear families.

The absurdity of presenting nuclear families as the norm to West Indian children requires no comment. Massiah (1983) has shown that not only is a high proportion of Caribbean households female-headed, varying from 46.6 per cent for St Kitts/Nevis to 22.4 per cent in Guyana with its large population of East Indian descent, but that most of these lie in the occupation levels which are in the majority in the texts. While the sociological data suggest that many women wish to marry, and that for women, "married" is perceived as a superior status to single, most Caribbean mothers are not married and 70 per cent of children are born to unmarried mothers. Parents, male or female, who are unmarried, widowed or divorced are beyond the pale in these texts. In only one series does divorce appear (NEC 4). The ideals of marriage and the nuclear family were and are in stark contrast to the Caribbean reality. The ideal has been preached by the church for 300 years, since marriage is a sacrament. The Caribbean reality has, however, continued to be interpreted mainly through European eyes. Thus, for example in 1741, Abel Alleyne, the manager of the Codrington Estates, reported on "polygamy" which he said was "as impossible to prevent as any one thing in the world as the men were lustful and also hoped to get more food by having more wives".

Although not directly relevant, I cannot resist referring you to the dilemma this created for the church, since Bishop Coleridge concluded subsequently that the "imposition of monogamy . . . might prove too heavy a burden . . . then we would have converted the ignorant polygamist into the self-convicted adulterer". (Drayton 1984:5)

Alleyne in fact called "polygamy" what we call a "visiting relationship". Of interest is his observation of its economic base, that is the male need for food in an impoverished society, a point discussed by Rohlehr (1988) in his analysis of calypsos of the 1930s. Examples of Caribbean reality interpreted through European male eyes abound, in which general area see, for example, Dann's 1987 study, *The Barbadian Male Sexual Attitude and Practices*. The phenomenon of black Caribbean male internalisation of European created stereotypes is interesting for our analysis.

Male/female relationships—"Nature has so ordered"

The male and female relationships between adults and between adults and children all appear in the texts. By and large relationships are characterised by fear and distrust, and by the inability of males and females to communicate. There are three instances where, dominated and controlled by men and feeling helpless, women commit suicide.

Fear and distrust begin in childhood. We find the small boy surprised and disturbed to find his friend speaking to a girl (*Days Gone By*, EL2). Inability to communicate is poignantly illustrated in Roger Mais's *You Gotta Go Home* in two series (LL3 and NEC4). In one extract, although Pedro and Christina are deeply in love, Christina cannot tell Pedro she is carrying another man's child and commits suicide (EL4). Saphira in *Creatures* (EL 2) kills herself because of unrequited love and the woman in John Wyndham's *Chrysalids* also commits suicide because she cannot take her defective child home to her husband: "Henry will turn me out I think. He'll find another wife who can give him proper children" (NEC 4). A different and irritating kind of helplessness appears in the woman who wants her husband to fire the maid. "She thinks she can defy me because I am only a woman. Please darling you do it for me."

Domination and control appear in the man who beats his wife because she tells the neighbours their son stole (NWE 3). Adults also beat children severely as, for example, in the extract from D.H. Lawrence's *The Rainbow*. Females, although in much smaller numbers, dominate and control males. This is apparent in the harshness of some mother and son relations, such as in *Days Gone By*; and of the mother in Jet, *A Gift for the Family* (EL 2), and also Miss Fan in *Creatures* (EL 2). Miss Fan feels that she alone must look after her lover but she berates, browbeats and abuses him in front of all. The black migrant wife in *Jet* is bossy and unreasonable in contrast to her patient, gentle husband.

There are still some examples of reasonable relationships; one appears in William Cobbett's *Advice to Young Men* in which the obsrvation is made, "nature has so ordered that "men shall become less ardent in their passion after the wedding day and women shall not" (NEC 4: 148). Overall, however, the textbooks do not present relationships where males and females mutually respect and trust each other and are interdependent and equal in status.

Images of women: "A thing to be seen and defined objectively"

One author begins a section of language exercises with this statement: "An abstraction is . . . not a thing to be seen and defined as objectively as a girl or a car" (LL 5:20). Girl and car are thus revealed as comparable concrete objects. Whether this author sees males as abstractions does not emerge.

The sexist socialisation has already been noted in social reproduction work, but here is a father's advice to his daughter. "Learn to make (bakes) good, girl, because when you married if you can't give your husband good food hell will roll." (Goose & Gander, NWE 3:54)

The stereotype of a woman with strength and endurance superior to a man and therefore able to endure suffering better, whether that suffering be physical, mental or emotional appears. Here for example is an extract from *The Pearl*: "Kino had wondered often at the iron of his patient fragile wife. She who was obedient and respectful and cheerful and patient could bear physical pain with hardly a cry. She could stand fatigue and hunger almost better than Kino himself. In the canoe she was like a strong man." (LL 2: 167)

The writer cannot let well alone. Kino's wife is not like herself, she is like a strong man. Apart from the distortion, this image is harmful. All human beings, regardless of sex, have the capacity to learn to deal with hardship and pain; it is not a genetically determined female capacity. If children do not learn that they alone have power and control over their responses to life situations they will also never learn how to be truly independent.

Unpleasant females like Miss Fan, Mrs Chandles, Sono's mother and others stalk the textbook pages, but one other persistent female stereotype must be addressed, that of woman the destroyer. Ever since Aphrodite burst out of her father's testicles to be born in the sea, women have been seen as the downfall of men and indeed of the human race. In the King James's version of the Bible it is Eve who caused Adam to be disobedient. (Adam clearly did not have access to Cobbett's advice.) Implicit in this well-known imagery is the patriarchal teaching that sex is evil and wicked. Sex is often symbolised as a "snake" which is also often a symbol for Satan, who is the destroyer. Thus in the mythology women have been equated with sex as a major socially destructive force. This image of woman is visible in Miss Lou in *Dan McGraw* (EL 2); Miss Lou's two lovers shoot it out and kill each other. Here it is again in an extract from Roger Mais's play, *The First Sacrifice*, where Cain is trying to explain why he murdered Abel.

Adam: How have you come to this?

Cain : I made a sacrifice for a sin, offering unto God and it lacked everything, wanting blood.

Adam: A sin offering?

Cain : Yes, for the sin of my coming here out of this woman [i.e. Eve] (LL3: 69)

Male and female role models

The West Indian male and female role models in the textbooks are few and far between. Two series include extracts from Harold La Borde's book, *All Oceans Blue*, which tells the story of the crossing of the Atlantic and the voyage around the world made by himself, his wife and his son. The Trinidad family's courage and achievements need to be more widely known. "Men to remember" include Galileo and Newton who have a unit devoted to them in one text (NW 2) and Uriah "Buzz" Butler, early leader of the Trinidadian oilfield workers, appears in an extract. Three American and one Russian astronaut also appear. Male models put forward have all been living men. By contrast this is true of only one female.

Mrs Manley, the mother of N.W. Manley, is presented in an extract from his *Autobiography*. The image is an attractive and engaging one of this woman who almost singlehandedly brought up her children, and she is described by her son as a "woman of immense energy and vitality". Merle Hodge's schoolgirl in Millicent is another attractive person, as is Mother Rebecca Silvera in Jean D'Costa's *Sprat Morrison*. She solves the problems and copes while the men and children look on. Perhaps the finest female model is the mother of *Alleluia Morning* in John Wickham's story. Although the mother is created through the daughter's narration she emerges as a person who recognises the importance of developing high self-esteem in her child. She teaches pride in one's identity and independence. Three of the females are fictitious characters and models of mothers. The effect of this selection is to imply that there are no women whose achievements in the public domain, whether in politics, science or the arts, are worth recording and reporting. The European (white) bias of the male selections must also be noted.

6. The language

Language used to describe or refer to males and females was analysed fully in only two series: *English for Life* and *Growing with Language*. The second is the most literary of the series surveyed. The task needs to be undertaken for all series before generalisations can be made. Suffice it to say that males are intelligent, lucid, tough, and daring (GL 3 12), small and wiry but heedless, careless of danger (GL 3). The male has "shameless pride and in his physical strength", is "built like an Adonis" (EL 4). The male is a "brilliant administrator", a "sound scholar", an eloquent debater and an incorruptible public servant undaunted by opposition.

Females are fat or exceedingly fat. Here is one of my favourites: "A negro woman of the people, short and rather fat, quite unremarkable. She waddled away indifferent to the son she had just brushed past . . . The last book he had been reading was The Heroes—what a difference between the mother of Perseus and this mother." (NWE 3:159, extract from *Mimic Men*).

Females are, of course, over-sensitive, sharp-tongued and short-tempered.

Discussion

This analysis was undertaken to determine the social content of English-Language texts written in independent Caribbean territories for the new Caribbean Examination in English which replaced the English examining boards' examinations in 1978. It is based on the premise that knowledge is not neutral and that it is specific social groups and classes that determine what is legitimate knowledge at different historical periods (Apple and King 1977: 342). The knowledge that schools distribute is therefore "a form of the larger distribution of goods and services in society" (Apple and King 1977: 3). Since English language is a compulsory subject in all Caribbean schools, and the texts analysed are the existing CXC text series, it can reasonably be concluded that almost all Caribbean children receive the knowledge distributed in these texts.

The analysis revealed the overwhelming sexist bias of the texts. The findings on sexism resemble those of a large number of studies on children's books of all kinds in many countries. In our case the concern is not that texts should not have sexist characters and sexist situations because these are after all part of life and literature. It is the lack of perspective or critical comment in editors' introductions and presentations of extracts. Units on the language and techniques of bias and on advertising appear in all the texts, with the greatest proportion in the two series by Cecil Gray, *Language for Living* and *English for Life*, but it is only in one textbook, *New English for the Caribbean*, that a serious article on sexism is presented. The extract is adapted from Gloria Royale's study of 40 advertisements shown on a West Indian TV station and called *Adam's Rib: Sexism in Advertising*. Ironically the main author of this series is Rhodri Jones, headmaster of a London boys' high school, and the four co-authors are women.

The stereotypes of weak, inferior women and strong superior men are harmful to both men and women. It permits the relegation of women to a subordinate status and demands the existence of strong, macho men who must not cry, show feelings or reveal weakness. Male socialisation into these stereotypical behaviours begins early. In young children's books it has been found that the only males who cry are frogs, toads and donkeys (Weizman *et al.* 1972, in Zimet 1976).

The stereotype also prevents serious analysis of class exploitation among women, which in the Caribbean is the exploitation of black women mainly by white and "light" women. It has masked the different social relationships which exist between one class of women and another and, what Anyon (1979) calls the "differences in the ideology of what is appropriate female behaviour". This last is obviously of enormous concern in Caribbean schools which are now open not only to the social elites but also to the masses of the people. It needs to be recognised that codes of acceptable female behaviours differ not only among individuals but among classes and that one central area of conflict in schools is between middle-class and working-class values.

Class as a concept important to social relations is invisible in the texts and this is why occupations were grouped by levels and not by class. The most explicit references were probably represented by Sparrow's "Capitalism Gone

Mad" (NWE 4), by the extract on "Butler and the 1937 Riots", extracted from Eric Williams (EL 3), and by the extract from the *Ragged Trousered Philanthropists* (NEC 4). The problems of individuals are presented mainly as individual and not as social or class problems. The capitalist emphasis on individualism and competition over cooperation is therefore implicit and poverty and crime are individual failings rather than "the result of an inequitable and racist economy". (Carnoy 1974:365)

The groupings by level and by sex did enable us to see that among the 12 male and female occupations with the largest numbers (Table 7) there are no owners of the means of production. There are, however, a vast majority of wage and salary earners among the 95 per cent males and 4.8 per cent females in occupations. The analysis of occupations also enabled us to see that in comparison to males, few women are shown in high-status or leadership roles. The *Leisure Code* not only presented an extreme example of male and female stereotypical behaviour but it enabled us to see that in young boys certain basically criminal behaviours such as stealing are justified. They are presented as amusing and appear to represent what is perceived as an essential part of boy days. The largest numbers both males and females looking on or watching (130 males and 21 females) were found in the *Leisure Code*. The stereotype of the passive female was expected but this analysis presents the image of a passive people. Inactive and reactive behaviours are engaged in by 6.5 per cent of the numbers in the texts. Passive people don't rock the boat and may not see the necessity to be participants in bringing about the social changes necessary to improve their lives. Passive people have internalised the ideology of domination and subordination which enables ruling groups to hold on to power.

The social reproduction code and the analysis of family together show women's unwaged work and males as family bread- winners. While the sexual division of labour did not arise with capitalism the particular forms in which we know it are a product of capitalism. The texts provide glimpses of the historical dimension of the sexual division of labour in the nurse from *Romeo and Juliet* and the *South African* and of its international dimension in the Skokian, the South African female seller of illicit liquor, they present an old and perhaps conservative view of West Indian society, as the match with actual statistics illustrated. It is interesting that in the occupations all the vendors are the traditional market vendors who do not represent the 67,000 Jamaican higglers whose economic power is now important in the Jamaican economy and is being seen as a threat by some Jamaican businessmen (Witter 1989). Traditional vendors are no threat to the established order, but perhaps this new breed of vendor is.

If all or most families are nuclear, with male bread-winners then only males need to earn real money. In this way the wages of female labour can be maintained at very low levels. The high representation of women at the lower level of the dual labour supply can therefore be rationalised and women are subordinated in both an institutional and cultural way. The lives of poor people are romanticised in the textbooks, which never reveal the institutional bases of poverty. Analysis of the shift in World Bank policy since 1973 show that "there is profit in investing in the poor" (Bennholdt-Thomson 1988) and this is confirmed by Boserup (1970) and Rogers (1980). In small enterprises and family enterprises, since wages are kept low in order to sell products, the costs of the physical reproduction of labour are kept low and self-exploitation occurs. The international sexual division of labour requires a large proportion of cheap labour and a male and female workforce which will engage in small business enterprises where waged work is not available.

The most surprising finding was with regard to racism in the texts. It is not the overt, crude, stereotyping of blacks in older texts, but it is there as the image of people who never achieved or discovered anything. It is not that the achievements of European inventors and discoverers should not be made known to our children, it is that the major achievements held up for admiration are by white males, and there are no comparable achievements by women, by blacks, nor by West Indians celebrated in the textbooks. A racist view of knowledge is also the effect of the lack of editorial comment on text such as the following:

> There were people in the swaying crowd who had been in Africa . . . they had travelled back to that dark continent tonight and were worshiping some sinister deity with power and will to harm . . . He could understand how devotees in pagan lands were moved at times almost to madness by the call and compulsion of their strange and horrible religions. (NEC 1:105).

English textbook writers focus on grammatical knowledge and on the skills of listening, speaking, reading and writing. While these are the responsibility of English teaching they are not conducted with value-free content and it is essential that textbook authors review selections and include editorial organisation and comment to address this serious problem. To a great extent the textbooks continue to interpret the West Indian reality through European eyes, the subject of Winston Bailey's brilliant composition, *Columbus Lie*. The colour of the knowledge of the textbooks is white and their sex bias is male.

References

Anyon, J. "Ideology and United States History Textbooks". *Harvard Educational Review*, Vol. 49, No. 3, August 1979.

Apple, M. and King, N. "What do Schools Teach?". OISE *Journal of Education 1977.*

Barrett, M. "Women's Oppression Today" in *Problems in Marxist Feminist Analysis* London: Verso 1980.

Beckles, Hilary. *Afro-Caribbean Women and Resistance to Slavery*, London: Karnak House 1988.

_______. *Natural Rebels. A Social History of Enslaved Black Women in Barbados*. London: Zed Books 1989.

Beechy, Veronica.*Unequal Work*. London: Verso. 1987.

Beneria, L. and Sen, G. "Accumulation, Reproduction and Women's Role in Economic Development: Boserup Revisited". *Signs, Journal of Women in Culture and Society* 7 (2), Winter 1981, pp. 279-98.

Bennholdt-Thomson, V. "Investment in the Poor: An Analysis of World Bank Policy". in Mies, M. *et al.* (ed). *Women: The Last Colony*. London: Zed Press. 1988. pp. 51-63.

Boserup, E. *Women's Role in Economic Development*, New York: St. Martin's Press. 1970.

Bowles, S. and Gintis, H. *Schooling in Capitalist America*, New York: Basic Books. 1976.

Carnoy, M. *Education as Cultural Imperialism*, New York: Longmans. 1974.

Council for Inter-Racial Children's Books "Sexism". In *Basal Readers and Other Textbooks*, New York. 1983.

Dann, Graham. *The Barbadian Male, Sexual Attitudes and Practices* Macmillan Caribbean. 1987.

Dalla Costa, M. and James, S. *The Power of Women in the Subversion of the Community*, Bristol, UK. 1982.

Drayton, Kathleen. *The Development of Higher Education for Women in the Commonwealth Caribbean, with Special Reference to Barbados*. Paper presented to 6th Berkshire Conference on the Hisotry of Women, Smith College, USA (unpublished). 1984.

Falcon, N. "The Oppressive Function of Values, Concepts and Images in Children's Books". In Prieswick, Roy (ed.) *The Slant of The Pen, Racism in Children's Books*. Geneva: WCC. 1980.

Hooks, Bell. *Ain't I a Woman?, Black Women in Feminism* London: Pluto Press. 1981.

Jackson, E.P. "Effects of Reading on Attitudes toward the Negro Race" *Library Quarterly*, 14, 1944, pp. 47-54. Cited in Zimet, *op. cit.*

James, Selma. *Sex, Race and Class, Housewives in Dialogue*, London. 1986.

Kelly, Joan. *Women's History and Theory, The Essays of Joan Kelly*. Chicago: University of Chicago Press. 1984.

King, Ruby (1979) "The Jamaica Schools' Committee and the Development of Secondary Education", in *Development and Disillusion in Third World Education; Ed.* Vincent Doyley and Reginald Murray (eds.), Ontario Institute for Studies in Education, Symposinm Series 10, Canada.

Mair, L.M. *Women Field Workers in Jamiaca During Slavery*. 1986 Elsa Goveia Memorial Lecture. Department of History, UWI, Mona. 1987.

Massiah, J. "Women's lives and livelihoods. A view from the Commonwealth Caribbean" *World Development*, Vol. 17, No. 17, 1983, pp. 965-77.

______. *Women as Heads of Households in the Caribbean: Family Structure and Feminine Status*. UNESCO. 1983.

Michel, A. "Sex differentiated Socialisation in French Schools". In Secretariat of the Council of Europe (ed.), *Sex Stereotyping in Schools*. Strasbourg 1982. pp. 91-103.

Mies, M. "The Social Origins of the Sexual Division of Labour" in ed. Maria Mies et al. *Women, The last colony*, London: 1988 Zed Books Ltd.

O'Jon, Eirene. "Some Comparaisons between Educational Development in British Guiana and Jamaica in the later Nineteenth Century". In D'Oyley and Murray, *op. cit.* 1979.

Purves, A.C. and Beach, R. *Literature and the Reader* 1972. Cited in Zimet, *op. cit.*

Reddock, R. *Women, Labour and Struggle in 20th-Century Trinidad and Tobago: 1898-1960*. PhD Thesis, University of Amsterdam. 1984.

Rogers, B. *The Domestication of Women. Discrimination in Developing Societies* London and New York. 1980.

Rohlehr, G. "Images of Men and Women in 1930s Calypsoes. The Sociology of Food Acquisition in the Context of Survival". In Mohammed, P. and Shepherd, C. *Gender in Caribbean Development* UWI Women and Development Studies Project. 1988.

Turner, T. "Objectives and Provisions for Trade and Technical Training: The Case of Colonial Jamaica, 1867-1920". 1979. In D'Oyley and Murray, *op. cit.*

Weitzman, L.J. *et al.* "Sex-role Socialisation in Picture Book for Pre-school Children", *American Journal of Sociology*, 77, 1972, pp. 1125-49. Cited in Zimet, *op. cit.*

Witter, M. (ed). "Higglering, Sidewalk Vending, Informal Commercial Traditions in the Jamaican Economy". Proceedings of a Symposium. UWI, Department of Economics, Occasional Paper No. 4, Jamaica. 1989.

Zimet, S.G. *Print and Prejudice*, UK: Hodder and Stoughton 1976.

Columbus Lie

Winston Bailey (The Shadow) 1989

Columbus was a mighty sailor
He sailed the open seas
He went down in the Caribbean
And he called it West Indies
He said he found a new world
And he expect me to believe
But how could this world be new
When its much older than Adam and Eve.

Chorus
Columbus lie (3) Columbus lie, lie, lie
He said he discovered
The whole of America
He never tell nobody
How he had to run from Apache
Columbus lie (3) Columbus lie so bad
I believe Columbus was mad

The man with the Santa Maria
Was as grave as a man can be
He sailed on to Venezuela
For another discovery.
He said he discovered new lands
And he thought that I wouldn't know
He discovered a lot of Indians
Who discovered the lands before.

Chorus
He took all the glory.
For many discoveries
The truth of the story
those lands were discovered already
Columbus lie
And if you concentrate
You'll discover the man was late.

Women in School Administration

Exclusion and Isolation

Ewart Taylor

This paper will look into the existence of the phenomena of exclusion and isolation which are perceived to be associated aspects of gender discrimination against women as educational administrators. Exclusion is taken to mean the total or near total prohibition of access to major administrative posts and their related duties. Isolation, on the other hand, is seen as a prevention from, or a numerical and substantive reduction of, participation in mainstream activities such as decision-making, policy formation, publication or research work. The paper uses three examples which manifest themselves worldwide and will examine:

1. some educational data from Trinidad and Tobago;
2. published themes listed in the British Educational Index; and
3. the composition of editorial boards of these educational administration journals.

The paper will present specific instances of exclusion and isolation for examination. Firstly, an answer to how exclusion and isolation manifest themselves will be essayed. Secondly, the quantitative contributions of women in areas of research associated with educational administration will be put forward and assessed against a description of the gender composition among gate-keepers (the editors and board members) of three journals. Finally, the theoretical perspectives in which isolation and exclusion may be explained are presented.

Manifestations of Exclusion and Isolation

A literature review on the subject of women in administration reveals that there are both deliberate as well as unconscious attempts to exclude and isolate women from educational administration. Whereas the deliberate attempts can be easily observed in the formal, but less so in the informal, organisation, the unconscious and subconscious efforts to undermine the contributions of women are less discernible by the uninitiated. Much of the explanation for the existence of these behaviours in men is attributable to the personal agenda developed through the ways in which men are conditioned or socialised. The more typical indicators of isolation and exclusion, like under-representation of women, salary inequities, powerlessness and confinement to low-status staff positions, are the more blatant forms with which this paper is concerned, but it restricts discussion mainly to one variable: under-representation.

Traditionally women have had limited opportunities for selection and entry into administrative positions based on criteria and job descriptions written to favour the hiring of men. Women are also assigned to the nurturing roles in primary school systems which tend to have flat structures that inhibit occupational mobility (Pounder 1988; Revere 1987; Yeakey, Johnston and Adkison 1986; Shakeshaft and Hanson 1986; Kanter 1984).

If or when promoted, the more advanced age of entry of women into administrative posts may be a disadvantage because of the efforts and energies required for such jobs. This is especially true since women tend to be given the most difficult assignments with little support and resources (Maienza 1986; Revere 1987). On the average, career paths for women tend to be longer and may be exacerbated by the claimed male tendency to withhold recognition of their competencies, commitment, etc, while their male colleagues engage in fault finding, victim analysis and the creation of surplus repression, which tend to be applied differentially to each sex (Davies 1987; Maienza 1986; Yeakey, Johnston and Adkison 1986).

Men are informally given the benefits of sponsorship, mentoring and alliances as they climb career ladders. Only a few women are so fortunate as to have these 'privileges', and the majority suffer the indignities of a male-dominated organisational culture. Any attempts to achieve success by women in administration or by those who aspire to be in administration are severely criticised. Women tend to be put down and traits seen as virtues in men are labelled flaws in women. These flaws are often the core of male jokes about females.

Hanson (1979) recorded some stereotypical assertions which compare male and female administrators: for example, "a male administrator is dynamic", "a female administrator is aggressive"; "he is confident", "she is stuck up"; "he has the courage of his convictions", "she is stubborn"; "he exercises authority diligently", "she is power mad" (p. 232). This is a situation that reinforces negative sanctions in the formal organisation that make women feel that they do not belong in administration (Yeakey, Johnston and Adkison 1986; Adkison 1981). Even worse is the situation of the black woman in the USA who suffers the double jeopardy of sex and race discrimination (Revere 1987).

Both Davies (1987) and Yeakey and her associates (1986) report the way in which research on women can be biased against them. Davies (1987) was mainly concerned with the imposition of first-world conceptions and models on the problems of third-world women. Yeakey and associates (1986) and Shakeshaft and Hanson (1986) concur with the position that stresses the urgent need to use critical and conflict theories as well as phenomenological approaches much more. These researchers fear the perpetuation of androcentric biases in present mainstream research themes, methodologies, conceptual frameworks, language usage and the data reported and conclusions drawn.

Under-representation of Female Administrators: The case of Trinidad and Tobago

International data have seemed to indicate a gross under-representation of women in high-status administrative positions. It has been observed in some African countries as well as in England (Davies 1987). Although some research reports in the USA have claimed that there have been improvements in representation at the upper administrative levels, there is still a gross imbalance which favours men. Yeakey, Johnston and Adkison (1986) reported national data supplied by the American Association of School Administrators (AASA) which showed a decline of male administrators from 80.8 to 68.27 per cent, and an increase of white women from 11.8 to 18.9 per cent. Revere (1987) counted only 29 black women who held superintendencies in 1985, a mere 0.18 per cent of all such posts in the USA. This nevertheless was an increase from three in 1970. The international trend of under-representation, but with modest increases in the quota of women, seems to be clear. What then is the position in the Caribbean? The case of the twin-island state of Trinidad and Tobago is examined.

The trend towards increased representation of women was reported among primary-school principals (PIs) in the *Statistics on Public Education of the Ministry of Education* (1980, 1984, 1985, 1987). Data here show that female principals increased from 148 (31.9 per cent) in the academic year 1980/81 to 182 (39.6 per cent) in the academic year 1987/88 (see Table 1). These figures show that a decline occurred in the relationship between the number of males and the primary-school principalship position, as the chi square value fell from 13.1 ($p < .001$) to 4.3 ($p < .05$). A clear increase in female representation was evident during the decade.

The picture seemed more encouraging for females among the primary-school vice-principals (VPIs). At the start of the decade of the 1980s the number

Table 1 *Gender ratios of principlas and vise-principals in government and assisted primary and secondary school of Trinidad and Tobago 1980–88*

Academic year	1980/81				1981/82				1982/83				1984/85				1987/88			
Post	M	F			M	F			M	F			M	F			M	F		
	(No)	(No)			(No)	(No)			(No)	(No)			(No)	(No)			(No)	(No)		
	%	%	χ^2	p	%	%	χ^2	p	%	%	χ^2	p	%	%	χ^2	p	%	%	χ^2	p
Principal I (PI)	(316)	(148)			(286)	(168)			(298)	(169)			(298)	(167)			(278)	(182)		
(Primary school)	68.1	31.9	31.1	<.001	63.9	36.1	7.8	.01	63.8	36.5	7.6	<.01	63.5	36.2	7.3	<.01	60.4	39.6	4.3	<.05
Vice-principal I (VPI)	(66)	(130)			(68)	(116)			(53)	(116)			(40)	(88)			(46)	(119)		
(Primary school)	33.2	66.8	11.3	<.001	37.0	63.0	11.4	<.001	31.4	68.8	13.8	<.001	31.3	68.7	14.0	<.001	27.9	72.1	19.5	<.001
Principal II (P II)	(68)	(21)			(66)	(23)			(66)	(25)			(71)	(24)			No			
(Secondary school)	76.4	23.6	27.9	<.001	74.2	25.8	23.4	<.001	72.7	27.5	20.2	<.001	74.7	25.3	24.4	<.001	Data			
Vice-principal II (VPi)	(67)	(37)			(53)	(32)			(82)	(34)			(69)	(43)			No			
	64.4	35.6	8.3	<.01	62.4	37.6	6.14	<.02	69.7	32.1	12.8	<.001	61.6	38.4	5.4	<.02	Data			

Note: Chi Square values were computed at ldf.
M = Male.
F = Female.

of female vice-principals was 130 (66.8 per cent) but increased in relative terms to 119 (72.1 per cent) by 1987/88. This seeming anomaly may be a reflection of the delays in appointments within the system. Gender representation favoured a significant relationship between the number of females and the vice-principalship category, and the magnitude of this relationship rose from a chi square value of 11.3 to 19.5 ($p < .001$). If seniority remains the dominant criterion in the promotional procedures, then it will be only a short time before more female principals are appointed. Eventually therefore, more female school supervisors (SS Is) in the primary-school sector may be appointed. The inevitability of this was guaranteed only on the assumption that the share of the mid-decade female teacher population of 71.93 per cent (Ministry of Education 1985) was maintained or increased.

A slight overall increase was also shown in the representation of females as principals (P II) and vice-principals (VP II) at the secondary level (see Table 1). A small number (21-25) of females (23.6 per cent to 25.3 per cent) were incumbents in principalship positions. Male principals were significantly greater in their representations which showed chi square values ranging between 27.9 and 20.2 ($p < .001$) during 1980-84. Female representation as vice-principals was numerically better during the same period when their share of the membership varied between 32 and 43 (37.6 per cent and 38.4 per cent). These figures had chi square values ranging from 12.8 (p .001) in 1982/83, to 5.4 ($p < .02$) in 1984/85, thus demonstrating an erratic pattern of representation.

The (1993) *Report of the Task Force on Education: Draft Policy Framework (1993-2003)* strongly recommended that expertise gained through accredited professional development programmes should replace seniority as the major criterion for promotion in the proposed Educational Service (Ministry of Education 1993). Provided that the optimism for the implementation of these proposals remains, the competencies gained in educational administration on the Diploma in Education programme will be used as a major qualification for secondary-school principalship positions. It thus appears that males will continue to dominate in the upper echelons of the educational system. This conclusion follows as a consequence of the imbalance favouring male membership in the educational administration classes at the Faculty of Education (University of the West Indies, St Augustine) over the period 1986-90. By using the figures of members enrolled only from co-educational schools, the male/female ratios were computed to be 5:1, 5:2, 3:2 and 9:0, whereas the enrolment on the entire programme and in the teaching concentrations (curriculum and instruction) during the same time span revealed a predominance of females. This tendency resembled the US pattern where women's representation on educational administration programmes was 12 per cent and 18 per cent at the state level and 19 per cent and 32 per cent at the national level for 1976 and 1979 respectively (Stockard and Kempner 1981). These data predicted that the upper-level administrative hierarchy in Trinidad and Tobago would continue to be male-dominant for some time unless some new criteria were used in the promotional structure.

An examination of the middle and upper management levels (that is, above the level of School Supervisor II - SS IIs, head of a primary-school district within the central administration framework of the educational system) also confirms the paucity of female membership in meaningful decision-making positions. From information supplied by the Educational Planning Unit of the Ministry of Education, it seems that there had never been a female appointed to the top post of Chief Education Officer (CEO) or who had acted in it.

Directorships of the departments of school supervision, curriculum development and educational planning were traditionally held by males until the appointment in 1990 of a female as the director of the Department of Curriculum Development. At about the same time the headship of the Measurement Unit passed from a male member to a female. Apart from these seeming aberrations, three females successively held the headship of the Guidance Unit since its inception in 1979. Similarly, all five previous heads of the library service were females. Such bits of information support international data and practices on staff positions relating to types of perceived gender-related traits. At the level of secondary school supervision (SS IIIs), the highest level in the field, which administers directly to the eighth educational division, there were only male incumbents. The trend in the nature of the representation was in men's favour and followed the pattern of most of the data already presented.

At the tertiary level the University of the West Indies (UWI), St Augustine campus, is examined here for gender imbalances in faculty administration. The campus was not necessarily typical of all UWI campuses, nor representative of the tertiary sector in Trinidad and Tobago. Data gleaned from Departmental Reports of the University of the West Indies for 1974/75, 1979/80, 1983/84 and 1987/88 were a bit sketchy. Nevertheless, the available figures showed the dominance of men in administration at the St Augustine campus. In fact, almost all deanships and headships were occupied by men in most faculties and their departments in the academic years selected. The preponderance of men as deans or heads in faculties and departments offering programmes in the hard sciences (physics and chemistry), mathematics, in technological areas (agriculture, engineering, management studies) and Social Sciences adds very much to the evidence of gender bias not only in the under-representation of women in school administration, but also of the bias in subject choices at the secondary-school level. The exceptions to this pattern of male hegemony were found in the headships in the English (1974/75, 1979/80, and 1983/84), French and Spanish departments (1979/80); and a deanship in the Faculty of Arts and General Studies (1987/88).

The under-representation of women in school administration in Trinidad and Tobago, mirrors the pattern in some countries of the West. The only apparent difference from the more global experience that emerges here is the equity that is demonstrated in the local primary schools with respect to the vice-principalship. The greater numerical dominance of men at the higher administrative echelons of the educational system is clear.

Women in Administration-related Research

Investigation of the exclusion and isolation of women was made in the area of research writing related to educational administration. In order to do this the British Educational Index, a reputable reference source, was selected because it provided in most cases the first and last names of authors from which gender could be ascertained. The entire yearbooks of 1980, 1985 and the April-June 1989 issue were selected to give some idea of change in gender representation of contributors to articles during the decade of the 1980s.

Pages in the author index section were systematically sampled at one in every ten pages (1980 and 1985), and one in every three pages for the April-June 1989 volume. Titles of alternate articles were then selected on the sampled pages and their authors' first names were used for gender identification. Since a large majority of these were known English names, the gender of the contributors was not difficult to detect. Nevertheless, where the first name could have indicated either gender, or where detection of gender was not clear, the particular article was excluded from further consideration. Theme analysis was then done on the basis of the face validity of the titles under the assumption that they reflected the central concern of the publication.

The method of theme classification used was adopted from the Educational Administration Abstracts. The gender ratio of contributors was then determined by theme and finally for total publications on all themes. Although there were some obvious limitations to this approach, it was felt that care in name selection reduced the incidence of gender mis-classification. Methodologically, the analysis would have been enhanced if data on submissions and rejections had been available. This is a regrettable omission that must be taken into account with respect to conclusions.

Table 2 illustrates some trends that characterise the themes on which male and female contributors chose to research and publish. An examination of each of the 14 themes reveals that men are the significant contributors to journals. In 1980 the contributions in 12 categories favoured male authors and showed chi square values greater than 12.96 ($p < .001$). The other 2 categories—"Community, Society and School" and "Theory and Research"—also favoured contributions from men, but these data showed smaller chi square values of 3.03 ($p < .1$) and 7.84 ($p < .01$) respectively. The pattern of male domination of publications repeated itself in 1985, except that only in "Counselling" ($\chi^2 = 5.48$; $p < .02$) and "Staff Development" ($\chi^2 = 4.00$; $p < .05$) were male contributions reduced. For 1989 some equity emerged in "Personnel", and some numerical advantage was experienced by female writers in the area of "Student Personnel" ($\chi^2 = 4.00$; $p < .05$).

Slight increases occurred in female contributions to themes in 1989, but these changes neither significantly challenged nor disrupted the general picture of male dominance. Female representation of 25-60 per cent was seen in all themes at some time during the decade, but the share of themes to which they contributed was generally below 35 per cent. The "Government, legal and financial issues" was consistently the only one with a less than 25 per cent female sponsorship.

Table 2 *The ratio of women to men on research literature related to educational administration as cited in the British Educational Indexes of 1980, 1985 and 1989*

	Themes	1980				1985				1989			
		M	F			M	F			M	F		
		(No)	(No)			(No)	(No)			(No)	(No)		
		%	%	χ^2	p	%	%	χ^2	p	%	%	χ^2	p
1	Administrative structure and process	(70)	(19)			(134)	(41)			(120)	(55)		
		78.6	21.4	32.7	<.001	76.6	23.4	28.30	<.001	68.6	31.4	13.94	<.0001
2	Personnel	(17)	(8)			(25)	(6)			(5)	(5)		
		68.0	32.0	12.96	<.001	80.6	19.4	37.45	<.001	50.0	50.0	.00	
3	Curriculum: theory, teaching, learning, testing	(355)	(136)			(543)	(232)			(208)	(100)		
		72.3	27.7	19.89	.001	70.1	29.9	16.16	<.001	67.5	32.5	12.25	<.001
4	Counselling	(29)	(14)			(66)	(41)			(21)	(13)		
		67.4	32.6	12.11	<.001	61.7	38.3	5.48	<.02	61.8	38.2	5.57	<.02
5	Professional preparation and certification	(13)	(4)			(36)	(10)			(10)	(4)		
		76.5	23.5	28.09	<.001	78.3	21.7	32.04	<.001	71.4	28.6	18.32	<.001
6	Staff development	(4)	(1)			(6)	(4)			(16)	(6)		
		80.0	20.0	36.00	<.001	60.0	40.0	4.00	<.05	72.7	27.3	20.61	<.001
7	Polices, programmes, planning inplementation	(31)	(11)			(58)	(21)			(53)	(14)		
		73.8	26.2	22.66	<.001	73.4	26.6	21.90	<.001	76.1	20.9	33.87	.001
8	Performance and programme evaluation	(10)	(3)			(13)	(5)			(22)	(7)		
		76.9	23.1	28.94	<.001	72.2	27.8	19.71	<.001	75.9	24.1	26.83	<.001
9	Community, society and school	(27)	(19)			(62)	(28)			(74)	(33)		
		58.7	41.3	3.03	<.10	68.9	31.1	14.29	<.001	69.2	30.8	14.75	<.001
10	Student persommel	(13)	(3)			(10)	(4)			(8)	(12)		
		81.2	18.8	38.93	<.001	71.4	28.6	18.32	<.001	40.0	60.0	4.00	<.05
11	Materials, equipment, facilities	(16)	(4)			(21)	(1)			(28)	(10)		
		80.0	20.0	36.00	<.001	95.5	4.5	82.81	<.001	73.7	26.3	22.47	<.001
12	School services	(6)	(1)			(10)	(0)			(9)	(5)		
		85.7	14.3	50.98	<.001	0.00	0.00	—	—	64.3	35.7	8.18	<.01
13	Government, legal financial issues	(6)	(1)			(7)	(0)			(6)	(0)		
		85.7	14.3	50.98	<.001	100.0	0.00	100.0	<.001	100.0	0.00	100.0	<.001
14	Theory, research	(16)	(9)			(24)	(4)			(43)	(16)		
		64.0	36.0	7.84	<.01	85.7	14.3	50.98	<.001	72.9	27.1	20.98	<.001
15	All themes	(6.07)	233			(1005)	(97)			(623)	(280)		
		72.5	27.5	20.25	<.001	73.4	26.6	21.90	<.001	69.0	31.0	14.44	<.001

Overall Table 2 shows that male contributions were favoured for publishing, and the overall chi square values, 20.25, 21.90 and 14.44 ($p<.001$) for all themes during the respective years sampled emphasised that the pattern of male over-representation is present in the areas of research and publications. The consequences of this for theory and practice of educational administration are that androcentric biases (Shakeshaft and Hanson 1986) would most likely have dominated almost every theme.

The gate-keeping function

Whenever it becomes part of the cultural tradition for any group of people to regard the exercise of certain social functions as their exclusive domain, that group tends deliberately to set up buffers against infringements of their control. This dictum tends to be true also for the groups of men who on a worldwide scale have ascribed rulership status on to themselves in educational systems. Fortunately, these situations are not irrevocable, as history demonstrates that women can breach the "Berlin Wall" around so-called male territory through such 'victories' as winning the adult suffrage and gaining membership in exclusive men's clubs. What prevents the rapid or sudden collapse of these walls is the protective functions of those who act as gate-keepers. With respect to publishing in the field of educational administration, there are formal and informal groups such as selection boards and executive committees at local, regional and national levels, and the alumni or "old boys' networks" connected with them, all of which have a bearing on the exclusion and isolation of women. It is particularly interesting to find out whether such editorial boards and committees are male-dominated and have been associated with the reduced contributions of women to some research and publications activities.

In testing the proposition of male dominance in this area, the gender composition of editorial boards and executive committees of three popular journals, *Educational Leadership (EL)*, the *Journal of Educational Administration Quarterly (JEA)* and the *Educational Administration Quarterly (EAQ)*, were chosen for scrutiny. Issues from 1980, 1985 and 1989 were sampled for examination of the male:female ratios during the 1980s decade. Gender was again determined as described before. Only in the case of the *JEA*, where members' initials were used for several first names, was it difficult to accurately determine gender composition of the entire body, and therefore consideration was given only to that part of the board that could have been gender-resolved.

Table 3 describes the gender composition of the boards of each of the three journals. There is an overwhelmingly male membership of the editorial boards (see row a) of each of the journals, which is expressed by the fact that eight of the nine chi square values reveal that these compositions would occur by chance in less than 1 out of 1,000 cases. It was only by 1989 that female membership of the editorial board of the *EAQ* had become about one-third that of the male membership ($\chi^2 = 4.00$; $p<.05$).

Table 3 *Gender composition of editorial boards, editors, management committees of and contridutors to the popular journals: Educational Administration Quarterly (EAQ), Educational Leadership (EL) and Joural of Educational Administration (JEA) in 1980, 1985 and 1989*

Journal	Composition of (a) educational boards (b) editors (c) management committees (d) contributors														
		1980					1985					1989			
		M (No) %	F (No) %	χ^2	p		M (No) %	F (No) %	χ^2	p		M (No) %	F (No) %	χ^2	p
Educational Administration Quarterly (EAQ)	(a)	18	0			(a)	12	1			(a)	15	10		
		100	0	100	<.001		92.31	7.69	71.60	<.001		60.00	40.00	4.00	<.05
	(b)*					(b)	11	2			(b)	10	3		
							84.62	15.38	47.94	<.001		76.92	23.08	28.99	<.001
	(c)*	No executive on management committee named													
	(d)	45	6			(d)	44	4			(d)	19	4		
		88.2	11.8	58.37	<.001		91.7	8.3	6956	<.001		82.6	17.4	42.51	<.001
Educational Leadership (EL)	(a)	5	2			(a)	5	2			(a)	5	2		
		71.43	28.57	18.37	<.001		71.43	28.57	18.37	<.001		71.43	28.57	18.37	<.001
	(b)	2	5			(b)	4	3			(b)	3	5		
		28.57	71.43	18.37	<.001		57.15	42.85	2.03	<.2		37.5	62.5	6.25	<.02
	(c)	7	6			(c)	6	7			(c)	7	6		
		53.85	46.15	.59	<.5		46.15	53.85	.59	<.5		53.85	46.15	.59	<.5
	(d)	155	57			(d)	156	78			(d)	50	39		
		73.1	26.9	21.3	<.001.		66.7	33.3	5.58	<.02		56.2	43.8	1.54	<.3
Journal of Educational Administration (JEA)	(a)	11	1			(a)	14	1			(a)	15	3		
		91.67	8.33	69.45	<.001		93.33	6067	75.05	<.001		83.33	16.67	44.40	<.001
	(b)	**	—	—	—	(b)	—	—	—	—	(b)	—	—	—	—
	(c)	**	—	—	—	(c)	—	—	—	—	9c0	—	—	—	—
	(d)	33	8	—	—	(d)	27	8			(d)	30	5		
		80.5	19.5	37.21	<.001		77.1	22.9	29.38	<.001		85.7	14.3	50.98	<.001

* No names were published under these categories.

** The gender compostions of management committees and editors could not be determined initials rather than first names were supplied.

Some data about editors (Table 3, row b) are missing and therefore a full picture is not possible for the period under review. In spite of this, the trend in the gender imbalance favours males ($p < .001$) in the *EAQ*. A significant development in this category shows that there were more women than men editors, and this difference reveals chi square values which vary in probabilities from $p < .02$ to $p < .001$.

Although it was difficult to extract or get data on the composition of the entire executive committees of the *EAQ* and the *JEA* (Table 3, row c), the trend in the disproportionately fewer opportunities for women seems to be maintained here. Again, the data from *EL* (Table 3, row c) show that this journal has attempted to move towards some measure of gender equity ($p < .05$), as is exhibited in a consistent 7:6 (male:female) ratio on its executive council during the decade.

The next question posed related to whether or not the journal with the most equitable gender ratio among editors, boards and committees does reflect a more equitable contribution to articles published. To measure this aspect, the articles from each journal in the respective years (1980, 1985, 1989) were examined, and the male and female contributors were listed only where their genders could be clearly determined by their names. Each member of a jointly written article was regarded as a full contributor, and if the gender of one member of a team could not be determined, the entire team was disqualified from the sample. Also, where an issue was unavailable for scrutiny, the male:female ratio was assumed to be affected only minimally for the period studied.

When rows a, b and c of Table 3 are examined individually, the conclusion that *EL* approaches gender equality in terms of representation is demonstrated more than it is in either the *EAQ* or the *JEA*. Generally, the smaller chi square values for *EL* in each row bear testimony to this. In fact, row b of *EL* shows that female editors outnumber their male counterparts, a reversal of the general pattern of gender representation.

Row d, Table 3 attempts to examine whether the contributions by either gender approaches a 'better' numerical balance. Without exception, each of the journals favours male contributors. But whereas the male proportion of writers was 77.1-91.7 per cent in the *EAQ* and *JEA*, their representation in the *EL* was 73.1 per cent in 1980 and 56.2 per cent in 1989, showing a progressive representation for women during the decade. Another look at the data reveals that a less than .001 level of significance in the *EAQ* and the *JEA* indicated that there was a very high chance of male authorship of these publications, whereas the *EL* reflected an increase in the probability (from $p < .001$ to $p < .3$) that gender was becoming less related to the chance of being published.

A further test of the relationship between gender and the chance of being published was carried out with the *EAQ* after a spate of pro-feminist articles in and after 1986, which seemed to have alerted the managerial personnel of this journal to the plight of females in the world of publication. There seems to have been an almost immediate improvement in female membership on the editorial board of the *EAQ* (see Table 3, row a 1989). The years 1988, 1989 and

1990 respectively had 23.4 per cent, 17.4 per cent and 22.7 per cent female contributions. Each of these had chi square values of 28.30, 42.51 and 29.81 (($p < .001$) favouring men, but these were considerably less than the 1980 and the 1985 statistical indices ($\chi^2 = 58.37$; $p<.001$ and $\chi^2 = 69.56$; $p<.001$). The change in these indices seems to demonstrate some marginal and not very significant improvement in the relationship between females and their chances of being published.

In view of the evidence from the data provided for *EL* (and to a lesser extent *EAQ*) the gate-keeping functions exercised by male personnel appear to limit the contributions by women to these publications. The existence of a more equitable gender composition on managerial boards does appear to reduce the possibility of isolation and exclusion of women. The explanation of the status of women as isolated and excluded in terms of numerical representation will now be put forward. This will be done by examining some of the literature which describes the discrimination against women.

Explaining Isolation and Exclusion

This section presents a compilation of the various ways in which discrimination of women in school administration may be explained. It suggests that no single perspective provides a complete view of the problem, but rather supports the notion that for a full understanding the entire range of explanations should be considered even though they do not appear to be mutually exclusive.

The low status of women in organisations has been traditionally explained by sex-role stereotyping and socialisation. This approach describes the characteristics which keep women in their place and contributes to the realisation of the inherent self-fulfilling prophecies about women in organisations. Females have been socialised according to the woman's place model, a compliance to which serves as the basis of rewards via certain minimal psychological and social comforts in the workplace. This approach to understanding under-representation is considered insufficient, as it explains very little of the variance of the low organisational status of women. Any complete understanding must include the examination of other variables (Adkison 1981; Pounder 1988; Revere 1987; Yeakey, Johnston and Adkison 1986).

An extension of our understanding of the phenomena, may be accomplished by looking at ways in which sex-role stereotyping and socialisation are linked to conceptions of administrative behaviour and performance which are used to judge women. These judgements are based almost entirely on male-oriented values, characteristics and behaviours deemed to be beneficial to the organisation. The genesis of such a feature is in ideas of the rational model of organisations in terms of mechanistic structures which are assumed to operate logically according to scientific management principles. These ideas, propagated chiefly by males, exclude women and their perspectives from the mainstream of the organisational life of school systems (Adkison 1981; Kanter 1984; Rimmer and Davies 1985).

There is also a need to look at reasons why, in spite of widespread governmental action to institutionalise an equal place for women for more than two decades in the USA, the problems of isolation and exclusion still persist. Adkison (1981) attributed this to a resistance to the implementation of policies at the operational level of recruitment and selection which are largely controlled by male networks in educational systems. This state of affairs even created a reduction of female principals from 15.2 per cent to 12.9 per cent in the USA, at a time when the Equal Employment Opportunity and Affirmative Action programmes were in force in the 1970s. The situation is made to look even worse when there are reports of a more than threefold increase in enrolments in masters and doctoral programmes in educational administration by women during the decades of the 70's and 80's. It is necessary, therefore, to include within the explanatory framework on the status of women the informally institutionalised practices that maintain a male hegemony in the organisational life of educational systems.

In order to examine the institutional practices, it is important to change the investigatory approaches in research in order to understand the cultural patterns controlled by men. The use of conflict and critical theory, ethnographic approaches, changes in conceptual frameworks, research designs, etc (Davies 1987; Yeakey, Johnston and Adkison 1986; Kanter 1984; Shakeshaft and Hanson 1986) must be used to understand how cultural patterns, male sponsorship and alliances, etc., deny the development of female role models and any signs of emergent anticipatory female socialisation, which are compounded by the apparent ubiquitous practice of the denigration of women (Adkison 1981). It is instructive to synthesise the empirical findings on gender differences for acquiring a total view of discrimination against women (Jones 1990).

Any effort to revise or propose new perspectives on organisational life must include an analysis of the outmoded notion that the structural characteristics of formal organisations fail to explain the place of women within them by claiming objectivity and neutrality. There must be a re-examination of recruitment and selection processes; career patterns; the isolation of women from organisational uncertainties that require strategic decision-making and policy formulation; as well as such features as the flatness in educational structures that deny occupational mobility to women (Adkison 1981; Kanter 1984; Maienza 1986).

The caste-like status of women in organisations and their reduced competitive capabilities when compared with their male counterparts must be viewed in relation to powerlessness. Without power, women are denied an essential ingredient for accessing and effectively using the resources of organisations. They are also denied any visibility and access to those in power. This relates to their lack of credibility that they are accorded, and it limits their opportunities for control and sponsorship. The understanding of traditional and current values attached to the sharing of power, opportunities and relative representation may hold the key to the differences in organisational behaviours between men and women (Adkison 1981; Kanter 1984; Maienza 1986).

Another area that may have some potential for explaining the exclusion and isolation of women by men is in the psychoanalysis of individual men. This approach looks at inequalities arising from personality development and gender identification. It highlights the need for men to break away from female domination as it is suggested that they fear the power of and dependency on women—mothers, wives, teachers—in their lives. Men's need to express their machismo in organisational life is seen to emerge from this aspect of male experience. Empirical support for this conception is lacking and will be difficult to obtain, but the idea should not be discredited as a possible area of investigation into gender discrimination issues.

Recommendations

A brief outline of some suggestions for action will be pursued here. At the risk of repeating what is already being done elsewhere, this paper modestly claims only to reinforce efforts to rectify any real biases against women in educational administration.

The most obvious ploy seems to be the conscientisation and mobilisation of women in all communities and at all levels related to the general problems of living in modern or modernising societies, and the need for the unique inputs of females into the resolution of these problems. Even in this attempt women must be sensitised and be made to develop a resistance to present and future efforts to devalue them (women) as persons and to trivialise their contributions. A good starting point is to seek the knowledge and understanding of the potential administrative ideal self that will best promote the female viewpoint. This means that women must take up much stronger ideological positions on organisational issues (Rimmer and Davies 1985). It is advisable to develop strengths and reduce weaknesses while preparing to use coping strategies as "stigmatised" women, and to use all the expertise at their disposal in attaining their goals (Marshall 1985).

Women need mentors to sponsor them in effective decision-making positions. They must therefore establish the necessary relationships while demonstrating their capabilities to administrate. Since most mentors in educational systems are male, the task of evoking empathy for women's views and circumstances must also be managed in the process (Dodgson 1987). Even while women seek to be protégées, they must develop peer support groups for nurturing the necessary collegial and professional affiliations in helping to achieve a shift in the balance of power with and within the 'old boys' networks (Levine 1987). Such efforts must be bolstered by a constant vigilance, especially in areas of female concerns, so as to influence governmental policies which will affect the quality of life for all positively. (Kelly 1987).

Additionally, students of women affairs must seek to explore more incisively the fields of research and development (Kelly 1987) as well as publish material that will help to alleviate the prejudicial conditions which still seem to exist in their organisational and administrative experiences. There is need for corrective actions concerning the under-representation of women in publications. The buttresses for male dominance and biases in this area also should be attacked in the ways that Shakeshaft and Hanson (1986) have suggested. The gate-keeping functions of men on editorial boards call out for further study with a view to dismantling the male biases that limit the views of women, thus impoverishing the total set of works published.

The impact of the relationships of new approaches and designs for research on the present status of women should not be under-estimated. Critical theory and hermeneutic approaches should complement the old positivist views which previously contributed to the isolation and exclusion of women. There must be greater encouragement for the choice and careful use of holistic conceptual frameworks which express the total image of the culture of organisations.

References

Adkison, J. A. "Women in school administration: A review of research." *Review of Educational Research*. 51 (3). 1981. pp. 311-43.

Davies, L. "Research Dilemmas concerning Gender and the Management of Education in Third World Countries." *Comparative Education*. 23 (1), 1987, pp. 23-34.

Dodgson, J. Do Women in Education Need Mentors? *Education Digest*. 52 January, 1987, pp. 30-31.

Hanson, E. M. *Educational Administration and Organizational Behaviour*. Boston: Allyn and Bacon. 1979.

Jones, B. K. "The Gender Difference Hypothesis: A Synthesis of Research Findings." *Educational Administration Quarterly*. 26 (1), 1990, pp. 5-37.

Kanter, R.M. "Women and Power in Organizations". In Fischer, F. and Sirianni, C. (eds.). *Organization and Bureaucracy*. Philadelphia: Temple University Press. 1984. pp. 241-69.

Kelly, G.P. "Setting State Policy on Women's Education in the Third World: Perspectives from Comparative Research". *Comparative Education*, 23 (1), 1987, pp. 95-112.

Levine, S. L. "Peer Support for Women in Middle Management". *Educational Leadership*. 45 (3), 1987, pp. 74-75.

Maienza, J. G. "The Superintendency: Characteristics of Access for Men and Women". *Educational Administration Quarterly*. 22 (4), 1986, pp. 59-79.

Marshall, C. "The Stigmatized Woman: The Professional Woman in a Male Sex-typed Career". *Journal of Educational Administration*. 23 (2), 1985, pp. 130-152.

Ministry of Education. *Statistics on Public Education*. Educational Planning Division: Port-of-Spain. 1980.

Ministry of Education. *Statistics on Public Education*. Educational Planning Division: Port-of-Spain. 1984.

Ministry of Education. *Statistics on Public Education*. Educational Planning Division: Port-of-Spain. 1985.

Ministry of Education. *Statistics on Public Education*. Educational Planning Division: Port-of-Spain. 1987.

Ministry of Education. *Report of the Task Force on Education: Draft Policy Framework (1993-2003)*. Educational Planning Division, Port-of-Spain. 1993.

Pounder, D.G. "The Male/Female Salary Differential for School Administrators: Implications for Career Patterns and Placement of Women'. *Educational Administration Quarterly*. 24 (1), 1988, pp. 5-19.

Revere, A.B. "Black Women Superintendents in the United States: 1984-1985". *Journal of Negro Education.* 56 (4), 1987, pp. 510-20.
Rimmer, C. and Davies, B. "Women principals in education departments in high schools in Victoria". *Journal of Educational Administration.* 23 (2), 1985, pp. 153-89.
Shakeshaft. C. and Hanson, M. "Androcentric Biases in the Educational Administration Quarterly". *Educational Administration Quarterly.* 22 (1), 1986, pp. 68-92.
Stockard, J. and Kempner, K. 'Women's Representation in School Administration: Recent Trends'. *Educational Administration Quarterly.* 17 (2), 1981, pp. 81-91.
University of the West Indies. *Departmental Reports:1974/1975.* St Augustine: University of the West Indies. 1975.
University of the West Indies. *Departmental Reports:1979/1980.* St Augustine: University of the West Indies. 1980.
University of the West Indies. *Departmental Reports:1983/1984.* St Augustine: University of the West Indies. 1984.
University of the West Indies. *Departmental Reports:1987/1988.* St Augustine: University of the West Indies. 1988.
Yeakey, C. C., Johnston, G. S. and Adkison, J.A. "In Pursuit of Equity: A Review of Research on Minorities and Women in Educational Administration". *Educational Administration Quarterly.* 22 (3), 1986, pp. 110-49.

Part FOUR

Gender in Language, Poetry and Prose

Gender in Language, Poetry and Prose

Introduction

Barbara Bailey

The three papers in this part were originally presented at a disciplinary seminar held in Trinidad in 1988 which focused on gender issues in the humanities.

Bernadette Farquhar's contribution is concerned with linguistics and the semantics of gender of the Romance languages. The particular focus is with French, the national language of many Caribbean territories. Gender assignment in the French language and the inconsistency of the paradigm of French nouns of professions are the focus of the discussion. Several examples of nouns are cited where the feminine form is lacking and subsumed under the masculine. This limitation of the paradigm, she argues, creates a form of sexual discrimination which could be considered prejudicial to women.

The work of a government body established in France in 1984, mandated to devise ways of removing this sexual bias from the French language in order that the role of women could be more adequately recognised, is examined in the light of criticisms made of its recommendations. The writer concludes that the commission's work up until the time of writing had not resulted in any marked change in the French language, for two reasons: there was not a significant enough number of French-speaking persons, specifically women, who regarded this as an important area for linguistic reform; and the deliberate intervention of an authoritative organisation does not necessarily bring about change at the pace desired.

Edward Baugh's paper centres on an analysis of poems by Lorna Goodison, a Jamaican poetess, in the context of feminist criticism. In his exposition he tests claims of feminist critics concerning the actuality of Goodison's poems. This exercise brings into focus the problems attending the cross-cultural application of mainstream feminist criticism and its relevance as a framework for analysing the contributions of black female writers and, moreso, black female Caribbean writers.

Baugh contends that, although Goodison intuitively articulates some of the concerns, impulses and tropes which have been identified by feminist critics as characteristic of women's writing, the variousness and nuances of her sensibility and vision prevent her work from fitting into some of their generalisations. This disjuncture, he opines, may be pointing to a need for a black feminist criticism and even, perhaps, to consideration of what might be distinctive about Caribbean women's writing.

Jennifer Rahim attempts to trace and account for the pattern of the female literary tradition in Trinidad and Tobago from the 1930s through to the 1960s. She addresses two interrelated phenomena: the disproportionate representation of female writers; and the dilemma they have faced writing in the context and confines of a dominant patriarchal culture.

The under-representation of women writers, particularly black and Indian writers, is attributed to the discriminatory colonial education system and to the influence of the domestic ideology which, she argues, was perpetuated and reinforced through schooling.

Rahim shows that the influence of the patriarchal culture was evident in the interplay between gender and writing as expressed in the differences between male and female writing during that period. She contends that the early female writers tended to imitate the literature of their 'masters' and to uphold the dominant Victorian ideology and concept of womanhood. The female literary output of that period therefore displayed a conservatism in terms of subject matter and its treatment of and lack of concern for women's issues. The author suggests that these features of female writing indicate the influence that sociological factors in Trinidad and Tobago had on the creative output of women writers and reflects the relationship between self-perception and literary form.

The French Language and Women's Quest for Equality

Bernadette Farquhar

The Semantics of Gender in the French Language

An issue arising out of the feminist movement of recent times, which has implications for linguistics and related fields, is the call for women to be recognised in their own right in the workplace and in society at large. As a result, attempts have been made to examine aspects of language that are predicted on gender, in order to remove all instances of sexual bias.

In the case of the Romance languages, the semantics of gender, to which the question of sexual discrimination in language is ultimately related, became the subject of scholarly discussion well before this century. Some 100 years ago, the meaning of gender markers in Romance was being explored. Researchers were calling attention to the existence of a small but significant corpus of feminine nouns by derivation, in which the feminine was augmentative, that is to say, that it served to indicate that the derivative referred to an entity of greater size than that entity which the base noun designated.[1] Conversely, they also cited instances of a masculine diminutive, in contrast to what the nature of the masculine gender is intuitively felt to be.[2]

The absence in French of the feminine of certain names of professions (or occupational terms as they are called by R. Lakoff) is another gender issue of rather long history. Early French writers used unestablished feminine forms in their writings, sometimes tongue in cheek, sometimes with serious intent, and several grammarians, among them J. Damourette and E. Pichon, pointed out that *lucanae* in the paradigm of nouns denoting professions were an instance of discrimination against women. One observer even declared in 1924, with reference to the French language: *La feminisation des noms de notre langue importe plus que la réforme de l'orthographe.*[3] The concerns that these early positions expressed were brought into sharper focus by the feminist movement of recent decades. They are not unlike those of women on the other side of the Atlantic, where such terms as 'chairperson' and 'Ms' have been created, but the debate that they have engendered is possibly more intense because grammatical gender is so deeply implanted in the vocabulary and syntax of the French language. Indeed, that characteristic of the language makes reform in the area of names of professions a simple process, since gender specification can be signalled through morphological variation and the use of determiners. But the same characteristic can be an obstacle to reform for those who consider masculine gender to be an immutable property of a noun (such as *juge*) and who thereby make no allowances for changes in the speaker's perspective.

That gender can change in spite of etymology is seen in the fluctuation of the gender of certain words during their early history. *Honneur*, derived from a masculine Latin noun, became feminine in Old French, the masculine in Middle French because scholars wanted to restore the masculine to those nouns that were of that gender in Latin. In modern French, *pamplemousse* (grapefruit) is listed as masculine by some dictionaries, and masculine or feminine by others. Moreover, there are instances of nouns of the same origin differing in gender from one Romance language to another: the French words *fin* (end) and *sel* (salt) are feminine and masculine respectively, as opposed to their Spanish equivalents *fin* and *sal*, the first of which is masculine, the second feminine.

Such gender shifts support the theory that at the synchronic level this grammatical category is largely an arbitrary feature of the noun. Of course, gender does overlap with sex to a significant degree in the case of animate nouns. Because they designate the male of the species, the French words *oncle* (uncle), *roi* (king) and *coq* (rooster) are predictably masculine nouns, whereas *tante* (aunt), *reine* (queen) and *poule* (hen) are feminine. Even in this category of nouns, however, sex and gender do not always intersect. French is replete with epicene nouns; nouns of a single gender which designate both sexes. Thus, the items *victime* (victim), *vedette* (movie star, leading figure) and *souris* (mouse), all feminine forms, refer to the male and female as do the masculine nouns *témoin* (witness) *successeur* (successor) *éléphant* (elephant).

The Work of the Commission on Language

A number of occupational terms in French are epicene nouns that are masculine. The masculine is then said to be generic. They inevitably became the focus of attention in the move towards political correctness in language. Many women, especially contributors to women's magazines, took matters into their own hands by using such seemingly aberrant forms as *une écrivaine* (writer) and *la ministre* (minister of government) as a matter of course. The creation in 1984 of *La Commission de Feminisation des Noms de Métiers* by Yvette Roudy, then Minister of Women's Affairs, was an attempt to give acceptability to neologisms in this section of the French vocabulary and to propose guidelines for further creations. The Commission was made up of linguists and representatives from the media, the various ministries of government and the Haute Comité de la Langue Française. It defined its role as that of responding to *"la demande en matière de feminisation des noms de professions, à fin d'eviter le sexisme dans les offres d'emploi, et, d'une manière générale, de faire des propositions necessaires pour éviter que la langue française ne soit porteuse de discriminations fondées sur le sexe."*

In these words the Commission expressed its desire to free the French language of sexual bias, which was particularly noticeable in the texts of job announcements, where the use of the generic masculine was pervasive, by providing guidelines which would make the feminine of every occupational term possible. What it is responding to can be seen in the following list of names of professions chosen at random.

Masculine	**Feminine**	
un acteur	une actrice	actor; actress
un assistant social	une assistante sociale	social worker
un avocat	une avocate	lawyer
un caissier	une caissière	cashier, bank teller
un chauffeur de taxi	-	taxi driver
un chef	-	chef
un chirurgien	-	surgeon
un directeur	une directrice	head, manager
un débardeur	-	dock worker/stevedore
un éboueur	-	sanitation worker
un écrivain	-	writer
un haut commissaire	-	High Commissioner
un huissier	-	bailiff
un ingénieur	-	engineer
un juge	-	judge
un mannequin	-	fashion model
un médecin	-	doctor
un metteur en scène	-	film director
un ministre	-	minister of government
un pasteur	-	pastor
un pilote	-	airline pilot
un professeur	-	teacher

un receveur	une receveuse	bus conductor
un technicien	une technicienne	technician
un violoniste	une violoniste	violinist

French is not without morpho-syntactic devices which permit the formation of some feminine forms absent from this list and from the language as a whole. That such forms have hardly gained acceptance is due in part to the connotations they have: the feminine of some nouns of this category usually refers to the wife of someone employed in a given position rather than to a woman who is so employed[5] and the use of *femme* in such compounds as *femme pilot* (female pilot) and *femme écrivain* (female writer) has generated as much adverse reaction as has the use of the corresponding English compounds in some English-speaking countries. A similar treatment is bestowed on the suffixes.

The Commission took these factors into account when it began its work in 1984, guided by the newly formulated principle that all names of professions were to have dual gender. Its proposals were generally in keeping with the structure of the language. They will be summarised here with reference to the examples listed above.

On analogy with *documentaliste* and other nouns ending in 'e' which have dual gender, *pilote* would also be masculine or feminine, according to the Commission's recommendations: *un pilote, une pilote*. The addition of 'e' to the masculine, which is the basic principle behind the formation of the French feminine, would apply to all nouns of the category whose masculine ends in a vowel other than 'e'; *un delegué, une deleguée*.[6] The same principle coupled with modification of the stem of the masculine produced such established forms as *un caissier, une caissière* and *un technicien, une technicienne. Une chirurgienne, une huissiere,* patterned on these examples, would also come into being as a result of the Commission's proposals.

The situation was not as simple in the case of the feminine of occupational terms ending in -eur, -teur and those with a final consonant rather than 'r'. Already well inscribed in the rules of the language is the principle that with a few exceptions, the suffixes -eur and -teur change to -euse and -teuse respectively if the noun in question is derived from a verb whose present participle stem is also the stem of that noun. This process yielded *receveuse*, which has long enjoyed acceptability, but should also produce *metteuse en scene*, according to the wishes of the Commission.

The Commission retained the rule that where no such relationship exists between the noun and the verb from which it is derived, the suffix *-teur* becomes *-trice* in the formation of the feminine:

Present participle	**Occupational term**
dirigeant	un directeur; une directrice

Left to be considered are nouns in *-eur* that are not related to any verb and those ending in a consonant other than *'r'*.[7] The Commission recommended simply that such forms be accorded dual gender without a change in spelling, their accompanying modifiers taking the mark of the feminine:

un éboueur	une éboueur
un médecin	une médecin
un professeur	une professeur[8]

To some, the Commission was little more than a group of women at afternoon tea intent on emasculating the French language. In some cases its intentions were deliberately distorted with thinly disguised sexual allusions, as when its members, erroneously presumed to be all female, were jokingly referred to as *des membranes,* a word which purports to be the feminine of *membre*. But there were also serious concerns that it was advocating the use of forms that ran counter to the nature of the French language. The view was expressed that: *"l'article ne s'impose, ni par la logique, ni par aucune nécessité, mais par l'histoire, voire la prehistoire du français."*[9]

If this position of obduracy ignores changes in gender in the history of Romance languages, it must be conceded that items such as *une médicin,and une pasteur* present a strange configuration (notwithstanding such forms as *une ardeur, and une ampleur*, which are abstract nouns and not of the category being discussed here) that users of the language will take some time to assimilate. This is perhaps one explanation for the failure of the proposals to gain wide currency. Two years after the Commission received its mandate, its proposals were published in the *Journal Officiel de la Langue Française* of 16 March 1986, as recommended language policy to be followed by the various ministries of government. While the directive to the ministries did not have the force of law, it did nonetheless articulate national policy. However, this appears not to have resulted in an overwhelming shift towards the direction mapped out for the French language by the Commission. Indeed, one observer writing some four years after the publication of the findings, was confident enough to conclude that *"les categories de genre et de nombre restent ce qu'elles sont"*, in effect asserting that gender in French had not undergone any significant change.[10]

Except for women's magazines, in which, for obvious reasons, a determined effort would be made to adhere to the intentions of the Commission, a perusal of other publications would probably reveal that little has changed. A perfect opportunity to test the extent to which the generic masculine has declined would have been provided in the person of Edith Cresson, former prime minister in the Mitterrand administration. As late as 1994, she was referred to as *"l'ancien Premier ministre"* in some sources, the adjective *ancien* indicating that *ministre* is masculine despite its application to a female.[11] This persistence of the generic masculine is reflected even in the *Journal Officiel de la République Française* in its 1994 edition, which is also a glossary of approved neologisms in the French language. While the glossary dutifully reproduces the directive of 11 March 1986 concerning the feminisation of occupational terms, it does not apply the principle to all new nouns of this category. Among those for which it offers no feminine forms are the following:

attaquant	:	raider (on the stock market)
cabliste	:	television cable operator
cadreur	:	movie camera operator
chef des navigateurs	:	leader navigator
chef des pilots	:	leader pilot
courtier	:	broker
essayeur	:	person who tests equipment
radioamateur	:	amateur radio operator
répartiteur	:	dispatcher
squatteur	:	squatter
usager	:	user (in telecommunications)

While the words listed above designate professions generally engaged in by men, it is difficult to draw any inferences from this since the glossary also gives *sourceur/sourceuse* (sourcing expert) and *un spationaute/une spationaute* (space explorer).[12] Inconsistency rather than a policy of gender bias would therefore seem to be the explanation for the retention of the generic masculine in this official government publication.

There are other reasons why today, some ten years after the La Commission de Féminisation des Noms de Métiers began its work, its proposals have not led to marked changes in this area of the French language. The negative connotation associated with the feminine of some nouns of the category under discussion here is one such reason. It is also possible that the number of French-speakers, women in particular, who consider this to be an important area of linguistic reform is not as significant as is generally thought. Another explanation can be sought in the idea that the deliberate intervention of an individual or authoritative organisation does not necessarily bring about linguistic change at the pace desired by the intervener. The campaign by the French administration to expunge all unauthorised anglicisms from the French language illustrates this point most vividly: draconian measures having the force of law had to be relaxed at least temporarily when it was realised that anglicisms persisted nonetheless.

Linguistic Reform: Additional concerns

The quest for linguistic reform in gender also has to contend with the fear that such reform has no limits. Is it conceivable that women might take exception to the fact that the nouns *cruauté* (cruelty), *haine* (hate), *faiblesse* (weakness) and *décadence* (decadence) are feminine? Will the first names which are both masculine and feminine without a change of spelling or pronunciation (*Dominique*) and the first names which are pronounced identically with a difference in spelling signalling a difference in gender (*Michel/Michèle*) come under feminist scrutiny?

The latter question, if it became an issue, would be in keeping with the debate about whether a woman needs to assume her husband's last name after marriage and relinquish hers. It has the merit at least of raising the question of identity. The first lies in the realm of the ridiculous and would only engender a sterile debate that detracts attention from serious issues of concern to women.

Endnotes

1. Meyer - Lubke, *Italienische Grammatik*, 1890, is one of the earliest sources in which the question of the feminine augmentative and the masculine diminutive is raised. For a chronological listing of studies dealing with this topic, see Malkiel (1975).
2. By the mid-twentieth century, when the question of the feminine augmentative had become a widely debated topic, Hasselrot was to write:

   Le féminin augmentatif, bien qu'assez répandu comme nous venons de le voir, constitue tout de même, réflexion faite, une anomalie. Dans plusieurs langues, c'est au contraire le masculin qui peut assumer une fonction augmentative et puisque l'homme, normalement, est plus grand et plus fort que la femme et que le même existe entre le mêle et la femelle dans la plupart des espèces, cela paraît plus normal, plus conforme à la nature des choses.

   He saw the feminine augmentative, however frequent, as an anomaly for two reasons: first, because in several languages it is the masculine which has that function and secondly, because in most species the male is stronger than the female. The quotation above concludes that the masculine augmentative is therefore "more in keeping with the nature of things".
3. Quoted in Houdebine (1987), p. 26. This comment ascribes more importance to the need for reform in the area of French vocabulary under discussion here than to orthographic reform. Both aspects of the language have been subject to scrutiny in the last 20 years.
4. *Professeuse* is said to have occurred in the works of Voltaire. From my experience, it is the most common aberrant form produced by students of French as a result of over generalisation of the rule which derives feminine forms in -euse from the masculine -eur.
5. *Ambassadrice* (ambassador), for example. At a meeting held at the University of the West Indies, Barbados, in November 1994, I was among representatives of the Barbados Association of Teachers of French when they were advised by a visiting specialist from the French overseas department of Martinique to ascertain whether the female principal of a teacher's training college in that island did not object to being addressed as *Madame la Directrice* before sending her correspondence so labelled.
6. The feminine form *deleguée* has long existed but there is a tendency not to use it to designate a woman occupying a substantive administrative political post.
7. These were treated differently in Quebec and in a manner which resulted in configurations which would seem more acceptable to users of the language: The feminine is signalled by a change in the accompanying modifiers and by the addition of 'e' to the masculine: *un professor/une professeure*.
8. European French usage has long recognised the use of the feminine pronoun elle with *professeur* (masculine) as its antecedent, possibly because the teaching profession is predominantly female. *La prof*, a shortened form of *la professeur*, is very much in use in popular French.

9. George Dumezil in *Le Nouvel Observateur* of 7 September 1984, quoted in Houdebine (1987). The claim being made here is that the gender of the noun and therefore the gender of the article which accompanies it were determined by the early history of French.
10. Verdelhan-Dourgade (1991).
11. There appears to be the feeling in France that French women, unlike the women of Quebec, are not bold enough to insist that the new feminine forms be applied to them instead of the generic masculine. Louise Beaudoin is referred to in an October 1994 issue of the magazine *l'Express* as *"Mme la Deleguée Générale du Quebec en France"*. The section in which this reference is made also explains that Madame Beaudoin simply informed officialdom in France of her preference for such a label: *"Pour avoir droit a son titre au feminin elle avait tout simplement saisi le Haut Comité de la langue française"*
    The article goes on to attribute this forthrightness to "un feminisme militant, insolent, canaille même" (an insolent, militant, almost coarse feminism) *"inscrit dans les gênes des Quebeçoises"*. Edith Cresol is referred to as *"l'ancien Premier ministre"* in the same edition of *l'Express.*
12. All the nouns of the category in question which are listed in the glossary appear to have a feminine form if they refer to activities in the field of sports.

References

Aebischer, *V. Les femmes et le langage*. Paris: Presses Universitaires de France. 1985.

Cornish, Francis. *Anaphoric Relations in English and French: A Discourse Perspective*. London: Groom He. 1986.

Damourette, J. and Pichon, E. *"Des mots à la Pensée: Essai de Grammaire de la Langue Francaise."* Paris: Collection des linguistes contemporains. 1930-49.

Dubois, Jean. *Grammaire Structurale du français: Nom et Pronom*. Paris: Larousse. 1965.

Elcock, W.W. *The Romance Languages*. London: Faber and Faber. 1960.

Ervin-Tripp, Susan. "What do Women Sociolinguists Want?: Prospects for a Research Field". *International Journal of the Sociology of Language*, 17, 1978, pp. 19-28.

Grevisse, Maurice. *"Le Bon Usage*. Paris-Gembloux Editions Duculot. 1980.

Houdebine, Anne-Marie. "Le Francais au Féminin". *La Linguistique*, Vol. 23, fascicule 1, 1987, 13-34.

Lakoff, R. *Language and Women's Place*. New York: Harper and Row. 1975.

Lakoff, R.T. *Talking Power: The Politics of Language*. New York: Harper Collins Publishers. 1990.

Malkiel, Yakov. "Gender, Sex, and Size". In Hogiwara, Michio Peter (ed.) *Studies in Romance Linguistics*. Rowley, Massachusetts: Newbury House Publishers. 1975, p. 254-77.

Massian, M. *"Et si l'on Ecrivait Correctement le Francais?"* Paris: Hachette. 1985.

Verdelhan-Bourgade, M. "Syntaxe du Français Branche". *Revue de la Societe Internationale de Linguistique Fonctionelle*, Vol. 26, 1991, pp. 53-70.

On Becoming One's Mother

Goodison in the context of Feminist Criticism

Edward Baugh

All women become like their mothers. That is their tragedy. No man does. That is his.

Oscar Wilde

Freeing yourself was one thing; claiming ownership of that freed self was another.

Toni Morrison, Beloved

Lorna Goodison has said that the title poem of her second volume, "I Am Becoming My Mother", has two levels of meaning. At both levels the poem throws light on certain considerations, indicating aspects of the poem which might otherwise be overlooked, and at the same time, through testing these considerations against the actuality of the poems, brings into relief some of the problems attaching to feminist criticism, which feminist critics have themselves shown awareness of at one time or another.

Feminist criticism proves to be a futile context in which to appreciate Goodison's work. As it were, intuitively, she articulates some of the concerns, impulses and tropes which have been identified by feminist critics as characteristic of women's writing. At the same time the variousness and nuances of her sensibility and vision prevent her work from fitting easily into some of the generalisations of feminist criticism. In this regard the disjunction may be germane to the issue of the need for a black feminist criticism and even, perhaps, to the question of what is distinctive about Caribbean women's writing.

At its more obvious level of meaning, "I Am Becoming My Mother" is about a woman's sense of identity through identification or bonding with the mother, with the female line of ancestry, and with whatever suffering and strength distinguish it. This awareness is described as a process of becoming; through this process the persona comes fully into being, becomes herself. She grows towards her birth, a psychic birth which complements her physical birth. The dynamism of the process is enhanced by the fact that it is two-way. "My mother is now me"; the mother is growing into the daughter just as the daughter is growing into the mother.

Goodison explains all this in simple terms of personal observation and popular belief:

> Barbara [her sister] will say something and I say, "But that is Mama!" I mean that's exactly what Mama would say. Or I look at my hands and they look like my mother's hands ... My helper, who has worked with my family for many years, a lot of times she will say, "You know, Miss Lorna, you really take after your mother." And a lot of women say that, because they realize, the older they get, how much they take from their mothers. It's natural; it's very good.[1]

Even in the deployment and relationship of characters in this domestic narrative - the female speaker, her sister, her female helper, her mother-present-in-spirit -we feel the idea of a self-energising woman's world, the idea of a special womanness which women most naturally perceive, and which has to be explained to men: "So they always tell men that if you want to know what your wife will look like, you must look at her mother."[2]

"It's a very natural; it's very good." The mood of fulfilment and affirmation with which the poet becomes her mother ("becomes" also in the sense of "being becoming to") is remarkable in that "alienation from and rejection of the mother" were identified as features of women's writing before the 1970s, cultivated in women by the institution of patriarchy. Elaine Showalter tells us that "[much] women's literature in the past has dealt with 'matrophobia' or the fear of becoming one's mother". However, "Female literature of the 1970s goes beyond matrophobia to a courageously sustained quest for the mother, in such books as Margaret Atwood's *Surfacing*, and Lisa Alther's ... *Kinflicks*."[3]

So Goodison is presumably a true child of the post-1970 period. However, since she hardly has to undertake any "quest for the mother", let alone a "courageous" one, perhaps her case provides an example to support the idea that definitive generalisations in matters like these always need qualifying. It might also prove useful to inquire whether there may be a racial-cultural explanation for any differences between Goodison's work and Showalter's generalisation. Such an inquiry would have some bearing on the case for a black feminist criticism. All the women writers to whom Showalter refers on the point of matrophobia are white.

But can we generalise about black women writers on this issue? Alice Walker's "In Search of Our Mothers' Gardens" is a joyful recognition of the models of creativity which mothers may represent for daughters. But the very title of the piece is consonant with its suggestion that daughters have had to cut through a tradition of imposed obfuscation in order to recognise this bequest. And if Paule Marshall's heroine in *Brown Girl, Brownstones* eventually achieves a similar recognition, what the novel details is the painful process which this achievement involves, the misunderstanding and even hatred which have to be displaced. Jamaica Kincaid's *Annie John* depicts another problematic, ambivalent relationship between daughter and mother.

The second, less obvious meaning which Goodison attributes to "I Am Becoming My Mother" is that in some essential sense one has to become one's own mother, that is one has to create or produce oneself:

> This is what I would say to any young person. Don't let the world tell you who you are to be. You don't have to do what everybody also is doing. . . . But in order to do this you're going to have to give birth to yourself—because the world not going to help you . . . Therefore you have to become your own mother.[4]

Although this statement may be read as yet another version of the idea that everyone, "any young person", must strive to be himself or herself, the idea has never been expressed in quite these terms, or with such radical urgency, in the patriarchal tradition. In the male-oriented tradition of *Bildungsroman* the hero seeks to assert himself, to resist wrong values in the quest for his best self, but there is never any doubt that he has a separate self, a privileged niche of selfhood. Woman cannot repose in any such sustaining idea. She finds herself in a world where her identity is determined for her by an androcentric consciousness. She is merely the created, not herself a creator. She is, in another feminist formulation, the text written by the male creative mind. She therefore has virtually to invent herself anew, or, to use the more organic and therefore more desirable image, to give birth to herself, in order also to find her own creative springs. And since to give birth is the biologically female activity, it is fitting that woman's finding of herself and her creativity should be expressed in the metaphor of giving birth.

Incidentally, in "Survivor", from the *Heartease* collection, Goodison takes a sardonic swipe at the notion of women as the creature of male consciousness, by way of reference to the biblical story that God created Eve from Adam's rib —"and you know how creative/God is with ribs."[5]

This train of ideas finds remarkable concurrence in recent feminist discourse. In a comment on Rachel Du-Plessis' poem-sequence "Eurydice", Alicia Ostriker observes:

> The heroine not only resents ... the loss of herself to a husband whose powerful sex and art define her "like a great linked chain" but is herself the snake "whose deepest desire was to pierce herself". Withdrawing from her husband, far back into the moist stony "fissure" and "cave" of herself, she becomes a self-generating plant and finally, amid an efflorescence of organic images, her own mother, giving birth to the girl child who is herself—or, since the sequence can be read as an allegory of female creativity, her poem. The idea of giving birth, unaided, to the self is also the conclusion of Adrienne Rich's "The Mirror In Which Two Are Seen As One".[6]

Ostriker's comments indicate that in the poems she is discussing sexuality is a crucial factor in the idea of giving birth to oneself. The rejection of the male is accompanied by a joyful auto-sexuality. This idea of the rejection of male sexual dominance can also lead us into the question of lesbianism, an important topic of feminist debate. Ostriker sees in the work of some recent women poets the notion of embracing one's (woman's) sexuality as an integral factor in becoming and accepting oneself, in achieving the wholeness and joy of self-realisation and creativity:

> A muse imagined in one's own likeness [as in Denise Levertov's "Song For Ishtar"] with whom one can fornicate with violence and laughter, implies the extraordinary possibility of a poetry of wholeness and joy, as against the poetry of the "age of anxiety" in which Levertov was writing. That a sacred joy can be found within the self, that it requires an embracing of one's sexuality; that access to it must be described as movement downward or inward, in gender-charged metaphors of water, earth, cave, sea, moon: such is the burden of these and many other poems by women.[7]

This "embracing of one's sexuality" as a necessary part of woman's experience of a full, free self, is symbolically enacted by Goodison in "On Becoming A Mermaid". Here again we notice the focus on the idea of becoming, the metamorphosis of self, re-birth. And again it is a kind of self-engendering. The persona imagines herself changing into a mermaid and thus, in effect, being released from (hetero) sexual entanglements, demands and frustrations. She undergoes a sea-change into something rich, strange, self-delighting and still essentially, utterly female.

We may read the poem at one level as an impossible dream prompted by a bitter awareness of actuality, a version of the Keatsian temptation of being "half in love with easeful death"; but there is too much vitality and delight in the imagery for us to rest at this level. True enough, the poem begins with the persona being drawn into the reverie that "drowning must be easy death/just let go and let the water carry you/away and under".[8] The "salt" (water) which buoys her breasts may suggest tears, grief, as it often does with Goodison. Furthermore, there is a kind of regret in the final image of her "sex sealed forever" as it "closes finally/on itself like some close-mouthed oyster".[9] But the persona does not really die; she is metamorphosed, and there is much that is vibrant, beautiful and pleasurable in this new "underlife". (my emphasis).

The achievement may be more properly described as that of woman laying claim to her sexuality, treasuring it in an access of that "wholeness and joy" of which Ostriker speaks. It is remarkable too, in view of Ostriker's observations, that the metamorphosis involves a descent into watery depths. And the sexual, generative and recreative connotations of the water imagery are a significant characteristic of Goodison's poetic vision. So, in the drama and tensions of the poem's imagery, out of death (drowning) comes life, in descent is buoyancy, and a locking-away or self-denial becomes a new freedom and self-fulfillment:

Your sex locked under
mother-of-pearl scales
you're a nixie now, a mermaid
a green tinged fish
fleshed woman
thing. . .
breasts full and floating buoyed up by the salt
and the space between your arms now always filled.[10]

Some of the dramatic force of the poem derives from the fact that it proceeds from a strong sexuality, the theme and dynamic of many Goodison poems. In other words, the condition from which the woman escapes by becoming a mermaid is, despite its painful vulnerability, a condition that has its own powerful attractiveness for her, a power which is still felt at the end of the poem. For Goodison, "embracing one's sexuality" is also a matter of simply being free to acknowledge and explore with candour that sexuality, to articulate those drives and desires which women, according to conventional wisdom, were not supposed to feel, or at least talk about- "to accept the erotic woman within herself".[11]

These considerations have a bearing on the issue of the relationship between lesbianism and feminism, since a poem such as "On Becoming A Mermaid", with its seeming impulse towards a self-contained female sexuality, could be easily accommodated by the lesbian vision. For some feminist critics "lesbian" becomes a paradigm for feminist, and woman's writing is, by implication, seen as somehow "better" than men's writing in so far as it exhibits certain virtues which are defined as characteristically lesbian.[12] This tendency no doubt provides one example of that "monolithic vision of shared female sexuality" which Ann Rosalind Jones questions:

> A monolithic vision of shared female sexuality, rather than defeating phallocentrism as doctrine and practice, is more likely to blind us to our varied and immediate needs and to the specific struggles we must coordinate in order to meet them. What is the meaning of [the] "two lips" [of the vulva, as theorized by Luce Irigaray] to heterosexual women who want men to recognize their clitoral pleasure—or to African or Middle Eastern women who, as a result of pharaonic clitoridectomies, have neither lips nor clitoris with which to jouir?[13]

While Goodison, as I have tried to suggest, may be seen as freely "embracing her sexuality" and enacting the notions of sisterhood, female-bonding and self-delighting, it would seem unnecessary and nonsensical to stretch the meaning of "lesbian" so far as to characterise her work, however metaphorically, as lesbian, in the same way that it seems unnecessary and ultimately unhelpful for Barbara Smith to define Toni Morrison's *Sula* as a lesbian novel.

Goodison's mermaid is also a reworking of the traditional mermaid of legend. The latter, also beautiful and mysterious, is usually envisioned as threatening and destructive, luring men to their deaths. As such, she is a creation of the male imagination. Goodison's mermaid is wholly involved with the joy of her self-creation and self-discovery, and not at all with any desire to do men in. To this extent she exemplifies the female re-visioning of myth which is the subject of Ostriker's essay, as illustrated in the passage on the muse quoted earlier.

That passage seems, for instance to depict a re-(en)gendering of the myth of Narcissus, with more positive, dynamic and creative values attaching to the female version. Narcissus' hopeless love for his own reflection in the pool was a punishment inflicted by the gods for his having spurned the advances of all would-be-lovers, both male and female. The lack of response from his reflection drove him to suicide. No frustration, and therefore no likelihood of suicide, is contemplated in the situation of female poet and a "muse imagined in [her] own likeness" as described by Ostriker.

There is another powerful, teasing Goodison poem about "becoming", which also in its way, revises the Narcissus myth. "On becoming a Tiger" is another poem about wholeness of self, about the fulfilment of woman, truly seeing herself and coming to the gratifying knowledge of her inner beauty and power. The persona first sees the splendid tiger, which "was actually always asleep/inside her", when she "stared/for seven consecutive days into a tall mirror":

Her focus had penetrated all exterior
till at last she could see within her
a red glowing landscape of memory and poems,
a heart within her heart
and lying there big, bright, and golden
was the tiger, wildly darkly stripped.[14]

The idea of engendering and a continuity of female inward knowing are suggested in the fact that at night the persona dreams that "her mother/undresses her and discovers" her tigerness. This is the only person who is imagined as sharing her secret self-knowledge; but by the end of the poem she is "living an openly/tigerly life".[15] Here, then, is a mythopoeic enactment of "claiming ownership of (the) freed self", and another figuration of the woman poet imagining the muse in her own likeness.

That female poets have to redefine the muse is a corollary of the traditional male-centred concept of the muse. Female poets must undertake this re-vision in order to liberate their creativity. The idea of "a muse imagined in one's own likeness" leads itself to being imaged in terms of both the auto-sexual and self-generative and lesbian terms. In an article entitled "Re-Vision of the Muse: Adrienne Rich, Audre Lorde, Judy Grahn, Olga Broumas", Mary J. Carruthers observes:

> The muse traditionally is female and the poet male. He addresses her in terms of sexual rapture, desiring to be possessed in order to possess, to be ravished in order to be fruitful. The language of violent sexual encounter, of submission and dominance, describes a relationship both of possession and enslavement . . . In the myth of the Lesbian poets, the muse remains female. This completely changes the relationship of the poet to the poetry. Because the muse is female, she is not Other but Familiar, material and sororal, a well-known face in the poet's community. Their relationship is not one of possession but of communal bonding.[16]

Ironically, while Carruthers notes an absence of "the language of violent sexual encounter" in the poetry of the women she discusses, Ostriker identifies with approval, in the work of other women poets, "a muse imagined in one's own likeness, with whom one can fornicate with violence and laughter". Carruthers' formulation of the lesbian relationship with the muse seems comparatively idealistic, defused of some of the very sexuality which is its basis. Still, her point about a radical shift of vision is well taken.

Be that as it may, it should be possible and allowable for some women poets to re-vision the muse as male, although this option might be resisted by the kind of feminist rhetoric which advocates a radical break with anything having patriarchal or phallocentric associations. The option of a male muse envisioned by a female poet may therefore be the most problematic and complex of the options. One of Goodison's more enigmatic poems, "The Mulatta and the Minotaur", seems at one level if the interpretation to be an exploration and affirmation of female creativity and sexuality, with the minotaur as the female persona's muse. In any event, in this re-vision of the myth, woman is no longer seen simply as the passive, sacrificial victim of male sexual power and the male imagination.

But if we can read Goodison's minotaur as a male muse, we should set beside him, or as an alternative to him, the female idea or essence which the poet names "Asi itra", in "Star Suite", a sequence from her third collection, *Heartease*. Here the ideas of sisterhood and a female ideal inspiring woman is given a metaphysical, indeed almost mystical presence:

Asi itra woman star
beams in pleased with being

. . . this lady
who is in charge
of all women
told her
"go to her (me)
remind her I'm who gave her flowers."

star skirted
moon stone belted
silver striped tresses,
Miss Beauty Queen of all stars
Sister, Asi itra.[17]

This delight in the beauty of a "sister" is part of the womanist "embracing of one's sexuality" which we noted earlier. Asi itra is Goodison's conception of a "woman spirit" which is the guardian of women and, as such, a key figure in a new feminine myth. Still, God, as hymned in the incantatory "A Rosary of Your Names" and "A Rosary of Your Names (II)", both from *Heartease,* is male, the traditional symbol of power and authority, the ultimate creator:

The one in charge
Superior Almighty
All knowing
Large
There is no God but God
He lit the first flame
Orchestrator of Dawns and Sunsets
Chant a rosary of His names.[18]

Do we conclude, then, that Goodison's feminism, such as it is, is self-contradictory or flawed, since it still invests in patriarchal notions? Or do we say that the many-sidedness of her imaging of gender relationships reflects the complex actuality of her world, rather than a doctrinaire or separatist feminism, and that this complexity may be fulfilling rather than limiting? Presumably a "free" woman should be free to worship a God imagined as male. The God of "A Rosary of Your Names" bears no resemblance to the soul-destroying masculinity of, say, "Ceremony for the Banishment of the King of Swords" (*Heartease*).

Like "The Mulatta and the Minotaur", "The Mulatta as Penelope" is an instance of that "revisionist mythmaking" which Ostriker finds to be an important feature of recent poetry by women. Hurt by the departure of her lover/husband, the persona (the Mulatta) refuses to take on the role of Homer's Penelope, ever faithful, ever forbearing, waiting chastely and patiently for her man to have his adventures and then return "with tin souvenirs and a claim to [her]".[19] By this language the persona rejects the male "claim" and the cheapness with which it is bought.

Moreover, this Penelope is rejecting the claim not just of the particular man. Unlike the classical Penelope, she will not make herself accessible to the predictable procession of suitors, whether to prove (like the classical Penelope) how faithful she is by resisting them (thereby allowing herself to be made into the subject/victim of a male test), or to prove her freedom by having a fling. No, she will opt out of the male-fixed game altogether: "I will not sit and spin and spin/the door open to let the madness in".[20] The madness is the androcentric sex game and woman's subservient acceptance of her part in it.

The classical Penelope, true to the conventional idea of "woman's place", wove as she waited. But "spin" is precisely the metaphor which Goodison needs. It connotes woman as plaything, being given "the go round",[21] with the psychic confusion which may attend this condition.

It may be argued that the final image of Goodison's Penelope is one which subsumes a conventional, male-centred view of woman. She will find solace in the love of her child, the child presumably fathered by the man who has left her. And she "will sit in the sun and dry [her] hair" while the child sleeps. We may seem to have here an example of the West Indian version of Penelope, another example of the "Brown Skin Gal", as depicted in the folk-song of that title, who will "stay home and mind baby". True, the Mulatta is not about to throw out her maternal instincts and pleasures along with the baby, nor will she deny that she grieves over the departure of the man. But she does so on her own terms. She lays claim to herself. The final image of her drying her hair in the sun is one of self-delighting wholeness.

As Maggie Humm explains, feminists have come to acknowledge that motherhood is not incompatible with feminism.[22] Adrienne Rich, for example, rationalises this awareness by way of her distinction between motherhood as "experience" and motherhood as "institution". Goodison has no anxieties on this score. She has been reported as saying that pregnancy and childbirth proved to be "one of the most spiritual and profound experiences" for her: "I have never felt so close to my woman spirit before".[23] Besides, there are the Goodison poems which celebrate pregnancy, childbirth and mothering, poems like "Dream -- August 1979" and "Songs For My Son".

Maggie Humm observes: "Feminist critics take Graeco-Roman myths to be masculine constructs whose changing narratives only reflect changes ... within the male psyche."[24] Not surprisingly therefore, the revisionist mythmaking of some female writers and critics is a matter of turning away from the Graeco-Roman to "more specifically female" mythologies. "Virginia Woolf's preference for the pre-Greek myths of Egypt and Isis iconography is an early example of a feminist rejecting the patriarchal obsession with Greek myths and their male heroes."[25] In this context, Goodison's fondness for an Egyptian iconography and setting may represent an intuitive groping towards an alternative mythology. And her "King of Swords", appropriated from the Tarot cards, is rich with mythopoeic possibilities.

"Ceremony for the Banishment of the King of Swords" (*Heartease*) is woman's definitive and ritual "song of release", release from the false and male-centred myths that have oppressed her. It is important to notice that the King of Swords is not a force purely external to her; he is also that pardonable error and weakness in her which make her conspire in her own undoing. So to banish the King of Swords is to have achieved knowledge, self-knowledge, the knowledge of one's true value, the knowledge that is power and protection. The "Ceremony" is a female crucifixion-and-resurrection ritual:

You can get up now
leave the tomb empty
leave the broken sword there

here is the chant of light
the new source of singing
this is the ending
this is the beginning.[26]

The process of becoming one's own mother, the process of self-invention, of finding one's woman spirit, issues in the incantatory glow of light and vision which illuminates *Heartease*. It is a world-embracing condition in which the poet is free and empowered to speak for all, of whatever gender, whose being and becoming are threatened or denied, whether the "bag woman/pushing rubbish babies/in ridiculous prams" ("This Is A Hymn"), or the man on the Kingston mini-bus "with the name *'Levi'* written across the front of him creppe". And the poet surmises that that "must be/his rightful name".

For sometimes it would suit a one
to write him name upon himself
In case Babylon stop you
and fraid claim your tongue
in which case you could just
look down and remind you eye
and say "Yes oppressor
I name is Levi".[27]
("Upon a Quarter Million")

Goodison's work is typical of the emergent mainstream of Anglophone Caribbean feminist discourse in that it does not exhibit any of the separatist or isolationist tendencies which some metropolitan feminist critics have found it necessary to regret in their sisters. And here we should observe that Goodison also gladly acknowledge paternal influence in her making and self-discovery:

. . . look see me rising, lighter
in the name of my father, dreamer
who said I should be
Of all worlds and a healer
source of mystery
and a morning star -
hear all, I will be.[28]
("My Father Always Promised Me")

Showalter argues that woman's writing does not accord with "current theories of literary influence", such as that of Harold Bloom, which posit that the text is "fathered". She quotes Virginia Woolf's dictum that "a woman writing thinks back through her mothers", then says, "But a woman writing unavoidably thinks back through her fathers as well; only male writers can forget or mute half of their parentage."

The position which Showalter attributes to women writers is no doubt the more wholesome, the more admirable. But I doubt that men, whatever their explicit rhetoric, are really as oblivious of half their parentage as Showalter thinks. At the same time, it is probably only natural for men to emphasise the male line of literary influence and women the female. In any event, the more urgent and revolutionary achievement of contemporary women writers is the declaration of the female line of creativity, the discovery, to use Alice Walker's luxuriant metaphor, of their "mother's gardens". Thus they come into their inheritance as makers. And so, for example, the women in Goodison's "Bedspread" who weave the bedspread "in the colours of our free Azania", are not only freedom fighters in their own way, and providers of solace and support for their men, but also artists in their own right, practising imagination and craftsmanship; and they become symbols of woman's artistic capacity and tradition. And so woman artist (the poet) salutes woman artist (the needleworker and quilt-maker) and woman as artist takes her rightful place in the effort of the tribe. Through her, also, the tribe becomes articulate.

Which brings us back to "I Am Becoming My Mother". It is also a poem about woman's recognition and celebration of her inheritance and power as artist. In a general way, giving birth may be read as a metaphor for artistic creativity. But, more specifically, the idea of giving birth is imaged in the active terms of "birth waters", which suggest not only fertility and creativity (water) but also continuity (flowing). And these birth waters are a joyous, beautiful, vitalising utterance: "her birth waters sang like rivers" (my emphasis). Besides, the mother is also imaged as artist in that she "raises rare blooms". Goodison, like Walker, has also "found" her mother's garden - and she is identified with beautiful works of art, albeit domestic, her "linen dress/the colour of the sky" and her "lace and damask/tablecloths". And since the poet has become her own mother, it is she who now "raises rare blooms" (her poems); it is her work which sings like rivers.

References

1. Lorna Goodison, interview with Pearl Wallace, recorded 1988 (unpublished).
2. *Ibid.*
3. Showalter, Elaine (ed.). *The New Feminist Criticism.* (London: Virago Press. 1986, p. 135.
4. Lorna Goodison, interview with Pearl Wallace.
5. Goodison, Lorna. *Heartease.* London: New Beacon. 1988. p. 16.
6. Ostriker, Alicia. "The Thieves of Language: Woman Poets and Revisionist Mythmaking". In Showalter, Elaine *op. cit.*, pp. 319-20.
7. *Ibid.*, pp. 320-321.
8. Goodison, Lorna. *I Am Becoming My Mother*. London: New Beacon. 1986. p. 30.
9. Showalter, *op. cit.*, p. 323.
10. See, for example, Smith, Barbara, "Towards a Black Féminist Criticism", in Showalter, *op. cit.*, and Carruthers, Mary J., "Revision of the Muse," in *Hudson Review*, *36*, Summer 1983.
11. Jones, Ann Rosalind, "Writing the Body: L'Ecriture Feminine", in Showalter, *op. cit.*, p. 371.
12. Goodison,Lorna . *Selected Poems*. Ann Arbor: University of Michigan Press. 1992. p. 134.

13. Ibid., p. 135.
14. Hudson Review, 36, Summer 1983, pp. 295-96.
15. *Heartease*, p. 13.
16. Ibid., p. 60.
17. *I Am Becoming My Mother*, p. 25 .
18. Ibid., p. 25.
19. Ibid., p. 15.
20. Humm, Maggie, *Feminist Criticism*. Brighton: Harvester. 1986. p. 98.
21. Sandy McIntosh, "Lorna Goodison: "It's Not Enough to Just Write What You Feel", *Sunday Sun*, 31 August 1980, p. 24.
22. Humm, Maggie, *op. cit.*, p. 93.
23. Ibid., p. 94.
24. *Heartease*, pp. 54-55.
25. Ibid., p. 27.
26. Ibid., p. 9.
27. Showalter, Elaine, *op. cit.*, p. 265.
28. *I Am Becoming My Mother*, p. 43.

Trinidad and Tobago Women's Writing, 1929-69

What Manner of Voice?

Jennifer Rahim

The history of the female literary presence in Trinidad and Tobago, as in England and America, is characterised by under-representation, gaps and silences. These features are particularly outstanding for the period 1929-69, which is the scope of this paper. The first recorded literary publication by a woman writer appeared in 1929, when Olga Comma-Maynard published the first in a series of nine booklets of local poems and short stories entitled *Carib Echoes*. During the 1930s a handful of local and expatriate women writers had work published in the literary journals of the time: *Forward*, *Trinidad* and *The Beacon*. The most prolific were Olga Yaatoff and Kathleen Archibald. *The Beacon*, which was the widest circulated and longest lasting magazine of the period, published about 32 female-authored poems, stories and plays in comparison with 145 written by men. This was followed by a long silence in the 1940s and 1950s when most of the pioneering writers, with the exception of Olga Comma-Maynard, just seemed to disappear from the literary roster. All the major literary publications by women appeared in the 1960s and these amounted to a mere five.

Women's Writing: The 1930s

What are the reasons for the course that our female literary tradition has taken? Is it an indication of an attempt by the male world to keep women out of their traditional field of dominance? Susan Gilbert and Susan Gubar have traced in their work, *The Madwoman in the Attic,* a history of patriarchal thought which has projected writing as an essentially male endeavour, a sort of extension of the male generative act. They claim: "the patriarchal notion that the writer 'fathers' his text just as God fathered the world, is and has been all-pervasive in Western literary civilization".[1] But to claim that the under-representation of women writers is evidence of an attempt by male publishers to keep women out of the literary world is too simplistic in any context. The instigators and developers of the creative writing movement in Trinidad from the outset placed the emphasis on the promotion of national literature, regardless of the sex of its creators. In one of the early editorials of the magazine *Trinidad,* Alfred Mendes made it clear that: 'Our aim is to afford our fellow men and women an opportunity to self expression and expansion, and if the assistance required is forthcoming to touch life at all available points.'[2]

There are however, hindrances to potential women writers that are specifically gender-related. Janet Fullerton suggests that the disproportionate representation of female creative writers is a reflection of their restriction by their roles as wives, mothers and home-makers: 'The bulk of the literature in Trinidad and indeed the entire Caribbean has been written by men. The majority of our women have been too busy caring for their homes, husbands and children to consider their intellectual development and creative ability or even to entertain the thought of writing.'[3]

While the demands of domesticity, child-bearing and rearing present recognisable difficulties for the woman who may be interested in a writing career, Fullerton overlooks other factors which further complicate matters for the woman. These include: inequalities in education, lack of privacy, pressures of social expectations which dictate to the woman the type of person she should be and if she does write, the type of writer. Equally important are the factors of race, colour and class which are of particular relevance to the West Indian context. All of these play a part in accounting for the under-representation of women writers, the lapses and silences that have typified the female literary tradition in Trinidad and Tobago.

The nature of colonial education significantly contributed to the disproportionate representation of women writers in the 1930s when local literature was beginning to get off the ground. Kenneth Ramchand has already made the fundamental connection between the birth and growth of West Indian literature and the expansion of popular education which began with the Negro Education Grant.[4] However, what does not emerge in Ramchand's discussion is the relationship of sex, education and literary production. The fact that the first major works of West Indian writing were produced by men is not at all surprising when one examines the sexual politics that informed the development of educational systems and the social attitudes relative to the acquisition of knowledge.

After emancipation, the introduction of the capitalist mode of production brought with it the sexual division of labour which designated to man the role of breadwinner and to woman the role of housewife. Integral to the capitalist system was the domestic ideology which was in itself a justification of the sexual division of labour. It is necessary to view girls' education with respect to the division of labour because in many ways the latter helped to shape and consolidate the former. Rhoda Reddock's study of women's colonial education in Trinidad and Tobago and women's labour policies show how the state sought to bring about the 'housewification' of women or to restrict them to certain fields of occupation.[5]

It is true that the colonial education system above the primary-school level was exclusive and that access was available on the basis of race, colour and class. As a result the vast majority of the black population was unable to attain higher education. From the outset, however, girls suffered doubly because they were not given the same opportunities as boys to excel academically. The influence of the domestic ideology was apparent in the girls' curricula, which discouraged the academics and concentrated on subjects that would better prepare them for their careers as good wives and mothers. Such subjects included domestic science, needlework, the rules of good taste, polite literature, hygiene, French and religion. There were also fewer secondary school for girls than for boys. For the entire nineteenth century and up to the 1920s St Joseph's Convent was the only secondary school for girls on the island and it was attended primarily by girls of French creole extraction. For boys there were the Queen's Royal College, St Mary's College and Naparima College.

Before the 1930s there was no equivalent for girls of the government exhibition examinations available to boys since 1870. Because of the high cost of education, parents who wanted to educate their children without a government grant, chose the boys to educate because girls were considered a poor investment. Social expectations about the roles of women made parents adopt the attitude that education was of secondary importance to their daughters, since their future lay in marriage. Reddock notes a lag in girls' school attendance at both the primary and secondary levels compared with the boys.[6] After the 1930s the figures gradually began to balance off. The imbalance was particularly pronounced among East Indian girls who were more likely to make early marriages and amongst whom it was considered that education was unnecessary.

Given this education system and the strong influence of the domestic ideology, it is easy to see why such a remarkably small number of women participated in creative writing during the 1930s. These women came mostly from the white upper and coloured middle classes. The most famous of the former was Olga Yaatoff, who was of French and English parentage. Although she was not a Trinidadian, some of her writing attempted to depict local experiences, hence the reason for including her in this discussion. She was also by far the most prolific of the early writers. Kathleen Archibald was from the coloured middle class. Olga Comma-Maynard came from the black middle class.

The apparent absence of women writers from the black lower class group is no doubt a reflection of their exclusion from the higher education system. The same applies for the East Indian women, although they suffered more acutely from cultural hindrances. In the first half of the century there was only one woman writer of East Indian descent, Amanda Nobbee-Eccles. Jeremy Poynting writes:

> One woman included in the 'Who's Who', Amanda Nobbee, is described as a part-time writer of 'amusing articles on tropical subjects' which appeared occasionally in the press, a collection of pieces called *English with Tears* (c. 1940), and some time later, a collection of children's short stories, *For Small Fry* (1957). Apart from the symbolic step of 'being' a writer, no great claims can be made for either the literary quality or the interest of this work.[7]

East Indian women made no significant impact on the local literary scene up to the 1960s. For the period under study, they have produced no novels or poetry collections, nor have they appeared in any of the major literary journals, a phenomenon which can be linked to their educational history and the rigid role restrictions which have been part of their ethnic experience.

Interplay between Gender and Writing: The 1930s

When the genre of the West Indian short story began to develop through writers like C.L.R. James and Alfred Mendes, the bourgeois public criticised the editors of *Trinidad* for publishing immoral literature. "Barrack-yard" literature, as it was called, focused on the social, economic and physical environment of the black lower classes. One of the striking features of this literature was its description of the sexual habits and values of the yard dwellers. "Triumph" by C.L.R. James and "Sweetman" and "Her Chinaman's Way" by Alfred Mendes, are examples of these popular barrack-yard stories. The use of material based on the black lower classes was at once a response to the search for literary independence and authenticity and an outright attack against the conventional, Eurocentric values of bourgeois society.

This was a revolutionary period, an open revolt against Victorianism, particularly in the sexual sphere. The editors of *Trinidad* and *The Beacon* seemed to revel in the controversy that the journals provoked. Mendes, for instance, dismissed the charges of obscenity against "Triumph" as irrelevant, claiming that the artist's function was to create an aesthetic from his material even if that material were what may be considered conventionally obscene. Mendes wrote in "A Commentary". "It all depends on what literary treatment they receive, though it does not necessarily mean that, so treated, they shall be no longer obscenities; it simply means that they shall be obscenities presented for reasons other than raising the disgust or sexual desires of the reader."[8]

> The stories by women in the 1930s differ significantly in both form and content from the "barrack-yard" stories written by the men. Commenting on the collection of stories that appeared in *Trinidad* and *The Beacon*, Reinhard Sander notes: 'With the exception of Olga Yaatoff and Kathleen Archibald's impressionistic pieces of Trinidad life, "Gasoline Station" and "Clipped Wings", the short fiction published in *Trinidad* and *The Beacon* is conventional in form.'[9]

Mendes replied:

> We hadn't as yet arrived at the stage where we were so avant-garde as not to have a beginning and an end. This was to come later with George Lamming, Wilson Harris and others. James and I departed from the convention in the selection of our material, in the choice of a strange way of life, in the use of a new dialect.[10]

Looking at the stories written by Yaatoff and Archibald, their style as Sander rightly observes differs from the conventional form used by their male contemporaries. It moved away from the traditional and applied characteristically modern techniques to the presentation of their themes and concerns. For instance, they do not use the linear plot development. Structure is fragmented. The narrative bears the qualities of the stream of consciousness mode of narration. So that while the barrack-yard stories may be original for their presentation of a strange way of life, the stories written by the women are significant for their stylistic experimentation.

Olga Yaatoff's "Gasoline Station"[11] is an observation of the social life of the upper and middle classes in Trinidad society. The gas station is the point where life is condensed as people move in and out of the gas station on their way to various venues. The moral emptiness, the pain and violence of life are brought into focus. What we are presented with is a stationary setting, the gas station, where the characters constantly change. One is more aware of emotional states and attitudes than of persons. Characters communicate more by their silences, facial expressions and physical appearance than by words and actions. There is no plot development, but a steady flow of scenes that combine to create a sense of purposelessness and futility that is concretised in the attendant George's final comment: "Nothing ever happened anyway."

Kathleen Archibald's "Clipped Wings"[12] explores the theme of poverty and the limitations it places on one's aspirations. Here too, we see a disregard of the linear plot structure. The story is divided into four sections, each dealing with various aspects of the life of the poor. The first three sections are linked by the experiences of a boy named Willy. However, there is a break in the growth section, which switches to a scene depicting scavengers at work. This sudden shift is jarring. While Archibald can be faulted for inconsistency, it seems that the development of a linear story line is subordinated to an attempt to present images of poverty, the emphasis being on entering the psychic states of the poor. In the second section, we are given a sensitive account of the hardship suffered by the lower-class woman who expresses her frustration by unjustly beating her son, and who later shows great tenderness by skipping dinner so that her children can have enough to eat.

These stories lack the romanticism, brawling, fast-moving, jovial atmosphere of the barrack-yard stories. Instead, there is a display of sobriety and seriousness in the treatment of social realities. Openness in dealing with gender relations and sexual behaviour is absent. In "Gasoline Station", for instance, the narrator hints at the sexual lives of her characters, leaving the reader to draw conclusions. The subject is never directly addressed. The barrack-yard stories exhibit a greater degree of freedom in this respect. Emphasis is placed more on atmosphere and emotional and psychological states than on action, speech and setting.

What accounts for the difference between stories written by males and females? Is it mere coincidence or rather evidence of a possible relationship between gender and writing? The concept of difference is one of the most controversial areas of feminist criticism. There is no ideology or methodology with which to decipher the interplay between gender and writing. Showalter has identified four approaches: biological, linguistic, psychological and cultural.[13] Each approach has its own method of differentiating women's writing from men's. The major problem of defining women's writing is that it is easy to fall into the trap of essentialism. There are theories which see women's writing as a product of an innate femaleness, assuming that woman is a homogenous category and ignoring factors of race, class, nationality, culture and history which affect women differently. This is precisely what feminist criticism is trying to avoid because it limits the creative process and establishes stereotypes of femininity.

The major criticism of radical French theorists who have proposed biological, psychological and linguistic theories of women's writing is that of essentialism.

In an attempt to avoid essentialism, Showalter has advocated a cultural approach to women's writing. Although she does not completely debunk the other approaches, she feels:

> A theory based on a model of women's culture can provide . . . a more complete and satisfying way to talk about the specificity and difference of women's writing that theories based in biology, linguistics or psychoanalysis. Indeed, a theory of culture incorporates ideas about women's body, language and psyche, but interprets them in relation to the social context in which they occur. The ways in which women conceptualize their bodies and their sexual and reproductive functions are intricately linked to their cultural environments. The female psyche can be studied as the product or construction of cultural forces. Language, too, comes back into the picture, as we consider the social dimensions and determinants of language use, the shaping of linguistic behaviour by cultural ideals. A cultural theory acknowledges that there are important differences between women as writers: class, race, nationality and history are determinants as significant as gender.[14]

It is not possible to speak of West Indian women as a homogenous group. They may share basic similarities of their sex—menstruation, pregnancy, sexual discrimination—but Marjorie Thorpe points out:

> The nature of the West Indian experience has militated against the emergence of any single set of characteristics which might be said to describe the West Indian woman. West Indian history of several different peoples who have come from countries that are racially and culturally very dissimilar, one from the other. Only their Caribbean experience links the members of the ethnically-diverse West Indian population, and this Caribbean experience has not been the same for the various immigrant groups.[15]

Pat Ellis reminds us of other areas of difference: "Although the lives of women in different parts of the region do not differ greatly, Caribbean women are not a homogenous group. Divisions of race, colour, class, social and economic status and place of residence affect their perceptions of themselves, their role and their contributions to the development of their countries."[16]

These considerations must be taken into account before formulating any theory about West Indian women's writing. A cultural approach would be most effective in attempting to decipher qualities of difference in West Indian women's writing.

There can be no categorical conclusions about such an elusive phenomenon as creativity. It would be misleading to assume that creativity is replicated on the basis of race, nationality or even sex. To do so would welcome the temptation of trying to force all women's writing into restricted categories, so leaving no room for difference. Some critics, through comparative textual analysis, have been able to identify areas of similarity which make it possible to distinguish an imaginative continuum characterised by recurrent themes, images, stylistic devices and patterns. Yet how certain can one be that these commonalities are solely due to sex and are not influenced by factors like race, class or literary trends? The search for a female style holds exciting prospects for the uncovering of a female tradition and for exploring the interconnections between women writers across all boundaries. But the barriers are many and the path still remains uncertain.

The difference in the female fiction of 1930s is the result of socio-cultural factors that placed expectations on the female sex. They were less able to join in the overt challenge that their male contemporaries were making to the Victorian ideals and values of their society. The women were still under pressure to conform to the ideals of Victorian womanhood. Their subject material would have been influenced by the social expectations of their sex. In her essay "Professions for Women",[17] Virginia Woolf writes about the forced censorship which inhibits the woman writer's freedom of expression. She contends that every woman writer faces the dilemma of reconciling "The Angel in the House" (who represents and upholds the values of patriarchy, including its assumptions about femaleness) with her own perceptions and feelings about her world and her sexuality. Woolf observes that women are "impeded by the extreme conventionality of the other sex. For though men allow themselves great freedom in these respects, I doubt that they realize or can control the extreme severity with which they condemn such freedom in women."[18]

For these reasons women may have felt more inhibited than men about writing the gender relations and sexual habits of the black lower classes. The lives of the lower classes would have been alien to women writers, who came from the middle stratum of society. Although the men were from the same class, they acquired their knowledge of the lower classes by actually integrating themselves into barrack-yard communities. Alfred Mendes, for instance, took up temporary residence in a barrack yard in order to get the atmosphere, dialect and behaviour of the people. Such an experiment would have been unthought of for a woman. This is perhaps why, with the exception of Kathleen Archibald's "Clipped Wings", all the stories written by women describe middle-class life. Arichibald was in a position to know more about barrack-yard life because her middle-class home on Picton Street was next to a small barrack-yard. However, in her story she chooses to focus on children and on the economic hardships of the poor. No mention is made of their sexual lives.

One of the characteristics of Showalter's "Feminine" stage is the tendency for the woman writer to uphold the social structures and to even support the existing stereotypes of women. Two stories, "Beyond the Horizon" by Kathleen Archibald and "Obituary for Doolarie" by Doreen Hamilton, display these characteristics. Archibald returns to the theme of poverty, not the poverty of the lower classes, but that of a middle class family who lack sufficient funds to support the middle-class lifestyle. Archibald explores how economic want affects the woman who must sacrifice self for the welfare of her family. Her youthful dreams of travel are never realised. Her condition is one of restriction and dissatisfaction which is blamed on her financial situation: "Her life was like a curtain. Once it had rippled, now it was still and only waiting until a little money should pass by and touch it with its hand."[19]

The story opens with a flashback scene where Mary Tulley, the protagonist, as a young woman is aboard a ship. A conversation about travel takes place between the young woman and an older man. While we learn that she has never left the West Indies, her companion has travelled to several countries such as England, France and Germany. But she has plans of her own. She wants to visit the countries of the East. She seems determined, yet one knows even before the second section begins that these dreams will not be realised. Perhaps this is because of the stillness of the atmosphere; the author makes the reader aware of how still the young lady sits. Or maybe it is because of the obvious contrast created between the man's freedom of movement and the woman's inertia. Mary is placed in a position of dependency since she must resort to seeing the places that her companion speaks of through his eyes, "His experiences were hers."

The second section of the story shifts to the present condition of the protagonist as a married woman with two daughters. There is no surprise that the state of inertia persists. Mary suffers silently, subordinating her own desires so that her daughters can have theirs fulfilled. The restriction and discontent that she feels are attributed to financial want. Marriage itself is not the problem. There is no more talk of travel, but one wonders what had prevented her from realising the dreams of her youth. Was it because of financial reasons or marriage, or a combination of the two? We are asked to accept the first.

This poses a problem because initially one gets a clear sense that Archibald is exploring male freedom as opposed to female restriction. However, this is somehow lost in the second half of the story. Through a switch in the direction and content of the narrative, Archibald alters the trend of her tale in what seems to be an effort to assure the reader—and possibly herself—that she never intended to make any complaint about the woman's condition or about the institution of marriage. In the obvious attempt to reverse what was potentially a protest story by highlighting the woman's problem as a financial one, rather than a gender issue, Archibald displays a reluctance to challenge the social structures and to raise questions central to the woman's condition.

The reserve and reticence that the women writers of fiction exhibited in addressing gender issues and sex also apply to the poetry. The poetry written in the 1930s covered a variety of themes and concerns: nature, history, religion, art, love. These poems bear the faults common to West Indian poetry of the period, such as imitativeness, clichés and romanticism.

The first woman who is recorded to have published her poetry in book form is Olga Comma-Maynard. In 1929 she funded herself the printing of a collection of poems and short stories entitled *Carib Echoes*. Mrs Comma-Maynard's poetry was targeted mainly at children. In fact, her inspiration to write came from her observation as a teacher that the poetry taught to the children under the colonial education system had no relevance to the local environment. Her poetry, then, was very much a response to the growing national consciousness ignited by the black consciousness movement of Marcus Garvey and the reform movement. The spirit of nationalism sought expression in the creation of a literature that celebrated the local landscape, language, culture, folklore and life style. Comma-Maynard was among the first local writers and the first woman writer to begin experimenting with local material. Her verse is patriotic with a tendency to romanticise West Indian life. Even the village washerwoman is presented as an exotic figure. Comma-Maynard's most successful pieces are "A West Indian Year Song", "The Keskidee", "Lullaby" and a short story called "The Marriage of the Saman".

Poems that dealt with the woman's experience were not very popular. Those dealing with love were in the same vein as Victorian romantic poetry. Only two poems exhibit the explicit use of sexual imagery: "Lines Written for a Certain Poet" and "Myself to the Muse of Poetry", both written by Olga Yaatoff. The former describes a sexual encounter between a poet and his lover, while the latter attempts to deal with the mystic union between the poet and the muse, which is made analogous to a sexual union. However, in dealing with the sex act Yaatoff makes an obvious effort to distance herself from the poems. This is evidence, I think, of a social conditioning that sanctions such topics as taboo for the woman.

In "Lines Written for a Certain Poet",[20] for instance, Yaatoff chooses to distance herself by making the "I" persona male. The poem is about a poet's declaration that his craft is his first love. He apologises to his lover to whom he had made devotional pledges in the heights of his passion. The poem concludes: "For I'm a poet to whom nothing is sacred save his Art."

Yaatoff uses the camouflage of the male persona to voice her own commitment to her art. By making the speaking voice male, she is also afforded the freedom to enter into a graphic description of the sexual experience. The explicitness of Yaatoff's imagery prompted one critic to describe her treatment of the love scene as "mildly pornographic",[21] a phrase which is suspect. Why should the critic use the word "pornographic", which suggests something unwholesome and morally twisted? Is it because the critic felt that the imagery was too coarse for a woman writer?

The poem "Myself to the Muse of Poetry"[22] provides even greater interest. What is curious here is the use of sexual imagery to symbolise the fusion between the artist and the muse. This is by no means new to poetry; however, in this poem we have a female artist who is seeking union with a muse who is traditionally presented as a woman. Unlike "Lines for a Certain Poet' where Yaatoff is claiming to be writing on behalf of another poet, in this poem she directly addresses the muse using the first person "I". Yet there is ambiguity about the sex of the "I" persona. Although it is quite obvious that the personified muse is female, it seems that Yaatoff may have assumed a male persona. But this seems contradictory, given the title which uses the reflexive pronoun "myself" and the use of the first person. The ambiguity surrounding the poet's sex is another attempt at distancing.

Shifts in the Quality of Women's Writing: The 1960s

The 1960s saw the re-emergence of women writers after a 20-year period of comparative silence. Five books written by women were published: *Tomorrow will Always Come* by Clara Rosa De Lima (1965), *Bird At My Window* by Rosa Guy (1966), *Among the Potatoes* by Barbara A. Jones (1967), *The Evil Spirit* by Veronica Fonrose (1967) and *Cheers* by Yvonne Jack (1966). Poems and short stories also appeared in literary journals and magazines such as *Voice*, *Bim* and *Caribbean Quarterly*. The outstanding women who appeared in these were Judy Miles, Marguerite Wyke, Barbara Jones and Lorain Rostant.

The mysterious silence that occurred in the 1940s and 1950s, when our women just seemed to drop out of the literary scene, can be viewed as an incubation period for the women writers who emerged in the 1960s. Several factors combined to facilitate the sudden burst of creativity. The women writers who emerged in the post-independence era came from amongst those who were benefitting from the improved education system and the increased opportunities for girls to obtain a secondary and university education, with the granting of government scholarships for girls, the establishment of more schools, both single-sex and co-educational, and the opening of the Senior Cambridge Examinations to girls.

Changes in attitudes to the role of women in social production and an awakening of a new self-perception among women about their potential and their contribution to society may have encouraged their re-entry into the field of creative writing. Assisting in the transformation of self-awareness in our women would have been these factors: The granting of universal suffrage; the black consciousness movement started by Marcus Garvey; the work of women like Amy Ashwood and Una Marson who encouraged women to participate in the movement; nationalism and the struggle for independence led by the People's National Movement (PNM); the formation of the PNM Women's League and the contribution and example of Audrey Jeffers and the Coterie of Social Workers recorded by Reddock; the growth of trade unionism which motivated women to fight for their rights as workers; and the revival of the women's movement in the USA and the UK.

Women's writing, according to Elaine Showalter, can be regarded as a subculture within the framework of a larger society, in relation to the evolution of women's self-awareness and to the ways in which a minority group finds its own direction of self-expression in the dominant society.[23] She identifies three stages in the development of women's writing which correspond to that of other literary subcultures: the feminine, the feminist and the female.[24] The stages are not rigidly defined but the transition from one stage to another is marked by external changes which encourage and accommodate change in women's self-perception. The reforms brought about by the women's liberation movement and its role in raising the consciousness of women were of key importance in the progress of British women's writing, from its imitativeness and internalisation of patriarchal values in the feminine stage, to their rejection of them in the feminist stage, to the discovery and celebration of the female experience in the female stage.

Women's writing can be seen as a process by which women undertake through art a pilgrimage of self-discovery and self-awareness that involves a rejection of male paradigms of female experience. Intimately related to what women as writers put upon the page is their socialisation, which is translated into a literary form which reveals time, place, culture and race. This can be seen in Showalter's analysis of women's writing in the West Indian context, where women are in the position of being twice removed as members of a subculture within a larger subculture that has had a history of domination from the culture of the European imperialists.

Hamilton's "Obituary for Doolarie",[25] which appeared in 1964, comes out in strong defence of the conventional values of womanhood. For the time it was published, in the 1960s when attitudes about the roles and potential of woman were undergoing change, the story's Victorian point of view is surprising. "Obituary for Doolarie" pays tribute to a woman whose life was characterised by hard work, child-bearing and suffering. According to the narrator, Doolarie's life was redeemed by a certain quality of spirit that made her, "a light shining through the hardship, the injustice, the confusion of our present existence". These qualities amount to gentleness, self-sacrifice, a capacity to suffer, ignorance, docile acceptance, non-participation, social invisibility and silence.

Hamilton writes: "True, many of the means of participation were denied her, but she did not look for, nor create, them. She merely lived the life which had been given her and was content that others should struggle for power to manipulate the mechanisms of society: that is to say, for education, for money, for social prominence."[26]

Her other admirable quality was her physical plainness: "she had never tried to enhance her appearance with cosmetics . . . or with conscious care".

Hamilton, whose authorial voice is felt throughout, is sentimentalising about the types of qualities which can redeem an age darkened by power struggles, injustice and greed. But the very qualities she upholds and cherishes in Doolarie are those that have facilitated the subordination and oppression of women throughout history. The story therefore reads like a patriarchal white paper on womanhood. The irony, however, lies in the fact that the story commemorates the death of a woman who epitomised the qualities of patriarchal womanhood.

The literature of the 1960s showed a greater maturity in style and content than that of the 1930s. There is a move, albeit a tentative one, towards more open exploration of the woman's experience and sexual relations. But as before there is no real attempt to connect ethnicity with the woman's situation, except for the poem "My Sister" in Jones's *Among the Potatoes*, which looks at the black migrant experience. Overall, however, women writers seemed to mesh with the male voices in bringing expression to the growing discontent and social unrest that began in the 1960s and climaxed in the 1970s.

Events on both the local and international scene contributed to the state of national consciousness that found expression in what Gordon Rohlehr described as "the troubled cataract of poetic statement which has characterized the decade".[27] These included the dissolution of the West Indian Federation, the growing dissatisfaction with the *status quo* and the black power movement. On the international scene there was also evidence of discontent with the existing systems, for instance the hippie cult, the peace movement that protested against the Vietnam war, the black civil rights movement in the USA and the second wave of the women's liberation movement.

Articulating a certain state of human spirit took precedence over the woman-centred protest that Showalter indicated as a characteristic of her feminist stage. The sentiments of discontent expressed in dealing with sexual relations were too weak to be identified as the voice of protest. Perhaps this is because they were so few that they lacked collectivity. But there was certainly a more adventurous spirit in exploring sex, which was probably an indication of the changes in social attitudes which also brought women courage to deal with taboo subjects.

Judy Miles was the most prolific and accomplished writer of the group. Her poems expressed a sense of futility and spiritual sickness. In her first published poem, "Holocaust",[28] Miles contrasts the commitment and purposeful action of the Vietnamese monks who sacrificed life in loyalty for the case, with the Caribbean situation where there was fragmentation and lack of real commitment or belief in any cause:

And I mourn that the springs of their faith were curled tight to
hurl them to such deeds. But our faith is whirled, driven
As dust in an endless drought
Defying cycles.[29]

Society was infected with a spiritual sickness that had roots in the commercialism that had taken the country by storm in the 1960s when Trinidad began its rapid economic expansion. It is also characteristic of the modern existentialist dilemma, so giving the verse a universal aspect. Marguerite Wyke in "On Remembering Immortelles"[30] laments the loss of a past of innocence, beauty and security, a time when love was symbolised by the flaming red of the immortelle blossoms, and freedom of movement was a "dancing space". The present however, has lost all that, being a "dim lit, dark-wood time".

Miles' poem "The Room"[31] presents a microcosm of the society. The room is occupied at the four cardinal points by various characters and objects. At the southern end a thin young woman lies on a bed reading Descartes. Her thinness alludes to a lack that surpasses the physical. To the east there is a Cyclopean representative of the rising sun, which heralds a new day founded on the "doctrine/Of sex, the dollar and the gun". In the western corner, there is a newspaper whose headlines read "Three Murders in One day". The red of the setting sun meshes with the blood of the murders. Finally, in the northern corner, a group of men converse on trivial subjects reflecting the intellectual and spiritual emptiness of the time.

Human relationships are also defiled by the moral and spiritual sickness that permeates the society. Love cannot flourish. It fails to be consolation and union, as in the poem "*At Two o'clock*":

You are alone
Between you
And that other body upon the bed
Distance is hard and tangible
The soul cannot be reached

Loneliness,
Harsh as sandpaper
Scrapes the heart.[32]

Individual loneliness and alienation prevent communication and communion. The sense of individual aloneness is part of the modern dilemma which has characterised the experience of twentieth-century man.

Rather than love, only lust seems to breed in this decadent age. In "Summer and Kitsilano Beach",[33] lust and decay become synonymous. The poem begins with images of decay, "rotting heads" and "vomit". Then the scene focuses on a girl who unknowingly becomes the target of male lust as the man who is walking along the beach sends out his "tentacles of lust" that move to destroy her. Barbara Jones in an untitled poem depicts how the lustful stares of male desire tarnish innocence like smoke rising out of a chimney to pollute the sky. They

make brownish
grey the
cleanliness

of some
maiden's breast
left naked
by their
gaze.[34]

Male and female relations are associated with distrust and discomfort. Women are presented as being easy victims of sexual violation. This sense of threat is also communicated in Rowena Scott's "Across the Table"[35] and Janice Bain-Mottley's "Casual Meeting".[36] In the former, male compliments induce anxiety and suspicion in the woman who senses danger. The latter depicts the uncertainty of the future of a developing relationship which can either become a lasting love union or a casual sexual encounter.

"The Promise"[37] and "My Evil Ones"[38] by Lorain Rostant bring a previously unexplored aspect of the woman into focus: not the woman as victim, but her capacity to be victimised and her potential for evil. Her writings indicate a movement towards a more balanced and honest portrayal of woman.

In the poem "The Promise" the woman is depicted as hunter. It describes a scene in which a woman is in a closed room awaiting the arrival of her lover. The woman sits in expectant stillness, poised like a predator stalking its prey. She is likened to a cat as she moves around the house "on cunning cats'/Paws".

The story "My Evil Ones" in theme as well as style shows that the writer is breaking new ground. It is an attempt to articulate the woman's discovery of a facet of her personality which she calls her "Evil Ones". While she is intrigued with these presences, she feels compelled to suppress them because they delight in behaviour that goes against what is socially accepted. The qualities they display resemble those associated with the unconscious forces of the *id*.

Rostant opens "My Evil Ones" with the line: "The problem is, though, how does a woman describe her fear without writing a full length novel 'around' it."[39]

Fear of what? Perhaps it is the fear of self-discovery or the fear of exposing the "dark side" which contradicts the socially prescribed attributes and behavioural codes associated with womanhood. Rostant is interested in the woman's problem of coming to terms with these aspects of her personality. Fear of full self-encounter and of upsetting the social norm are perhaps what lead to avoidance, deviation and suppression. Rostant indicates a connection between the woman's conflict of self with a style that is exemplified by circularity and illusiveness. These qualities have been recognised in women's writing elsewhere and can be linked to the sociocultural condition of women, which has encouraged fear and repression.

Conclusion

This is a preliminary survey of women's writing in Trinidad and Tobago for the period 1929-69, in an attempt to account for the patterns that our female literary tradition has taken. The barriers that have inhibited the participation of our women in creative writing do not vary greatly from those of women elsewhere.

The gaps, silences and the small trickle of writing that characterised our female literary history up to the 1960s, reflect the restrictions that patriarchal attitudes have forced upon women. I have linked the disproportionate representation of women in the period between 1929 and independence to the discriminatory Colonial education system and the influence of the domestic ideology which sought to keep women within the home. The burst of creativity in the 1960s came from women who benefited from an improved education system and the change in attitudes about women.

Because women's writing is the expression of a subculture it is caught in the dilemma of writing within the confines of the dominant culture. The development of West Indian literature has had a similar experience. The early writers tended to imitate the literature of their masters. Eventually there was a move towards a search for authenticity, self-celebration and discovery. Trinidadian women, particularly in the first half of the twentieth century, were socialised to uphold the dominant Victorian ideology and its concept of womanhood. Although it was a reality attainable by only a small section of the society, it was still the ideal. The women who wrote, especially in the 1930s, came from the sector of society that would have been most deeply entrenched in the dominant Victorian attitudes of their time. Therefore the manner of voice that they brought to their creative output was influenced consciously or unconsciously by their sociocultural conditioning and the social expectations of their sex.

In the 1930s women writers showed a marked reserve in dealing with gender issues. They lacked the freedom of their male contemporaries who challenged the Victorian ideals of their society by creating a literature that openly debunked conventional values. The rapid and wide-ranging changes on the local and international scene had some effect on the quality of women's writing in the 1960s. Writers showed an awareness of and concern for the sociopolitical climate and there was evidence of the beginning of exploration into the issue of ethnicity which had been absent in the previous period. In the area of sex and sexuality some writers exhibited a willingness to be more open and honest; however, the transition was too tentative to be described as revolutionary.

The literary output of women in Trinidad between 1929 and 1969 displayed a conservatism in terms of the choice of subject matter, its treatment and the lack of concern for women's issues that reflects the nature of their self-awareness and their absorption into the society's gender definitions. Significantly, Rhoda Reddock found in her research of the pre-independence women's movement in Trinidad and Tobago a conservative element which was evident in the reluctance or neglect of the women in the forefront of the movement to challenge the existing sexual division of labour and the power hierarchy and in their failure to address crucial questions relevant to women's roles and sexual inequality. Commenting on the contribution of Audrey Jeffers in her capacity as an activist and politician representing the issues of women, Reddock writes:

"Jeffers represented a clear example of feminist conservatism which at the same time that it sought to change the system, worked actively for its maintenance."[40]

The lack of a radical approach to women's issues that characterised the women's movement in Trinidad and Tobago up to the 1960s, is reproduced in the literature of that same period. The correlation is not coincidental; it indicates the influence that sociological forces have had on the creative output of our women and the relationship between self-perception and literary form.

References

1. Gilbert, Susan and Gubar, Susan. *The Madwoman in the Attic*. New Haven and London: Yale University Press. 1979. p. 4.
2. Mendes, Alfred. *Trinidad*, Vol. 1 No. 2, Easter, 1930, p. 57.
3. Fullerton, Janet. "Women in Trinidadian life and Literature", *The New Voices*, 5 (9), March, 1977, p. 9.
4. Ramchand, Kenneth. *The West Indian Novel and Its Background*. London: Heinemann Education Books, 1983. 2nd edn. Chapter 2.
5. Reddock, Rhoda. "Women, Labour and Struggle in 20th-Century Trinidad and Tobago 1898-1960". PhD dissertation. The Hague. 1980, Chapter 3.3.
6. *Ibid*. pp. 220 and 225. Reddock notes that girls comprised approximately 45 per cent of the primary-school enrolment figure for 1937. The number of girls receiving secondary education rose from none in 1903 to 922 in 1937, whereas for boys the increase was from 375 to 1,215.
7. Poynting, Jeremy. "East Indian Women in the Caribbean: Experience and Voice", In Dabydeen, David and Samaroo Brinsley (ed.). *India in the Caribbean*, London: Hansib Publishers 1987 p.235
8. Mendes, Alfred. "A Commentary". *Trinidad*, Vol. 1. No. 2 Easter, 1930, p. 65.
9. Reinhard Sander in King, Bruce (ed.). *West Indian Literature* London: Macmillan Press. 1979. p. 51.
10. *Ibid*., p. 51.
11. Yaatoff, Olga. "Gasoline Station". *The Beacon*, Vol. 1 No. 12 April, 1932, pp. 10-11.
12. Archibald, Kathleen. *'Clipped Wings'*, Trinidad POS 1937, pp. 45-54.
13. Showalter, Elaine. "Feminist Criticism in the Wilderness". In Showalter, Elaine,(ed.) *The New Feminist Criticism: Essays on Women, Literature and Theory*. New York: Pantheon Book. 1985. p. 249.
14. Ibid., pp. 259-60.
15. Thorpe, Marjorie. "Beyond the Sargasso: The Significance of the Presentation of the Woman in the West Indian Novel". PhD dissertation. Queen's University, Kingston, Ontario, Canada. 1975. p. 38.
16. Ellis, Pat. "An Overview of Women in Caribbean Society". In Ellis, Pat (ed.). *Women of the Caribbean*, Jamaica: Kingston Publishers. 1986. p. 1.
17. Woolf, Virginia. "Professions for Women". In Eagleton, Mary (ed.). *Feminist Literature Theory: A Reader*. New York: Basil Blackwell. pp. 51-53.
18. Ibid., p. 52.
19. Archibald, Kathleen. "Beyond the Horizon", *The Beacon*, Vol 1, No. 3, p. 29.
20. Yaatoff, Olga. "Lines for a Certain Poet" , *The Beacon*, Vol. 2, No. 7, 1932, p. 38.
21. Ayers, Peter K. "Introduction to Sander", Rienhard (ed.). *From Trinidad*, London: Hodder and Stoughton. 1978. p. 18.

22. Yaatoff, Olga. "Myself to the Muse of Poetry", *The Beacon*, Vol. 2, No. 7, 1932, p. 35.
23. Showalter, Elaine. *A Literature of Their Own: British Women Novelists From Bronte to Lessing*. New Jersey: Princeton University Press. 1977. p. 11.
24. *Ibid.*, p. 13.
25. Hamilton, Doreen. "Obituary for Doolarie", *Voices*, Vol. 1, No. 1, 1964, p. 9.
26. Ibid., p. 9.
27. Rohlehr, Gordon. "My Strangled City: Poetry in Trinidad 1964-75", *Caliban*, Vol. 2, No. 1, 1976, p. 50.
28. Judy Miles, "Holocaust", *Voices*, Vol. 1, No. 4, 1965, pp. 2-3.
29. *Ibid.*, p. 2.
30. Wyke, Marguerite. "On Remembering Immortelles", *Caribbean Quarterly*, Vol. 5, No. 3, 1958, pp. 225-26.
31. Judy Miles, "The Room", *Voices*, Vol. 1, No. 6, 1966, p. 16.
32. "At Two o'Clock", *Voices*, Vol. 1, No. 4, 1965, p. 13.
33. *Ibid.*, "Summer and Kitsilano Beach", *Voices*, Vol. 2, No. 1, 1966, p. 12.
34. Barbara Jones, "Untitled Poem", *Voices*, Vol., 2, No. 1, 1969, p. 20.
35. Rowena Scott, "Across the Table", *Voices*, Vol. 2, No. 1, 1969, p. 18.
36. Janice Bain-Mottley, "Casual Meeting", *Voices*, Vol. 1, No. 4, 1965, p. 5.
37. Lorain Rostant, "The Promise", *Voices*, Vol. 1, No. 1, 1964, p. 14.
38. *Ibid.*, "My Evil Ones", *Voices*, Vol. 1, No. 1, 1964, pp. 13-14.
39. *Ibid.*, p. 13.
40. Reddock, Rhoda, *op. cit.*, p. 612.

Part FIVE

Gender and Health

Gender and Health

Introduction

Elsa Leo-Rhynie

Three of the papers in this part were presented at the Women and Health Seminar held in Barbados in October 1992. The fourth paper, by June George, was presented at the seminar on Gender, Science and Technology in February 1994 in Jamaica. Health as a crucial factor in economic and social development and the vital importance of women in the maintenance of the nation's health are the major concepts with which this part is concerned. In the first paper some of the challenges which the health needs of Caribbean women present during the 1990s are examined.Two papers look at research into women's health generally, and specifically as it relates to sexually transmitted diseases (STDs). The effectiveness of health education in meeting its objectives of changing behaviour, which is one of the assumptions on which recommendations for reducing the incidence of STDs are offered, is explored in a case study which looks at the interplay of information from conventional science with traditional health beliefs.

The need to recognise the importance of women's health and maintaining it at a high level is pointed out by Gloria Scott, who notes that not only is this vital for the well-being of the woman, but also at the most basic level the well-being of men and children is closely linked to and dependent on the well being of women.

She uses this to provide a strong rationale for identifying, and trying to meet women's health needs. The argument is also a powerful one for researching women's health and educating women about good health practices. Another argument, which is also emphasised in the papers by Joycelin Massiah and Caroline Allen, is that failure to meet the health needs of women today has long-term consequences which may not surface until the twenty-first century. Among the challenges to be faced in the 1990s is the recognition that Caribbean women do not constitute a homogeneous group in terms of their lifecycle position, or their social background, and that this has implications for meeting needs, and establishing priorities in the provision of health care. The role of the state and of non-governmental organisations in offering health services is considered in the light of the lack of resources in the countries of the Caribbean region.

This lack of resources is noted also by Massiah, who identifies structural adjustment as the major factor threatening the level of health and health care in the Caribbean. She notes that Caribbean countries have surpassed the standards set by the World Health Organisation in terms of maternity and child health, and also that they have performed favourably in other established health indicators; she warns, however, that the poor economic indicators evident in these countries and which result in reduced government spending on health care could well change this. This is particularly worrying in light of the new diseases such as Acquired Immune Deficiency Syndrome (AIDS) and those which are stress-related or generated by environmental change.

Massiah emphasises that researchers should stop conceiving of women's health needs solely in terms of maternity and child health, and calls for a reconceptualisation of what constitutes women's health, and for research to support this reconceptualisation. She identifies the medical research strengths in the Caribbean and urges consideration of five major questions which should be addressed by research:

1. What is to be researched?
2. By whom?
3. For whom?
4. How?
5. With what?

Caroline Allen's paper concentrates on research on sexually transmitted diseases (STDs), and her paper reflects one of Massiah's concerns about the methodology employed when conducting research with women on personal topics such as these. The importance of quantitative methods in providing an overview is recognised, but even more so is the use of qualitative methods to obtain the type of information which helps understand the forces that are associated with high-risk behaviours which often result in women contracting

STDs. Sexuality is intricately bound up with male-female power relationships, and women very often lack the power to insist on the practice of safe sex by their partners. The sort of information necessary to confirm such a hypothesis can only be obtained when the questions posed by Massiah have been thoroughly considered in the planning of the research, and the sensitivity of the issues must be taken into account in conducting interviews as well as gathering other data.

It is essential to unearth such information if effective public education campaigns are to be planned and implemented. Allen stresses that the motives that guide behaviour must be understood in order to facilitate behaviour change, and points to the pervasive nature of traditional health beliefs, their effect on health behaviour and the spread of STDs.

The interplay of traditional beliefs and conventional science in health care behaviour is vividly portrayed in the case study presented by June George, who explains that new knowledge is very often received and linked to prior knowledge in such a way that the learner can make sense of the new information and can be comfortable with it. This link is clear in her conversations with Mrs S. which bring to life the melding of concepts which emerge from the reception of new information and its linkage to accepted traditional knowledge. She notes the implication of this for health education geared towards adults, who already have a 'lay' understanding of a wide range of health concepts.Her view is that this understanding should be treated with respect, and that it is important for the facilitation of learning that those who are designing educational material and programmes for this group try to determine what such an understanding is, and how it may be used when new ideas are presented.

The role of women as both recipients of health care and as health care providers emerged in all the papers, and the need for medical training to focus on gender as a variable in the design and implementation of health care programmes was one of the priorities identified.

Health Needs of Caribbean Women

Challenges for the Nineties

Gloria Scott

Introduction

To be healthy is a basic human right of all people. Physical, emotional and mental well-being is a prerequisite for energy and physical strength as well as for the intellectual harmony which facilitates productivity and creativity and enables individuals to contribute to and benefit from personal and societal development. Also, good health is a primary resource for national development. Health is also defined as a state of positive well-being. Having control over one's health means possessing knowledge of what needs to be done in order to be healthy, as well as having access to resources and facilities to meet those needs and the capacity to make the necessary decisions.

The determinants of health are not completely clear. They include purchasing power over certain goods and services (this depends on income and on prices); the health environment, climate, standards of public sanitation and prevalence of communicable diseases; and people's understanding of health, nutrition and hygiene. These determinants apply to all but there are particular dimensions of each which have special relevance for women. Health problems affecting women arise from a complex combination of factors and can be understood fully only in the context of a broad definition of health related to women's roles and positions in society. Traditional values and attitudes that place a low value on women are important determinants of their health, as are many elements of poverty and underdevelopment. Strategies for improving women's health require fundamental structural and attitudinal changes.

It is important to recognise that Caribbean women are not a homogeneous mass. While there are many ethnic and cultural similarities throughout the region, differences among women are marked by socio-economic, cultural, political and locational factors which affect and are affected by their health. There are differences, too, according to the phases of women's life cycle. What we do when we speak about Caribbean women is to attempt some generalisations as a starting point for a more penetrating examination. It is important to bear in mind that women are not an isolated group in society. For instance, at the most basic level the well-being of men and children is closely linked to and dependent on the well-being of women.

This paper examines health conditions of Caribbean women and the consequent needs and challenges for the remainder of the 1990s. Many health conditions have long-term consequences; and health needs of one period, if not met adequately, will ripple into subsequent phases of the lifecycle as well as subsequent periods of time. These challenges will be at individual and family or household level, at community level and at national level. While it is interesting to try to separate these levels, they intertwine and challenges occur concurrently. Ways in which satisfying needs at one level are reflected at other levels depend on complex factors. The first section will identify some of the most common health concerns, including those arising from their high or increasing prevalence, the burden they represent for women and the lack of relevant services and facilities. The second section will discuss the challenges of these concerns, including institutional, organisational and resource issues. An issue which should be clarified is the role of the state vis-à-vis other actors in providing and facilitating health care and ensuring that equity of access is preserved. A brief third section will encapsulate some priorities and suggestions for action.

Common Health Concerns

The decade of the 1980s witnessed an increased awareness of the importance of women's health: (i) women's exposure to health risks and their ability to deal with health problems differ from those of men; (ii) women's health needs are often neglected and the resultant ill-health carries a heavy price for the individuals, their families and the community; and (iii) the poor health of women inflicts a high cost on the entire economy and hinders its development and progress. This section will identify some of the major health risks of women.

There are two overriding features of the health situation in the Caribbean. Firstly, over the past 20 or 30 years there have been dramatic changes in the pattern of diseases. As advanced public health technology and greater awareness have controlled the most serious infectious diseases, chronic non-communicable diseases have become the leading cause of death, the main contributors to premature mortality and the main causes of morbidity and chronic disability among adults. Indicators such as life expectancy, infant and maternal mortality have become increasingly positive and the Caribbean in general has been registering levels comparable with the advanced Western countries. The second feature is that in many areas the progress in health conditions is being reversed, especially within the decade of the 1980s, because of the deteriorating economic situation and serious erosion of national and individual purchasing powers. These two features have particular implications for women.

Mothers and children make up two-thirds of the population of the region. It is well known that women are sick more often and require more medical attention than men, although there is evidence that these differences are associated much more with behaviour patterns than with biological factors. It is also well known that women neglect their own health as a symptom of their low self-concept and their social conditioning. Despite women's child-bearing functions, men have a higher occupancy rate of hospital beds than women. Although women generally face the same health problems as men, they suffer from additional risks due to their lower socio-economic status, their limited access to basic resources, the time and energy demands of their double day combining household maintenance and economic production, and also the physical demands of reproduction.

The mid-year 1990 population of the English-speaking Caribbean region was 6.74 million and is projected to reach 6.9 million by the year 2000. The average annual rate of population increase in 1987-90, was 0.8 per cent with a range of 0.3 per cent per year in Montserrat to a high of 6.2 per cent in the British Virgin Islands. This growth of population means that there are more people to make claims on health services, which have generally been contracting, not expanding. Also, there are more people to make claims on natural resources and create environmental health hazards.

Overall, life expectancy at birth has increased from 55 years in the mid-1960s to 72.4 years, with Guyana demonstrating the low of 64.2 years and Barbados the high of 75.1 years. There is an average differential of three years in the life expectancy of males and females: 77.7 years for Barbadian females and a low of 67.1 for females born in Guyana. This means that the population of the Caribbean is ageing and that the proportion of females in the older population is increasing. In fact at older ages women significantly outnumber men. In addition to the presence or absence of various either genetic or behavioural risk factors, the health of older women is a product of their risk exposure throughout the earlier years of their lives. Their health shows the effects of years of stress, excessive workloads, malnutrition, repeated pregnancies, etc. The reference to older women is made here to signal a population group of growing significance whose needs for health and general well-being until recently have been ignored.

Cancer is now the second leading cause of death in the region. Rates of incidence are not uniform throughout the region, reflecting true differences in prevalence and also differences in reporting, but the excess of women among persons with cancer is constant and striking. Cancers of the uterine cervix and breast are the leading malignancies among women. Cervical cancer is most common among women who have had multiple pregnancies and there is evidence that it is likely to develop in females who commence regular sexual activity at an early age. While there appears to be some doubt still as to whether it is truly a sexually transmitted disease, it has been noted that cervical cancer occurs in women with a history of exposure to multiple sexual partners. Precision is lacking on the contribution to this incidence of the promiscuity of the male partners. Among both sexes lung cancer seems to be registering the most rapid increase in prevalence. The lack of facilities for early detection and treatment of cancer in a number of countries results in unnecessary mortality; in countries where these facilities exist, cutbacks in personnel, supplies and maintenance of equipment limit their effectiveness and their ability to respond to programmes increasing cancer awareness. Women from countries without facilities face additional stress from the need to travel to seek treatment, away from their families and with little social or economic support. There is a need to improve the availability of detection and treatment facilities and for social support for patients coming from other territories.

Hypertension is another of the highly prevalent chronic non-communicable conditions which is more common among women. The increase in hypertension in women over 50 years old is associated with the menopause as well as with their diet. Somewhat less prevalent but rapidly increasing and also a serious health concern is diabetes mellitus. Some 15 per cent of the adult population over 35 years old is affected and there is an excess of women in the diabetic population. Obesity, which is a growing problem in the region, even among adolescent females, is closely related to both these diseases which frequently remain undetected and uncontrolled until they strike down adults at the height of their productive capacity. Undiagnosed, they are a serious health risk for pregnant women. Obesity is also identified in the pathogenesis of some cancers. Ethnicity and cultural factors have been linked to obesity in females. These are reflected in food consumption patterns, images of desirability, etc, changes in which would be an important element in any strategy to control non-communicable diseases. Women's roles in promoting these behavioural changes towards more healthy lifestyles need to be strengthened.

In the deteriorating economies of the Caribbean there is increasing pressure on women. Many of the services to women in their non-producer roles have been reduced. There has been no compensating assistance to them in their producer role. Women must compensate for cuts in services and face increasing pressure to earn income, both of which force them to work more hours and juggle the uses of their time. The resultant stress should be considered as a health problem, together with those of the occupations which women are entering in increasing numbers. Many women have found employment in Export Processing Zones (EPZ) where working conditions such as long hours and infrequent bathroom breaks have harmful effects on their health. Many of the jobs women do are high-demand, low-control jobs and new technology has added another risk factor to their already high levels of stress.

Disease patterns have been identified in occupations in which women predominate. Risk factors include: contaminant dust, dyes, machine noise (textile workers); hair dyes, solvents, standing (beauticians); chemical pesticides and herbicides, poor personal hygiene facilities (agricultural workers); and food allergens, temperature extremes, ergonomic stressors (food service workers). Lack of protective clothing is common. A response to the economic situation has been a burgeoning of the informal sector, in which women are heavily involved. Many of their activities and the conditions in which they work present health risks: for instance, there is no control on their materials or tools, many of which may be hazardous. Another area of women's work which entails health hazards is inter-island trade. Contracting out or place work, which many women do, often has unrealistic performance expectations which place great pressure on women working in poor conditions. As in the case of street food vendors, exposure to dust and fumes of leaded gas have a deleterious effect on health. In addition to affecting the health of the women workers, many of these factors also can affect the health of unborn children, and contaminants carried home (such as on clothing) can affect household members.

There is a common perception that the focus of concern on women's health is almost exclusively reproductive health: obstetrics, gynaecology, sexuality, child-bearing, lactation and birth control. Recently, because of increased life expectancy, the reproductive health concern has become extended to the menopause. Child-bearing continues to be a cultural imperative for Caribbean women and in some countries there is still pressure to prove femaleness by bearing a child. This has contributed to teenage pregnancy which is a serious health as well as social problem. Births to mothers under 20 years have risen as a proportion of total births and represent 80 per cent of first births. Pregnant teenagers run a disproportionate health risk and many of their babies have limited life chances. The mothers are frequently emotionally and socially unprepared to raise children, and child-bearing disrupts their education, their personal maturation and development. Among teenagers of both sexes there is limited understanding of human sexuality and they are shackled by myths regarding pregnancy and reproduction.

Birth rates in the region have been declining. In 1991 Belize had the highest rate at 38 per 100 population and Barbados the lowest at 16 per 1,000 population, and the Caribbean is approaching the state at which excessive child-bearing will cease to be a predominant health concern. The present concerns are that for a variety of reasons (including fear of how they are treated by nurses), many pregnant women refuse to seek prenatal care until late in their pregnancy. Thus they are not screened for potential complications during delivery or for sexually transmitted diseases, and are not immunised. Another concern is that maternal mortality is unnecessarily high and is higher even than the level indicated by official statistics. A third concern is that many maternity facilities are overcrowded and understaffed. Only some 60 per cent of births are attended by trained personnel.

Sexually transmitted diseases (STDs) have increased substantially throughout the Caribbean. The number of cases of AIDS is relatively small but is increasing rapidly enough to be a serious worry. The prevalence of STDs among adolescents is high. A response to the economic situation has been liaisons between schoolgirls and older men who often infect them. The incidence, prevalence and health impact of STDs on women is not known fully because of difficulties in diagnosis in women, deficiencies in notification and the quality of the information obtained from the notification. It should be noted that women are vulnerable to STDs not so much because of their own sexual behaviour but because of the behaviour of their partners; male promiscuity is commonly accepted as the norm by Caribbean women at all socio-economic strata. One of the spectres facing older women is the responsibility they will face when sons and daughters, the productive members of the family on whom they are supposed to be dependent, have died from AIDS.

Caribbean women are concerned that, in tandem with the marginalisation of males because of high unemployment and other elements of the recession, there has been an explosion of violence against women: sexual violence, battery and other forms of abuse. This violence is seldom acknowledged as the health issue it is even if it results in no apparent physical damage to women. The full extent of the long-term emotional damage to the victims and its health and productivity implications are perhaps not fully understood. It is a contradiction that in a region where in many ways women are independent and resourceful, they perceive themselves as having no choice but to accept the violence because of their economic and social dependence on men.

Many other important health conditions such as mental health and malnutrition also merit inclusion here. Their incidence is significant and they have long-term effects. There are many health issues related to the environment which have particular interest for women, such as exposure to dust and caustic wastes in bauxite areas.

Challenges related to Health Concerns

The panorama of the health conditions of Caribbean women in the previous section suggests several groups of challenges which relate to existing persistent needs as well as to new ones. Some of the challenges derive from inadequacies in the health sector, inadequacies of services, facilities and resources, including human resources, information and understanding. As noted in the introduction, the challenges could be addressed to one or more levels of actors and institutions.

Women's health care needs are constantly changing with society, and health care needs are emerging in domestic and productive work settings which are not taken into account in the provision of health services. The broad challenge is to incorporate into the policy and programming institutions mechanisms to provide surveillance of women's health, their access to health care services and facilities and the realities of their lives, which will ensure that they respond to their needs. Related to this is the challenge to health administrations to integrate health concerns—and specifically concerns related to women's health—into the national policies of all sectors. Many of the causes of ill-health go far beyond the health sector and these causes can only be addressed in the context of overall development policy. These are national challenges, but the information needed for formulating the policies must trickle upwards from the individual and household levels at which levels the challenge is not only to provide realistic information, but also to seek the information which will enable them to influence public health policy.

There are many gaps in the services, limitations on access and non-responsiveness of design in health services. Merely providing additional services (if there were resources for them) along the same lines would not necessarily lead to higher utilisation or an automatic improvement in women's health. The challenge is to ensure much greater community involvement in the design feasibility of health services, to ensure that they respond to the needs of local women. The provision of primary health care services depend heavily on the efforts of local women, but their involvement in the planning of such services has been inadequate. A further necessity is to study the impact on health services of the recession, the restrictive policies introduced with structural adjustment, many of which are not in the health sector but have implications for health, and reductions in budget allocations. This information should be aired and fed into national policy and planning. Another area of planning health services which has not received adequate attention, both because of political implications and also because of lack of information, is the targeting of health care services to particular groups.

There are indications that public health is being neglected in some areas. This is of particular concern to women who must provide front-line health care for their families when they become ill from the contagious diseases, such as measles, that are again emerging or from malaria which had been eradicated, or from typhoid or other waterborne diseases. The challenge is to try to recoup the progress that has been lost in recent years and also to strengthen health awareness and health promotion programmes. It is particularly important that women, who have a significant role as agents of change, be provided with the information and tools with which to effect change.

The human resources to undertake these tasks are a major problem. A large number of the service providers in the health care system are women, many of whom are discouraged by adverse conditions of work—high vacancy rates, low pay, inadequate supplies and equipment—and many patients regard them as hostile. This is the first part of the challenge: to redeem these persons and encourage their initiative and job satisfaction. The second part of the challenge is to update their training and to hone their communication skills. Many health personnel at all levels have not been exposed to some of the health situations they are now facing, and many have an off-putting approach to women, both as patients and as colleagues. This situation in its most undesirable form is represented by foreign doctors whose culture is different from that of the Caribbean.

Women's reproductive health also presents some challenges. Declining availability of resources for family life and population education makes it critical to use the limited resources to maximum effect. One solution would be streamlining family life education at an early age in schools for both girls and boys, training teachers, counsellors and peer group advisers. The scope of the education would include population, human sexuality, responsibility and behavioural change. Parents of both sexes should be involved in order to reinforce the education message. Some countries may soon have no external funds for family planning programmes. Ways will have to be found to continue the distribution of condoms which have been an important preventive measure against AIDS and other STDs. Caribbean fertility rates have declined but their continued decline depends in large part on increasing contraceptive prevalence, which is unlikely unless family planning programmes can be stepped up.

In all the countries of the region there is women's machinery and there is a Women, Health and Development (WHD) mechanism. Although they are both mandated to provide advocacy and outreach for women's issues, there has been little collaboration and in the health field their effectiveness has been limited. The University of Guyana and the University of the West Indies have women's studies programmes which could make a significant substantive contribution to furthering awareness and understanding of the issues discussed in this paper. Many women's non-governmental organisations and umbrella organisations are operating to some effect. Focusing their attention and their commitment to pursing priority health concerns of women is a major challenge. Funding for research tends to be biased against research on specific women's health concerns and funding for research on women in general is much more limited than that for "hard science". Collaboration in order to change this is important. As funding becomes available, these organisations should ensure that research findings are policy-relevant and presented in ways that would make them intelligible and usable by the various parties interested in such information for policy, programming and public information.

Priorities for Action

Caribbean women contribute heavily to the economy and the family and often lack resources and opportunities to work at full efficiency. This is compounded by poor nutrition and nutrition-related diseases, such as anaemia, which affect energy as well as by other health disorders. Women and their children, for whom they take principal responsibility, represent the largest and most vulnerable group in society and the group with the least power. The Caribbean health ministers have endorsed a Plan of Action on Women, Health and Development, 1990-94. Its implementation leaves much to be desired, but the six goals which were elaborated in considerable detail are in keeping with the concerns of this paper and suggest these priorities.

1. Strengthening the capacity of countries to ensure development of gender-sensitive health policies and programmes.

2. Improving the identification of the principal health problems affecting Caribbean women and the development of gender-specific indicators.
3. Ensuring the availability and accessibility of health services appropriate to the needs of Caribbean women.
4. Facilitating the ability of women to make informed decisions and take appropriate action regarding their health.
5. Promoting good mental health as an essential element for total well-being, with particular emphasis on its significance for women.
6. Reducing health risks and risk factors for women in the working environment, both in and out of the home.

References

Alleyne, Sir George and Sealey, K.A. *Whither Caribbean Health?* 1992.
Caribbean Development Bank. *Annual Report 1991, Barbados.*
Hagley, Knox R. 'Chronic non-communicable diseases and their impact on Caribbean women'. W. I. Medical Journal, 30, 1990, p. 4.
International Women's Health Coalition. "Reproductive tract infections in women in the Third World." *National and international policy implications.* 1991.
Pan-American Health Organisation. *Health Conditions in the Americas.* (mimeo).
______. *Mid-Life and Older Women in Latin America and the Caribbean.* 1989 (mimeo.)
Scott, Gloria L. "Notes on Women and Health and Development in the English-speaking Caribbean". 1992. (mimeo)
_______. "Mission Report: Women Health and Development in the English speaking Caribbean." 1992. (mimeo).
______. "Social Indicators of Development." 1991-92.
World Bank. *World Development Report.* 1992.

Researching Women's Health

Joycelin Massiah

One of the surprising aspects of the women and development dialogue in the Caribbean region so far has been the late interest which has been displayed in the matter of women's health. Given the recent admission by development specialists of the relation of health to development, perhaps it should not be surprising that the relation between women, health and development has been so long in being understood. Why this should be so may be a function of the high health standards in the region since the 1940s and 1950s. An element of complacency may have been the result, or there may have been an assumption that other, more pressing matters need to be placed on the development agenda. After all, every development plan in the region attaches significance to health.

The extent of that significance is what is at issue. There are those who see health as an essential good in itself; those who see health as an integral component of human resource development; and those who see health as a welfare arm of structural adjustment policy. It is perhaps this last group which has been most instrumental in drawing public attention to the need to review approaches to the delivery of health care, the training of health practitioners and the conceptualisation of health as a contributor to economic improvement. Foremost among this advocacy group have been women.

The shock of the economic events of the 1980s in at least four territories of the region (and several others since then) has thrown into sharp relief the links between health and development and women's place within that equation.

A process of social disinvestment involving reduction in the provision of social services, including health care, has resulted in the displacement of health workers, shortages of medical supplies, deterioration in the maintenance of the physical stock and equipment, increases in the cost of services in the private sector and the introduction of user fees for in—and outpatient care and medical supplies in the public sector. All of these factors threaten the high standards of health and health care to which the region has become accustomed. Pockets of social deprivation are beginning to emerge, the region is becoming vulnerable to new epidemic diseases. Indeed, in recognition of this, the West Indian Commission has made a specific recommendation that Governments, in designing structural adjustment programmes, whether with the World Bank and the IMF or otherwise, maintain the integrity of primary health care and community health programmes, and of facilities and infrastructure that guarantee public health.

Women have experienced many negative effects as a result of these changes. Growing unemployment in the health sector, in which substantial numbers of women are usually employed, and in other sectors as well, has meant the inability to provide children with basic meals, clothing, school books and transport to school. It has meant an inability to find the money required for transport costs in order to seek and obtain medical attention and supplies for themselves and their children. It has meant that in their anxiety to seek other means of providing these services to their families, women are tending to pay even less attention to their own health, resulting in succumbing in greater numbers to stress-related disorders.

Although it has been argued that the impact of the economic downturn on health may not necessarily have been negative in the short term, it is also accepted that the full impact is unlikely to be apparent immediately. One estimate places a time lag of 1-4 years between national economic downturns and deterioration in the overall health status of the population. In the intervening period some of the major health indicators suggest no marked deterioration in health status (Le Franc, 1990). Life expectancy for both sexes has risen in every territory, and in some cases even approaches levels obtaining in the developed world. Infant and early child mortality rates of boys and girls have, with few exceptions, generally been declining. To the extent that data allow a conclusion, it appears that levels of malnutrition warrant concern, though no clear case can be made for full-scale increases throughout the region. The incidence of communicable diseases amenable to immunisation control has declined to the point of insignificance.

Why then is there concern? For one thing, the epidemiologic transition has been compressed into a much shorter period than in the developed countries. As a result, other components of the development equation have had insufficient time to "catch up", as it were. In fact, it has been said that as far as the social indicators show, our region has not done too badly compared with other developing regions and indeed compares quite favourably with the developed world. But our economic indicators reveal poor performance, suggesting how difficult it is to sustain a favourable social infrastructure.

On the purely health side there has been a worrying increase in a number of communicable diseases previously thought to be under control. These include: gastro-enteritis in several territories, and malaria in Guyana; diseases for which there had almost been no reports previously, for example viral hepatitis. Furthermore, a number of chronic non-communicable diseases and diseases associated with poverty have shown unmistakable signs of rises. So, too, have diseases associated with lifestyle. Diseases associated with an ageing population—thus degenerative and chronic diseases, cancer, diabetes—represent the three principal causes of mortality in most territories. In addition, there have emerged new infectious diseases, such as Acquired Immunity Deficiency Syndrome (AIDS), for which the medical technology and infrastructure have been unprepared; new environmental problems associated with particular forms of development activity and leading to unfamiliar health problems; and forms of behaviour associated with the economic crisis which are producing increases in stress-related behaviour and illnesses, such as violence against women and children and drug abuse.

Where do women fit into this scenario? Traditionally, women's health has been equated with maternal and child health (MCH), an interpretation which only sees women in their societal roles of mothers and mates. But in this region not only is this inappropriate, if ever it was appropriate, but it may even be counterproductive. Not only is it incorrect to assume that those are the only two roles which women perform which have health implications, but it is also incorrect to assume that the MCH budgets, most of which are directed at child health, necessarily improve women's health. Further, the Caribbean has long surpassed the standards set by the World Health Organisation (WHO) in the area of maternal and child health. To continue to focus on this as the main, some would say sole, area of concern for women's health goes against reality. In addition, it ignores the very real health needs of women in other areas.

If attention is to be paid to women's health, it is necessary to understand the synergistic relationship between women's health and children's health; the levels and trends in morbidity and mortality among women as distinct from that prevailing among men; the position of women in the delivery of health care; and the gender sensitivity of medical and paramedical personnel. For us the main issues surrounding women's health should include the following:

1. The transformation of health systems in such a way as to take into account the total health of the woman.
2. Educating women to take responsibility for their own health as well as that of those in their care.
3. Assisting governments to recognise and constantly review the implications of policy decisions.
4. Working with donor agencies to include a gender perspective in their programming.

Underpinning this thrust towards a reconceptualisation of women's health is, of course, the need for research. And here there are many advantages which can be exploited. Among these may be these:

1. A tradition of medical research, which although limited by a bias towards disease-focused research, provides a base on which our present concerns can be built.
2. A network of institutions involved in collaborative research initiatives and constantly seeking ways to strengthen that kind of research.
3. The availability of research databases and the proposals for the establishment of new ones.
4. The growing recognition amongst the medical fraternity of the need to link the medical and behavioural sciences in future research.
5. The growing strength and impact of women's organisations within territories and across the region.
6. The increasing interest in health issues being displayed by development non-governmental organisation (NGOs) and women's NGOs across the region.
7. The number of health-based NGOs expressing an interest in conducting research.
8. The presence in each Ministry of Health of a Women in Development (WID) focal point intended to work with women's bureaux and women's groups to effect policy changes in the health system which would benefit women.

All of these represent opportunities to build coherent collaborative research programmes which draw on the strengths of the various organisations. At the same time, the particular mix of interested organisations can bring fresh approaches to the conduct of the kind of research required to address the issues. The particular stage of social evolution in which the Caribbean finds itself—and here I include both the revolution in the status of women and the epidemiologic transition—requires innovation in all stages of research.

I should like now to focus on five issues which I consider to be relevant to this discussion of researching women's health.

What Research?

Here the concern is with the topics for research. It is not the intention to present a list, merely to indicate that the holistic approach requires a broad range of topics to be investigated at several levels and to cover several areas. The latter would include: economic issues, for example, the gender impact of stabilisation and structural adjustment programmes on health; sociological issues, for isntance, factors contributing to higher illness prevalence among women than among men; policy issues, the review of the implementation of the Alma-Ata agreement with reference to women's access to primary health care; and service delivery issues, like the perceptions and attitudes of male and female health workers and the impact of these on patient compliance and community participation.

It is important to remember that at their 1986 meeting ministers of health in the Caribbean Economic Community (CARICOM) introduced a strategy for Caribbean cooperation in health which included action on seven (subsequently increased to eight) priority areas. These included chronic non-communicable diseases, maternal and child health and population, AIDS, food and nutrition, environmental protection (including vector control), health manpower development, strengthening health systems and substance abuse. Up to April 1992 some $50 million had flowed into these priority areas through both national and regional projects. None of the priority areas are directed specifically at women but women are affected by every single one of them. Those persons interested in research on women in any of these areas would be advised to work with and through agencies which are already involved.

Research by whom?

Conventional medical research has concentrated on investigating the process of disease using primarily laboratory methods. Invariably this has essentially been either a one-person operation or a team of two or three, emanating from the University of the West Indies (UWI), the Faculty of Medical Sciences, (FMS) and the Tropical Metabolism Research Unit (TMRU), and a number of regional institutions, notably the Caribbean Epidemiology Centre (CAREC), Caribbean Food and Nutrition Institute (CFNI), Caribbean Environmental Health Institute (CEHI) and the Medical Research Council (MRC). By contrast, the small quantity of research which has recently begun to emerge from the social sciences has tended to be team-based, covering disciplines from both the social and medical sciences and dealing with both behavioural and medical issues. But, in both instances little attempt is made to draw into the research process those to whom health problems first become apparent, for instance: the health care workers in the field who can quickly identify a potential problem because of their familiarity with an individual or a community; the NGOs and community groups which are much more closely in touch with the people in the community and their individual circumstances; and the statistical clerks in the ministries of health who can tell from the trends in the figures that a problem is worsening or improving. All of these people represent a valuable resource which can be used alongside the professional researchers, in the design, implementation and evaluation of research projects.

Research for whom?

The results of conventional medical research in the Caribbean have been used primarily by colleague medical practitioners, researchers looking for more research and by governments pursuing policy changes. Social science research has shared much the same fate. Researchers need to pay more attention to the ethical issues concerning the right of the research subjects to know the results of the research. Researchers working with women and women's issues have been specially conscious of this and there are several instances of researchers going back to the communities to disseminate research findings, such as the Women in the Caribbean Project (WICP). Researchers such as the Caribbean Association for Feminist Research and Action (CAFRA) have also been involved in assisting community members to lobby for the kind of changes which the research indicates are necessary if women are to truly benefit. This emerging practice must be followed scrupulously in the area of research into women's health. The women deserve it. And our consciences demand no less.

Research how?

Apart from the general question of the methodology of data-gathering and analysis, there are three other considerations worthy of mention. First is the question of coordination of the kind of collaborative research which is being advocated. Among women's groups the so-called participatory methods have assumed considerable popularity. The technique is said to ensure that the research process becomes a tool of empowerment which enables community members to take control of their own lives. While this proposition is yet to be tested in the region, it is appropriate to note that whether the approach is to put together a team of academic researchers, para-professional health care workers or community members, single person coordination (or facilitation) needs to be exercised if the whole effort is not to degenerate into confusion. It is very important to choose this person with extreme care.

Also of importance is the need for flexibility, which will allow the research to inform and be informed by the needs of the wider community. At the same time, it always has to guard against the temptation to dilute the rigour of the statistical requirements if it is to be able to defend its findings and use them to design policy recommendations. This is crucial if planners and policy-makers are to be persuaded to utilise the results of research in an area to which they have not attached much priority.

Finally, there is the question of communication and dissemination of research results. Here the media are crucial. More and more frequently analysts are expressing concern that the messages being transmitted by health educators are either not being received at all or are being received in a form other than is intended. Doubt is also being expressed about whether and how those messages are being further transmitted into the recipient's social setting and with what effect. Here the question of culture looms paramount. For example, research tells us of the rising incidence of obesity among women in the region and of its deleterious effects on their health. At the same time, cultural values place a high premium on a woman "looking good and thick". Should we therefore be surprised that the rising obesity is being found among young girls also? Where are they learning this from? I believe that carefully constructed education programmes using up-to-date media technology can be a tremendous help in addressing these issues. Every option must be used to carry the message to the public that women's health, like men's health and children's health, is vital to the development of our communities.

Research with what?

This refers to the vexed question of resources. Traditionally, health services have been provided by our ministries of health but few, if any, of them have supported health research of any kind, much less research on women's health.

One or two of them have taken the initiative to find funds from external sources for specific research enquiries, but this tends to be on an *ad hoc* basis rather than being a sustained effort. Research from the regional institutions has been funded by external agencies almost without exception, a process which, though unsatisfactory, is unlikely to change within the foreseeable future. But donor funds are shrinking inexorably as the international financial crisis continues. Thus both the quantum and the range of donors willing to fund health research is growing smaller.

Three options are available to those interested in undertaking research into women's health. Become more aggressive in seeking research funds from overseas, try to link into existing research projects, or concentrate on small-scale research projects for which local funds may be available but policy impact and potential to change behaviour may be limited. These are not necessarily mutually exclusive. But each of them takes time and none of them is guaranteed to succeed. What can succeed is the application of the combined talents and determination of a number of persons in a single collaborative effort. No longer can we afford the luxury of the distinctions between the health care practitioners, the policy-makers, the researchers and the women and development specialists. Collaboration between all of these groups on a continual basis must be seen as the tool which will not only bridge the gap between these groups, but will also strengthen the ability of our region to preserve the health gains secured over the past 50 years and enable us to prepare to face the uncertainty of the future.

References

Figueroa, J. Peter. "Is Serious Research Possible in the Caribbean?" *Ethnicity and Disease*, Vol. 1, Fall 1991, pp. 368 – 78.

Kandrack, Mary-Anne, Grant, Karen and Segall, A. "Gender Differences in Health Related Behaviour: Some Unanswered Questions". *Social Science Medicine*, 32 (5), 1991. 579-90.

LeFranc, Elsie. *Health Status and Health Services Utilization in the English-speaking Caribbean*. ISER, UWI, Kingston, Jamaica, 1990.

Massiah, Joycelin. "Economic Change, Structural Adjustment and Women in the Commonwealth Caribbean." Background document prepared for Commonwealth Secretariat Caribbean Regional Meeting on "Structural Adjustment, Economic Change and Women." Barbados, 21 – 23 May, 1990.

________. "Collaborative Health Research in the Commonwealth Caribbean." Paper prepared for CCMRC Essential National Health Research Workshop, Curaçao, 27 – 28 April, 1992.

Raikes, Alanagh and Kabeer, Naila (eds). "Gender and Primary Health Care: Some Forward Looking Strategies". *IDS Bulletin*, 23 (1), 1992.

Scott, Gloria L. "Women, Health and Development in the Caribbean". Report prepared for PAHO/WHO. Barbados, 1989. (mimeo).

The West Indian Commission. *Time for Action*, 1992 (mimeo)

Researching Sexually Transmitted Diseases in the Caribbean

Caroline Allen

As this conference is devoted to the topic of women and health, I have concentrated upon the issues of most relevance to women and their health in researching sexually transmitted diseases (STDs) in the Caribbean.

STDs cause major problems for the health of women, but their impact goes far beyond this. In their effects on female reproductive capacity and in signifying sexual mobility or infidelity, they strike at core aspects of feminine identity.

Especially since the advent of the Acquired Immune Deficiency Syndrome (AIDS) epidemic, it has been recognised that it is necessary to address the behavioural rather than simply the physiological consequences and causes of STDs. Public education has been the major vehicle for inducing behavioural change in the Caribbean. Research has been carried out to measure knowledge, attitudes and beliefs concerning the diseases and their prevention and to assess their effects upon behaviour. The results of this research have been fed into the public education drive. This research, however, though useful in providing descriptions, has been limited by its assumption that health education will by itself provoke a change in attitudes and behaviour. Biomedicine is not the only source of beliefs about health, and it may interact with alternative or even competing belief systems, which should be explored. Furthermore, factors outside the individuals' control may be more powerful than health education in determining behaviour. Social mores concerning sexuality and sexual behaviour, gender and economic power are all forces to be reckoned with. Their interaction with health beliefs should be examined if we are to make sense of behaviour contributing to the spread of STDs.

This argument has implications for methodology. The implied model in much of the existing research has been behaviouralist, with the assumption that people react passively to external stimuli such as health education. Thus research has been essentially quantitative, concentrating on measurement of the impact of this stimulus. Another approach sees people as actively interpreting information from public education within their existing frame of reference. This information is combined with other knowledge, attitudes and beliefs before the person decides whether to use it to guide behaviour in the way which best suits him or her. I shall argue that qualitative methods are necessary in order to understand the motives that guide behaviour.

The Importance of STDs to Women in the Caribbean

The fact that AIDS is an international public health emergency has been highlighted by many, and strenuous efforts have been made at the regional level to catalogue, cope with and control the spread of the virus (Narain et al. 1990; Narain and White 1991; Walrond 1991). It has been noted that AIDS is more easily transferred from male to female than *vice versa* (Desai 1989; Padian 1987), so efforts have been made to raise awareness and safeguard the health of women (Panos Institute, 1990).

In contrast to AIDS, other STDs can usually be cured and most are not life-threatening and have not achieved the prominence of AIDS in recent public health policy discussions and research. However, biological research has shown that the presence of STDs or local infection in the penis or vagina increases the risk of contracting the HIV virus (Desai, 1989). The director of AIDSTECH writes that the presence of an STD can increase the chance of HIV transmission by up to 100 times in a single act of intercourse (Lamptey, 1991). The lesions caused by some STDs, such as syphilis or chancroid, make people who are exposed to HIV more vulnerable to infection (Holmberg et al. 1988; Plummer et al. 1988). Such research has highlighted the need to integrate AIDS and STD prevention and treatment programmes (Family Health International, 1991). As women are biologically more susceptible to infection by certain STDs than men (Barnes and Holmes, 1984), this makes them additionally vulnerable to AIDS.

STDs other than AIDS may, at least in their early stages, present only mild symptoms, such as itching and odour, if they cause symptoms at all. However, they can have a very serious long-term impact, especially if not treated at an early stage. Women are disproportionately affected (Aral and Guinan, 1984). Although STDs "cause health problems for both sexes, in women they are less

* PLEASE rewind films / videotap
****

Van

L 9442699

004134

001640.

004601

003255

003196

003173

HC/59/.71C32

likely to be symptomatic, are more difficult to diagnose and are more likely to cause serious, long-term consequences" (Althaus, 1991).

These include higher risks of genital cancers, pelvic inflammatory disease (PID), ectopic pregnancy, adverse pregnancy outcomes and neonatal health problems (Althaus, 1991). Most cases of PID are caused by chlamydia or gonorrhea (Cates *et al.* 1990), but unfortunately many go undetected as they are asymptomatic (Wolner-Hanssen *et al.* 1990). STDs can affect the health of children born to infected mothers through fetal wastage, congenital infections and low birth weight (Althaus, 1991). They are thus an important issue in maternal and child health.

Thus STDs can have extremely serious effects on the health of women. However, policy-makers are likely to be unaware of the quantitative scale of the problem. Statistics on STD prevalence in the region rely on STD clinic attendance, figures which underestimate prevalence if (as is likely) not all infections are reported.

STDs sap the energies of women in particular and add to the burden of caring for their families, presenting further barriers to female education and career (WAND, 1991). In marginalising people from full participation in the labour force, they deprive society of wealth. Women's labour within the household is also curtailed, which affects their ability to provide services essential to the sustenance of the workforce. Because STDs are often not treated as early as they could be, expensive health service resources are used where prevention and early treatment would be more efficient and reduce suffering (Faundes and Tanaka, 1992).

STDs impair the quality of women's lives through their interaction with social mores. A woman's status within her family and community is frequently determined by her fertility, particularly in places where educational and career opportunities for women are limited (Panos Institute, 1990). A woman's reproductive role is endorsed at the expense of her productive role (Zeidenstein, 1989; Shorey-Bryan, 1987). Barren women are frequently ostracised and abused (Althaus, 1991) and abandoned by male partners (IWHC and WAND, 1992a). To the extent that STDs lead to infertility, they can cause major discord between partners and great personal suffering.

We can hypothesise that people rendered infertile by STDs are heavily stigmatised in the Caribbean. Durant-Gonzalez (1982) shows that Caribbean women derive status principally from their role as mothers, and that educational advancement and political participation, for example, are not so highly prized. MacCormack and Draper (1987) argue that seeking status through procreation results in part from limited opportunities in other spheres. Indeed,

> child-bearing and child-rearing are identified as important instrumental areas of the female role. It is in these activities that women find the greatest opportunities to exercise independence, responsibility, decision-making autonomy and control over self and others. In the above domains they may be said to surpass men in status. (MacKenzie, 1982)

Failure to bear children is viewed as having negative consequences for physical and mental health (Durant-Gonzalez, 1982; MacCormack and Draper, 1987). This is one of the explanations for the high rate of teenage pregnancy combined with low educational achievement by some women in the Caribbean (Jagdeo, 1984; MacCormack and Draper, 1987). Investigations of male attitudes in the Caribbean show a similar emphasis on procreation as an indicator of manhood. Thus infertility causes great suffering to victims of both sexes. Investigations of the experiences of people suffering from infertility would be useful both in indicating the urgency of preventing and treating STDs at an early stage and in suggesting avenues for counselling and social support.

STDs are often seen as signs of sexual infidelity (Bang *et al.* 1991). A person may be infected by his/her partner and develop symptoms although his/her partner has none; this can place a substantial strain on the relationship. Women are usually under more social pressure than men to be faithful. On the one hand, therefore, they are less likely to be unfaithful, while on the other they suffer greater indignity when so accused. A woman who has only ever had one sexual partner may be accused of infidelity although she has caught the infection as a result of her partner's sexual dealings, past or present (IWHC and WAND, 1992a). Bang *et al.* (1991) show that women are sometimes in a no-win situation; when a man's infidelity is admitted his partner is scorned "as it is taken that the woman's husband is not satisfied with her and hence he is wandering out".

The physical symptoms of STDs, such as discharge or odour, are unpleasant and adversely affect the sex life of many couples. There are cultural beliefs surrounding particular symptoms. They function as symbols of social incapacity or malaise and can be stigmatising. For example, Bang *et al.* (1991) found that people in the Gadchiroli district in India believe that a white discharge in women leads to weakness: "This 'weakness' is an all-encompassing term - it is physical, mental and sexual weakness."

White discharge had a more serious impact on the lives of these women than was appreciated by service providers.

Research reveals that the symptoms of STDs can be stigmatising because they can operate as signs of sexual infidelity or weakness. Ethnographic research by Jones (1990) in St Lucia shows how the ethnomedical belief system allows the symptoms of STDs to be interpreted as arising from "sitting on a hot stone" or "eating cold rice". Biomedical interpretations are also accepted by some, which are blame-oriented as they imply infidelity by one of the partners. She reports that some men use these belief systems selectively, saying that they caught the disease from "sitting on a hot stone" or "eating cold rice", while their wives have caught it from them or an "outside man". This appears to conform with the double standard of sexual morality said to prevail in Caribbean culture (Barrow, 1982; Massiah, 1986).

It would be useful to investigate how the biological effects of STDs are viewed by victims and how they feel this affects their social relationships, particularly with their sexual partner. We could investigate the social impact of the biological effects, ranging from unpleasant symptoms such as itching to serious illness such as genital cancer.

Research on Socio-economic Factors Contributing to the spread of STDs in the Caribbean

Here I examine studies of factors contributing to the spread of STDs in the Caribbean and abroad, and combine these with theory from medical sociology. I argue that social research on STDs in the Caribbean should examine alternative health beliefs, questions of power and resources and the social mores governing sexual activity and how they affect knowledge, attitudes, beliefs and practices (KABP) contributing to the spread of STDs. Survey research which has been used to guide public policy has explored limited aspects of KABP and policy has been guided by the assumption that an improvement in the level of biomedical knowledge will translate into improvements in medically recommended behaviour. There is a need for more challenging research and analysis.

Caribbean surveys on STDs have measured levels of accurate biomedical knowledge about the diseases and their transmission along with attitudes to safe sexual practices such as condom use. They have concentrated on biomedical knowledge and have not explored alternative or competing health beliefs. It is as if no correct biomedical health beliefs equals no health beliefs. Biomedicine recommends certain attitudes and practices such as sexual monogamy or celibacy and condom use to prevent the spread of the disease. Thus survey questions have tended to explore attitudes and practices relating to these issues and have not explored attitudes relating to other belief systems. There has been little analysis of the role of gender and economic power issues, although significant differences in responses by gender have been found (Wickramasuriya and Adu-Krow, 1990a).

Measures of accurate biomedical knowledge indicate that there are improvements to be made (Walrond, 1991; Wickramasuriya and Adu-Krow, 1990a and 1990b). However, the research shows important and wide gaps between knowledge and practice. Wickramasuriya and Adu-Krow, (1990a and 1990b), carried out a detailed survey in Barbados of specific STD related knowledge, attitudes and practice. They constructed indices of knowledge, attitudes and practice with higher scores indicating "better" or "higher levels of" biomedically recommended knowledge, attitudes and practice. They found positive correlations between knowledge and attitudes and between attitudes and frequency of condom use, but no correlation between knowledge and recommended practice, which remained disappointing (for example, only 18 per cent of men and 10 per cent of women had always used condoms for sexual intercourse in the past six months). It appears that greater knowledge will only lead to improved practice if knowledge improves attitudes. A survey of Barbadian schoolchildren found a sharp disparity between knowledge and practice, with 75 per cent of the children claiming they knew how to use a condom and 77 per cent knowing that condoms could be used to avoid getting AIDS, while only 35 per cent indicated they used anything to protect themselves from getting AIDS when they had sexual intercourse (Otley 1991; Walrond 1991). The research lacks analysis of mechanisms by which health knowledge may be translated into health behaviour and the obstacles between the two. It indicates that we need to pay attention to the factors influencing attitudes and motivation in order to make public education more effective.

A way of understanding the relationships in KABP is to look at the concepts of health beliefs and health behaviour and how they interact with social mores and the power of the individual to determine her or his own destiny. The point is that there may be tension between the former and the latter such that one cancels out the other. Health beliefs will only prevail in determining behaviour if, either they are more forceful than the weight of social mores and power issues, or if there is no tension between the two, that is, if health beliefs and social mores or power issues both prompt a certain behaviour. My main theoretical contention is thus that the individual's health beliefs interact with the mores and power structure of the wider society to determine the sexual behaviour which affects the spread of STDs.

Let us unpackage this statement. I shall first examine the roles of health beliefs and health behaviour in affecting the spread of STDs. I shall then study issues of power and social mores and how they interact with health beliefs to determine behaviour.

Health beliefs can be defined as "the common sense views held by laymen in reference to health, illness and the health services. These beliefs are made up of a number of elements, including experience, expectations, political views and ideas taken on board from the media and 'significant others". (Cant 1988)

Knowledge, attitudes and beliefs about STDs can all be categorised as health beliefs.

Health beliefs determine behaviour, which is "any activity undertaken by a person believing himself to be healthy, for the purpose of preventing disease or detecting it in an asymptomatic state" (Kasl and Cobb, 1966). In the case of STDs, biomedically accurate health beliefs about the means of disease transmission and ways of preventing or halting such transmission would lead logically to the adoption of health behaviours such as abstinence from sexual activity, reducing the number of sexual partners or safe sexual practice such as condom use, especially if medical advice recommends these practices.

We should however consider a very important component of health beliefs: perceptions of risk (Calnan, 1987). Where people believe that their risk of infection is low, they have less incentive to adopt health behaviours than in cases where they perceive risk to be higher. Thus knowledge of low STD prevalence rates may lead an individual to think that his or her risk of infection is low. He or she may respond to publicity about groups "at risk", such as intravenous drug users, commercial sex workers or male homosexuals in such a way as to believe that his or her risk of infection is low as he or she does not fall into any of these categories. From this point of view it is important that people have an accurate perception of risk. Thus estimates of prevalence should not be based solely on the number of people presenting themselves for treatment and data on groups "at risk" should be continuously updated and disseminated. Efforts on this front are being made in the Caribbean, at least in relation to AIDS. But it is important to acknowledge that perceptions of risk may lead some people to adopt risky behaviours as they believe they will be able to get away with it. Research of KABP in relation to STDs should study perceptions of risk.

As public education programmes have focused on AIDS, it is likely that ignorance about other STDs is widespread and leads to misperceptions of risk. These misperceptions may affect AIDS transmission itself given that STD infection increases the risk of AIDS. People often do not recognise STDs when they have them, especially as some can be asymptomatic. Where a problem is identified it may be dismissed as minor and care will not be sought, although the later consequences of STDs can be very serious. People may be unaware of which behaviours carry particular risks of STD and of preventative measures such as the use of condoms for intercourse (IWHC 1991).

Specific health beliefs and practices concerning STDs can contribute to their spread. Some traditional remedies and beliefs may introduce or exacerbate infection. For instance, in parts of India it is believed that white discharge is caused by: "bursting out of heat inside the body . . . Consumption of food supposed to be hot can cause or aggravate this heat. Unfortunately, most of the nutritionally rich foods such as milk, cream, egg, meat, are avoided by already malnourished women." (Bang *et al*, 1991)

We saw above that some St Lucians believe symptoms of STDs result from "sitting on a hot stone" or "eating cold rice" (Jones, 1990). She writes that the ethnomedical belief system there is based on the hot and cold dichotomy. Thus prevention of STDs would involve avoiding certain situations exposing the body to hot or cold. Unless biomedically accurate health beliefs can complement or replace such beliefs, health behaviour will not conform to those currently approved by the medical profession. We need research on ethnomedical beliefs on STDs throughout the Caribbean.

This should be complemented by research on lay knowledge of human physiology, reproductive processes, reproductive technology and beliefs about the relationship of STDs to all of these. MacCormack and Draper (1987) explored lay understanding of the body's form and functions with a sample of women in Jamaica. By persuading respondents to draw the female reproductive organs in outlines of the female form, they were able to find out how much the women knew about their own bodies. Not surprisingly, they found that less formally educated women living in isolated rural communities were less likely to draw accurate pictures. Such women are less likely to understand educational messages on STDs if such messages assume biomedical knowledge of reproductive physiology. Such research may suggest a more radical and extensive programme of reproductive health education.

Thus far it is clear that public health education has a part to play in disseminating current biomedical knowledge and advice which will tend to slow the spread of STDs. However, we must acknowledge that forces outside the individual's control may prevent him or her from translating accurate health beliefs into appropriate health behaviour.

Sex and diseases associated with it are often taboo subjects and the cultural settings where they can be discussed without embarrassment are limited. They are marginalised to specific areas of life. The norms governing debate of these topics vary. The IWHC and WAND (IWHC, 1991; IWHC and WAND 1992a and 1992b) argue that where a repressive culture of silence surrounds STDs it is a major contributor to the spread of infection and a major barrier to both prevention and cure. Silence prevents knowledge about effective strategies of prevention and cure and stifles use of these strategies. Thus we should examine the mores governing open debate of STDs in the Caribbean and how these are gender-related.

The high sexual mobility of men often exists unchallenged and not open to discussion. The culture of silence is imposed in a context of double standards of sexual morality. "Women in the general population are frequently vulnerable to these infections not so much because of their own sexual behaviour, but because of the behaviour of their partners: male promiscuity—multiple partners and use of commercial sex workers—is often the norm." (IWHC 1991)

Thus we should consider the Caribbean social mores governing sexual behaviour. Much work has been done on the nature of relationships between men and women in the Caribbean, which points to certain hypotheses about the spread of STDs. The existence of socially sanctioned male sexual mobility and the double standard (Barrow 1982; Massiah 1986) has implications for the spread of STDs here as in other parts of the world. The phenomenon of "male-sharing" is common in the Caribbean (Durant-Gonzalez, 1982) and women often have a number of sexual partners (though not usually simultaneously) throughout their lifetime (Safa, 1986). In this respect West Indian women differ from those in many areas of the world where the norm is for women to have sex only with their husbands and to have only one husband throughout adult life. Furthermore, Caribbean youth tend to initiate sexual activity at a young age (MacCormack and Draper 1987; Morris 1988; Remez 1989). The Caribbean pattern encourages the spread of STDs via multiple sexual partners. Further attention should be paid to how such social mores affect reproductive health.

We must consider issues of power in analysing these matters (Massiah 1986). Some sociologists, led by Max Weber, have observed that the social actor cannot pursue rational action in pursuit of his or her objectives unless he or she has power. Knowledge, attitudes and beliefs concerning STDs will be ineffective in determining practice if the social actor has no power. Objectives may differ between men and women, and where men are more powerful, their wishes will probably prevail.

Thus we must consider the issue of how sexuality is entrenched in gender-power relationships. Women may be keen for their partners to use condoms for intercourse or adopt non-penetrative sexual practices in order to protect their health. However, women often lack "the power to determine whether, when, and with whom they have sex" (IWHC 1991). We could add that women often lack the power to determine how they have sex. Men may be unwilling and women may not be in a position to demand safer sex. In cases of male sexual violence such as rape or child abuse this is very clear. Commercial sex workers find it difficult to determine how sex will take place. But this is not confined to such extreme cases; submission to male sexual preferences is a day-to-day reality for many women.

MacKenzie (1982) argues that it is precisely in the domains of "sexual and emotional involvement with men, the fathers of their children and their (sometimes) breadwinners, that [Caribbean] women appear to be the weakest.". Data from the Women in the Caribbean Project (Shorey-Bryan, 1987) show that "in spite of the fact that 40 per cent of households are headed by women, many of the women neither had a positive self-concept nor self confidence; they experienced a low level of autonomy and had little control over their own lives in relation to their fertility and child-bearing capacity." Under such circumstances women are in a weak position to defend their reproductive rights and health. Thus it is essential to consider male attitudes to sex and reproduction even if our principal focus is upon women's reproductive health.

Jones (1990) demonstrates the role of gender power in determining condom use in St Lucia. Approximately one-third of the women with whom she conducted depth interviews at STD clinics reported that they did not want their partners to use condoms because "men put holes in them". She writes:

> The women said that men were 'vicious' and that if you asked them to wear a condom they would put a hole in it . . . When I asked men about this they confirmed what the women said—men do or are at least perceived capable of putting holes in condoms ... St Lucian men do not like wearing condoms and they particularly don't like women telling them to wear them. Women who challenge men by asking them to use a condom risk and jeopardize future economic support. Consequently, 'holes in condoms' assures that not only will women not ask men to use condoms, but very often they will discourage them from doing so.

Clearly, in this Caribbean example, male power was asserted at the expense of reproductive health, particularly that of women. Handwerker (1992a, 1992b, 1992c) provides further examples from Antigua and Barbados which demonstrate the role of gender power in determining sexual behaviour and thus the spread of STDs. For example, he shows that the number of sexual partners taken by women in the last five years was raised significantly for women who had been sexually abused during childhood (1992a).

IWHC (1991) recommends assessment of "women's strategies for self-esteem". The Women in the Caribbean project provided some particularly useful data on how women build supportive social networks, partly in response to perceived deficiencies in the supportiveness of men (Massiah, 1986, and Powell, 1982). It would be interesting to investigate whether the access to and the extent of such networks bears upon sexual practice by empowering women.

Finally, women's inferior access to economic resources has been shown to be a powerful determinant of behaviour leading to a higher risk of STDs. In the Caribbean rates of unemployment, poverty and insecure informal labour are higher among women than elsewhere (Allen and Bailey 1993; Gordon 1989; Le Franc 1989), although they are expected to be able to provide food and sustenance for their families. Income differentials between men and women are at their highest among working-class people (Miller, 1991), demonstrating the particular vulnerability of poor women. Men are seen as "gate-keepers" to the resources women need to maintain themselves and their families (Handwerber, 1992c) and women often give up their sexual and reproductive autonomy in order to gain access to these resources (Worth, 1989). Handwerber (1992a, 1992b, 1992c) argues that a wide range of extreme manifestations of male power, such as domestic violence, child abuse, physical and emotional abuse of members of the family and use of commercial sex workers can be explained by men's role as gate-keepers.

A study of Haitian women's role in sexual decision-making confirms the importance of economic factors (Vlin *et al.* 1993). Haiti is the poorest country in the western hemisphere, and female unemployment is extremely high. The research was conducted in two neighbourhoods where over 70 per cent of women had no independent income.

Both women and men expressed the belief that men have the prerogative to have more than one partner, but women do not. Furthermore, women only have the right to refuse sex under certain circumstances such as illness, and then only for limited periods. Women in stable or married relationships do not have the right to demand that their partners use condoms; neither do women who have no children or whose partners want more children. Challenges to any of these norms could result in sanctions imposed by males such as violence, sexual infidelity, withdrawal of financial support or abandonment. But male ability to impose sanctions was seen to relate to control over resources: "The single most important barrier to the efforts of Haitian women to effect positive behaviour change is their subordinate status in the economy." (Vlin et al. 1993, p. 77)

The comments of several women are useful in demonstrating this:

> You can refuse the man [sex], and for a whole week he will not give you food or pay the rent. He might tell you that you have other men who are feeding you. (p. 35)
>
> Every decision a woman makes depends on the money she has in her hand. If she does not work and the man does, he will always be the head of the family. (p. 41)
>
> If the woman is fooling around and she is my friend, I will tell her to stop so she won't get AIDS. But there are some who will curse you. They will say you don't understand, because you don't have their financial problems, and if you did, you would never refuse the little money a man offered you. (p. 62)

Chambers and Mitchell-Kernan (1993) carried out a study of female low-income workers in Jamaica, and their findings provide further evidence that access to resources is a powerful determinant of sexual behaviour. However, the women in the Jamaican focus group tended to be more proactive than those in Haiti in bargaining sexual favours for money or goods: "For working women with low and/or unstable incomes, and with children, there is imbalance in the bargaining terms. Some use sex as the unit of exchange, and offer or withhold based on receipt of money or goods - even within the context of [stable] relationships." (p. 2)

This acquisitive behaviour is termed by the authors "transactional sex". Some of the women saw money and goods as compensation for the suspected or known infidelities of their menfolk.

Some women, including schoolgirls, were said to engage in "red-eye sex" with an open trade of sex for money. This resembled commercial sex work, but respondents emphasised that women who practised "red-eye sex" already had their basic subsistence needs taken care of, but wanted extra money for status items such as fine shoes, clothes and earrings. They offered sexual services because they wanted to look good, thus showing a connection between the acquisitive nature of popular fashion in Jamaica and sexual behaviour. Comparison between the Haitian and Jamaican studies suggests that the culture of extreme poverty makes Haitian women generally more vulnerable to abuse, and that it is necessary to look at the status attached to certain modes of behaviour and material goods in each cultural context.

The implications for the spread of STDs in the Caribbean are far-reaching. Female poverty exists throughout the region and in some areas it is widespread. Foreign media tend to encourage the desire for material status symbols. Tourists enter poor areas apparently loaded with money and looking for a good time. No research has been done yet on the implications of the expansion of tourism for the spread of STDs, possibly because such research would be politically sensitive. Moreover, it is widely understood that some unemployed young men make a living from consorting with tourists; some of these men also have local girlfriends or wives.

Data on such power imbalances must inform research on health beliefs and be considered when making educational recommendations. They may suggest supplementary strategies, such as changing the organisation of policy-making so as better to reflect the interests of oppressed groups, and women in particular, or offering increased resources to such groups. Hence it will be important to study the access of research subjects to resources and their perceived ability to take effective decisions in their own interest both on the domestic front and outside. Thus structural variables such as income, social class and level of education should be included, and it is important to study how individuals themselves think such variables affect their behaviour. Intrinsic to the research on STDs should be a study of barriers to rational action in pursuit of reproductive health.

Implications for Research Methodology

The previous section argued that further research should be carried out to provide explanations of behaviour that contributes to the spread of STDs. Quantitative surveys have provided useful descriptions of the state of KABP and they should be continually updated. However, some have revealed apparent inconsistencies between levels of biomedically accurate health knowledge and levels of medically recommended health behaviour. This begs the question of why such apparent inconsistencies exist; a number of explanations have been advanced to guide future research efforts. We should explore the causative links between social variables even where no such inconsistencies are found. These links lie in the motivations of social actors, and we should use methods suitable to discover them.

Our choice of research method should aim to provide explanations, not simply correlations between variables indicating, for example, a strong association between knowledge and practice. Yin (1984) argues that the choice of research method is usefully guided by the nature of the research question to be asked. Quantitative research usefully answers questions of how much, which and where. In essence it looks at what can be observed and measured. It measures the actions of individuals, including their responses to interview questions. Qualitative research is more appropriate to questions of why and how. It emphasises the inner world of the values which motivate human behaviour. Human motivation links external forces with personal behaviour (Weber 1949). Thus health education, as one of many external forces, must lead to a change in the motivation of individuals if it is to effect behavioural change. It is clear that qualitative research is needed to go beyond a description of KABP. This is not to say that description is useless. It is particularly useful in providing a picture of the baseline from which we must progress. However, it does not show us the processes at work behind the figures; it does not give us the mechanical knowledge necessary to make progress (Walker 1989).

Examples of quantitative methods include social experiments and surveys with structured interview schedules. The approach is consistent with that used in natural sciences, including medicine. There are similar emphases, for example, on subjecting data to experimental or statistical controls and ensuring sufficiently large random samples to account for variability in subject matter and ensure adequate representation of the population studied. The philosophy behind qualitative research, on the other hand, is that human beings differ in one fundamental way from the subjects of natural scientific experiments; they have free will (Lessnoff 1981). Thus what is important is in the mind. Research methods aim to understand the contents of this mental domain, and it is believed that this necessitates the social interaction of researchers with the subjects of research. Thus unstructured depth interviews, group interviews and participant observation are favoured. Supporters of the qualitative approach do not generally seek to deny the importance of representative samples and reliability, but would sacrifice these ideals if they threatened the ability of the researcher to explore personal motivation. The emphasis in qualitative research tends to be on depth of understanding rather than breadth of coverage; it is *vice versa* for quantitative research. Thus quantitative and qualitative research may be used in complementary ways, the first aiming to provide a representative and reliable description of the characteristics of the population studied, while the second aims to provide valid explanations based on human motivation (Allen 1990; Kirk and Miller 1986).

Highly structured questionnaire research of course fails to provide answers to questions which are not in the questionnaire. The questionnaire is structured according to the initial interests of the researcher and is not responsive to data which lie outside these interests (Bryman, 1988). This makes the method unsuitable for exploratory research where the objective is discovery and the generation of new ideas. Qualitative research may be used to complement surveys by providing a testing ground for ideas incorporated in interview schedules. The marginalisation of open discussion of STDs means that a limited amount is publicly known about the social causes and consequences of the diseases, making exploratory research essential. Furthermore, highly structured questionnaire research is unlikely to pick up idiosyncracies and local variations. These are likely to be large given the diversity of Caribbean culture.

Existing research on STDs in the Caribbean has been primarily quantitative in character, in part because it has been spearheaded by people with a medical training who would favour this approach. The arguments above suggest that social scientists could make a major contribution to research on STDs by applying qualitative research skills which aim to discover the sociological reasons for behaviour.

The subject matter of STDs lends itself more readily to qualitative research. I have argued that the cultural settings in which STDs may be discussed are limited, especially for women. Open discussion of STDs is marginalised to certain areas of life. Respondents need to feel comfortable and to trust the researcher before they will divulge such personal information. Thus the location of the interview may be important in determining the validity of the response. Ideally, respondents should be able to choose a time and place where they feel comfortable discussing such subjects. Symbols of power, status and cultural differentials between researchers and their subjects should be absent if possible (Lupton, 1989). Thus items such as questionnaires, laptop computers and expensive clothes may make some respondents hesitate to give personal information. In the Caribbean the impact of racial differences between researchers and subjects should be considered. These issues are more readily addressed in qualitative research where the researcher spends time getting to know respondents and more emphasis is placed on understanding and respecting the cultural mores of the respondent. Survey interviewers tend to spend less time with research subjects and the latter often have little or no part in shaping interview conditions.

Linked to this is the issue of gender power and how it affects research on STDs. A respondent may find it more appropriate to answer truthfully if the researcher is of the same sex. A women may be actively prevented from answering by a male relative or partner, or the mere presence of such a person during an interview may inhibit or shape a woman's response to certain questions. Similarly, men may hesitate to answer certain questions in front of their spouse or partner. Again, because of its emphasis on understanding the feelings of respondents, qualitative research is more likely to ensure that the gender issues of importance to respondents shape the research process (Oakley, 1990).

The small scale of many Caribbean societies makes the establishment of trust both crucial and problematic. Respondents may be especially suspicious of research commissioned by official authorities such as government. Fear of negative feedback on their own lives may prompt them to give false or distorted answers to some questions, especially if the questions concern socially stigmatised subjects such as homosexuality. The smaller the society, the more fear there is likely to be that people will be able to identify the responses of an individual. Thus it is vital to ensure confidentiality, and to convince respondents that they will not be identified. During qualitative research, investigators are likely to build up a relationship with respondents over a period of time, which is more conducive to trust than the sudden appearance of a survey interviewer with a clipboard and pen. The establishment of trust, however, carries with it the moral obligation not to break this trust. Thus the researcher must make every effort to maintain confidentially (Punch, 1986).

We saw above how Jones (1990) provided useful information about ethnomedical knowledge of STDs and the role of gender relations in condom use in St Lucia. MacCormack and Draper (1987) used drawings by research participants to reveal women's knowledge about their own bodies in Jamaica. Both used qualitative methods, aimed at gaining new understandings of knowledge, attitudes and beliefs. The results of both have policy implications, indicating, for example, the need for far-reaching programmes of reproductive health education for women in order to combat the spread of STDs. Further research of this nature is needed to complement descriptive survey research.

Conclusion

STDs can have devastating effects on women's health and their social status. Educating women on the accurate biomedical causes of STDs and on strategies for prevention or cure empowers them to take rational decisions to protect their health. Much of the policy and research effort in the Caribbean, particularly that led by the medical fraternity, has focused on public education. I have argued that women are subject to outside forces which often prevent them from making and implementing decisions which would best benefit their health. These forces include social mores regarding sex, gender and economic power issues. Research on these should be conducted to discover the forces at work in determining the spread of STDs. During research women should give their own accounts of these forces: how they are interpreted and how, or whether, they motivate their actions. I have argued that quantitative research can describe forces which may be relevant, but qualitative research should be used to explore personal motivation, which is essential in explaining human actions. The objective should be to choose concepts and research issues which are relevant to women's experience and to select methods which will best reveal this experience.

References

Allen, C. "Evaluating qualitative research with reference to the criteria of validity and reliability." Assessment for the degree of MA in Social Research, University of Kent at Canterbury, UK. 1990.

Allen, C. and Bailey, *W. A Situational Analysis of Reproductive Health in the Caribbean,* Institute of Social and Economic Studies (Eastern Caribbean), University of the West Indies. 1993.

Althaus, F. A. "Reproductive Tract Infections and Women's Health," *International Family Planning Perspectives,* Vol. 17, No. 4, December 1991, pp. 145-150.

Aral, S. O. and Guinan, M. "Women and Sexually Transmitted Diseases". In Holmes, K. K. et al. (eds.) *Sexually Transmitted Diseases.* New York: McGraw-Hill. 1st edn. 1984.

Bang, R. A., Bang, A. T. and SEARCH Team. "Reproductive Tract Infections: Rural Women's Point of View". Paper presented at the National Council of International Health meeting, "Reproductive Tract Infections Among Third World Women: Challenges for Practitioners and Policy Makers." 23-26 June 1991, Washington, DC, USA.

Barnes, R. C. and Holmes, K. K. "Epidemiology of Gonorrhea: Current Perspectives". *Epidemiologic Reviews,* Vol. 6, No. 1, 1984.

Barrow, C. "Male perceptions of women in Barbados". Paper presented at Women in the Caribbean Project conference, University of the West Indies, Cave Hill Campus, Barbados. 12-16 September, 1982.

Bryman, A. *Quantity and Quality in Social Research.* London: Unwin Hyman. 1988.

Calnan, M. *Health and Illness: the Lay Perspective.* London: Tavistock Publications. 1987.

Cant, S. "Why Believe Health Beliefs? An Examination of the Contribution of Lay Health Beliefs to an Understanding and Evaluation of the Health Care System." Dissertation submitted for the degree of MSc in Sociology with special reference to the Sociology of Medicine, Royal Holloway and Bedford New College, University of London. September 1988.

Cates, W., Rolfs, R. and Aral, S. O. "Sexually Transmitted Diseases, Pelvic Inflammatory Disease and Infertility: an Epidemiologic Update" *Epidemiologic Reviews,* Vol. 12, No. 199, 1990.

Chambers, C. and Mitchell-Kernan, C. "Transactional Sex: AIDS-Related Issues for Low Income Workers in Jamaica." Caribbean Studies Association Conference, Kingston and Ocho Rios, Jamaica. 24-29 May, 1993.

Desai, B. T. "An Ongoing Tragedy: the Acquired Immune Deficiency Syndrome", *Manushi* (New Delhi, India), No. 54-55, 1989, pp. 44-46.

Durant-Gonzalez, V. "The Realm of Female Familial Responsibility". In ISER *Women and the Family,* Women in the Caribbean Project, University of the West Indies, Cave Hill Campus, Barbados. 1982.

Family Health International. "STD/AIDS prevention: New Challenges for Family Planning Programs", *Network,* Vol. 12, No. 3, December 1991.

Faundes, A. and Tanaka, A. C. "Reproductive Tract Infections in Brazil: Solutions in a Difficult Economic Climate". In Germain, A., Holmes, K.K., Piot, P. and Wasserheit, J., (eds.) *Reproductive Tract Infections: Global Impact and Priorities for Women's Reproductive Health,* New York: Plenum Press, 1992.

Gordon, D. *"Women, Work and Social Mobility in Post-War Jamaica",* in Hart, K. (ed.) Women and the Sexual Division of Labour in the Caribbean, Consortium Graduate School, University of the West Indies, Mona, Jamaica. 1989.

Handwerker, W. P. *Gender Power Differences may be STD Risk Factors for the Next generation*. Program in Anthropology, Humboldt State University, Arcata, California, USA. 1992a.

_______. *Sexuality and 'De fas life' in Barbados*, Program in Anthropology, Humboldt State University, Arcata, California, USA. 1992b.

_______. *'Sexual Tracking: Inter-generational Influences on Women's Adolescent Sexuality*, Program in Anthropology, Humboldt State University, Arcata, California, USA. 1992c.

Holmberg, S. D. et al. "Prior Herpes Simplex Type 2 Infection as a Risk Factor for HIV Infection", *Journal of the American Medical Association*, Vol. 259, No. 1048, 1988.

International Women's Health Coalition (IWHC). *Reproductive Tract Infections in Women in the Third World: National and International Policy Implications.* Report of meeting at the Bellagio Study and Conference Center, Lake Como, Italy, 29 April- 3 May, 1991, co-sponsored by the International Women's Health Coalition and the Rockefeller Foundation.

International Women's Health Coalition (IWHC) and Women and Development Unit (WAND). "Reproductive Tract Infections Among Women in the Third World: Ending the Culture of Silence." Conference co-organised by IWHC and WAND, 16-18 March, 1992, Paradise Beach Hotel, Barbados. 1992a.

International Women's Health Coalition (IWHC) and Women and Development Unit (WAND). "Call to Action by the Barbados Consultation for New Alliances Between Women and Men to End Reproductive Tract Infections". Paper from conference, "Reproductive Tract Infections Among Women in the Third World: Ending the Culture of Silence," co-organised by IWHC and WAND, 16-18 March, 1992, Paradise Beach Hotel, Barbados. 1992b.

Jagdeo, T. P. *Teenage Pregnancy in the Caribbean*, New York: International Planned Parenthood Federation, Western Hemisphere Region. 1984.

Jones, R. *The Political and Economic Dynamics of Sexual Diseases*, Southern Methodist University, USA. 1990.

Kasl, S. V. and Cobb, S. "Health behaviour, illness behaviour and sick role behaviour". *Archives of Environmental Health*, 12, 1966, pp. 246-66.

Kirk, J. and Miller, M. L. *Reliability and Validity in Qualitative Research*, Sage University Paper Series on Qualitative Research Methods, Vol. 1, Beverley Hills, USA. 1986.

Lamptey, P. "How Intervention Projects Affect Sexual Behaviour". *Network*, Vol. 12, No. 1, June 1991, p 2.

Le Franc, E. "Petty Trading and Labour Mobility: Higglers in the Kingston Metropolitan Area". In Hart, K. (ed.) *Women and the Sexual Division of Labour in the Caribbean*, Consortium Graduate School, University of the West Indies, Mona, Jamaica. 1989.

Lessnoff, M. "Minds and Social Science", in Brown, S. Fauvel, J. and Finnegan, R. *Conceptions of Inquiry*, London: Open University Press. 1981.

Lupton, C. "Feminist Research into the Organisation and Practice of Social Work: The Dilemmas of a Contract-Based Research Worker." Paper presented to the British Sociological Association Annual Conference, 20-22 March, 1989, Plymouth Polytechnic, UK.

MacCormack, C. and Draper, A. "Social and Cognitive Aspects of Female Sexuality in Jamaica". In Caplan, P. (ed.). *The Cultural Construction of Sexuality*, London: Routledge. 1987.

MacKenzie, H. "Introduction: Women and the Family in Caribbean Society". In ISER *Women and the Family*, Women in the Caribbean Project, University of the West Indies, Cave Hill Campus, Barbados. 1982.

Massiah, J. "Women in the Caribbean Project: An Overview", *Social and Economic Studies*, Vol. 35, No. 2, June 1986, pp. 1-29.
Miller, E. *Men At Risk*. Kingston, Jamaica: Jamaica Publishing House. 1991.
Morris, L. "Young Adults in Latin America and the Caribbean: their Sexual Experience and Contraceptive Use", *International Family Planning Perspectives*, Vol. 14, No. 4, December 1988, pp. 153-58.
Narain, J. P. and White, F. M. M. "AIDS Epidemic in the Caribbean: Trends and Initiatives" *West Indian Medical Journal*, Vol. 39, Suppl. 1, 1991, p 28.
Narain, J. P., White, F. M. M., Kimball, A. M., Zessler, L. and Zacarias, F. R. K. "Combatting AIDS in the Caribbean: a Coordinated Subregional Approach". *Bulletin of PAHO*, Vol. 24, No. 3, 1990, pp. 335-40.
Oakley, A. "Interviewing Women: A Contradiction in Terms". In Roberts, H. (ed.). *Doing Feminist Research*. London: Routledge and Kegan Paul. 1990.
Otley, J. "Sexuality and Sexual Practices amongst Children of School Age". In Project Hope, AIDS in the Caribbean: Presentations and Teleconferences. AIDS Information centre, Ministry of Health, Barbados. 1991.
Padian, N. S. "Heterosexual Transmission of Acquired Immune Deficiency Syndrome: International Perspectives and National Projections". *Reviews of Infectious Diseases*, Vol. 9, No. 947, 1987.
Panos Institute. *Triple Jeopardy: Women and AIDS*. London: Panos Dossier, Panos Publications. 1990.
Plummer, F. A. *et al.* "Co-factors in Male-Female Transmission of HIV." Paper presented at IV International AIDS Conference, Stockholm, Sweden. 1988.
Powell, D. "Network Analysis: A Suggested Model for the Study of Women and the Family in the Caribbean". In ISER, *Women and the Family*, Women in the Caribbean Project, University of the West Indies, Cave Hill Campus, Barbados. 1982.
Punch, M. *The Politics and Ethics of Fieldwork*, Sage University Paper Series on Qualitative Research Methods, Vol. 3, Beverley Hills, USA. 1986.
Remez, L. "Adolescent Fertility in Latin America and the Caribbean: Examining the Problem and the Solutions". *International Family Planning Perspectives*, Vol. 15, No. 4, December 1989, pp 144-48.
Safa, H. "Economic Autonomy and Sexual Equality in Caribbean Society". *Social And Economic Studies*, Vol. 35, No. 3, September 1986.
Shorey-Bryan, N. "Policy issues affecting women and the family". Paper presented at UNESCO/ISER (EC) seminar on "Changing Family Patterns and Women's Role in the Caribbean." University of the West Indies, Cave Hill Campus, Barbados, 24-27 March 1987.
Vlin, P.R., Cayemittes, M. and Metellus, E. *Haitian Women's Role in Sexual Decision-Making: the Gap Between AIDS Knowledge and Behaviour Change*, AIDSTECH, Family Health Internationa, North Carolina, USA. 1993.
Walker, R. "We would Like to Know Why: Qualitative Research and the Policy Maker". *Research, Policy and Planning*, Vol. 7, No. 2, 1989, pp 15-21.
Walrond, E. R. "Targeting Behaviour Change in AIDS Prevention and Control". In Project Hope, "AIDS in the Caribbean: Presentations and Teleconferences." AIDS Information Centre, Ministry of Health, Barbados. 1991.
WAND. *Annual Report*, 1 August, 1990-31 July, 1991, School of Continuing Studies, University of the West Indies, Cave Hill Campus, Barbados.
Weber, M. (1949) in Shils, E. A. and Finch, H. A. (eds.). *The Methodology of the Social Sciences*. Toronto: The Free Press.

Wickramasuriya, T. V. and Adu-Krow, "W. Sex Differences in Knowledge and Attitudes with Regard to the Use of Condoms for AIDS and STD Prevention in Barbados. Paper presented at IV International Conference on AIDS Education, San Juan, Puerto Rico, 6 August, 1990. 1990a.

_______. "A Survey of Knowledge, Attitudes and Practices with Regard to the Use of Condoms for AIDS and STD Prevention in Barbados." Paper presented at Regional Meeting on Behavioural Interventions for AIDS and STD Prevention, Kingston, Jamaica, 12 December, 1990. 1990b.

Wolner-Hanssen, P. W., Kiviat, N. B. and Holmes, K. K. "A Typical Pelvic Inflammatory Disease: Subacute, Chronic or Subclinical Upper Genital Tract Infection on Women", in K. K. Holmes et al. (eds.,) *Sexually Transmitted Diseases*. New York: McGraw-Hill. 2nd edn. 1990.

Worth, D. "Sexual Decision-Making and AIDS: Why Condon Promotion Among Vulnerable Women is Likely to Fail". *Studies in Family Planning*, Vol. 20, No. 6, Nov./Dec. 1989, pp. 297-307.

Yin, R. K. *Case Study Research: Design and Methods*, Applied Social Research Methods Series, Vol. 5, Sage Publications, Beverley Hills, California, USA. 1984.

Zeidenstein, G. "Adolescent fertility and the health and status of women". Paper presented at International Conference on Adolescent Fertility in Latin America and the Caribbean. Oaxaca, Mexico, 6-10 November, 1989.

The Interplay of Conventional Science and Traditional Knowledge in the life of a Rural Woman in Trinidad

June M. George

Introduction

The case study reported in this paper is part of a bigger study undertaken in a rural village, which will be called "Seablast", on the north-eastern coast of Trinidad. The bigger study was designed to document and analyse some of the traditional practices and beliefs existing in the village, with a view to ascertaining the degree to which young people and adults in the village were committed to them. The ultimate aim is to make these findings available for use in science curriculum development and in the delivery of adult health education programmes.

The case study described in this paper focuses on one of the key informants in the village, who will be referred to as "Mrs S", and it explores how she makes use of both conventional science and traditional knowledge in conducting her life. The findings are compared with practices in adult health education delivery systems and the paper highlights the need for personnel working in this area to explore further the ways in which official knowledge is treated by lay people as they attempt to use it in practical action.

The Role of Prior Knowledge

The psychologist D. Ausubel asserted that the single most important factor affecting learning is what the learner already knows. He argued that one should first ascertain the learner's prior knowledge and then teach him or her accordingly (Ausubel 1968). A large part of science education research since 1970 has been based on this principle. It is now generally agreed that learners come to the classroom with firm ideas about how the world functions and that such ideas can influence their attempts to make sense of school knowledge (Driver and Erickson 1983; Hewson and Hamlyn 1984; Osborne and Cosgrove 1983).

The research work cited above has focused on the learning of conventional science by students in primary and secondary schools. However, there exists a related line of research work with adults in which attempts are being made to understand the prior knowledge of adults with a view to using this knowledge in adult education delivery systems. This approach is now being pursued in health education (Cumming *et al.* 1991; Eisenbruch 1990; Rubenstein *et al.* 1992), and its importance has been recognised by researchers studying the understanding of science by young people and adults (Furnham 1992).

The research paradigms used to analyse the understandings of the world held by lay people have been reviewed by Furnham. He has identified four common not necessarily exclusive themes that underlie research in this area. The first theme is a focus on how little lay people know and how wrong they are. The second theme is the attempt to find the cause(s) of this state of affairs, for example, texts and the media. The third theme focuses on the macro-system and seeks to identify the consequences of lay ignorance for economic growth and development. Finally, the fourth and most recent theme sees the lay person as a "skeptic and pragmatist" rather than as an "ignoramus or philistine" (Furnham 1992: 42).

This study is closely aligned to the fourth theme identified by Furnham. It is based on a conviction that lay people and the understandings that they hold are to be treated with respect. The aim of research into lay understandings is thus not to denigrate them but rather to understand them; to understand how lay people use them when exposed to new ideas and to suggest ways in which they may be exploited for educational benefit in adult education programmes.

The Interaction of Lay Understandings and Formal Knowledge

Much of the work done on students' conceptions prior to instruction has been undertaken from a constructivist perspective in which the main tenet is that knowledge is not passively received, but is actively built up by the subject (Wheatley 1991). The resulting constructions are continually tested against experience and modified if necessary (Driver and Oldham 1986; Wheatley

1991). Some have argued that these constructions are not only personal; there are important social influences on them as well (Kaiser 1993; Solomon 1987). Whether personal or social in origin, these prior constructions are likely to shape what happens when an individual is exposed to formal knowledge.

Different theories have been advanced to explain the interaction between lay understandings and formal knowledge. Hawkins and Pea (1987) as well as Hewson (1988) draw on the work of Toulmin (1972) and borrow the notion of "niche" from biological theory. They suggest that knowledge develops as a result of the interaction between an individual and his or her environment in much the same way that organisms are biologically adapted to their space or niche. For Hawkins and Pea (1987: 294) the child's environment is the cultural setting surrounding the child which they define as "objects and events, people, media, informal learning situations, and the practices of such institutions as schools". They view science as being defined by the problems it works on and suggest that the problem niche of scientific thinking is quite different from that of everyday thinking. Although both of these forms of thinking embody the common feature of explanations, Hawkins and Pea (1987: 297) suggest that more precise explanations are required in scientific thinking: "The explanations offered by the natural sciences are often orders of magnitude more precise than the explanations offered in everyday life. They are more precise because the theoretic principles of scientists in their problem niches demand such precision."

When the two cultures meet, the child must be made to realise that his/her everyday explanations are inadequate:

> the problem is one of creating conditions for compelling conceptual change, to impel the child to adapt his or her understanding to deal with the new explanatory standards of the problem niches of the communities of science. The child must induce that his or her explanations are inadequate in terms of precision, completeness, coherence from the perspective of canonical science." (Hawkins and Pea 1987: 296).

Implicit in this account is the idea that any changes that must be made by the child must be made in the direction of conventional science. This orientation is related to the first theme identified by Furnham (1992).

A different view of what is desirable when lay understandings and conventional science come into contact is provided by Hewson (1988). She discusses this in terms of knowledge from the Western world and knowledge from developing countries: "Critical dialogue between the West and the developing countries should promote conceptual change of the knowledge bases of both, and allow for the emergence of a new type of science that is effective in meeting specific problems at a range of levels in developing countries and possibly in the West as well." (Hewson 1988: 317).

Although Hewson ascribes some value to knowledge from the developing world, there is a suggestion that the amalgamated knowledge that she is proposing is likely to be of less value to the West than to developing countries.

Some evidence for the form of interaction proposed by Hewson is provided by Layton (1991). Layton deals not with the interaction of knowledge from developing countries and knowledge from the West but with the interaction of scientific knowledge and lay understandings and dispositions of adults. He reviewed several qualitative studies aimed at exploring the public understanding of science. One of the findings from the review was that scientific knowledge available to the public is often not used in its pure form, but is instead integrated with other types of knowledge:

> the researches indicate that the scientific knowledge offered or accessible to people is rarely usable without being reworked and contextualised... This is not to say that scientific knowledge is not important. Rather, there is an interaction between the knowledge which emanates from science in relation to a particular situation or problem and the understandings and dispositions which people themselves bring to bear. It is clear, however, that the cognitive deficit model, with its assumption of a one-way flow of scientific knowledge from producers to consumers, is an inadequate description of the relationship. (Layton 1991: 58-59).

Support for this position is also provided by Pines and West (1986) who see the integration of the two types of knowledge as "genuine science learning" from a constructivist viewpoint.

Some interesting parallels can be found in the report of Bebbington (1991) on the ways in which indigenous farmers in Ecuador deal with modern agricultural concepts to which they are exposed. Bebbington found that there are three ways in which such farmers tend to react: they may replace existing ideas and values with the new knowledge; they may reinterpret existing ideas; or they may incorporate the new knowledge into their existing system of knowledge.

What is emerging from this brief review of the literature is that lay adults do not simply absorb conventional science ideas that are presented to them. Instead, an interactive process takes place in which some sifting and sorting occurs, resulting in a form of knowledge with which the lay adult feels comfortable and which he or she perceives will result in successful action. This study sought to explore this interactive process in a specific instance by seeking answers to the question of what is the nature of the interaction between conventional science and traditional knowledge in the life of a rural woman in Seablast.

The Research Setting

The society of Trinidad and Tobago is a cosmopolitan one, but there are two main ethnic groupings: people of African descent and people of East Indian descent. The first of these two groups was brought by the British to Tobago and by the French and Spanish to Trinidad to work as slaves on the sugar plantations during the latter half of the eighteenth century. The second group was also brought to work on the sugar plantations, but as indentured labourers. They arrived in 1845. In addition, there are other smaller groups such as the descendants of former British and French landowners, the Syrians and the Chinese.

Seablast is a rural village with a population of a few hundred people of African descent in the main. The main occupations in Seablast are fishing and agriculture. Typically, women in the village are engaged in housework and agricultural pursuits. There is no formal industrial activity. The area is served by three primary schools and one secondary school. Although the primary schools have a long history in the district, the secondary school was established only as recently as 1977.

The village is also served by a health facility at which minor complaints can be treated. More serious cases are referred to the hospital in a nearby town. Other government departments such as a postal agency and the Works Department can be found there. In addition, agricultural extension officers serve the area. Adult education programmes are mounted by these officers as well as by the nurse in charge of the health facility.

Methodology

The qualitative case study research design (Merriam 1988) was adopted and this sub-study may be considered as a case within a case. The overall selection strategy used was referred to by Goetz and Le Compte (1984) as "sequential sampling". The larger case study has as its unit of analysis the bounded system comprising villagers of Seablast. Mrs S is a woman within that unit, chosen because she was assessed as a typical representative of persons in the larger study who had had a fair amount of exposure to conventional science alongside her traditional knowledge base. Traditional knowledge is here defined as those practices and beliefs which emanate from people's experiences as they conduct their daily lives and which are passed on, usually in the oral mode, from one generation to the next.

With this type of research design, data sources are usually documents, field notes from observations and interview data. Established literature on Seablast and its occupants is almost non-existent. Direct observations were not done to any significant extent because of time constraints and the difficulties of travelling to and from Seablast. In-depth, fairly unstructured interviews were therefore used as the sole data-collecting strategy.

In a typical interview, one or two questions were first asked to initiate discussion on how an informant conducted his or her life. Thereafter, the direction in which the interview proceeded depended mainly on what the informant had to say. The interviews were audio-taped, transcribed and entered verbatim into the computer. Six interviews in all were conducted with Mrs S at intervals during the period 1989-93. During that period interviews were also conducted with more than 40 other villagers.

Data were analysed in the grounded theory tradition, employing the various levels of coding and category development and using the constant comparative process (Strauss and Corbin 1990). Word processing and data management computer programmes were used as tools in the analysis. Links with conventional science emerged as a prominent category in Mrs S's data.

Findings

The Subject

Mrs S was 61 years old at the time of the first interview in 1989. She had recently retired from a job at the senior citizens' home in the district where she had spent almost 23 years taking care of the older villagers. By the time she retired, she was a senior member of staff at the home. Before this Mrs S had been employed as a female worker in a road maintenance crew, a cleaner at the district post office and an assistant at the district health facility. In this latter post she had functioned as a helper to the nurse and the pharmacist. In addition to whatever formal job she held, Mrs S also did housework and some gardening.

Formal education for Mrs S consisted of primary schooling and four months at a secondary school in the capital city, Port-of-Spain. She was forced to curtail her secondary schooling because she had to return home to the village to help take care of an ailing relative. At the primary school, Mrs S was introduced to the British Red Cross Society and she subsequently had substantial exposure to their teachings and practices.

It is evident that Mrs S has developed an interest in gaining information from texts over the years. She is a member of the Seventh Day Adventist church in the district and she has acquired a couple of texts on health education published by that organisation. She also owns a few texts on first aid and nursing published by the British Red Cross Society.

Mrs S is the mother of two grown children. She has four grandchildren and one great-grandchild. Since retiring, she has been spending most of her time doing housework and taking care of her grandchildren and great-grand child. She still does some gardening on a small scale.

Interaction of Traditional Knowledge and Conventional Science

A constant theme that has pervaded all of the discussions with Mrs S is that we need to take care of our bodies if we are to remain healthy. She sums up her philosophy by saying: "Every bad sickness depends on how we are cared."

There are several preventive measures that Mrs S advocates for ensuring good health. Some of them are drawn from conventional medicine, for example eating "good" food, drinking a lot of water and taking walks in the "fresh" morning air. At times, Mrs S makes specific reference to conventional science terms and conventional science sources when giving these admonitions.

> *A:* We don't keep our children in, neither cloak up. Morning walk, you walk with a blanket, an umbrella in case of rain because they are young. But you have them in their little nightie exposed. As I tell you, always keep their feet warm because is there you taking the cold from. You have your blanket and your umbrella, if you could

afford, and you walk your baby. You go to the sea and stand up to the head of the sea with your baby and the breeze hitting it. You inhaling the iodine. The iodine from the sea have you perfect.

Q: You mentioned how people used to give cassava porridge. Some people have told me that they use flour porridge and you parch the flour.

A: Some people parch their flour; we use it ordinary.

Q: Why do they parch the flour?

Q: They say from the starch, too much of starch in the body. But we use it so. Remember if you give the baby a balanced diet, starch can't overpower it.

Q: So, they say that parching the flour gets rid of some of the starch?

A: So they say.

Q: I see.

A: But having a baby with a balanced diet . . . because a baby can't eat, eh. When it on porridge form, you get honey and give your baby: you get cod liver oil and give your baby, your baby can't blind.

Q: So what do you think ensures having a healthy baby, like what you should do during pregnancy to have a healthy baby?

A: Eat proper food. Liver, all kind of pumpkin for cooling. But how you get two babies and you eh know these things. You pulling my legs man!

Q: I am not sure the things I do are the same things you do.

A: With a pregnancy you drink a lot of milk and all these things. With pregnancy you have to eat good food. Not any and any thing. As soon as you feel you pregnant you go to a doctor and an ante-natal clinic. And then you eat proper food. A lot of fruit juices, drink water, plenty water. Water is very essential.

Other preventive measures are based mainly on traditional knowledge. The most prominent of these are measures to avoid catching a cold and measures to control the amount of "heat" in the body. Mrs S, as well as many of the other villagers, subscribes to a hot/cold classification system with respect to food and the functioning of the human body. If one eats too many "heated" foods, the blood becomes hot, resulting in illness. To prevent this, one must use "cooling" foods regularly.

> **Q:** Tell me some of the things that will make your blood get hot.
>
> *A:* The food, plenty of starch.
>
> **Q:** When you say starch, what do you mean? Dasheen and so?
>
> *A:* Excessive starch then. When you eat a lot of dasheen, cassava, anything that you think have starch in it then. You run a heat in the body. I think sweets too. Sugar, or when you have diabetes then, it comes from a heat. When your body overrun you get diabetes and thing, because the other parts come low to that. It overwhelm the body. In order to keep out those things you use bran bread.
>
> **Q:** What kind of bread?
>
> *A:* Bran.
>
> **Q:** So the whole wheat . . .
>
> *A:* Yes, the whole wheat, or put a little bit of bran in your white flour. White bread is not wholesome. Mix your flour with whole wheat or bran and that keeps the body in subjection.
>
> **Q:** Besides the bran, are there any other cooling foods then?
>
> *A:* Cress, cabbage—cabbage has water in it. And the yellow food, pumpkin and carrots.
>
> **Q:** And you said that cabbage has water in it.
>
> *A:* It is watery.
>
> **Q:** So it is the watery foods that have the cooling in it?
>
> *A:* Because pumpkin has water, and carrots, they are cooling for the body. Well bran hasn't water but still it cools down the blood.

In the above conversation, one can also detect reference to conventional science terms even though the reason for taking this particular preventive measure is not part of conventional medical science. In addition to the more modern preventive measures outlined above, Mrs S also advocates the use of traditional measures such as cooling teas made from herbs such as "vervine" and "olive leaf".

Mrs S outlined preventive measures for conditions recognised in conventional medical science, for example the post-partum state of mothers, but these were given different interpretations in the traditional knowledge system.

A: You have a baby, remember it forms from you. It in you and it forms you; your blood and the things you eat and everything. That is how you get a healthy baby. Your body is healthy, you clean it out with molasses and everything and you tonic your body, and you get pregnant, you get a healthy baby and you, yourself heal quick. This baby, when it comes out, your pores open. Your first baby, you take the chances to do everything—not in winter. In summer you do everything. You walk barehead and everything—climatise your body. But, you have to clothe your body too. When you go out barefeet. . . . Rain ent go fall whole night and you go out barefeet and you just have a baby. Or, rain wouldn't fall whole night and you just got up from your bed and rush out barefeet. You still have to put something on your head and something on your feet. Well, sometime you might have an accident—you know it does have accident in everything—you rush out and may get a cold and you careless with it, well, it stays in you. It either form arthritis, which they call rheumatism, or it form all different things. Sometimes it go to your lungs and form all different infection in your body. But, if you care it and take proper medicine to root out that cold, it don't form in you; you don't have lining cold. Every bad sickness depends on how we are cared.

Q: So, the lining cold is especially after mother gives birth?

A: Or you careless with a common cold, the flu then. You know flu go around.

Q: And if you don't take the precautions.

A: Right.

Q: Now, I thought when they said lining cold, especially since they talk about that with the mothers who just had their babies, I thought it meant that something happened to your womb or . . .

A: No, but sometimes it goes to the womb too. You understand? Well, you know poor people. They have their babies and they have to go to work. Rain come, and according to the work, you know, extracting coconut, you have to sit down on wet bags so that cold goes in them. Even self your natural body, cold goes in and if you don't work it out, it turn a lining cold. It not particularly mothers.

Q; Anybody.

A: Anybody.

Q: Right.

A: You meddle in the wet and you didn't care it, it turn a lining cold.

In all of these admonitions there is the overarching theme that one needs to take care of one's body. In fact, Mrs S invokes this same theme in dealing with the new disease, AIDS.

Q: I wanted to find out, also, how people in the village deal with some of the new sicknesses. Now, you know all the things we have been talking about are sicknesses that have been around a long time. But some of these new things that are coming up, I wanted to find out how people deal with them. Like, for example, AIDS, what people think about AIDS in the village. What do you think about AIDS?

A: Well, let me tell you something, we born with every disease in our body. All the consumptions and thing they say about disease, we born with them; we make up with them. But, remember, is the same thing if we didn't care our bodies, we ruin ourselves. Now, for instance, everything you overdo, you get sick. A man drinks and drink a lot, he gets sick. Another smoke extremely, he get sick. So, AIDS is just like the different . . . sick men get. I feel it is so. They didn't care their body and these things come on you, so it spread.

Not all traditional preventive measures are accepted by Mrs S. Preventive measures dealing with menstruation problems were rejected by her even though she did soften her rejection by admitting that people have different tolerance levels. This principle with respect to tolerance levels was used in other parts of the data as well.

Q: You know what I want to get at. They say when you are menstruating there are certain things you mustn't do.

A: Like what? Name them. I will tell you.

Q: Like climbing fruit trees.

A: Well, me do everything. I climb fruit trees. I pitch marbles. I do all kind of thing. They say girl mustn't skin up and they must be neat.

I do everything. I plant. They say you mustn't plant. I plant and do everything.

Q: And nothing happened?

A: I ent see nothing happen yet. And it can't happen again because I am 61 years.

Q: They say you mustn't be bathing . . .

A: Well, some people . . . anything. Things does affect you when your resistance low. I think I have strong resistance. There are plenty things I could do but don't overdo. You know your period on, you use a little lime juice and you won't use it the whole time for your period. You might use it a day to two and stop. Any acidity. . .

Q: What happens? Does it hurt your belly?

A: Well, you see your blood in action. It can affect you right, and some people might bathe and get sick and you will get cold and all these things. Well, me, I bathing right through . . .

In the same vein, she sometimes rejects conventional science outright.

A: Another thing we fooling we self with is ice water. That gives you a lot of heat and people don't know. More you drink ice water, more you have a thirst. A crave for water. Water all the time. That never happen to you?

Q: I'm not a water drinker.

A: Water is very good. You must drink water. You hear? Yes. It flushes the bladder and keep the bladder cool and everything. We suppose to drink how many pints or bottles of water per day? We learn that in elementary.

Q: Eight glasses per day.

A: Alright. Take care you come to pull we legs, you know.

Q: No, no, no!

Again here there is a softening of the rejection as she draws on other aspects of conventional science.

This dynamic movement along the traditional knowledge and conventional science continuum are also reflected in the courses of action suggested by Mrs S for dealing with illnesses. Four different courses of action were identified. There is the method of treatment which uses traditional medicine as a temporary first-aid measure until medical assistance can be obtained.

A: I work in the senior citizen home. I work social welfare, works and I care for the aged. I resigned just in June this year, so I worked 22 years, say 23 because July would make me 23 years experience. When they get sick I give them first aid to the best of my ability by using some of the herbs that I know could help if I couldn't get on to the doctor as fast as I can. That help them on and I would go to the doctor and they will give me the privilege of the ambulance in the district to carry them to hospital and I care for them, like their clothing and thing. Every day I take clothing for them, to see how and pick up and when they reach a certain stage of home caring again they would send them up with the ambulance. The county hospital send them to the senior citizen home and I care the balance.

Q: What do you use vervine for?

A: Colds on the chest and clean the body and wild coffee.

Q: What does the wild coffee do?

A: Clean your bladder and all kind of thing, your blood, and I will use those first aid until I get to the doctor. They help me a lot; the doctor and the nurses. Sometimes they have ulcers and they come in and dress and they give me dressing to dress them because I did a little first aid—Red Cross.

There is the method which uses traditional medicine primarily, particularly in the treatment of "heat", which is a condition that conventional medicine does not recognise.

Q: When you used to be in the health centre . . . not the health centre, the old people's home..

A: I work there too you know.

Q: You worked there too? And the old people's home. Did the doctors give anything for cooling and so? Did they recommend anything?

A: No. Well they never meet with the upstairs of . . . When they come in, sometimes their lips red. Bachelor buttons too is a good cooling and is good for stoppage of water. Coconut water cools the blood too. So, when you coming to my home, I notice your body and your mouth does show the heat too. It does be extra red and sorey. So I would give you medicine to suit and then I will give something that will purge you, like a little senna in your tea. We have senna leaves. You draw it, that purge you. So when you drink the cooling a certain amount of days that take out that heat. Sometimes even your rectum does be red, red. When you going off, it burns, it pains. After the cooling, you would see it. All the mouth start to come pale and you continue until it come to the natural. Well, you eh go use it regular, regular, regular, to weaken. You rest off and you take again until you come to the natural.

Sometimes the sickness is diagnosed in conventional medical terms, but the treatment is traditional.

Q: Tannia is easy to come by here?

A: Yes. It have a lot of tannia here.

Q: And that is used a lot for the babies?

A: Yes, tannia. They say not to give them cassava. You know, long time people dry the cassava, pound it and make porridge and grow their children strong and lusty. If you see their hands, their legs. They condemn all those things and give artificial food, but now I see they are turning back. We give them fresh milk, but the best milk is goat milk. Even for us, goat milk is the richest milk and it helps you in different sicknesses. Like, babies does get . . . the name slip me . . . Marasme. Their skin does be quality. But it is very good for that. You bathe them with a bush called Congolala. I say that is malnutrition. Maybe the mother body not form up properly to have a baby, and then she get pregnant and then the skin get quality. But they bathe them with a bush called Congolala.

Q: And they give them goat's milk.

A: Yes. And they skin come back to this nice texture and they come nice.

Conventional medical science treatments are sometimes used if the traditional treatment fails to achieve the desired results.

Q: What you took for it?

A: Oh God! I ain't know what I took. I went to doctor and took tablet till I get fed up. Sometimes when I know my period time coming I would just sit down and cry. Painful menstruation. I drink Lady-a-pink-come ... I do all kind of thing. I went to Dr. Lynch. They say he is a boss for that, but he dead. And he explain to me. Now, when I was growing, I was very thin, very, very thin. My bracelet went over my arm, to tell you how thin I was, and I grow thin. So when I meet the age of menstruation, my tube was small, but for my thinness my parents tonic me. I am a one child. So they say I had a full amount of blood. So, every time for the blood to flow, it chokes. That is why I was getting the pain. So, Dr Lynch put me to sit down and he told me. So don't take nothing, eat everything. When you vomit, you wash your mouth and you eat again. Because you will still have the pain and you will still be sick. And when you get married everything will be over and it is true. It is marriage life that ease my pain.

And for some illnesses, only conventional medical treatments are used

Q: How about purge and so on? What did you give them old people for constipation?

A: Well, you see constipation is most in your diet. You drink a lot of water ....

Q: No bush for that?

A: No. I don't take bush for that. But I use P-L tablets. You know when you eating and you want a purge, I use P-L tablets. But constipation, old people suffer a lot with constipation. But I give them a lot of fruits and fruit juices. Less salt. Less sugar.

Throughout her conversations Mrs S used conventional scientific terms and in so doing exhibited varying levels of understanding of their meanings. At times she used these scientific terms alongside traditional concepts.

Q: Someone told me that pregnant women are supposed to eat ochroes.

A: Yes. Is cooling. Not only pregnant women. Everybody is suppose to eat ochroes. First in your joints you have to have a certain amount of . . . How they call it again? I learn. Some gristle or so.

Q: Cartilage.

A: Right. Ochro help to give you that.

Q: It helps to build up that.

A: And your joints free. It have the amount to spin. And you find old people in the country just boil we ochro so and we eat it. And it keep the body cool.

Q: Some people say they use sea water to make medicine for the cold. Do you know about that?

A: No. I know they use sea water to purge your blood, clear out your blood system, your blood cells.

On one particular occasion Mrs S used the same word, "balanced", with both its traditional knowledge meaning and its conventional scientific meaning in the same explanatory statement.

A: So, if you eat plenty corn, you find you get a rash, you scratching and rashes would come out.

Q: That is how you know you body is heated?

A: Yes. Pimples on your face, your hands will be itching, all your body a little rash and so. Sometimes, the rash come from the water you bathe in and all these things.

Q: So, it could come from outside?

A: Yes. It could come from outside and it could come from within. You now have to care your body. Your body needs care. You wash your clothes, you press it and you put it on. You bathe. Well, that is outside, but remember inside. The heat of the weather, you contract a heat; your food you eat, so the body must need a balance. Same way you eating a balanced food, your body needs a balanced cleansing—in and out. So, you take a little cooling. For some time you will drink a little carrot water. You will eat carrots and thing, different cooling food and have the body healthy.

There are also parts of Mrs S's discourse which indicate that sometimes she incorporates traditional knowledge into conventional science. The following extract illustrates this with respect to the functions of the kidney. The kidney is thought to be damaged by hot water as well as "heat" from rum.

A: When I was working, doctors scare. They only visit because they have to do it but they does tell me: "Dr S, go ahead nah man." Well you see, you have to learn from nursing. To keep a healthy body, you have to know a lot of home nursing—the type of lukewarm bath. Mostly in the evening you take a lukewarm bath after the judging of the day. Like you now, you travelling up and down. When you go home, you take a lukewarm bath and you find you feel ok. You find at the time you reach home you feel tired: "Oh I tired drive today; Seablast Road long." But you take a lukewarm bath, not a hot bath—it have a time for hot and a time for lukewarm—lukewarm relieves tensions, tiredness. Even though you worry and you take a lukewarm bath, it refreshes you. You know when you worry you miserable, you look old. And you take a lukewarm bath, squeeze a little lemon in the water and you take a bath. And after you could take a little warm tea also.

Q: When should you take a hot bath?

A: When the muscles sick. When you feel like a backache, you give a hot treatment. You have to be careful too. Not too hot because remember your kidneys. Your kidneys is the filter for the body so when you scorch it up it sick. You see rum drinkers suffer mostly with their kidneys—the heat of the rum.

Mrs S described two practices in which a product from conventional science was mixed with a traditional product in the attempt to reduce the negative side-effects of the scientific product:

Q: How about making coconut oil?

A: You grate your coconut and you wash it with cold water. Some people wash it with warm water, that is if you are doing it this month so. Winter it does come a cloudy way. You know how the oil does sleep in the bottle. It sleeps in the husk. The juice sleeps in the husk. You wash it in a little warm water to get out the fat. And you leave it to settle and then you skim the top.

Q: You don't strain it?

A: Yes. When you wash it, you strain it. And then you have it in a container and after a certain hour you have your fireside or stove or whatever you boiling it on and you skim it and put it in a pot. And it boils until it comes right down to oil. It make a little "dong". Some people, if it crispy, they eat it.

Q: The "dong"?

A: Yes.

Q: And you feed it to fowl and thing?

A: The husk.

Q: The husk?

A: You could dry it and the feed you buying you mix it up and feed your fowls. And like it cuts the chemical too because they don't even taste like a bred fowl. It taste like a yard fowl. A sweetened taste.

Q: How long the coconut oil will last?

A: If you boil it good, you know, boil it clean and it have no fat in it, when I say fat, it ain't have this milky thing. Some people does boil their coconut oil white, white. You know, it rancid quick, but if you boil it brown and nice, it last a good time. You put it in a very clean bottle. I have to boil some for my little grandson and they.

Q: To rub them down and so?

A: Yes. It very good for your hair and keep your skin smooth and thing, but now it have cream all you ain't using coconut again. All you living like England. But the grease we put in our hair, the Vaseline, it clogs the pores, the hair root. But when you mix it with the coconut oil it have a thing like it healthy and smooth.

In contrast, Mrs S used conventional science to legitimise beliefs:

A: Yes, yes. You never had a flu and you go to the sea and bathe and you sneeze out the cold?

Q: I know when I have the asthma and I come up to Seablast, or whatever, the fresh air helps the breathing.

A: You see that! The fresh air helps you and I have a cousin who died, when he comes to Seablast he gets asthma. But I know it is something in his body that causes that because an airy place with plenty breeze keeps your body healthy. It helps because oxygen is air. And when you have it hard and you go to the hospital, the first thing you get is oxygen and that beats it down better than an injection.

There were instances when traditional procedures described by Mrs S could be totally explained by conventional scientific principles, but she seemed to be unaware of them. This was particularly striking with respect to the technological procedures described below. The conventional science process here is one in which wood is burnt in a limited supply of oxygen to produce coals.

Q: You know how to make coals?

A: Yes. You dig a place and you cut your wood to length and you lay it. Sometimes, you have three layers to length . . .

Q: The length of the pit?

A: Yes. And then you cover it with bush and straw.

Q: Green bush or dry?

A: Green and dry. And then you make a barrier right around. Lay it and tie it and you get dirt and cover all that wood inside the barrier. The barrier make like a cage then.

Q: A cage around the hole?

A: Yes. It is not a deep hole. It is a shallow hole and then you pack your logs there and then. You put wood across lengthwise like a square business like a picket and you get your bush string and thing and tie it up.

Q: You tie the pickets?

A: Yes, on to the square logs like how you lay the bricks . . . and then now; you dig a place again and take all that dirt and cover the wood. That is called "stifling the wood" to make the coal. So, you leave a hole now to light it and when it well light up, the wood catch and thing, you cover that hole well because if it burst the wood would burn away and you get no coal. So this earth is to make the coal. You stifle the wood so it baking then until all bake out to be coal.

Q: What kinds of woods give you the best coals?

A: All kinds. But you know some lighter than some so it would burn away quick. But, balata, water cane, those give hard coals and produce good heat.

In summary, these extracts show that there is a very dynamic interplay of traditional knowledge and conventional science in the life of Mrs S. Neither conventional science nor traditional knowledge is accepted wholesale. Rather, Mrs S reacts to different situations by using various mixes of the two types of knowledge. In the next section of the paper an attempt is made to identify the interpretative frames that she uses to do this.

Discussion and Summary

The interpretative framework that Mrs S seems to be making can be described at two levels: conceptual and procedural.

At the conceptual level there are some main ideas that seem to guide her thoughts and through which she seems to filter everything. The central idea that we must take good care of our bodies puts some responsibility on the individual. Since also Mrs S holds the idea that we are born with every disease in our body, the need to take good care of one's body is even more apparent. Mrs S reinforces this idea by her numerous admonitions to "build up" the body.

Coupled with these ideas is the notion that a "balance" must be maintained in our bodies. Mrs. S seemed to project two variants of this balance, one being the sub-set of the other. There is the balance between heat and cold which is controlled by using appropriate foods and drinks and by taking purges at intervals. This notion is not unique to Seablast and is widely documented in the literature (Ato and Minott 1977; Harwood 1971; Laguerre 1987). At the more global level there seems to be the notion that the body is at war with disease but as long as the balance point is in a certain position, the body remains healthy. However, "your body (is) lower to the symptoms", or "when your body (is) over-run", or "when the (body) parts come low" to disease, the disease "overwhelms" the body. As Mrs S sums up: "You know the body supposed to have everything in proportion, not too much, and when your body system low, these things diseases overpower you." A more specific concept that pervades Mrs S's thinking is the mechanism whereby a cold is contracted. She holds the view that colds enter the body, particularly through the feet. This process is facilitated by certain climatic conditions. Many of the preventive measures suggested are based on such convictions.

At the procedural level it is evident that Mrs S's exposure to conventional science as a member of the Red Cross, by reading texts and by exposure to institutional health care practices, has affected the ways in which she explains and processes information. Technical words are used, sometimes without full comprehension, and are incorporated into traditional explanations. The discussion becomes complex when the same term is used in both systems, but with different meanings.

The exposure to conventional science seems to have resulted in a method of operating similar to that described by Bebbington (1991) for farmers in Ecuador. There is evidence thatr Mrs S reinterprets old ideas using new terms. Thus, for example, Mrs S talks about "purging the red blood cells" and effecting a "balanced cleansing" to control the amount of heat in the body. Mrs S liberally uses the scientific terms with which she is familiar in her explanations.

Mrs S also has the capacity to reject either of the two forms of knowledge, based on authoritative backing. Typically, that backing is from her own personal experience. Thus, the traditional wisdom about practices during menstruation have been discarded by Mrs S because she "ent seen nothing happen yet". In the same vein, the conventional scientific notion that iced water is a cooling agent is rejected by her because her experience tells her that when her body is "heated", iced water does not help. Although most of the backing that she draws on is from her own experience, she does utilise conventional science, medical authorities and the knowledge that is taught in elementary school. The result is that Mrs S is not restricted to specific dogmas, but interprets and reinterprets as she sees fit.

The result of a case study such as this cannot be extended to refer to the larger unit of the village of Seablast. Its usefulness lies in the fact that it presents ideas of what may be happening in the larger society. It thus presents clues of concepts, procedures and ways of thinking that may be explored in the wider community. One of the key questions that adult educators may wish to pursue in the larger community is whether or not the dynamic interplay between conventional science and traditional knowledge exhibited by Mrs S is typical of adults in the village.

Answers to this question and others will have definite implications for adult education programmes, particularly in health. Typically in such programmes conventional medical science is presented to adults with little consideration of what they already know. This is probably as a result of blind faith in conventional science and the educators' conviction that their job is to pass on the official knowledge. A health educator at the health facility in Seablast explained her perception of her role as a health educator in this way: "Sometimes they ask me about these home remedies. Well, I heard about these home remedies growing up as a child, but I say, you see that, the Ministry (of Health) never advocate that to me. I have special guidelines that I have to go out and teach the people."

Interestingly, this health educator admitted to resorting to some of the home remedies in the privacy of her own home.

The results of this study suggest that the community health education personnel in Trinidad need to evaluate the effectiveness of their approach by exploring the ways in which villagers translate the health information that they receive and transform it for practical action. Another important and related need is for meaningful medical research into the effectiveness of the more prominent aspects of the traditional knowledge that are at variance with conventional medical science. Since women are the prime care-givers in Seablast, as in most communities, their involvement in such ventures is critical.

Endnote

The writer acknowledges with gratitude the financial assistance given by the Women and Development Studies Group, UWI, St. Augustine, for the collection of data for this project. She also acknowledges the valuable comments on the work in progress received from Dr Joyce Glasgow, Dr Edrick Gift, Dr Ian Robertson and Professor Nelson Haggerson.

References

Ato, W. and Minott, K. "Creole and Doctor Medicine: Folk Beliefs, Practices and Orientations to Modern Medicine in a Rural and an Industrial Sub-urban Setting in Trinidad and Tobago, The West Indies'. *Social Science and Medicine*, 11, 1977, pp. 349-55.

Ausubel, D. *Educational Psychology*. New York: Holt Rinehart and Winston. 1968.

Bebbington, A. "Indigenous Agricultural Knowledge Systems, Human Interests, and Critical Analysis: Reflections on Farmer Organization in Ecuador'. *Agriculture and Human Values*, 8 (1/2), 1991, pp. 14-24.

Cumming, D., Cumming, C. and Kieren, D. "Menstrual Mythology and Sources of Information about Menstruation". *American Journal of Obstetrics and Gynecology* 1, 64 (2), 1991, pp. 472-76.

Driver, R. and Erickson, G. "Theories-in-Action: Some Theoretical and Empirical Issues in the Study of Students' Conceptual Frameworks in Science". *Studies in Science Education*, 10, 1983, pp. 37-60.

Driver, R. and Oldham, V. "A Constructivist Approach to Curriculum Development in Science". *Studies in Science Education*, 13, 1986, pp. 105-22.

Eisenbruch, M. "Classification of Natural and Supernatural Causes of Mental Distress: Development of a Mental Distress Explanatory Model Questionnaire". *Journal of Nervous and Mental Disease* 178 (11), 1990, p. 719.

Furnham, A. 'Lay Understanding of Science: Young People and Adults' Ideas of Scientific Concepts'. *Studies in Science Education*, 20, 1992, pp. 29-64.

Goetz, J. and LeCompte, M. *Ethnography and Qualitative Design in Educational Research*. Orlando, Florida: Academic Press. 1984.

Harwood, A. "The Hot-cold Theory of Disease: Implications for Treatment of Puerto Ricans'. *Journal of the American Medical Association*, 216 (7), 1971, pp. 1153-158.

Hawkins, J. and Pea, R.D. 'Tools for Bridging the Cultures of Everyday and Scientific Thinking". *Journal of Research in Science Teaching*, 24 (4), 1987, pp. 291-307.

Hewson, M. "The Ecological Context of Knowledge: Implications for Learning Science in Developing Countries". *Journal of Curriculum Studies*, 20 (4), 1988, pp. 317-26.

_______ and Hamlyn, D. "The Influence of Intellectual Environment on Conceptions of heat". *European Journal of Science Education*, 6 (3), 1984, pp. 245-62.

Kaiser, R. "The Narrative-Focussed Interview in Educational Research: Its Features, Application and Evaluation". *Education*, 48, 1993, pp. 74-82.

Laguerre, M. "*Afro-Caribbean Folk Medicine*. Massachusetts: Bergin and Garvey. 1987.

Layton, D. "Science Education and Praxis: The Relationship of School Science to Practical Action'. *Studies in Science Education* 19, 1991, pp. 43-79.

Merriam, S.B. *Case Study Research in Education: A Qualitative Approach*. San Francisco: Jossey-Bass. 1988.

Osborne, R.J. and Cosgrove, M. "Children's Conceptions of the Changes of State of Water". *Journal of Research in Science Teaching*, 20 (9), 1983, pp. 825-38.

Pines, A.L. and West, L.H.T. "Conceptual Understanding and Science Learning: An Interpretation of Research within a Sources-of-Knowledge Framework'. *Science Education*, 70 (5), 1986, pp. 583-603.

Rubenstein, H., O'Connor, B., Nieman, L. and Graceley, E. "Introducing students to the Role of Folk and Popular Health Beliefs-systems in Patient Care'. *Academic Medicine*, 67, (9), 1992, pp. 566-68.

Solomon, J. "Social Influences on the Construction of Pupils' Understanding of Science". *Studies in Science Education* 14, 1988, pp. 63-82.
Strauss, A. and Corbin, J. *Basics of Qualitative Research: Grounded Theory Procedures and Techniques*. California: Sage. 1990.
Strauss, A. and Corbin, J. "Grounded Theory Methodology." In N.K. Denzin and Y.S. Lincoln (Eds) *Handbook of Qualitative Research*. Newbury Park, California: Sage 1994
Toulmin, S. *The Uses of Argument*. Cambridge: The University Press 1958
Wheatley, G.H. "Constructivist Perspectives on Science and Mathematics Learning". *Science Education*, 75 (1), 1991, pp. 9-21.

Part SIX

Gender Issues in Agriculture

Constructing Alternatives for Teaching, Research and Policy

Gender Issues in Agriculture

Constructing Alternatives for Teaching, Research and Policy

Introduction

Christine Barrow

As an academic discipline and a sector of Caribbean economies, agriculture has been described as one of the last bastions of male dominance. Male and female participants in this seminar issued a challenge to agriculture by focusing on alternative strategies for agricultural development, with emphasis on women and gender issues. The specific aims of the seminar were as follows:

1. to investigate women and gender issues in Caribbean agriculture as they have been taught and researched;
2. to create more effective, gender-aware, multidisciplinary perspectives;
3. to provide information through the findings and materials of the seminar to programmes taught and researched at the University of the West Indies.

Presentations and discussions covering a wide range of interests identified common fundamental questions as:

1. What distinctions exist between male and female farming systems and have these distinctions been reinforced by official policy?
2. In what ways does Caribbean women's contribution to agriculture compare with that of their sisters elsewhere in the third world and how is it unique?
3. How have development policies impacted on food security and agricultural sustainability and what are the alternative strategies?

The seminar, in particular the four papers selected for this volume, adds the distinctive voices and visions of Caribbean women and men to the global debate on agricultural development in the contemporary context of economic crisis.

Achola Pala Okeyo's keynote address set the stage for the conference, providing an overview of the changing perceptions and circumstances of third world women in general and women in agriculture in particular. Contemporary global geopolitics along with national economic, demographic, environmental and technological changes, provide both constraints and opportunities for women in agriculture. Responding to the challenge demands a more holistic understanding of the socio-cultural context of women's lives and new and innovative strategies which work towards gender equality and an increase in women's income, while ensuring family health, nutrition and welfare. Policies for sustainable agriculture that respond to locally identified needs, which harness indigenous knowledge and practice and which involve local participation and organisation must be given priority on the agenda for development.

The papers by Joan French and by Rhoda Reddock and Jasmine Huggins complement each other. The former reports the results of a project sponsored by CAFRA (Caribbean Association for Feminist Research and Action) on women's involvement in contemporary, small-scale food farming in the Eastern Caribbean territories of Dominica and St Vincent and the Grenadines; the latter provides a historical overview of women's roles in plantation agriculture in Trinidad and Tobago.

The innovative, participatory methodology adopted for the CAFRA project combined questionnaire surveys with in-depth techniques; researchers lived with farm families, developing intimate relationships with women farmers and closely observing their lives and involvement in agriculture. The results highlighted the low resource base, the non-viability of women's agriculture and their survival as an "endangered species". The project also acknowledged the importance of income-saving subsistence production for women and deconstructed the perception of women as housewives. Community workshops for project evaluation and popular cultural presentations to disseminate information were integral components of the research process. A link between research and activism was forged by training village women in feminist theory and research methodology and empowering them to take charge of change.

By tracing the changing contribution of women's roles in agriculture as African slaves, as East Indian indentured servants and as free labourers and farmers, Reddock and Huggins make a significant contribution to the task of adding women's history to mainstream Caribbean history. Their presentation addresses the contradictions between Eurocentric gender ideologies of femininity and woman's place, conceptualised in "housewifisation" and plantation capitalism, that is, profit-making through the control and reduction of labour costs. The complex interplay between these opposing principles manipulates women's work by defining and redefining their roles either as agricultural labourers or as homemakers and farmers' wives and daughters. In the process, both the incorporation and the exclusion of female agricultural labour are promoted and justified, as is the practice of equal labour for less pay for women. The flexibility essential to successful capitalist exploitation is thereby maintained.

The final paper was prepared as the rapporteur's report to the seminar. It provides an overview and synthesis of the main issues raised at the seminar, exploring the implications for both policy and research. The paper attempts to highlight the essence of Caribbean gender ideology and practice in agriculture and to initiate the construction of comparative theoretical perspectives for Caribbean women in agriculture.

The uniqueness and the paradox of Caribbean women in agriculture were addressed both directly and indirectly by seminar presentations. The following themes emerged:

1. While other regions devise strategies for the equal involvement of women in agriculture, the Caribbean appears to be reversing the process and undermining traditional gender equalities in agricultural production by marginalising women through the push of mechanisation and scarce resources and the pull of ideologies of female domestication, encouraging a retreat into the roles of wife and mother.
2. Matriarchal families and female-headed households are familiar features of the Caribbean social landscape, but women's status and power does not extend beyond the house and yard into the national economic and political arena.
3. Women's labour input into agricultural productivity is at least equal to that of men and women dominate national and regional food distribution, but agricultural policy and on farm decision-making are male prerogatives.
4. Women's food production is crucial to family nutrition and well-being and yet this remains invisible in the scramble for foreign exchange through export agriculture.
5. The contribution and potential of Caribbean women in agricultural production, food distribution and family nutrition is crucial, yet their very survival is threatened by misconceived national and global restructuring policies.

The heritage of dual and asymmetrical agricultural practice and policy in the Caribbean, evident as plantation versus peasant with monocrop export agriculture thriving at the expense of food for local consumption, now appears in new clothing, redefined as the contradictory pull of IMF and World Bank stabilisation and structural adjustment policies against strategies to ensure food security and agricultural sustainability. Adjustment packages demand agricultural production for export, the removal of food subsidies and the re-allocation of funds from social services and human welfare to debt repayment. Regional organisations, governments and non-governmental organisations (NGOs) struggle to construct agricultural policies which balance and, impossible as it may seem, reconcile the requirements of restructuring with the provision of human basic needs and an enhanced quality of life for Caribbean people. We need to understand more of the way in which women's agriculture is structured into this crisis and the relationship between female farming systems, food security and agricultural sustainability. What became very clear during this seminar is that Caribbean women farm first and foremost to feed their families. Therein lies the unique potential of women's agriculture, with appropriate programmes and resources, to respond to the challenge to put people, families and communities at the centre of agricultural policy and revive the human face of development.

Gender Issues in Agricultural Innovation

Reflections on the Future

Achola Pala Okeyo

This seminar has given me the opportunity for my first visit to the Caribbean, a region that I have longed to see since my college days. This feeling was later reinforced by encounters with a distinguished scholars, diplomats and leaders of the region with whom I have had contact over several years of the UN Decade for Women. For many years scholars from the Caribbean have brought important analytical insights to African development problems, a contribution which must not be obscured by time. I welcome the opportunity on the basis of our common descent and cultural heritage to conduct a dialogue with you on development. We share our African descent and, even more importantly, we share a history of triumph over the great traumas and tragedies of slavery and colonialism. We must, therefore, now act decisively and collectively to shape our common destiny in the areas of gender relations and development.

We should remember that the historical roots of gender inequality and our imaging of future options are very much tied up with those iniquitous processes that have characterised our regions from the sixteenth century to today. Our relationship with the international economic system continues to be an extractive and somewhat rapacious one with the developed countries getting the lion's share of the booty which we have historically hunted for together.

I have elected to title my Keynote Address "Gender Issues in Agricultural Innovations: Reflections on the Future" because I believe that the research undertaken in the last two decades, in particular, provides us with much food for thought. We therefore need to stop and reflect about what we know in order to face the twenty-first century. For this reason, I will touch on some historical, conceptual, ideological and methodological issues which provide the basic definitions for interpreting gender relations today and in years to come.

Conceptual Perspectives

I do not intend to spend much time recounting the litany of woes concerning how women as a group are disadvantaged. I want to focus attention on lessons learnt over the last decade and use these as a basis for reflecting on the future, following the theme of the seminar and its accent on alternatives. First, a little historical background may be in order. It will be recalled that the UN Decade for Women (1975-85) did much to advocate the improvement of the status and position of women in development, in general, and in agriculture in particular. The basic rationale for advocating gender equality during the decade (as well as before and after) was based on the premise that gender inequality, if allowed to persist, would deny humankind a fundamental development opportunity. Moreover, it was emphasised that women as people could not be free to contribute fully as members of society if their rights and freedoms remained severely curtailed; and that persisting gender inequality was both unjust in human rights terms and inefficient in economic terms.

Over that decade, however, we saw how the international geopolitical agenda and macro-economic policies and the problems of the developing world became even more knotted up with the inflationary trends of the 1970s and 1980s. Whereas the Mexico Conference (1975) indicated that the world community was ready to define a common agenda in the area of gender equality and act on it (albeit with differing approaches), the Copenhagen Conference of 1980 showed even more clearly the reticence of the developed world over political and economic power-sharing and called into question the ability of the world community to make a consensus even over a fundamental question like the status of women if the North continued to be dominant over the South. After that conference one came away with a clear and sad picture that the governments of the developed regions would want to participate in a world forum for defining the agenda to fight female subordination but that they would continue to push for these negotiations on their terms and conditions.

Perhaps because of the shock of Copenhagen, or because this was inevitable, the developing world in the ensuing period took a greater initiative in acting and networking in ways that were more amenable to creating changes on their own conditions. They also stepped up efforts to evolve their own strategies for solving sex equality problems in ways that were locally possible. These initiatives were galvanised by a growing women's movement in these regions and the recognition of the value of intensified South-South linkages as a response to the global power relations in which the South continued to be short-changed by the North.

By 1985, the world political climate had changed somewhat and the Nairobi Conference yielded greater consensus, placing emphasis on development as the major area of focus, to improve the condition of women, with equality and peace being seen as complementary.

The World Conference on Agrarian Reform and Rural Development (WCARRD), held in 1979, presented a chance for the international community to focus on women's roles and opportunities in agriculture and rural development. The obstacles identified by the WCARRD to women's equal access in agriculture remain valid. The WCARRD noted that women of the developing world were preponderant in agriculture and food production both as producers and workers, but they lacked access to the basic means of production such as land; they had little or no access to technological innovations and information; they lacked incentives such as credit and extension; and their limited membership in rural institutions could not really help them to improve their agricultural work. They also did not have overall policy support to enable them to contribute more efficiently to agriculture and food production. The WCARRD's analysis showed that women in the developing world would continue to be a substantial part of the stable rural agricultural population for some time and that national governments need to take women more into account in policies to expand agricultural production.

In the meantime, women of the developing world were also thinking. The launching of DAWN (Development Alternatives with Women for a New Era) during this period presented the developing countries with a new feminist development paradigm. Stated simply, DAWN took the view that, as women of developing countries, there was a need for feminist analysis that would link poverty alleviation efforts with improvement of the status of women while also increasing women's productivity, efficiency and power in the share of resources. Moreover, it was DAWN's conviction that gender issues should form an integral part of the development debate. The envisioned choices in the DAWN paradigm were that for development to benefit women it had to address the problem of structural inequality within countries, at the local and familial levels as well as at the international macro-level; that development should entail participation of all rural people and thereby empower women to participate in local organisations and decision-making on an equal footing with men; and that development should entail equality in sharing the benefits of common effort. The vision that DAWN invoked was that gender inequality could not be solved in and of itself, but must be addressed in the wider context of structural inequality which creates and sustains gender ideology and impediments to women.

The lessons we have learnt during the Decade for Women, in which problems of gender inequality have been discussed and analysed, are many. The following key points may be worth revisiting at this stage.

1. We have learnt that gender inequality is not biologically fixed, but rather socially constructed and therefore within our human means to transform. We are also learning that even biology is not that fixed and is amenable to change.

2. The experience of such organizational innovations like the Grameen Bank in India, Zimbabwe's Federation of Rural Savings Clubs, Kenya Women's Water for Health Organization, ADB/FAO credit programme for African women, SEWA (Self-Employed Woman's Association of India), WAND (Women and Development) in the Caribbean and AAWORD (Association of African Movement for Research and Development) show that women can be a major lever for change not only for themselves, but for their countries and local communities as well. Therefore, investing in women is probably the most direct way to invest in social and economic development.

3. We have also learned other fundamental things.

   a. Changing demographic and social patterns in rural areas have, in turn, led to greater diversification or need for diversified employment by rural dwellers and by women in particular. A study by Joycelin Massiah of 13 CARICOM countries has indicated that women are involved in a wide range of work, of which agriculture is but one component. Extended to the other parts of the developing world, this finding from the Caribbean means that, with varying degrees of emphasis, agriculture is one in a spectrum of economic activities undertaken by women. A better understanding of this range of work done by women is essential if strategies and options for improving women's agricultural work are to be pursued.

   b. Because of increased male migration in search of wage work, female-headed households are on the increase around the world. Some of these are caused by bereavement, abandonment and outright poverty. Evidence suggests that female household heads could well become major innovators in agriculture if they can receive the necessary incentives and policy support. The increase of female household heads need not be seen as deviant, but as a significant outcome of recent and current demographic changes.

   c. Increasing urbanisation may lead to a pattern of female migration which will put the latter in peri-urban areas where they become suppliers of labour to the urban domestic market while, at the same time, engaging in satellite agriculture (mostly horticulture) for the urban consumers.

   d. Increasing work loads due to male migration and stress from frequent child-bearing and child care can lead to the impairment of women's health.

4. Inflationary trends in many developing countries have had the impact of driving more and more women into the informal sector, with the result that more women will want to combine some cash- earning endeavour with their traditional agricultural roles.

5. Environmental degradation has meant a reduction in fuel wood used for domestic consumption with the result that many rural households, particularly in Asia and Africa, may eat less hot food and resort to less nutritious diets. This has implications for family health, in particular women's and children's health. It also means that women have to have access to cash for other energy sources.

6. Perhaps one of the most fundamental innovations in agriculture which stands to affect women's scope in agriculture is biotechnology. With its capacity to revolutionise production so very rapidly, the consequences for women farmers may be quite adverse. They could be quickly marginalised by agri-business based on new seed technology.

7. With the shrinking land base and problems of ownership already studied in Africa, Asia and here in the Caribbean, one cannot help reflecting that even the prospect of ownership entitlement for women which we have been arguing for over the past decade may probably be an unrealisable prospect in the long run and that we may need to rethink this issue of women's land rights over again.

Long-term Perspective: Options and Strategies

How does this knowledge help us to understand the current situation? The following suggest themselves:

1. Linking women agricultural producers to technological innovations directly without the use of intermediary extensions system, by which women can have direct access to mainstream knowledge, for example the science of crop and livestock improvement.

2. Discovering the range of work done by women for a livelihood in order to see how their agricultural work fits into the range and how it might be improved in relation to their other work and health needs. This calls for:

   a. An improved database on women's work so as to gain policy support to sustain their work effort in agriculture (and other fields).

   b. A better understanding of household dynamics and the trade-offs between male and female investment in the household economy and what this implies for agricultural work and women's uptake of new technology.

   c. A better understanding of the socio-economic and cultural context in which women work, so as to evolve strategies and policy responses which will target particular problems. Interdisciplinary collaboration would enhance health and agricultural links and would show the necessity to conceive of interventions to improve family and female health and nutrition as well as agriculture.

3. Improving women's access to credit facilities and banking could directly benefit agriculture in two ways: first, it would increase their capacity to invest in agriculture in places where they still have use rights to land or where land for rent is available; and second, it would encourage the beginnings of food processing and rural industrialisation while at the same time increasing women's income.

4. Support for informal-sector activities in trade, manufacture, food processing and packaging could lead to a higher financial leverage for women, since they are already engaged to a large extent in these activities.

5. One finding which has repeatedly come out of studies across the world is that as women gain access to more cash they invest the greater proportion of their cash earnings on family health and on improving household welfare. This would lead one to think that problems of female and child malnutrition could be addressed in relation to effort to increase women's cash income. The way ahead is likely to meet

with greater success if creativity accompanies innovation in programmes to deal with gender inequality.

6. Problems of gender inequality are not going to be successfully addressed and resolved through women's desks or bureaux acting alone. These women's desks have to work hand-in-hand with ministries, research institutions and financial organisations to begin to influence the direction of changes which will be sustainable in the future. Increased policy support could be achieved through greater collaboration in women's national machineries and other areas in which the controls for development programming and financing are located.

Summary and Conclusions

1. Emerging developing countries' perspectives place emphasis on grassroots organisation, strengthening indigenous knowledge and farming practices, and delinking the proof of land ownership with access to agricultural development incentives for women.
2. Emerging technological innovations, for instance biotechnology and its impact on the agricultural market, should be monitored especially with regard to what advantages or disadvantages women may face with these new developments.
3. Social innovations in understanding gender equality and support for them: men and women have to be innovative in relations between them to lessen the burden of responsibility for change on women.
4. We need innovative women's bureaux and national machineries which will collaborate in order to be strong and informed in the development debate.
5. Diversification and investment in agricultural production and marketing in the informal sector is an important area requiring increased support as a local response to structural adjustment constraints.
6. Organisation and solidarity, the basis for collective bargaining: women must strengthen their solidarity relationships in order to increase their capacity to bargain and to prevail over difficult structural and ideological problems.
7. Imaging women: sophisticated research is needed to show the way to linking women with mainstream development while safeguarding their freedom through organised and participatory procedures.
8. Influencing donor action: it is important for developing countries to indicate areas in which help is needed and not to accept money for programmes which they do not have simply because donor money is available. The long-term ideal is to get donors to respond to women's needs as seen by women rather than as donor-driven development agenda.
9. In the wake of changes in eastern Europe during the 1980s and the perspective that that region is to get greater support from the western industrial states, there is a need to strengthen South-South collaboration in creating new inter-regional markets and knowledge banks which can be shared widely among developing countries.

In conclusion, I should note that the gist of this presentation is that the rural world is changing and the geopolitics of the world is also changing. We, in the developing countries, need to understand these changes and how they affect women. The present world predicament of developing economies presents a rare opportunity to review how the changing situation can be addressed with gender awareness in mind. These opportunities can be used to strengthen women and to stem the deleterious consequences of the world geopolitical restructuring for the developing world, focusing on women as a lever for societal change both in the area of gender relations and in the area of development as a whole.

Gender Issues in Caribbean Agriculture

Methodology and Process in the Movement Towards Change

Joan French

Introduction

Women in Caribbean Agriculture (WICA)(1987-88) was the first major research project sponsored by CAFRA (Caribbean Association for Feminist Research and Action). Its aim was to find out about women's contribution and needs in an area fundamental to Caribbean economies. According to statistics, agriculture contributes more than 30 per cent of gross domestic product (GDP) in Dominica and approximately 20 per cent in St Vincent and the Grenadines (1986); 20 per cent of economically active females were recognised as working in agriculture in Dominica (1981), while in St Vincent and the Grenadines 54 per cent of the labour in agriculture was recognised as being contributed by women. These data are based on investigations which exclude women's subsistence production to a large extent and ignore that part of women's agricultural labour which is hidden within her definition as housewife and her work at the home base.

Dominica and St Vincent and the Grenadines were chosen because CAFRA wished to move the focus away from the big territories, which are often the focus of major research, to the smaller territories which have no university campuses and are often left out of major research projects. In addition, those territories had CAFRA members working within agencies committed and engaged in work with women. These were the Committee for the Development of Women (CDW) in St Vincent and the Grenadines, and in Dominica the Small Projects Assistance Team (SPAT) through its women's programme. These agencies were willing to collaborate in the project and to be channels for the development of action programmes arising from the research findings.

The project aimed to help to strengthen and develop the work which local agencies were doing with women. This is why the researchers were primarily activists, rather than academics. Their skills were upgraded through seminars in feminist theory and analysis, report writing, methods of popular dissemination and production of popular materials. The process also put them in contact with women in the communities in a way which made them into students learning from the women being researched. In these ways, the project strengthened the capacity of the local women's movement to carry out their own research and develop their programmes in responding to the issues.

Many agencies besides CDW and SPAT participated in the process as part of back-up teams which kept in touch with progress, gave advice, assisted in making arrangements in the communities and, at the end of the research phase, helped to design action programmes to respond to the needs of the women as shown in the findings.

Participatory Action Research: The Process

Three communities in each country were chosen for study, representing the main types of agricultural communities in the territory. Survey questionnaires were administered to women working in agriculture in 10 per cent of the households. Researchers also spent time living in selected households in the communities with the women, observing their day-to-day activities, recording how much time they spent on each, observing how work was shared within the household, and sharing life stories and concerns with the women. There were also workshops in which the women and other members of the community came together to hear about how things were going, to discuss the issues, to help clarify information and to make recommendations for action. The process meant that a really intimate relationship was developed over time between the researchers and the women who were sharing their lives.

After the information had been collected and analysed it was shared and discussed in the communities and at the national and regional levels with organisations working with women or involved in agriculture. Recommendations for action were made at all levels and these were put together and developed into programmes for follow-up action in both territories.

Gender, Race and Class

To speak about gender issues in agriculture is to speak about gender issues in general, for women in agriculture share with women in society a common subordination within a patriarchal system. However, in looking at the conditions of the women who are involved in agriculture at the very base, we look at how this common subordination manifests itself in their particular daily activities. We also look at issues of class: the two cannot be separated. While women small farmers and agricultural labourers operate at a systematised disadvantage to men of their class, we also see that both male and female small farmers and labourers are subject to subordination to the "bigger people", those who control the larger resources and have the most say. We also see that these "bigger people" are mainly men. Such is the nature of a patriarchal system. The issue of race, of course, also arises, and is clouded in some Caribbean territories by the unobtrusive mechanisms through which race control is exercised, such as credit institutions and banks. The same institutions that obstruct the ability of poor black people of whatever ethnic group to make progress are the same institutions that support the manipulation of gender in the interest of profit. The triple subordination of gender, race and class is therefore intertwined.

The purpose here, however, is to focus on the issues relating to gender, for while race and class have been for some time acceptable themes for progressive academics, the relevance of gender issues to social analysis is only just beginning to be recognised in the Caribbean. There is a major resistance among our predominantly male decision-makers and, where lip-service is given, implementation lags far behind. One reason is that those with the necessary experience, analysis and commitment are not yet in a position to effectively implement the necessary changes. It is therefore critical that while we continue to strengthen the various institutions created ostensibly to influence policy in this direction (women's bureaux, women's studies programmes, etc), we pay attention to the empowerment of those with most at stake: the women at the grassroots level whose daily existence is defined by the constraints of the system.

Methodological Issues

For this reason the project sought not only to generate data about women small farmers and labourers, but also to create the potential for action on the issues by the use of a participatory methodology:

1. linking the project to an activist institution in each territory to be studied;
2. choosing researchers from among women active in and committed to working for the advancement of women; as part of the design for the project, training in feminist theory and research methodology was provided for researchers;
3. involving the communities in data collection and evaluation through workshops;

4. involving community agencies working in agriculture and among women in facilitating the research, responding to the findings and defining action to address the issues that emerged;
5. developing a coherent action programme out of inputs from the community, the researchers and the local and regional institutions.

The process has been outlined here because research design is itself a gender issue. If we accept the premise that the aim of research with women is to change the subordination of women, the empowerment of women to take charge of that process must be one of the principal aims of any research project on gender issues.

It is necessary to point to some other methodological issues which are also important. The first is that the use of questionnaires was balanced and complemented by other methodologies. For example, researchers lived in selected households in each community for a period and were able through this method to get information on areas for which a questionnaire would be inadequate. In this way, the researchers were able to collect information about the amount of time spent on reproductive as well as productive work and by which member of the household: which productive tasks were carried out at the home base and the various strategies used by women to keep supplying the basic needs of the family. Information on man-woman relations, rape, incest and sexual harassment also came to the fore as researchers developed intimate relationships with the women.

This approach to the measurement of women's labour sought to challenge the traditional approach in which researchers look at the "farm family", without specific attention to the inputs and labour of the individuals within that family. In the "farm family" approach, the labour and subordination of women have been subsumed within an institution which is seen as the basic unit of agricultural endeavour. Only by using other approaches is it possible to see the over-exploitation of women through excessive hours of housework in which men do not participate, children participate minimally and girl children participate far more than boys. By using these methods we can also see the extent to which women and children are directly involved in agricultural tasks, both those that take place in the field and those that take place in the home and so-called kitchen gardens at the home base. Researchers in the WICA project lived in individual households and measured by observation the time spent on these various tasks by each member of the household. Researchers sought to find out which household member performed various tasks associated with agricultural as well as domestic activities. In this way they were able to see which domestic tasks were actually agricultural tasks performed at the home base, to what extent activities previously categorised as domestic were actually income-generating or expenditure-saving activities, the value of women's work at the home base, and the value of the contribution made by women through their labour at the home base as well as in the field. Produce used for home consumption was costed to arrive at the full value of the household's annual production. As this subsistence production is for the most part women's work, the result is to put a cash value on an area of women's production that has historically been ignored.

The decision to focus on activities at the home base as well as in the field in conducting occupation-related research was a new departure in social science research in the region. This was done because experience has shown that a large part of women's work is done at the home base, and there is a relationship between what goes on at the home base and what takes place in what has traditionally been regarded as the "workplace", that is, the place where women work for wages outside the home. In recent years, feminist social scientists have been developing methodologies to challenge the traditional division between the private and public areas of women's lives, and to show how much women work at the home base, how the invisibility of this work in the private realm is an essential element in the subordination of women and how the devaluation of women's labour outside the home is related to its association with her "natural" role in the home.

CAFRA drew on these methodologies as used by the Centro De Investigación Para La Acción Femenina (CIPAF) in the Dominican Republic, adapted them to the particular experience of the English-speaking Caribbean and the particular territories being studied and complemented them with popular participatory methodologies developed within the region. In this exercise, the assistance of WAND and Sistren as well as the women's programme of UN-ECLAC (United Nations Economic Commission for Latin America and the Caribbean) were critical. Through popular methodologies the information was shared with the communities after the data had been gathered and analysed. Charts, skits, poems, songs, booklets and videos were produced for the dual purpose of developing the skills of the researchers in popular dissemination methods and getting across to the communities in a direct and non-academic way the results of the research. Having taken this approach, what kind of information was generated and what issues did the information raise?

During the period of archival research, the researchers became conscious of the almost total absence of sex-differentiated information in population and agricultural censuses and other statistical publications of the Eastern Caribbean. The little sex-differentiated information that existed was extremely limited and ignored areas critical to an assessment of the true situation of women in relation to men. Additionally, farmers' organisations and most of the existing research assumed that farmers were male, and saw no need to differentiate their records by sex or to pay any specific attention to women as a group. There was an assumption that if women were farmers, they had the same problems and existed under the same conditions as male farmers.

Structural Inequities: The Findings

The findings of the WICA research project indicate that women farmers have specific concerns related to the particular way in which they are structured into society as women. Most of these arise from the assumption that man is breadwinner, while woman exists primarily to serve men and families.

First of all, women in the agricultural communities studied face the problem of basic amenities and infrastructure. The main problems are: poor roads into the communities and difficulty in reaching plots, especially in rainy periods; lack of transport, which is often available only from a distant main road and is expensive and infrequent; an inadequate water supply, with many households, especially in St Vincent, depending on rivers for water for domestic use; and the absence of any organised garbage disposal system. Pit latrines are the main form of human waste disposal. While most communities have health clinics and primary schools, they are understaffed and only the most elementary health care is available locally. Secondary schools are concentrated in the capital and large towns, except in the communities of Marigot in Dominica and Buccament in St Vincent.

The lack of these basic facilities affects women in particular, since they bear responsibility for washing, cooking, cleaning, child care, the maintenance of life and health and the care of the sick and the aged. The point is borne out by the fact that in the communities in Dominica where social infrastructure is more developed, women on the whole spend less time on domestic and other reproductive work. In St Vincent, household case studies show women spending 5-10 hours per day on this sort of work, with most households at the upper end of the scale; in Dominica, women spend 3-10 hours per day on it with more spending roughly 3 hours.

Table 1: *Domestic work of main women in hours per year*

	No. of households	
Hours per year	**Dominica**	**St Vincent**
4000+	1	5
2000-3999	3	4
1000-1999	6	2
Less than 1000	-	1

Land and Agricultural Services

The research shows clearly that women's access to land is mainly through men, that is, male spouses or male relatives. It is mainly women who squat, rent, lease and sharecrop land controlled by men, or are simply allowed to work the land at the discretion of the men, usually in exchange for services, for example providing food, helping the men with work on their land and looking after their common children single-handedly.

In Dominica, land ownership by males and females varies in different communities (see Table 2).

Table 2: *Land ownership (titled): Dominica (per cent)*

Community	Titles overall	Main woman	Male spouse	Other relatives
Grand Bay	14.5	36.8	47.4	7.9
Marigot	26.4	21.4	21.4	32.1
Giraudel	31.6	11.1	44.4	44.4

In St Vincent women have their names on the titles for the land in 25.6 per cent of cases: in over 60 per cent of cases the titles are in the names of males.

The dependence on men for the most basic resource, land, means that women's relationships with men are based primarily on economic and only secondarily on affective considerations, although it is also true that in practice women try to get the best deal, that is, to find someone they like who can supply economic support. The primacy of economic considerations, however, has serious consequences. Cases have been found of women tolerating incest because they are dependent on the men who are abusing their daughters; of women tolerating relationships because they have no alternative means of survival, and of fathers using the fact that their daughters are dependent on them for land to prevent them from establishing relationships based on affection and to force them to accept partners chosen by the fathers.

Dependence on men also affects women's access to credit. Few small farmers, women included, seek loans because they fear losing the little they have in case of natural disasters or a bad crop. Too much is at stake. The few women who do often have to get partners to co-sign if they have no land titles of their own. Most of the loan sources are non-governmental, and some non-governmental organisations (NGOs) such as CARDATS (Caribbean Rural Development Advisory and Training Service) have credit schemes which address these issues. The need for partners to co-sign is a reflection of the weak position of women in relation to collateral and the "guardianship" role which society gives men in relation to women. No males need to get their female partners to co-sign loans.

Another effect of women's position in relation to land is that the men keep the best land for themselves and use it to grow cash crops, mainly bananas. Women grow mainly ground provisions to feed their families, for sale on the local market and for export if there is a surplus. Cash returns are lower than for bananas.

Women's production, both in cash and in kind, goes primarily to family consumption. Men are therefore usually in a stronger position to get loans. Some women are waging a struggle to get more involved in banana production, but are up against the men's control of land and their decision-making power on how it is used.

Apart from the traditional methods, government land reform, the Integrated Rural Development Programme (IRDP) programme is the next most important mechanism through which women come to own land. Women get an unequal share of the land available through these programmes. Most of the land goes to men. Women are not considered if their male spouses get land and male spouses are given priority. In addition women are assigned the less fertile, less productive land. In the Grand Bay community in Dominica, of the 400 farmers targeted for land through IRDP, only 24 per cent are women. The situation is similar in all areas where land reform programmes exist. In Orange Hill, St Vincent, the only location in the sample which remains intact as an estate, there is the additional problem that land is going to outsiders rather than to the people who have lived and worked on the estate for generations. Of the 83 persons allocated land so far, only 24 are from Orange Hill and only seven of these are women.

As far as inheritance is concerned, family land seems to be of particular significance to women. Where family land is found, it is occupied primarily by women. In this African tradition the land is handed down from generation to generation and cannot be sold out of the family. Daughters and sons have equal right of use. This tradition has come under pressure from the British colonial pattern of male inheritance and this has come to affect the sense of security of women occupying family land when male potential contenders exist. The women's security is also being affected by the enhanced economic power of brothers or other (mainly male) relatives who have advanced through migration.

Extension services such as technical advice on fertilisers and spraying are available mainly for bananas. Women's main production (provisions and vegetables) gets little or no attention and they depend mainly on experience or on each other for information. The aerial sprays used for bananas are destroying their vegetables in some communities. Governments have shown little concern. The women are simply told to cover their vegetables with plastic if they want to protect them. Some NGOs are beginning to do surveys to determine who exactly is affected, with a view to helping with remedial measures.

Marketing services are also geared towards bananas. Women and men in provision or vegetable farming have to make their own arrangements. In St Vincent, a private firm, Eastern Caribbean Agencies, buys provisions from the farmers but the farmers complain that prices are low. Farm-to-Market Limited in Dominica also assists with marketing products other than bananas. In general, however, it is easier for women to market through women traders who come into the community and take responsibility for getting the goods to market and selling them. They retain a portion of the sales for themselves and give the rest to the farmers. Farmers often have trouble collecting as traders complain of spoilage and low returns.

Decision-making, Labour and Survival

While women most often do not own or have primary control over the land they work, everyday farm management and maintenance are most often left to them. In St Vincent women lead in making decisions about farm improvements, hiring labour and acquiring services. Men, however, lead in making the decisions about purchasing farm equipment. In Dominica women participate fully in decisions about farm improvements and labour, as well as equipment.

Men are cited as the main decision-makers when it comes to the type of crops to be grown, credit and agricultural services. The data suggest that while men control the land and determine policy in relation to crops, women bear the main responsibility for everyday farm management and day-to-day decisions. The situation mirrors somewhat a proprietor-worker relationship.

The absence of a spouse or resident partner does not mean that these relations do not exist, as the proprietor role is often held by a brother, a father or other male relative. The social contract is maintained without conflict where the woman honours the unwritten terms of the agreement, that is, her services in exchange for access and adherence to the policies determined by the male. Otherwise there is friction, frustration and sometimes separation.

Where women manage to establish an independent base, they make their own decisions in all areas, but the possibilities for this are very limited except for squatting on government land. Then the government moves into the role of male spouse or patriarch, and usually does not even feel it necessary to consult "his wife" or "his daughter". Most women who establish a base independent of the fathers of their children and discontinue sexual relations with them forfeit support for the children.

In-depth studies of ten households chosen to reflect the variety of situations in Dominica and 12 in St Vincent show that in 14 of the 22 households women have no resident partners and no partners assist in work in the field. This is because in Dominica, especially, women engaged in agriculture are mostly of an advanced age and, even if previously married, their partners have died. In St Vincent as well as the Marigot community in Dominica, households are mainly run by women without resident partners.

What this means is that, in most cases, women are doing their field work themselves, assisted by older male children and occasionally by hired labour. In St Vincent the resident male partners who assist spend significantly more time in work than the women. In Dominica this is not so: in fact, the women either do almost the same or more hours of work than the men.

In addition to doing this large amount of field work, the women carry the main responsibility for domestic work and the training and rearing of children in their households. While the research has not measured the time spent on socialisation, a mini-survey among 15-year-olds in the communities in St Vincent reveals that mothers are exclusively responsible for telling their teenage daughters about matters like menstruation and sex, for buying their clothes and for looking for jobs for them. The general survey shows that they are the main decision-makers in all matters concerned with the everyday care and rearing of children.

As indicated earlier, the women in Dominica sperd less time on housework than those in St. Vincent. It would be interesting to explore the link between the higher level of basic facilities in Dominica and the generally lower number of hours spent on housework. Men give little assistance with housework. The maximum assistance given by males in the five households where there are resident male partners is 156 hours per year or 24 minutes per day.

Most of the time spent on housework by the women is spent on child care (where there were young children), cooking and washing wares and washing and ironing. This is the same for St Vincent and Dominica. In St Vincent up to 65 per cent of domestic work time is spent on child care and up to 47 per cent on cooking and washing wares. In Dominica the figures are 38 per cent and 51 per cent respectively.

The long hours involved in child care means that there is a definite relationship between the age of children in the family and the amount of housework. Where there are young children, the amount of work is greater. Where girl children are old enough to help, they are made to do so and the women's work decreases. Where the older female children in households are relatives (the household case studies show these are always nieces) the bulk of the domestic work is passed on to them. This suggests that they are brought into the household specifically to help with domestic work. There is a relationship between the age of the children and the ability to work land. For example, a family which owns 10 acres is only able to work 3 acres because so much time is taken up with the care of the children, who are young.

In Dominica the majority of families (50-70 per cent in the three communities) comprise 1 - 5 persons. One-quarter to one-third include 6 - 10 children. There are very few families larger than that. In St Vincent 46 per cent have 1 - 3 persons, 47 per cent had 4 - 7 persons, and very few are larger than this. It is clear that family size in the Dominica sample is generally larger than that of St Vincent, yet children take up less time. This appears to be the result of better social conditions in the Dominican communities (availability of schools, water, etc) and perhaps a more effective extended family network given the high proportion of legal marriages which account for most of the extended families. Over 35 per cent of households in the two larger communities in Dominica are extended.

When working their own plots, both men and women tend to do the whole range of tasks. However, when working as hired labour, tasks are strictly divided according to sex. Both women and men hire men to plough, dig and clear, while men hire women to weed. Women rarely hire women to weed, which could either mean they do it themselves or rely on non-wage mutual aid mechanisms. Fertilising, sowing, harvesting and field picking are also done mainly by women. The application of chemical sprays is done by men. Where couples work land jointly, there is a tendency for men to do more of the "men's tasks" and for women to do more of the "women's tasks".

Tasks done by women are regarded as less physically demanding, but requiring greater care and skill. Tasks done by men are regarded as physically more demanding. In official literature and to a certain extent in popular language this is referred to as women doing "lighter" and men doing "heavier" work. The distinction hardly holds good. Even when only physical requirements are considered, the back-breaking task of weeding can hardly be said to be less physically wearing than digging or ploughing and the long-term physical effects can be far more damaging. The concentration required for sowing, harvesting and field-picking should place these above less mentally demanding tasks such as digging and ploughing. The definition of men's tasks as "heavy" and women's tasks as "light" is used to justify lower wages for women.

Tasks which require technical knowledge and skills, such as applying chemicals and sprays, are done by men. There are few female extension officers in either territory. Extension officers are involved almost exclusively in giving technical advice.

Although agriculture is their main income-earning activity, the household case studies suggest that most women involved in agriculture are unable to show cash profits from their agricultural activities alone. Women employ a variety of survival strategies to supplement income from their agricultural activities. The household case studies show that, in Dominica, women employ 1 - 3 other strategies to survive and 3 - 5 in St Vincent. The main supplementary strategies are wage work (which is primary, not supplementary, for women with no access to land), the receipt of remittances from abroad, trading in small goods (foods, sweets, cigarettes, etc), the rearing of small livestock and the exchange of goods and labour. As we can see, these strategies include not only income-earning activities, but also activities which substitute for the expenditure of cash. For example, excess produce and labour is shared with friends, but friends can also be depended on for similar help. Remittances are usually linked to past or present services of child care and household services. They constitute an informal "wages for housework" network in which women are the main donors and recipients.

Despite the use of these multiple strategies, the household case studies show that less than half of the households in St Vincent and just over half of those in Dominica are able to meet their basic needs and show a positive balance - but only just. The remaining 50 per cent of households are unable to maintain themselves from these activities even at a very minimal level and live in perpetual debt. The level at which households maintain themselves is generally very low. In all communities the bulk of expenditure is on food: an average of 70.5 per cent in St Vincent and 66.59 per cent in Dominica. Despite this, the nutritional content of the food is low.

In spite of poverty and debt, the women manage to put aside some cash savings for crises, primarily medical expenses (Dominica) and burial (St Vincent). In Dominica formal savings are kept mainly in the Credit Union and in St Vincent in the Friendly Society. Smaller savings such as subs (Dominica) and sou-sou (St Vincent) and the savings from medium livestock (on the Orange Hill Estate) go mainly towards fitting children out for school and purchasing or replacing household equipment.

So what of the future? What is women's participation in agriculture likely to be in the next generation? The majority of women presently involved in agriculture are over 35 years of age. The highest participation is in the age group of over 45 years old. In the communities surveyed there are two factors which determined the involvement of younger women: repressive conditions and the proven success of farming as an income-generating activity. On the Orange Hill estate in St Vincent, however, there are more women under 35 involved than women over 35. However, this is because Orange Hill is an estate with almost slave-like conditions where alternatives to wage labour on the estate are almost non-existent. Residents have no access to land for any substantial incomes for women. In this community there are as many younger women involved as older women. The same is true of the Giraudel community in Dominica where vegetable farming has proved very profitable and is controlled by women.

In general, however, returns from farming for women are so poor that they want neither their sons nor daughters to be totally dependent on farming. They prefer them to have some other skills as well. The women do not see farming as a viable activity by itself. With this proviso, 60 - 70 per cent are willing for their sons to be farmers, while only 40 - 50 per cent feel the same way about daughters. The highest preference for girls as farmers exists in those communities (Lauders in St Vincent and Giraudel in Dominica) where women are doing quite well as farmers. However, even where women say they want their daughters to be farmers, they do not involve them in agricultural work. They involve their sons. If they have to make such a choice, they will take a boy rather than a girl out of school. The main reason given is that a boy can get along in life without an education more easily than a girl. This finding is significant as it differs from findings for other regions of the world where there is usually a clear preference for giving educational opportunity to boys (Acker *et al.* 1984).

The education of the women interviewed is almost exclusively primary and often not complete because of having to look after young children or help in the field, or because of the distance of school from home. Most have become involved in agriculture in their early teens. This suggests that girls of an earlier generation were more involved in field work than nowadays. However, 28 of the 48 young women interviewed in St Vincent from a random sample said they assisted their parents in field work. Twenty-three of these young women said they would like to follow their mothers into agriculture, while 19 would not. The mothers, however, sometimes discourage their daughters from going into agriculture. For example, one daughter who declared her intention to go into agriculture did so in the presence of her mother. The mother confirmed that the daughter loved agriculture and worked the land with good results. However, she said she did not want that for her daughter and was making attempts to send her overseas. Most women in the survey saw the migration of younger family members as the best hope for improved standards of living.

What all this means is that unless agriculture can be made viable for women, unless its prestige can be raised and unless young women can win the necessary practical and propaganda support which women in agriculture need to overcome the obstacles to participation and success, including control of the land, women in agriculture may well be a dying breed.

Conclusion

However burning the issues and however persuasive the information, things will not improve for women in agriculture, or grassroots women anywhere, unless they themselves are empowered to take action on their own behalf. It will be up to the gender-oriented women's movement in all its ramifications –

grassroots groups and activists at all levels, including the University—to network, strategise, analyse and, most of all, to act to change the situation. In this we are up against walls higher and tougher than those of Jericho or Berlin. The walls of patriarchy in our society are not about to fall, but here and there they are showing signs of crumbling. The movement can be justly proud of its successes despite the limitations. As the walls crumble, however, the hardliners become even more brutal in their opposition to change.

It is up to the women's movement to capture the energies of all in favour of change, including the energies of men who understand that gender equity and the restructuring of society along non-patriarchal lines are indispensable, not only to women, but to the liberation of society as a whole, including men and children. The attempts at change being made at the university level through the Women and Development Unit (WAND) and the Women and Development Studies (renamed the Centre for Gender and Development Studies, CGDS) programme which it has helped to establish, as well as the work of CAFRA, are important elements in a many-pronged strategy to redefine the content of our efforts at development and to take gender as well as race and class into account.

This implies the removal of oppression at the grassroots level where the majority of our people live their daily lives. The work of university academics gender-conscious policy-makers and middle-class activists can best serve this purpose if it links to and supports the activism of ordinary women on their own behalfs. Challenging the separation of academic analysis from activism needs to be a critical component of any women's studies programme whose ultimate aim is to change the unjust structural limitations under which ordinary people live.

Reference

Acker. S. et al. (eds). *World Yearbook of Education, 1984: Women and Education*, London: Kogan Page, 1984.

Agriculture and Women's Place

The Impact of Changing National Policies on Women's Agricultural Work in Trinidad and Tobago

Rhoda Reddock and Jasmine Huggins

Introduction

Any effort to examine the reality of women's experience in agriculture and rural employment in the Caribbean today would be incomplete without an understanding of its history. This paper aims to trace chronologically the experience of women in agricultural production in Trinidad and Tobago. It will analyse processes in the various agricultural sectors as well as the effects of management strategies and colonial labour and economic policy.

This paper begins with the premise that the majority of women who entered Trinidad and Tobago during the eighteenth and nineteenth centuries did so as workers, as slaves or indentured labourers primarily for work on sugar plantations (or estates, as they were more commonly referred to). An important part of this paper will be to identify the process by which women were increasingly excluded from agricultural labour and defined as non-earning, dependent housewives.

While attempting to explain this, it should be noted that the explanation is not simple. Although women were initially withdrawn from full-time estate wage labour, this did not mark their total withdrawal from agricultural labour. On the contrary, women continued to work in cane farming, cocoa and coconut proprietorship and in domestic food production, often without recognition and without regular remuneration.

Although no explicit colonial policy on women's labour was ever stated, in practice a clear policy could be identified in terms of the division of labour in employment, education, wage rates and remuneration and authority structures. This policy, as would be expected, was directly influenced by British values of women's place and the sexual division of labour. At times this contradicted the more crude profit and loss strategies of the plantocracy. In the continued effort to hinder the tendency of the falling rate of profit, this group was much more willing to opportunistically manipulate the division of labour to most profitably benefit from women's subordinate position in society.

This historical exploration is important not only for the insight which it provides into the past; but also because many of the economic strategies used in the past continue to be used today. It is important that they be recognised and appropriate measures developed to deal with them. The period 1838 to the present has been characterised by a strengthening of capitalist relations of production in agriculture in what has been termed the modernisation process. As part of this effort, increasing pressure has been put on women to conform to Western European ideals of femininity and women's place. Both trends have served to increasingly alienate women from agricultural activity, a trend which continues to this day. As far as the modernisation process is concerned, this particular trend has usually viewed women as external to and therefore incapable of contributing to the process of national development and stimulation of the economy. Thus, while the contribution that sugar has made historically to the Trinidadian economy has been well recognised, the contribution that women have made in developing the sugar economy has always been perceived as marginal, despite evidence to the contrary.

At present, the reality of the contemporary period is such that increased local food production is of vital importance to Trinidad and Tobago if economic self-sufficiency and a reduction of the present food import bill is to be achieved. According to the CSO, "Statistics at a Glance", the food import bill was estimated at TT$896.7m for 1992 and TT$938.9 for 1993. The contribution of women to small-scale food production, as will be shown in this paper, remains largely invisible and under-remunerated and continues to be unrecognised even after the United Nations Decade (1975-1985) aimed at the "integration of women into development" which placed some emphasis on women's work in agriculture.

Over this century, the development of the petroleum industry as the main contributor to the economy sharpened the tendency to move out of agriculture and into other areas of work. Whereas men could move into other areas of economic activity, for women the alternatives were much less rewarding. For some time, up to the late 1940s, domestic service was a major employer of women. Others were self-employed as dressmakers, laundresses and petty traders while those mainly of the lower middle classes were employed as shop assistants and clerks. These alternatives presented some relief from the arduous painstaking work of agricultural production but significantly fitted much better into the scheme of 'women's work' but in the colonial mentality. Frances and Melville Herskovits, for example, in their publication *Trinidad Village*, noted that, although in the village of Toco in 1939 agricultural production and petty-trading of produce assured Afro-Trinidadian women of an independent income, this was not considered acceptable for the daughters of these women. "Whether she works to supplement a husband's income or as a principal support of her children, a woman's earnings are her own . . . If she works a garden, what she receives for the produce she sells is hers; if she works it with her husband, the receipts from what she sells in the market are likewise hers." (Herskovits 1974:49).

On the other hand, they found that:

> "There is one Toco code that is held to today by all mothers. Girls are not allowed to work on the estates. A mother will herself weed, but however great the need, she will see to it that her daughter will not 'go to the field'. As was explained, 'she will rather have them go with some lady or gentleman, who will keep the girl for the work she does'—without paying her a wage—so the daughter may learn 'better ways of living'." (Herskovits 1974 : 58).

From the above observations, it is clear that agricultural labour for women had attained a negative connotation, while work in the house was perceived as 'better'. Although by the 1970s, the low status attached to agriculture was beginning to rescind, the years of the 'oil boom', approximately 1973 to 1980, reduced what little viability it maintained as a form of economic survival. During this period, food imports increased and domestic food production and processing declined drastically.

The period since then, however, has witnessed a resurgence of interest in the agricultural sector and its significance as an avenue for employment as well as economic viability. In this new era, a greater understanding of the experience of women is surely needed, but largely absent. For reasons not examined in this paper, existing statistics do not provide an adequate picture of this reality and in depth investigation is relatively non-existent.

It is within this framework that this paper will proceed to trace the historical developments relative to women in agriculture production and rural employment in Trinidad and Tobago. Hopefully out of this discussion the possibility for further research and action in this area will emerge.

Early Sugar Plantation Production

The sugar plantation was, from its inception, governed and managed by the purely capitalist drive to produce sugar is in expensively as possible and gain maximum profit. All other considerations were secondary. Human labour was merely perceived by planters as another variable to be manipulated in the constant drive for profit and production. Female labour, as well as male labour, fitted squarely into this mode of production. Both sexes were therefore brought to the Caribbean for the sole purpose of working in the fields.

Although a sexual division of labour existed for most of the years of slavery, since its inception in the 1640s, it was not a strict one. This trend continued throughout the seventeenth and into the eighteenth centuries as well, with very little change even up to the nineteenth century. For close to three hundred years, therefore, African women were largely given the same tasks and the same daily work quotas as men, and were expected to produce as much. The bulk of work was done by both able-bodied men and women and this included both the back-breaking tasks of weeding, cutting, digging and carrying, as well as planting. Typically, labourers were divided into groups of three or four, known as 'gangs', which would be supervised by drivers who were nearly always men. The only exception was the gang made up of children, which was supervised by a woman driver.

While it is often believed that the majority of women dominated domestic activities on the plantation, occupying positions as cooks, cleaners and general servants, this was not in fact the case. According to Mrs. A. Carmichael, apologist for the plantocracy, from as early as age four, young girls were put into gangs to work on the fields, starting with simple tasks such as "collecting vines for the sheep". When girls matured enough to be considered adults, they were merely transferred to the adult gangs. Boys suffered a similar fate. As far as field work is concerned, female labourers did exactly the same work as male labourers (Carmichael 1969, Volume II: 138).

Women were, however, excluded from the skilled tasks which were few in number. These included work in the factory and the operation and maintenance of factory boilers and distillers. Patterson has argued that the exclusion of women from these highly skilled jobs was due to the women's physical incapability: the handling of factory work necessitated "frequent and periodic bursts of extraordinary strength" (Patterson 1982: 256) which, therefore, in his opinion explains the reason why women were not allowed to do this type of work.

Evidence suggests, however, that it is more likely a manifestation of the planter's belief in the subordinate position of women vis-à-vis men and their concern to maintain some minimal male privilege, which led to the above-mentioned trend. There is abundant evidence to suggest that the physical inferiority of women was an insufficient justification for the sexual division of labour on the plantations. The actual work done by women evinced their physical strength and resilience. Demanding tasks, strict discipline and long hours of work were conditions within which slave women in the fields worked and survived. Women invariably met their daily quotas and worked 16-18 hour days as did men and, in the British Caribbean colonies, manifested a higher survival rate (Craton 1978).

The above examples clearly show a trend that is worthy of note, since it is based on this accepted although conveniently manipulated belief in female subordination which later becomes institutionalised in policies which prevent women from being accepted as full-time labourers in any form of agricultural activity. Rather than any established sexual division of labour, for women did the same work as men in the fields, there seemed to be a division of tasks into high status and low status tasks, which, except that of driver, were skilled tasks. They were invariably all done by men. Women were thus nearly always relegated to doing non-prestigious tasks and this prevailed both in agricultural and domestic activity. This does not mean that no men did non-prestigious tasks; what it does mean is that the few positions of prestige based on a skilled occupation seemed to have maintained a degree of status hierarchy on the plantation between men and men and between women and men.

Towards the later years of slavery, in particular after the U.S. War of Independence, it had become more economically advantageous for planters to give labourers a small plot of ground for their own domestic food production than to pay to feed them entirely. This had also been one of the proposals contained in the 1789 Spanish Code for amelioration of conditions for slaves. Thus began the emergence of a germ of peasant agriculture side by side with plantation production. This development was precipitated, it must be noted, more by the economic need of planters to reduce costs, than by the quest to become self sufficient in food production.

Slaves were given small plots of ground and, in Trinidad and Tobago, grew ground provisions (root crops), fruits and vegetables, cocoa, coffee and coconuts. Although at first there were cases of slaves not receiving land where planters had none to distribute, during the later years of slavery, the surpluses grown by slaves could be sold at Sunday markets, with the effect of granting independence which planters fought against throughout the years of slavery and after. It is seen, for example, that when planters became dissatisfied with the Sunday market and the profits which accrued therefrom, appeals were made to abolish the system with the excuse that slaves needed to devote the day to worship.

There is further evidence of women being able to pay for their freedom as a result of this Sunday market activity, by re-selling food produce and/or food stuffs (higglering and huckstering) to slaves and other 'free citizens'. There is, for example, the case of 'C' (Carmichael 1969, Vol. II: 183) who by huckstering, giving dances and supplying supper for slaves during these dances managed to free herself in 1830 by manumission.

Post-emancipation Trends in Agriculture: The Development of the Peasantry 1838-1938

The emancipation of the slaves in 1838 opened up several possibilities for ex-slaves to employ themselves in varied areas of peasant agriculture. This, however, was a gradual development which did not follow immediately, Brereton notes that unemployment was, for some ex-slaves, a serious problem for many years (Brereton 1979: 123-4). That vagrancy was a serious evil in Trinidad during the last thirty years of the 19th century suggests that the possibilities for agricultural labour were often made unattractive for large sectors of the population. As Brereton states for one group: "The African immigrants rarely resided on the estates as full-time labourers after their indentureship[1]. Some were skilled craftsmen, women worked as domestics, vendors, hucksters; African wage labour to the cocoa estates. But possession of a plot of land, and economic independence were crucial to the Africans." (Brereton 1979: 134).

For the large masses of ex-slaves who migrated to Port-of-Spain after emancipation, unemployment or temporary employment seemed to be a way of life. Brereton notes that in 1874, of the 90 female prostitutes registered in Port-of-Spain, 60 were Trinidadian and this figure reflected the trend for San Fernando as well. Then again, only a "fraction" of prostitutes actually living in Port-of-Spain had been registered at all. The figures do suggest a lack of employment opportunities, at least for women concentrated in urban areas.

A different trend emerges for rural employment. As Brereton states, "the peasantry in Trinidad originated with the withdrawal of ex-slaves from the sugar plantations after 1838. Perhaps around 7,000 ex-slaves left the estates to become small holders. Of these, about five-sixths became owners of between one and ten acres of land, growing chiefly ground provisions and cocoa." (Brereton 1979: 138).

Along with cocoa cultivation, coffee and coconuts became important crops which provided employment for peasants during the later years of the 19th century. Early in this period (1890s-1900s), the viability of only peasant crop production was questionable, since it has been noted that peasants had to combine their own land cultivation with work on larger cocoa, coconut and sugar plantations. Furthermore, the fact that many larger cocoa estates were made up of a conglomeration of smaller land units which were bought over from peasants, suggests that the economic independence sought by peasants did not last very long.

Brereton notes, for example, that nearly all large cocoa estates in Trinidad in the late 19th century (1872-1900) were first established by peasant agriculturalists, who cleared land that they bought, planted cocoa and then resold both crop and land to planters when the harvest was ready. On this land, peasants planted both cocoa and food crops for subsistence, and, for additional remuneration, sold their labour to nearby estates perhaps mainly during harvests (Brereton 1979: 140, Reddock 1984: 204). From the start of cocoa cultivation therefore, there is evidence to suggest that peasant cultivation alone could not guarantee adequate subsistence. This is substantiated by the contract system described above which reduced the economic independence of the peasant farmer. Thus larger plantations, like "a sponge" absorbed smaller holdings, "with the dispossessed small cultivators going back into the forest, only to be brought out again in a few years, or reduced to mere wage labourers" (Brereton 1979: 141).

The Development of Cane Farming as Peasant Agriculture

As early as 1872, Governor Rennie had looked forward to and openly advocated the small scale production of cane on individual plots as opposed to estates. This became a reality for ex-slaves around 1884-1885 (Brereton 1979; 141). Cane farming had been established on a very small scale since 1870, but the crisis in the sugar industry of the 1880s was the key factor that precipitated its sudden development. Brereton notes that incentives were given to encourage unemployed peasants to attempt cane farming. Among these were the opening up of land for peasants, as well as the centralisation of factories so that production costs for planters were reduced even more (Brereton 1979: 141-142).

Statistics show that cane farming, as opposed to estate production, developed quite rapidly as a viable source of employment for a variety of persons, some of whom were former cocoa cultivators attracted to the greater profitability of cane. Between 1880 and 1890 mostly African ex-slaves were involved. However, the period 1890-1906 witnessed a changeover from mostly African to Indian proprietors (Brereton 1979: 142). Production during that time and beyond increased from 156,421 tons between 1898-1907, to 396,725 tons between 1928 and 1934 (Reddock 1984: 209). Cane farming was therefore an established source of labour for both African and East Indian labour for the late 19th and early 20th centuries.

Although, as noted by Brereton (1979: 21), "In this period 1880s - 1930s agriculture meant sugar and cocoa", the minor cultivation of coconuts and wet rice or padi were relatively important and as such deserve mention. Coconut production had begun since 1890 in Trinidad and even earlier in Tobago, where the coconut industry, in addition to cacao, was the most important one in terms of agriculture. These, however, it must be noted, were not government assisted schemes, but independent peasant projects which were successful. Much of the crop was exported. The Annual Register in 1895 recorded no less than 38 coconut estates (Brereton 1979: 21). That coconuts continued to be a relatively important crop up to the 1930s can be attested to by the fact that a 1938 census showed at least 2,751[2] persons employed in coconut cultivation. Of this number, approximately one quarter came from Tobago. While 2,751 peasants involved in coconut production does not compare very well with the 23,797[3] employed in the sugar industry, it does still prove that the industry had relative importance.

Women's Labour in the Cultivation of Cacao, Coconuts & Sugar Cane

As far as the sexual division of labour is concerned, women participated in all areas of activity, except those few tasks which were considered skilled. Thus, the division of tasks into skilled and unskilled categories did predominate as on the plantation during slavery. Peasant agriculture, however, differed from plantation, in that it manifested signs of a more strict sexual division of labour which became increasingly entrenched into the culture with time. The reasons for this development will be discussed. Although a clear sexual division of labour was established in peasant agriculture, it was, according to the Herskovits accepted practice rather than "inviolate rule". They found that "When need presses, a man or woman will do what must be done without great thought as to whether it is proper or improper of his sex to do it." (Herskovits 1947: 45).

Cocoa

Just as on plantations, peasant women did mainly weeding, cutlassing and picking on cocoa estates during the late nineteenth and early twentieth centuries. Men, on the other hand, cleared the land, prepared it for cultivation, dug, put the crop into bags and transported it to the markets. Both men and women were responsible for hulling the beans, "dancing" as it is known (Herskovits 1947: 45-47).

Coconuts

A similar division of labour was established on coconut estates. Men were in charge of collecting coconuts, breaking them open, bagging copra and transporting the crop to the markets. Women were responsible for "extracting coconut mean from their shells, and drying them". Both sexes were involved in planting and nursing young plants, but, like with several other crops, women were responsible for weeding (Herskovits 1947: 45-47).

Cane

On the private cane farms the sexual division of labour would have been less defined. Women often had more responsibility for overseeing farms, especially later on East Indian land, where the menfolk continued to work on the estates.

The Indentureship System

The focus in the above discussion on peasant agriculture has been limited to the experiences of ex-slave (that is African) women labourers. The separation between the experiences of slaves, later ex-slaves, and indentured labourers has been made because of differences in the development of their peasant and plantation agriculture.

While it is often believed that East Indian immigrants were brought to the Caribbean, Trinidad included, because of the lack of labour caused by the exodus of ex-slaves from estate sugar production, there is evidence to suggest that it was more the need of capitalist planters to continue to control labour at minimum wages, than lack of labour, which was the definitive factor. The decisive reason was, as Brereton (1979: 176) states, to procure a new, cheap, reliable and manageable labour force which the newly emancipated ex-slaves, clamouring for better working conditions, could not and would not supply. This point was supported by C. Kondapi when he stated that: "even in territories where ex-slave labour was available Indian labour was used to depress wages" (Kondapi 1951: 16).

Indentureship, therefore, was an attempt by the plantocracy to re-establish some of the power and control over labour which they had had during slavery.

It is, therefore, no surprise to find that female wage labour was considered merely another variable in the production process which could be manipulated at will for maximum profit and minimum cost. Indeed, this was the very purpose of the introduction of indentured labour and so the argument that indentureship was completely different from slavery is questionable, at least from the point of view of the planters' motives. Needless to say, indentured women like slave women were brought to the region primarily for the purpose of labouring on the sugar plantations.

East Indian immigrants laboured on the sugar plantations for a contracted number of years, usually five, although this was later changed to three years for women, after which they were supposed to be given free passage back to India. Very few immigrants returned. The effect of this was the establishment of large East Indian communities conglomerated around the sugar estates of Trinidad. By 1869, 37,440 Indians had come to Trinidad (Brereton 1979: 176). The final set of immigrants came as late as 1917, which was the last year.

Whereas no strict sexual division of labour had existed on slave plantations, by the time of the start of indentureship it had become established and therefore governed the allocation of tasks to men and women. Indeed, a comparison between the perception of female slave labour and female indentured labour proves interesting, since it reveals the contradictions in planters' attitudes and policies which are inherent in the capitalist system. Under slavery it was profitable to have a more flexible sexual division of labour, since female wage labour, then of course unpaid, could be exploited without any moral or ethical restrictions. Women were thus perceived to be as capable as men and did work which was as physically demanding and tiring. Under indentureship, however, where remuneration was an established part of the system, it was more to the planters' advantage to redefine female labour and place it in the same category as that of weakly men and children. Women were therefore paid the wages of weak and infirm men or of children. Thus the definition of female labour changed, as did the perception—although not the reality—of what female labour was physically capable of. It is clear that these contradictions were justified only by the motive to maximise profit by the exploitation of labour at minimum costs.

These new definitions were not only contradictory, but also defied reality. The sexual division of labour which existed on the indentured plantations was based on the assumption that able-bodied men could do full tasks in heavy work, while women, weak men and children could only do full tasks of light work. As in slavery, the highly skilled jobs were almost totally done by men. Women did mainly weeding, manuring, supplying and cane-cutting. Most able-bodied male labour was concentrated on forking, millworks, cane-cutting and truck-loading. Not surprisingly, women's tasks were the lowest paid, largely due to the fact that these were conceived as light tasks. Agricultural activity on estates was divided into 'tasks', or fixed amounts of work. Depending on the size of the tasks, these could be completed in one or more days according to the worker. As a rule, men and women were allotted equal tasks. Workers were paid according to the day or the task.

From the inception of indentureship, women were paid lower wages than men, even in the cases where equal work was done. In 1845 the following rates were recorded:

Category	Wages ($)
Male labourer	2.40 per month
Female labourer	1.45 per month

Source: Cumpston (1953: 99).

In 1870 and 1875, wages were as follows:

Category	Wages
Men	25 – 40 cents daily
Women	10 – 25 cents daily
Children	10 – 15 cents daily

Source: Comins (1893: 36).

This difference in remuneration existed despite the fact that women very often did the same work as men. As the planters had established it in the late nineteenth century, no matter what jobs women did, they could earn no more than 25 cents daily, despite evidence that the sexual division of labour was not constant and women often did what were considered 'heavy male' tasks such as truck loading.

The obvious discrimination in giving less pay for what was equal labour became even more blatant when, in times of financial crisis, planters found it necessary to increase the size of tasks for the same wage, with the effect that many tasks could not be finished within one working day. As late as 1934, for example, there is evidence that tasks were increased beyond the capacity of women, in order to get two day's work for one day's pay. For instance, Soogbarsie, being given 25 rods to do daily, complained that she took two and sometimes more days to complete one task of 25 rods; the manipulation is clear here (Trinidad and Tobago Report of the Labour Disturbances Commission 1934: 25).

The indentureship system thus managed not only to prolong control of planters over estate labour, but also managed to strengthen the partially institutionalised discrimination against female agricultural labour on plantations, a trend which continued throughout the nineteenth and twentieth centuries.

Wet Rice Cultivation, 1860-1900s

The cultivation of wet rice or padi was carried out chiefly by East Indian labourers. It developed as an outgrowth of peasant production, usually after indentured labourers had completed their contracted years on sugar estates and turned to rice as a means of subsistence (Brereton 1979: 21). Wet rice cultivation was carried out on parcels of land which were either given out to labourers by grants from the government or they purchased themselves. Between 1885 and 1895, 23,000 acres were sold; between 1962 and 1912, a further 31,766 acres were sold to ex-indentured labourers (Dookhan 1979: 61).

By the start of the twentieth century, wet rice cultivation had become an important activity for East Indian labourers, especially those who had settled in central and southern areas of Trinidad. Its profitability was questionable, since planters generally preferred Indian labourers to devote their labour to either cane farming which, as we have previously noted, became progressively an East Indian occupation after 1900s, or to remain as wage labourers. In other words, planters preferred for Indian farmers to labour in an activity over which they could maintain some economic control (Brereton 1979: 21).

There was a definite reason for the planters' wish to suppress rice cultivation. As already mentioned, many ex-indentured labourers were granted lands for cane farming during the late nineteenth and early twentieth centuries, but continued, nevertheless, to be part-time labourers on sugar estates for wages. This cyclical employment meant that labourers were left unwaged for long periods, during which they turned to their own lands for subsistence. In this situation women participated in cultivation, harvesting and whatever else was necessary to produce food crops (Ramesar 1979). This had adverse effects on the planters' estates, for labourers were no longer totally dependent on estate production. This cultivation, however, ensured that labourers could have food to eat and women could fulfil their gender-defined responsibility to feed their families. As Ramesar states:

> The labourers were expected to overcome their difficulties as best they could by making employment for themselves in rice planting and vegetable gardening . . . Turned adrift after a week's work, the labourer had to plant food crops for his family's subsistence and could not afford to accommodate the employer later on in the year by undertaking labour when it was offered during the planting season. (Ramesar 1979).

Thus peasant production of food crops threatened the planters' control over the labourers.

The establishment of incentives away from rice production and towards cane farming therefore had made rice a non-profitable crop for farming by 1906. Padi or wet rice production was never allowed to gain the importance it had developed in British Guiana (Reddock 1984: 205). Even though an estimated 6,000 acres of rice were reported for 1896, "supplying one sixth of local consumption" (Shepherd 1936: 23), this high level of production did not continue. An exception was made during the years of the First World War, when food self-sufficiency was important in order to feed the population. Thus between 1914 and 1918 padi "was facilitated by the extension of rice cultivation facilities to labourers as a means of retaining their labour" (Shepherd 1936: 23). After the First World War, rice was once again imported from India. The decreasing importance of rice as a separate industry in the twentieth century can be seen in Table 1, which shows the breakdown in land use for agriculture from 1920 to 1932. Rice no longer figures as a separate crop.

Table 1: *Acreage under principal agricultural crops in Trinidad, 1920-32 (acres)*

Crop	1920	1923	1926	1929	1932
Cacao	200,252	202,103	187,716	209,000	225,000
Sugar	43,265	34,719	32,874	44,000	60,000
Coconut	36,531	41,113	36,940	50,000	52,500
Mixed Cultivation[a]	16,829	11,568	35,951	12,216a	13,935a

aIncludes only coffee, rice, rubber, limes and grapefruit. Volume of rice acreage therefore not known.
Source: Shepherd (1936: 11)

The Emergence of the Housewife Ideology: Education and the Reduction of Women's Participation in Agriculture 1838-1950s

It has already been noted that female labour was important to estate and peasant agriculture during the periods of slavery, post-emancipation, indentureship and post-indentureship. This was true for both African and East Indian women. Whereas perceptions of women's labour were often responsible for the allocation of women to low-status tasks, these perceptions often contradicted the reality of women's contribution to agriculture.

Several historical trends contributed to the decrease in women's participation in agriculture. One of the most important of these was the development of education. The clamours of abolitionists during the later years of slavery for the education of slaves were translated into decisive measures after emancipation in 1838. More than merely educating the masses, however, the colonial government sought to impose measures on the newly emancipated slaves in order to make them conform to the new ideals of their status as free citizens. The need to educate, both formally and informally, was therefore considered urgent.

The Negro Education grant of 1834 was established to see to it that proper education was administered, proper education being "instruction in the doctrines and precepts of Christianity" (Gordon 1963: 20). Right up to 1933, therefore, the primary purpose of the educational system was to inculcate an awareness of and appreciation for the culture of the colonisers.

A clear-cut division of curriculum based on sex was not immediately apparent, although there is the suggestion that this division was understood and taken for granted. John Morton, a Presbyterian missionary, identified the aim of mission education as follows: "to teach the largest number of the three R's, a knowledge of the way of life and duty and to the girls sewing" (Morton 1916: 255).

This accepted assumption was to become the foundation of many policies on education for women.

The knowledge of the three Rs for a long time excluded agriculture as a subject. When it was finally considered, it was again subject to sex biases on the part of the educational decision-makers. The *Catholic News* of January 1889 stated: "So far little or nothing has been attempted in that direction. In consequence the students attending the higher educational institutions turn their attention to the learned professions and to government clerkships... We must endeavour to make agriculture a popular and remunerative career for *young men* in the West Indies." (Gordon 1963: 144) (emphasis added).

Agriculture did not seem to have the sympathies of students in those days and, as the attitude of the writer shows, if any attention was to be paid to it at all, it should be in relation to the male.

The curriculum established later reflected this attitude. After 1917 the curriculum for girls in government primary schools included domestic science, while boys did handcraft, a broad generic term for skills such as paper and cardboard modelling, carpentry, shoe-making, cane and straw work. If any agricultural work was done, "the girls usually worked in the flower and ornamental sections" (Reddock 1984: 219). Even this, however, was considered unacceptable by some parents. Parents of girls at Point Fortin, for example, did not allow girls to participate in this activity (Trinidad and Tobago, *Annual Report of the Director of Education*, No. 51, 1931: 25). Any education in agriculture for girls was limited to gardening.

Several later measures confirmed this trend. In 1935, the education code put in motion, among other things, programmes for teaching domestic science at special centres for girls only. This controversial code also concretised the exclusion of married women from the teaching profession. The Canadian Presbyterian missionaries in Trinidad had established girls' training homes for primary-level East Indian girls at the beginning of the twentieth century. The curriculum established for girls reflected ideas about the purpose of girls' education. It included, for example, "Hindi catechism, worship, Hindi writing, gardening and housework, arithmetic, English reading, sewing, writing, scripture, questions and answers in English and singing" (Morton 1916: 349). In the words of the Presbyterian missionary, John Morton, "washing, ironing, starching, scrubbing, gardening, sewing, and the housewifely arts were included in our course" (Morton 1916: 349).

It is clear, therefore, that the measures of 1935 were only official pronouncements of what had been subscribed to and practised long before. Whereas it is popularly believed that the educational system was put into operation in order to ensure equal access to opportunities in a democratic society, in reality the curriculum merely supported the existing prejudices of the then ruling class. One clear aspect of these prejudices was the unwillingness to have women trained to be agriculturalists and the concerted efforts to mould them into "respectable Christian housewives".

But the measures had far-reaching psychological effects which were more unfortunate. By establishing such sex divisions in education—domestic science for women, technical and craft training for men—early in the education system, the colonial authorities imposed values and orientations which were invariably anti-labour, especially for women, with the effect that every successive generation of women moved further and further away from agriculture. It is ironic that while women were still very active in agriculture in the first 30 years of the twentieth century, the years when definite policies were being made concerning education for women, their value orientations made them aspire to other forms of employment or to being housewives. Women were very active in cane farming, cocoa and coconut production, rice cultivation and other forms of peasant and plantation agriculture during the early twentieth century. At the same time girls were very much present at school, as Table 2 shows.

Table 2: *Primary-school enrolment in Trinidad and Tobago 1903 – 37*

Year	Boys		Girls		Total	% girls
	Gov't	Denom.	Gov't	Denom.		
1903/04	4,772	16,370	3,835	13,333	38,310	44.81
1914/15	5,963	22,778	4,725	18,031	51,497	44.19
1921	5,519	25,021	4,324	20,523	55,027	45.15
1926	33,078		26,335		59,413	44.33
1937	6,249	33,613	5,330	27,604	72,796	45.24

Source: Trinidad and Tobago Annual General Report (1926: 34).

From as early as 1903, nearly half the population of children attending primary school were girls and this percentage was consistent, although showing a slight annual increase between 1921 and 1937. Thus while female participation in both agriculture and education was obvious, consider, for example, the heavy labour input of East Indian women on estates. Both sectors instead of consolidating one another, did exactly the opposite.

The educational system imposed Western ideals on a young Trinidad and Tobago society, making women aspire to non-agricultural forms of employment or housewife status in marriage. From the end of the nineteenth century, at the same time as the emergence of peasant agriculture, women, previously wage labourers, were withdrawn from paid labour into the domestic economy. The pattern was different for African and East Indian women.

Employment options for African and East Indian women differed at the turn of the century. There was a growing tendency for African women to migrate to towns after having abandoned estate and/or peasant agriculture. The evidence is supported by the fact that most African peasant labour seemed to be non-Trinidadian, that is, mainly migrant labour from other West Indian territories such as St Vincent and Grenada (Shepherd 1936: 15). In Tobago peasant agriculture was concentrated in coconuts and cacao, and women were very much involved. East Indian female labour, however, continued to predominate in peasant and plantation agriculture.

Transformations in Plantation Agriculture and its effects on Women: The Sugar Industry, 1939-80

As early as 1906, the Night Work Ordinance based on recommendations put forward by the International Labour Organisation, was passed in Trinidad and Tobago which prohibited women from participating in 'Industrial Undertakings' at night. 'Night' was later changed to between the hours of 10 pm and 5am (Reddock 1984: 255). The ordinance was again changed in 1939 to prohibit all women from work at night, except in certain cases, thereby making agriculture and non-agricultural labour impossible for large numbers of women. This ordinance also consolidated the tendency for women to be expelled from certain sectors of wage labour, especially in factories.

The mechanisation of sugar cultivation and production established by landowners during the 1910s also led to the decrease in female labour, by this time primarily Indian. This had been forecast as early as 1898 by the replacement of animal mills with steam mills, the centralisation of factories to cover a wider area of planted land, the use of improved varieties of cane and most importantly, the use of ploughs, harrows, fertilisers and more complex irrigation schemes (Dookhan 1979: 38). The use of heavy equipment at least on the larger fields, is noteworthy, for such equipment was considered to be outside of the reach of women's labour.

This early rationalisation clearly militated against female labour, and continued throughout the twentieth century as estates attempted to curtail costs. Between the years of 1939 and 1948, for example, the value of agricultural machinery increased from TT$41,900 to TT$1,365,000 (Trinidad and Tobago *Annual Statistical Digest* 1955: 177), a fact which also explained the decrease in numbers of women employed in this industry. Large factories continued to modernise and expand, with increased concentration of ownership between 1939 and 1952 in the hands of the Tate and Lyle Sugar Corporation (Reddock 1984: 453).

The mechanisation of the sugar industry during the first half of the twentieth century and particularly just before the Second World War fits into the general development scheme of the time. This scheme made the rapid industrialisation of the Trinidad and Tobago economy a priority, both for monetary reasons and as a viable means of reducing the hold over the industry of large numbers of skilled labourers. Of particular importance was the growth of petroleum and manufacturing industries, whose contribution to the national economy increased rapidly, with the effect that agriculture lost the economic edge it had enjoyed during the previous century.

Industrialisation was to have lasting effects on women's employment, as it provided other avenues for wage labour outside the agricultural economy. It provided further incentives for women to discontinue their direct relationship with the land. The garment industry was one such avenue which was taken advantage of by women (Reddock 1984: 463). Thus mechanisation, industrialisation and institutional methods (night work ordinances) served to entrench the movement of women away from paid labour on sugar estates in the 1930s and 1940s.

There is, however, one outstanding example of a time when women were actively encouraged to participate once more in food production. During the Second World War, especially between 1942 and 1945, a drastic reduction in supplies of food to Trinidad and Tobago was experienced. The era of the wartime shortages, as it was popularly called, was a time when emergency measures were taken in an attempt to become self-sufficient in food, thereby feeding what would otherwise have been a starving population. Two factors contributed to this temporary return of women to agriculture. Firstly, the years 1939-45 witnessed the establishment of naval bases in various parts of Trinidad. As a result, large numbers of male labourers, formerly employed on sugar estates, got temporary employment in construction. The number of people employed on sugar estates fell from 25,000 to 16,700 between 1939 and 1943 (Brereton 1981: 212). Secondly, a 'Grow More Food' campaign was instituted by the colonial government in order to feed the population. Started in 1942, this campaign: "encouraged labourers to concentrate more time and energy on their private plots than on estate production" (Reddock 1984: 513).

As a result, normal estate labour was reduced. Women returned to sugar estate production during these years and managed to secure for themselves some degree of economic independence once more. Brereton (1981) notes, for example, that incentives were given to attract labour; individual tasks were reduced to make the working day manageable and wages increased. Furthermore, wartime bonuses were given of between 5 cents per day in 1941 and 15 cents per day in 1943.

It is interesting to note how, once again, the definition of female labour changed in order to meet economic demands. Similarly, notions of what women should and should not do according to their gender were easily eroded when the time was right. Women predominated in the fields during this time and did jobs which were then considered male tasks, such as cane cutting (Reddock 1984: 513). Typically, women during this period did tasks such as planting, weeding, hauling, fertilising and loading, as well as their traditional tasks of weeding and forking.

Food Production during the Second World War

Under the conditions of the wartime 'Grow More Food' campaign the peasantry thrived. The success of this campaign was largely due to the participation of female labour in the smaller farmholdings as well as on larger estates which temporarily turned to food production for subsistence and sale. Between 1939 and 1942 the acreage of land under food production increased more than twofold or, in numerical terms, 10,000 acres of land had been added to the total number of acres under food production by 1942. The main crops produced were rice, yams, sweet potatoes and corn, which sold at local markets and whose prices managed to compete successfully against foreign imported foodstuffs (Reddock 1984: 450, 513).

It is significant that the temporary return to agriculture for food production did not continue after the end of the war in 1945. Although the 'Grow More Food' campaign was successful, the priority given to food production was not maintained. As can be imagined, there was a subsequent decline in agricultural production, especially of non-estate crops or non-cash crops. Coconut and cocoa production, especially, suffered both economic and labour losses.

Female labour in peasant agriculture once again was relegated to the unskilled tasks in both cacao and coconut production. The only exception was that, with the nuclear family as the basic unit of peasant agricultural activity, the female labourer continued to work unpaid as wife or daughter of the farmer or head of household who was considered to be the man. Despite the clear evidence of female participation during the 'Grow More Food' era, it was ironically after the war that the 'housewifisation' ideology became even more entrenched.

A clear result of this housewifisation policy was that more females were defined as dependent and having male breadwinners. Women who before 1939 were seen as independent labourers gradually became perceived as wives of farmers, both on cane farms and cocoa and coconut estates (Reddock 1984: 468). The perception that women were wives and not farmers led to concrete results. Harewood (1975) notes that population censuses during the 1940s often referred to women as 'unemployed' while men were labelled 'farmers'. A comparison between numbers of women grouped into the 'unpaid family worker' category of 1946 and 1960 reveals this trend.

Type of Worker	1946	1960
Unpaid family workers	1,183	4,208
Percentage of total population	2.3%	6.1%

Source: Harewood (1975: 148).

While the numbers indicate a population increase as well as an increase of women in this category between 1946 and 1960, it is the increase in percentage which seems significant. Within the category of "unpaid family worker" was the assumption that women as wives, were "not gainfully employed" (Harewood 1956: 8-9). In reality, however, women continued to labour unpaid, and this was seen as a natural extension of their duties as housewives. Later agricultural policies have been based on the misguided notion that only men are active in agriculture, leading to a further denial of women's relationship to agriculture.

Contemporary Trends in Female Participation in Agriculture, 1960-80s: The Sugar Industry

The contemporary period manifests rather the results of trends established early in the twentieth century than any new developments. This section therefore shows the consolidation of policies and processes already discussed.

By the 1970s Caroni Ltd was a nationally owned sugar company comprising a conglomerate of all surviving sugar estates and factories. A review of the company in the twentieth century would show an increase in efforts to maximise profits, reduce production costs (including labour) and have output at optimum level. Obviously, an aspect of this continued rationalisation was the exclusion of unskilled labourers as far as possible and the employment of a capable workforce that could face the rigours of a changing economy. The former group would inevitably be the women. Their omission was due to both the increased mechanisation, already discussed, and the growing use of specially improved varieties of grain, both of which were monitored and developed solely by men (Harry 1980: 2). Rationalisation, therefore, was in effect a male- dominated process.

Harry stated that in 1978 6,176 men and 1,880 women were employed by Caroni. This was less than in previous years; for example, in 1969 6,245 male and 3,581 females were employed: "The reduction in females has been deliberate: the company has been reducing by attrition the number of women workers and has begun to mechanise most tasks in the cultivation process" (Harry 1980:2).

The effect therefore, is that women have been "almost completely withdrawn from cane cultivation... Female family members help with care-oriented tasks only if their labour is absolutely essential." (Harry 1980: 115).

Similarly, the Report of the Committee to Consider the Rationalization of the Sugar Industry, 1978 stated that most aspects of cane farming were being mechanised. The following trends were observed. In 1973 1,221 acres were cleared by machine, while 1,518 were done by hand. 1977 figures show that 2,842 acres were still done by hand, but machine-clearing increased to 1,313 acres. Female labour was often used to clear lands, especially in small holdings where mechanisation might not be viable. However, all land preparation was done by crawler tractors except for a very small operation done by hand. Thus women were largely excluded from this area of activity, became nearly all those trained to operate machinery were men (Harry 1980: 111). Planting was done by a combination of methods with operations continually being geared towards increased mechanisation: moving from manual to semi-mechanical, then to complete mechanical planting. As two out of three methods involved the use of machinery, it is clear that women were excluded from this task as well. Fertilising was done in the same way, with equal emphasis on mechanisation (Harry 1980: 111). Hauling of trash was apparently still manually operated, but weeding, traditionally the task of women, in some cases necessitated the use of sprayers to which, Harry states, women were averse. Much mechanical weeding was now done (Harry 1980: 130). Drainage and pest control were all 'high-status' jobs requiring training and specialised skills. Finally, harvesting was still done by animal-drawn carts and increasingly tractors. While women were known to prefer this type of work, this particular trend was changing (Harry 1980: 111).

A breakdown in task performance in cane farming according to sex shows the following:

Masculine	Feminine
Weed control	Planting
Burning, cutting	Fertilising
Transportation	Cutting mature canes
	Loading and hauling

Source: Harry (1980: 91).

It is noticeable that in 1978 typical female tasks like planting and fertilising were the ones which were in transition from being manual to being mechanised. Thus female labour for those tasks will eventually be phased out completely. Similarly, the only virtually unchanged task was hauling, noticeably still a manual task and noticeably still done by female labour. Weed control was now a completely male-dominated task. Previously this was the traditional forte of women. The breakdown thus shows clearly how and why the female labourer became gradually absent from sugar estate production.

Table 3: *Sexual division of labour according to crop*

Crop	Tasks	
	Masculine	**Feminine**
Cocoa	All tasks related to cocoa production other than those done by women	Gathering picked fruits
		Removing seeds from cracked pods
		Drying seeds
	"Dancing"[4]	
Cane	Weed control	Planting
	Burning	Fertilizing
	Cutting	Cutting mature canes
	Transportation	Loading of cut canes on to animal-drawn carts or tractors
Rice	Cutting ripened stalks	Planting
	Transporting rice stalks from fields	Cutting
	Beating stalks to separate from grains	Drying
		Winnowing the rice grains
Vegetables	Planting and harvesting	
	Nursery care	Fertilising
	Maintenance	Weeding
	Spraying	Tying plants to anchored stakes

Source: Harry (1980: 93-99).

Farmer and Food Crop Production 1960-80s

In the farming community women were perceived primarily as wives of farmers and only very rarely as farmers or owners of farms themselves. The few exceptions were women who inherited farms from deceased husbands. Of a total of 130 farms surveyed by Harry, for example, 26 were managed by women. Of these, only five were actually purchased, six were inherited, and 11 were rented or leased. According to Harry (1980: 63), "Most of the women managers were widowed or separated from their spouses."

The division of labour in the late 1970s on most peasant estates, that is, estates devoted to food crop production, showed little change from that noted for the first 30 years of the twentieth century. Skilled tasks were left for men, unskilled for women, except in cases of economic necessity where women were still expected to do unconventional tasks. Table 3 shows the sexual division of labour according to crop.

What is very noticeable in Table 3 is the continued prevalence of women in tasks such as planting, fertilising, cutting and weeding, while men did other jobs which necessitate some sort of technical or heavy apparatus, like spraying using sprayers strapped to the back. Women, however, continued to work predominantly in the field, very often as unpaid labour. The changes noted for plantation agriculture, therefore, took place much more gradually in the peasant sector. Of even greater importance, however, is the fact that, while women in the late 1970s were still labouring primarily in the fields, men seemed to control the decision-making, managing and marketing of food produce. The actual division of labour on fields remained unchanged, but again higher prestige or higher "skilled" jobs, were dominated by men, particularly to managerial or non-labour aspects of farm work.

While conditions for peasant farmers have improved gradually in terms of land tenure and possibilities for the private establishment of farms, the advantages for women of these improvements are questionable.

Table 4 shows the percentages of male, female and joint selling of major crops (that is, selling of crops according to the sex of the vendor).

Table 4: *Percentage distribution of major crop, by vendors, by sex and by product sector*

Vendor	Cocoa	Cane	Rice	Vegetables
Male	72.5	100.0	100.0	53.6
Female	20.0	--	--	21.4
Joint	7.5	--	--	25.0

Source: Harry (1980: 104).

The statistics for cane and rice marketing are significant, for they reveal the virtual exclusion of women from this economic activity, where the crop produced was a major income earner. Moreover, female cocoa vendors sold their crop to middlemen rather than directly to the markets (Harry 1980: 104), suggesting again that the unavailability of transport militated against their being more involved in all areas of agricultural activity. Where minor crops were grown, however, the participation of women in selling increased, especially vegetables.

Responsibility for decision-making (type of crops, time for planting, harvesting, etc) varied according to the nature of crop and who owned the farm. The typical line of distinction for who was responsible for crops between men and women was determined by the economic viability of these crops. Large decision-making, selling and marketing for major crops was a male activity; minor selling, marketing and cultivation was very often a joint responsibility. A generalised picture, however, can be gleaned from Table 5.

Table 5: *Percentage and frequency distribution of male, female or joint responsibility for farm by product sector*

Sex	Cocoa	Cane	Rice	Vegetables
Male	61.0	75.0	50.0	53.6
Female	22.0	13.3	25.0	17.9
Joint	17.1	6.7	25.0	28.6

Source: Harry (1980: 104).

With the exception of vegetables, it is clear that responsibility for crops was generally still dominated by men.

It was not only women who fared badly in the production of food stuffs, but also the producers in general. This of course, was due to the low profit margins of food crops and the continued reliance on cash crops for export. The little research that has been done in this area is very revealing. Anthony Seesahai (1983), stated that although root crops (cassava, yams, sweet potatoes, dasheen leaves, dasheen, eddoes, tannia) ranked eighth in commodity priority in Trinidad, they were granted merely 0.3 per cent of arable lands, while traditional export crops had 68 per cent. Research was done mostly on these traditional export crops, so that food production was further debilitated (Seesahai 1983: unnumbered document). Seesahai noted also that little development of farming practices had taken place, with the effect that '30-35 per cent of food crops are destroyed by pests during growth, harvesting and storage'. Very little institutional support has been given to root crop production.

Conclusion

This paper has sought to examine the historical relationship of women to agriculture, both peasant and plantation, in Trinidad and Tobago from the beginning of its modern history. The process identified is true not only for this country, but in many instances for other parts of the region. The mechanisms through which women were removed from agriculture and into a traditionalised domesticity have been noted, but many factors served to make agriculture a less than attractive occupation, initially for women but increasingly for most people.

It can be argued also that the large numbers of women who appear in the statistics as economically inactive or not in the labour force in Trinidad and Tobago reflect, among other things, the expulsion of women from agriculture and the inability of any other economic activity to fully take its place. So women are a small minority in plantation agriculture and labour primarily as unpaid labourers in family plots, and as a result are not documented as farmers in regional agricultural statistics. This continued exclusion of women from this field and their invisibility where they still exist is only one, but also a significant one, of the problems affecting Caribbean agriculture.

Notes

1. "After the British Parliament's abolition of the slave trade in 1809, slaves liberated by British naval patrols off the West African coast were often encouraged or forced into indenture. The majority of slaves at the time were Yoruba, Kongo and Hausa. The period of the most intensive introduction of African indentured labour into Trinidad was 1840-60" (Warner-Lewis 1979, p. 102).
2. *Submission of the Government of Trinidad and Tobago to the West Indian Royal Commission on Labour Statistics*, 1979.
3. *Ibid.*
4. 'Dancing': persons, moving, walking, and jumping on the dried cacao beans as part of the mode of processing.

References

Brereton, Bridget. *Race Relations in Colonial Trinidad 1870-1900.* Cambridge University Press, 1979.

Brereton, Bridget. *A History of Modern Trinidad, 1783-1963.* London, Heinemann, 1981.

Carmichael, A. C.. *Domestic Manners and the Social Condition of the White, Coloured and Negro Population of the West Indies* Vol. II New York: Negro Universities Press, 1969.

Comins, D. W. D. (Surgeon Major). *A Note on Emigration from India to Trinidad.* Printed Calcutta, Bengal Secretariat Press, 1893.

Craton, Michael. *Searching for the Invisible Man: Slaves and Plantation Life in Jamaica.* Cambridge, Mass: Harvard University Press, 1978.

CSO. *Statistics at a Glance.*

Cumpston, J. M. *Indians Overseas in British Territories.* London: Oxford University Press, 1953.

Dookhan, Isaac. *A Pre-Emancipation History of the West Indies 1492-1865.* Collins, 1979.

Dookhan, Isaac. *A Post-Emancipation History of the West Indies 1834-1975.* Collins, 1979.

Gordon, Shirley. *A Century of the West Indian Education,* London: Longmans, 1963.

Harewood, Jack. "A System of Labour Force Statistics". *Social and Economic Studies,* Vol. 5, No. 1, 1956.

Harewood, Jack. *The Population of Trinidad and Tobago,* CICRED Series, 1975.

Harry, Indra S. "Women in Agriculture in Trinidad", MSc thesis Alberta: Calgary, 1980.

Herskovits, Melville J. and Frances, S. *Trinidad Village,* New York: Alfred A. Knopf, 1947.

Johnson, Howard. "The Origins and Development of Early Cane Farming in Trinidad 1882-1906". *Journal of Caribbean History,* Vol. 5, November 1972.

Kondapi, C. *Indians Overseas.* New Delhi: Oxford University Press, 1951.

Knudson, Barbara et. al. *The Economic Role of Women in Small-Scale Agriculture in the Eastern Caribbean.* St Lucia, Extra-Mural Department, Pinelands, Barbados, 1981.
Maharaj, Deyanand. *Cane Farming in the Trinidad Sugar Industry,* Thesis University of Edinburgh, 1969.
Morton, Sarah. *John Morton of Trinidad: Journals, Letters and Papers With Illustrations and Maps.* Toronto: Westminster Company, 1916.
Patterson, Orlando. "Recent Studies on Caribbean Slavery and the Atlantic Slave Trade. A Review Essay". *Latin American Research Review,* Vol. XVII, No. 3, 1982.
Ramesar, Mariane. "The Historical Origins of the Unemployment Problem in Trinidad". *Caribbean Issues,* Vol. III, Nos. 2 and 3, August-December 1979.
Reddock, Rhoda. *Women, Labour and Struggle in 20th-Century Trinidad and Tobago 1898-1960,* The Hague: Institute of Social Studies, 1984.
Caroni Ltd. *Review Seminar on the Agricultural Aspects of Mechanization of S ugar-cane Production and Harvesting.* Proceedings of talks and discussions, 1977.
Seesahai, Anthony. *Root Crop Production in Trinidad and Tobago,* Centeno, Trinidad, Ministry of Agriculture, 1983.
Shepherd, C. Y.. "Agricultural Labour in Trinidad", *Tropical Agriculture,* Vol. III, Nos. 1, 2, 3, 4, 5, 6, 7. Printed by Government Printer, Port-of-Spain, 1936.
Trinidad and Tobago. *Annual Report of the Director of Education* Council Paper No. 51. 1931.
Trinidad and Tobago. *Annual Statistical Digest,* Vol. 1, No. 1, 1953-51, Port-of-Spain, Central Statistical Office. Revised edition. 1955.
Trinidad and Tobago. *Colonial Annual Report for 1926.* Government Printing Office. 1927.
Trinidad and Tobago. National Commission on the Status of Women. Port-of-Spain. 1974.
Trinidad and Tobago. *Report of the Labour Disturbances Commission,* Legislative Council Paper. No. 109. 1934.
Warner-Lewis, Maureen. "African Impact on Language and Literature in the English-Speaking Caribbean". In Crahan, Margaret Knight, Franklin (eds.). *Africa and the Caribbean. The Legacies of a Link.* London: John Hopkins University Press, 1979.

Charting the Future

Alternative Strategies for Policy and Research Rapporteur's Report to the Seminar

Christine Barrow

The process of condensing and synthesising the mass of new and exciting information and discussion that has taken place during this seminar in formal and informal sessions is a near impossible task. What this report does not attempt is to cover it all in chronological order. Rather what it endeavours to do is to select from the mass of facts, information and argument, the major issues which are of central importance in relation to the question of where we go from here. A list of semiar presentations is included as an appendix to this paper. The major directions for the future identified in the seminar were in relation to policy and research.

Policy

Four major dimensions are discussed here, namely: the question of the impact of development processes on Caribbean women at the macro-level; the provision of resources (especially land) for women in agriculture; the misplaced emphasis on statistical indicators for women in development; and the involvement of women in food production.

Thirdworld Development and Caribbean Women

Various statements repeated during this seminar have made it very clear that policy-makers (mainly men) have little clue about the implications of third-world development and official policy on the lives and wellbeing of Caribbean women. They have little or no idea about the impact on Caribbean women of colonialism, imperialism, modernisation, structural adjustment and the like, processes imposed from outside as strategies for the appropriation of third-world resources. We need studies to highlight this. Rhoda Reddock and Jasmine Huggins paper for this seminar gave us a good start with what they call a "broad sweep" of the history of women in Trinidad and the presentation by Gloria Thomas-Emeagwali provided a similar perspective for Nigeria.

But in order to fill the gaps in the minds of policy-makers, such wide-ranging studies must be short, concise and above all simple. They also need to be supplemented by specific case studies. This brings us to the second level, the importance of identifying specific resources for women in agriculture.

Women's Access to Resources for Agriculture

Land

A central theme running through this seminar was that development processes have in fact chipped away at the resource base of the poor in third-world countries and at the resources of women rather than those of men. And yet, paradoxically, it is this control over resources that is a major factor influencing women's autonomy and relationships with men. This is the fundamental point with which Wicky Meynen started her presentation. She pointed out that we must draw a distinction between *de jure* and *de facto* rights to land. Policy is generally based on rights in law. This may or may not parallel rights by custom at a normative level. Neither may reflect the real situation on the ground, so to speak. Women may thus be unable to convert formal land rights to substantive claims. The seminar explored a number of reasons for this.

Women's rights to land are generally vested in the family. We saw this for St Lucia in Michaeline Crichlow's paper, South-West Nigeria in Carlisle Pemberton's paper and St Vincent and Dominica in Joan French's presentation. Women have rights to land not so much as independent purchasers but through their positions in the family as daughters or wives. We also saw that these rights are generally communally held family or tribal land and that, while they often constitute usufruct rather than ownership rights, they are still relatively secure. As Wicky Meynen pointed out, within these contexts women are often able to manipulate the system, using their natal land rights as bargaining power in relations with their husbands.

Customary rights are threatened in many third-world countries. For one thing, the agricultural land base as a whole is shrinking through desertification, the encroachment by residential or tourist development, and so forth. The effective land base for individual farms is also being reduced by population pressure. The first to be moved off the land are women. For another thing, state policy which attempts to "rationalise" land, that is to individualise tenure thereby eliminating what is perceived as the anachronistic and wasteful system of communal or family land tenure, obviously has an immediate and drastic impact on women's rights. Governments need to be bombarded with information concerning the impact of these policies on women.

Before we leave the question of access to land, two additional points of significance were stressed during the seminar. Firstly, there is evidence from Wicky Meynen's paper that women are increasingly investing in houses, that is houses in their own villages, and through this investing in their family networks. The question is whether this implies a shift away from investment in land and if so what the implications of this on food production and the welfare of women and children will be. Secondly, there is the question raised by Achola Pala Okeyo's keynote address. Given the shrinking land base and increasing population pressure, should we, from a policy perspective, continue to pressure for land for women or balance this with pressure for agro-industrial development and employment plans for women in rural areas?

Labour, credit and training

Land is not the only resource required for development. Presentations and discussions at the seminar also examined labour, noting the special difficulties of women in finding labour. Credit was emphasised in Jean Craigwell's paper. She noted the assumption by banks and other lending institutions in Guyana that only men are credit-worthy, which has resulted in credit allocations to women which are very low compared with those to men. Another consequence is that women often are not bothering even to apply for credit.

The seminar noted the recommendations to broaden the definition of collateral to encourage indigenous "susu" types of savings mentioned in Selwyn Griffith's presentation.

Training was also mentioned. We heard critical views of agricultural programmes at the University of the West Indies (UWI), emphasising the need to incorporate management and computer training and to outfit students with the skills required to establish themselves in agri-business. Selwyn Griffith stressed that it would be appropriate now to establish a gender perspective in university programmes. The need to provide short-term outreach courses which appreciate women's heavy domestic and child care commitments was also mentioned. On this note we heard from Ann Rajack that this holistic perception of the reality of women's lives has still to be fully appreciated in extension services, despite the redefinition of method away from the traditional training and visits (T and V) paid to male model farms.

Cooperatives and technology

The importance of networking and organisation among women in order to provide a base for access to power structures was a recurrent theme of the seminar. The experiences of the Dominica Huckster's Association outlined by Heather O'Garro and illustrated in their video production *God Gives us the Talent* were very encouraging. We saw from Gloria Thomas-Emeagwali's account of the Nigerian experience that women's organisation into indigenous cooperatives has given them not only economic security and progress, but also a power base which counters the whole structure of patriarchy and, more specifically, a power base which is crucial in their selection and rejection of government policy on, for example, technology and crop varieties deemed inappropriate by the women. On a more informal level, the need for networking among Caribbean women, in particular among UWI graduates, was suggested in Lystra Fletcher-Paul's presentation. It was quite clear to those attending the seminar, if not to government and other policy-makers, that the problems with women and technology are not that women cannot learn, but that the structure of access is wrong. There is no inherent gender difference in the understanding and absorbtion of technical and scientific knowledge, that is once women get beyond that mental block against numbers and machines identified by Ena Harvey.

Another message for policy-makers is that women (and men) who work in the field have their own science. The need therefore is to bridge the knowledge gap: to de-mystify laboratory science and to work through the knowledge base, what we might call the "science for living" that is already functioning in the field.

We saw that innovative technology, from top down, either does not reach women or erodes their income and reduces their status to that of a labour reserve. Ena Harvey clearly pointed out the need to adapt technology. She stressed the need to develop technology that makes business sense: that does not price the end product (the crop) out of the market; protects against the hazards of noise and bad light, back straining and bending and carrying heavy weights; and fits with the whole round of women's lives, acknowledging the constraints that they as women face in attempting to combine agriculture with a range of additional responsibilities.

Multiplex roles

Finally we need to look at how women balance their involvement in agricultural production and distribution with all the other commitments that constitute their multiplex roles. What time and energy do women have for agriculture? Domestic chores and child care can be very time- and energy-consuming, especially if (as Carlisle Pemberton pointed out for South-West Nigeria) women are involved in collecting firewood and water and if the expansion of educational facilities removes the help they formerly received from their children. The enormous assistance given to women by programmes of rural electrification, by the provision of running water, and so on, needs to be made clear in policy formation. Women need relief, not only in production, but also in social reproduction. As Peggy Antrobus pointed out, we cannot expect women to spend more time in agriculture unless they are relieved in other areas of their lives.

Statistics

During this seminar we have been presented with an impressive array of figures, starting with a 42 per cent female enrolment in what was described as the "slave faculty" of agriculture at UWI. In addition, Daniel Thompson referred to the Eastern Caribbean Institute of Agriculture and Forestry and the impressive record of women not only in enrolment, but also in performance. Other presenters have added their contributions to the statistical record.

But we must be careful. There is a notion among policy-makers that development means, as the saying goes, "add women and stir", and that accordingly success is reflected in statistics. This seminar has seriously questioned the assumption that all that is needed is for women to gain access to male domains. However willing and committed these women are, their presence will initiate little or no change unless they themselves have developed gender consciousness and the ability to articulate these concerns. Gender consciousness is not a God-given something implanted at birth. It is developed by interpersonal contact and by training and reinforced by workshops and seminars like this one. And, one must add, it is not confined to women.

All too often women use their newfound positions as avenues for their own, albeit limited, social mobility, as pivots for moving into air-conditioned offices and away from the field, the hot sun and dirt under their finger nails. Or is the reason, as Peggy Antrobus suggested, that they are afraid of being labeled "feminist".

Women and Food

The final issue raised here concerning policy is what is arguably the most important message of this seminar, that is the crucial involvement of women in food production and distribution for domestic consumption, an involvement that continues throughout the food chain, from production to distribution to family nutrition and welfare. This theme was highlighted by Jean Craigwell, Joan French and Ann Rajack. Helen Thomas, herself a farmer, emphasised her involvement in food production, Heather O'Garro picked up the point from the perspective of distribution and it was echoed by Carlisle Pemberton for the African context.

Women's efforts in food production and distribution have been neglected by official policy. One bright spot, however, was the "Grow More Food" campaign for Trinidad and Tobago, which Rhoda Reddock and Jasmine Huggins mentioned for Trinidad and Tobago and which also occurred in other Caribbean territories during the Second World War. But this campaign was short-lived. In general agriculture, especially food production, as Hilary Robertson-Hickling articulated, is what we fall back on when all else fails. In a crisis, not only in the Caribbean but also in Nigeria, as Gloria Thomas-Emeagwali pointed out, it is agriculture that is called on to provide a solution.

The neglect of agriculture in general and women's involvement in domestic food production in particular has resulted in what we might almost call an inevitable situation. The Caribbean region faces a food crisis. As Curtis MacIntosh pointed out in his presentation, food imports into the region have escalated to EC$2 billion annually. Agricultural exports pay for less and less of the food import bill. Multinational corporations have penetrated not only at the levels of marketing and prices, but also in relation to inputs such as fertiliser, thus constituting an additional source of foreign exchange leakage.

The debt crisis has subjected many third-world countries to the strictures of the IMF, including imposed increases in the price of food staples and a further round of crisis in food supply for the local population. A number of solutions have been proposed:

1. Agricultural diversification to increase food production and food security and to lower the food bill by import substitution. We might ask ourselves, who is it that is centrally involved in food production and ensuring food security for the family? The seminar clearly identified the women of the Caribbean as having assumed this responsibility.
2. Increased trading in food within the region. We might ask what sector of the population is it that is most involved in this? Hugh Saul's presentation indicated that over 80 per cent of the intra-regional traders are women and that they control over 90 per cent of that trade.
3. A continuing attack on malnutrition. According to Curtis MacIntosh malnutrition in children under five years of age could be as high as 35 per cent in certain areas of the Carribean. And who is it that is responsible for feeding the children? Mothers, grandmothers, aunts, in other words, women again.

The paper by Frank Gumbs introduced us to a whole array of Caribbean policies to internalise food production and distribution. They include regional food plans, food and nutrition strategies and others put together by a range of organisations, such as the Caribbean Food Corporation, Caricom, the OECS and others. But nowhere was there any specific mention of women.

Research

Under the heading research we deal with two topics, namely methodology and model and theory building.

Methodology

One of the most crucial advances that women's studies has made in the Caribbean (and elsewhere) is to critically question much of the traditional social science methodology. Women's studies has made it abundantly clear to those who did not already know it, that the conclusions of any research project depend on the methodology. For example, if the researchers want in depth data, then they should not depend entirely on a questionnaire and if they wish to initiate change then reliance on the remote and "objective" methodology of traditional social science will be entirely inappropriate.

Women's studies in the Caribbean has been in the forefront of methodological development. Joan French's work with CAFRA and the work of WAND, as reported to the seminar by Peggy Antrobus and Jeanette Bell, have introduced us to these new and exciting methodologies. They identified a number of characteristics:

1. Working in and through local communities rather than assuming that all good things will trickle down to community level and spread themselves evenly through-

out. As Jeanette Bell put it, there is a need to involve women as collaborators in research rather than as recipients.

2. Adopting a participatory approach to the reality of women's lives and examining what women actually do rather than what they say they do. Many women who identify themselves to census and other interviewers as "housewives" in fact spend more time in agricultural pursuits.
3. Challenging concepts such as the farm family, which assumes homogeneity, gender equality and the pooling and sharing of resources.
4. Deliberately incorporating a component of consciousness-raising and public education on gender issues.
5. Using a variety of techniques, including theatre, sketches, video production and other visual methods.
6. Incorporating into the research a political dimension, that is empowering women and training them for leadership.

Model and theory building

The majority of papers presented during the seminar were heavily empiricist, very close to the data collected in fieldwork. This is not said in criticism, rather to recognise that such empiricism is important and necessary at this embryonic stage of theory building for women in the Caribbean. Research in relation to women in agriculture in the third world has produced a substantial body of information at the level of generalisation and theory for Africa, Asia and Latin America, but only a trickle for the Caribbean. More often than not researchers, following Ester Boserup's classic, Women's Role in Economic Development, append Caribbean women to Latin America with all the mistaken assumptions about "male farming systems" and similar lifestyles and conditions. It is more than time to put Caribbean women in agriculture on the map as Caribbean women. This seminar has made a substantial contribution to initiating this process. Thanks to the presentations from Carlisle Pemberton, Laurie Kelly and Gloria Thomas-Emeagwali on the African situation, we have begun the process of building a comparative framework which incorporates Caribbean women in agriculture.

Caribbean women in agriculture have much in common with their sisters elsewhere. But they are also unique in many ways and are definitely not an extension of Latin America. During this seminar we have identified some of these features which make them distinctly Caribbean, but more in passing than as a specific focus of attention. It is important, therefore, to highlight some of these characteristics.

1. For contemporary populations of the Caribbean, other than for the indiginous people the Caribs of Dominica and Guyana, there was no such thing as pre-capitalist small-scale agriculture. Their history begins with what was arguably the most severe capitalist system ever to have existed. It is difficult, therefore, to talk about the impact of colonialism on subsistence agriculture and on the pre-capitalist, complementary male-female relationships, subjects which are heavily researched in Africa and Latin America.

2. Slavery in the Caribbean in many ways was gender-blind for the black population and encouraged a marked degree of autonomy for women and equality in relations between male and female.
3. Female-headed households and matrifocal families are not new to the Caribbean, as they are for example to Latin America. For the Caribbean they date back to slavery and were reinforced by predaminantly male emigration in the early 1900s.
4. It also appears possible that Eurocentric ideologies penetrated far deeper into the black population in the Caribbean than in many other third-world populations that have survived colonialism and imperialism. As Rhoda Reddock and Jasmine Huggins' paper illustrated housewifisation or domestication was promoted in the Caribbean by the church, the school and the law. It became a sign of upward mobility for women to get married and stay at home. Agricultural women became farmer's wives. Thus Caribbean women who spend hours working on farms continue to describe themselves as 'housewives'. And although this seminar did not explore the fact, consecutive censuses in the Caribbean have recorded them as such, thus reinforcing their invisibility.
5. Caribbean male-female relationships may also be different. We must ask ourselves how the Eurocentric value complexes of respectability and domestication have affected the gender equality of the slave period. We might also ask whether the deference without submission which Achola Pala Okeyo mentioned for females in relation to males in Africa also exists in the Caribbean.

The search for Caribbean feminist models must be careful not to assume homogeneity among the women of the region. Race and class distinctions are very apparent and national socio-economic circumstances are in marked contrast. The video presentations during this seminar made this vividly clear. In this respect we welcome the presentation of material from St Vincent and Dominica from Joan French, Peggy Antrobus and Jeanette Bell and Heather O'Garro and St Lucia from Michaeline Crichlow. All too often Caribbean research has been dominated by Jamaica, Trinidad and Barbados.

Life cycle distinctions are also important. Although the research presentations for this seminar did not highlight this point, the videos made it quite clear that the life-style and involvement in farming of a woman in her twenties or thirties with young children is very different from that of a woman in her sixties or older. Model building for the Caribbean must not assume homogeneity in this respect either.

In the absence of models reflecting the reality of Caribbean women's lives, stereotypes have thrived. There are many such distorted images. Daniel Thompson referred to perceptions of women as submissive, as receivers of blows, non-thinkers, last in line and at home; Lystra-Ann Johnson reported perceptions of women in tattered clothes, bearing cutlasses and carrying bananas on their heads; and Helen Thomas referred to the stereotype of women as household entities to be protected from outside. Ena Harvey urged women not to reinforce these stereotypes with phobias about mathematics and machines. But we must remember that while persons attending seminars such as this see these as biased images to be countered and replaced by more realistic models, to many people they continue to be all too real.

It is vital that in our move to create models and build theories we operate on different levels. Women in agriculture in the Caribbean are not isolated from the national, regional and global processes of development (or indeed under-development). None of them is immune to these changes, nor have they ever been. Ann Rajack's presentation, in particular, pinpointed the need to understand Caribbean women within such a broad framework of analysis.

The models we build must be holistic. We stressed the need, for example, to examine women's health. Curtis McIntosh alerted us to the high levels of obesity and anaemia among Caribbean women and Ena Harvey to the impact of inappropriate technology on women's health. Our models must also move into environmental science, into technology, into the law and even into philosophy. This should not involve the acceptance of these disciplines as they are. We need to question the fundamental assumptions on which knowledge as we have learnt it is based. The exciting thing about women's studies is its ability to draw on threads and arguments from a wide range of disciplines and in turn to make an input into all areas of study—a truly interdiciplinary exercise, as David Dolly pointed out.

The need to reinstate culture in development models for Caribbean women was also perceived as essential. Culture as pleasure is one thing, but culture identified as a framework for development under one's own terms and conditions, much like the Ujamaa villages of Tanzania, and not as a copycat exercise in imitating North America, is quite another matter.

To go forward we must learn our lessons from the past. Achola Pala Okeyo has pointed the way. Her keynote address raised some general questions that we must answer in the Caribbean context. Our alternative strategies for agricultural development for women in the Caribbean must be based on visions alternative to the Judeo-Christian, Anglo-Saxon and even Victorian epistomologies which still plague our thinking. Planning for development in the Caribbean, a male prerogative, has up until now consisted largely of *ad hoc* responses to crises imposed from outside. As women we need, as Achola Pala Okeyo stresses, to image the future, to incorporate these images into our planning models and to will them for the future.

Note

There are many papers mentioned here that have not been included in the the section for publication, but which were presented at the seminar, and were important contributions to the formulation of the policy. A complete list is presented in the Appendix.

Appendix

List of Seminar Presentations

Papers

Antrobus, Peggy and Jeanette Bell:
Participatory Approaches to Gender in Rural Development :The Experience of the Women and Development Unit

Craigwell, Jean:
Historical and Contemporary Roles of Women in Caribbean Agriculture : A Guyanese Perspectives.

Crichlow, Michaeline:
New Perspectives on Family Land Tenure

Dolly, David:
Implications for Research and Postgraduate Studies in Agriculture

Fletcher-Paul, Lystra:
To Assess the Education and Training of Professional Women in Agriculture

French, Joan:
Gender Issues in Caribbean Agriculture

Griffith, Selwyn:
Implications for Teaching in Agriculture

Gumbs, Frank:
Regional Agriculture Development: Future Plans and the Role of Women

Harvey, Ena:
The Gender Variable in the Development of Post -Harvest Technology

Harvey, Winston:
Technological Innovations in Agriculture and their Awareness of Gender Differences

Kelly, Laurie:
Notes on Women's Contribution to the Planning of an Improved Cooking Stove Programme in Kenya

McIntosh, Curtis:
Food and Nutrition Security and the Gender Issue

Meynen, Wicky:
Women and Land Issues: Some Comparative and Theoretical Notes

O'Garro, Heather:
The Challenge to Produce Marketing in a Hurricane Prone Region

Pala Okeyo, Achola:
Keynote Address: Gender Issues in Agricultural Innovations: Reflections on the Future

Pemberton, Carlisle:
Factors Affecting the Allocation of Time to Farming: The Case of Women Farmers in South-West Nigeria

Rajack, Ann:
Extension Planning for Women in Agricultural Development as it Relates to the National Agricultural Policy.

Reddock, Rhoda and Jasmine Huggins:
The Historical and Contemporary Roles of Caribbean Women in Agriculture

Saul, Hugh:
Agricultural Export opportunities: Implications for Gender

Thomas, Helen:
An appreciation of the Contribution of Women to Agricultural Development

Thompson, Daniel and Lystra Sampson-Ovid:
Sex Stereotyping and Hindrance to Agricultural Development

Videos

An Unending Day (Caribbean Association of Feminist Research and Action (CAFRA) and Women in Caribbean Agriculture Project (WICA)

God Gives Us the Talent (Economic Commission for Latin America and the Caribbean (ECLAC)

Women, Land and Food Production: Small Farmers in Barbados
(Produced by Christine Barrow and Ellen Frankenstein)